Introduction to
CATALOGING
and
CLASSIFICATION

LIBRARY SCIENCE TEXT SERIES

Bohdan S. Wynar

Introduction to
Cataloging
and
Classification

5th edition

Prepared with the assistance of
JOHN PHILLIP IMMROTH

1976
LIBRARIES UNLIMITED, INC.
Littleton, Colo.

LIBRARIES UNLIMITED, INC.
P.O. Box 263
Littleton, Colorado 80120

Wynar, Bohdan S
    Introduction to cataloging and classification.

    (Library science text series)
    Bibliography: p. 412
    Includes index.
    1. Cataloging. 2. Classification--Books. I. Imm-
roth, John Phillip, joint author. II. Title.
Z693.W94 1976   025.3   75-44324

ISBN 0-87287-160-6
ISBN 0-87287-161-4 pbk.

PREFACE TO THE FIFTH EDITION

Since the publication of the first edition in 1964, this textbook has become widely known in the library profession in this country and abroad. It is both an introductory text for the beginning student in library science and a handy companion volume for practicing catalogers. Subsequent editions were published at frequent intervals, with the fourth revised edition appearing in 1972. At that time, most chapters were enlarged, and a new section was added to cover Expansive Classification, Subject Classification of James Duff Brown, Bibliographic Classification, Universal Decimal Classification, and Colon Classification. It must be kept in mind, however, that principles and concepts of cataloging and classification are constantly changing. Any text on this subject must incorporate these changes to some degree, so that at all times the teacher and the student can have the up-to-date material at hand in one volume. This new edition, reflecting our intention to keep pace with new developments in cataloging and classification, introduces a number of important changes and innovations: certain subjects are treated in greater depth than in previous editions; most chapters have been substantially revised and restructured; and the entire text in this new edition has been reset. New examples of LC cards have been provided throughout the book, and specific points exemplified by the cards are highlighted graphically. In this preface we will discuss only the most important changes in this completely revised edition, since we hope most libraries and library schools will keep the other edition at hand.

First, some comments about official changes in descriptive cataloging rules. Additions and changes from 1967 to 1969 were incorporated in a supplement to the paperback edition of AACR, North American text, reprinted in 1970. Current additions and changes are regularly published in *Cataloging Service*, a bulletin from the Processing Department of the Library of Congress. Up to the end of 1975 at least 38 rules have been changed and three chapters totally revised. Four rules (3, 4, 11, and 98) have been completely rewritten and two rules (5 and 99) have been deleted. In 1974 the revised Chapter 6, for separately published monographs (including photographic and other reproductions, formerly in Chapter 9), was published, and in 1975 a revised Chapter 12, for audiovisual media, was issued. This fifth edition of *Introduction to Cataloging and Classification* incorporates and explains all these changes, which reflect development toward the second edition of the AACR and an attempt to establish complete uniformity between the British and North American texts of the rules. Perhaps the most significant single change in descriptive cataloging has been the application of standards of bibliographic description based on International Standard Bibliographic Description (ISBD) for descriptive cataloging of monographs, audiovisual media, and special instructional materials. In addition, ISBD(S) (i.e., ISBD for serials) is being studied for possible use. Some libraries may implement only selected sections of these rules, while others may be in a position to use all the rules. Our discussion of the most important rules (Chapters 3 through 9), illustrated with actual card samples, is based on ISBD practice; to assist beginning catalogers with this problem, however, we also discuss in Chapter 1 the former (pre-ISBD) rules for descriptive cataloging, illustrated with card examples. Chapter 9 discusses cataloging of nonbook materials, covering Anglo-American cataloging rules for four distinct groups of nonbook materials: maps and atlases; audiovisual media and special instructional materials; printed music; and sound recordings. This chapter has been significantly revised and restructured. Other possible solutions (besides AACR treatment) for handling nonbook material are briefly discussed; we hope that many catalogers will find this information useful.

The chapters on classification and subject headings contain much new material. In response to many requests from faculty, the chapters on Dewey Decimal Classification and Library of Congress Classification have been expanded to include additional examples pertaining to number building, use of area tables, detailed explanations of DDC and LC tables and LC notations, etc.; needless to say, all the major changes in the Dewey Decimal Classification are also incorporated. A complete chapter on comparative classification has also been added. Here, using specific examples, we show the difference in treatment of a given subject in Dewey Decimal Classification, Library of Congress Classification, and five other classification systems—namely, Expansive Classification, Subject Classification, Bibliographic Classification, UDC, and Colon Classification. The chapter on Library of Congress subject headings, which takes into consideration all the major changes introduced by the eighth edition, has also been expanded. The chapter on centralized processing and cataloging routines presents a fuller treatment of such topics as Library of Congress services, centralized and commercial processing, the role of data banks and their impact on cataloging routines, the increased role of regional processing networks (e.g., the Ohio College Library Center), the evaluation of CIP data, etc. The new edition concludes with an expanded glossary of terms and abbreviations, a selected bibliography, and an index.

In the preface to the fourth edition, we indicated that this text was designed to meet the needs of beginning courses in cataloging and classification. Techniques of cataloging as practiced in good libraries in the United States are presented in conjunction with the underlying theory essential for a full understanding of these techniques. Other aspects—purely theoretical, highly technical, or of an administrative nature—are outside the scope of this text and should be reserved for advanced courses. However, it is our belief that from this foundation the individual instructor can build and elaborate as he desires. The additional references to other texts included in this new edition may be of some assistance in this task. However, it must be kept in mind that principles, and even the basic concepts, of cataloging and classification are changing. To keep pace with these developments, it is our intention to continue the periodic revision of this text.

This basic philosophy remains unchanged also in this new edition. Nevertheless, certain trends in the library profession today require a brief comment in a textbook of this type. Some library schools have ceased to teach cataloging and classification as a separate entity or as a basic course in librarianship. Instead, they incorporate elements of cataloging and classification theory and practice under the umbrella of such courses as information retrieval, data processing, organization and use of library collections, etc. So far, this trend has not been fully discussed in library literature. Occasional comments, however, point to the rationale behind this trend: there is no need to continue with traditional cataloging practices because larger libraries have access to automated bibliographical data bases and smaller libraries are using commercial or centralized processing services. This is a problem that needs to be discussed more fully in the library profession. Although we have no intention of starting such a discussion in this brief preface, certain facts should be pointed out. It is certainly true that two of the major and integrated aspects of the retrieval process are the traditional reference approach and a familiarity with organization of materials for potential use (which is actually a core requirement for cataloging and classification). As Sayers once said, we cannot reason, even in the simplest manner, unless we possess in a greater or lesser degree the power of classifying; or, to put it in simpler terms, we must first see things together before we can tell them apart. Thus, knowledge of a classification system is a prerequisite for the retrieval process, a fact well known to information scientists and reference librarians.

It is true that so-called original cataloging is being kept to a minimum, at least in most medium-sized and smaller libraries, since cataloging data for material for such collections is now widely available. Nevertheless, the mass production of cataloging data poses another problem. It is no secret to experienced catalogers that Library of Congress cards have, in recent years, contained more frequent errors in descriptive cataloging, insufficient subject headings, or even misleading classification numbers. It should be also kept in mind that even error-free LC cards need to be edited in order to meet the individual requirements of libraries of different sizes and different clientele. In a brief discussion of this problem by Frances Ohmes and J. F. Jones, they indicated:

> Now that LC copy is available for most library materials, the first phase of cataloging has been reduced in most instances to a few minutes; the cataloger examines the new work and if necessary edits the card to adjust any discrepancies between the card and the work. The second phase of cataloging, however, remains tedious and time-consuming. LC has specified the multiple entries under which the record is to be filed, entries which meshed with like entries in the LC catalog at the time the card was produced. They will not necessarily file in the same way in another catalog, or in the LC catalog of another date. Since the difference of a single letter or digit shunts a heading out of alignment, headings for the same person, place, or thing must be uniform. Each catalog contains its own unique assortment of vintage LC and local entries, and each library, therefore, must accomplish the coordination of old and new headings for itself.[1]

---

[1] Frances Ohmes and J. F. Jones, "The Other Half of Cataloging," *Library Resources and Technical Services* 17 (Summer 1973): 321.

We feel that the interpretive art of cataloging should continue in its own right as a separate discipline of library science. Some cataloging courses may need to be revised to emphasize this interpretive function, but we do not believe that they should be merged with information retrieval courses or courses in bibliography and reference. Hybrid courses can destroy or weaken the knowledge of each of the separate fields. Although automation and centralized processing may lead to a decrease in the number of professional catalogers in larger libraries, there should be an increase in the number of librarians who know how to interpret the catalog and its theoretical structure.

The constantly increasing publication rate of material in all fields places a greater demand on the library profession. It provides an entirely new set of objectives for library service in terms of transmitting this large volume of information to its potential users. In this new context the role of the traditional cataloger needs to be carefully reexamined. The paramount need is to continue the search for more efficient codes and classification schemes for organizing the available information, since, if they are used and modified in accordance with users' needs, cataloging codes and classification schemes can provide much needed guidance. This search should be undertaken not only by catalogers but also by reference librarians and information specialists, because these are the groups that are actively participating in designing an information system to meet the new requirements of our expanding universe.

It would be difficult to acknowledge all the resources that have contributed to the preparation of the new edition and all the fellow librarians who have encouraged the authors in this undertaking. Ms. Susan Wagner of Indiana University of Pennsylvania was kind enough to read the entire first draft and offer many helpful suggestions and corrections. Ms. Patricia Oyler of Simmons College made many useful suggestions for improvements from the previous edition, as did Sidney Jackson of Kent State University, Donald Lehnus of the University of Puerto Rico, M. Nabil Hamdy of the University of Denver, and Ellen Gay Defletsen of the University of Pittsburgh. The authors received sound advice from Blanche Woolls, of the University of Pittsburgh, for the chapter on non-book materials and its application to school libraries. We are further indebted, for their great assistance, to the Processing Department of the Library of Congress, under the direction of William Welsh, with special thanks to Joseph Howard, Benjamin Custer, and Edward Blume at LC. We are grateful to the senior editors at Libraries Unlimited, Richard Gray and Christine Wynar, for their careful and exacting readings of the revisions and their many valuable additions, especially in the chapters on filing rules and OCLC. Similarly, Ann Harwell's editorial work on this book has been invaluable. And finally we want to point out that this edition's improved appearance is due entirely to Judy Caraghar's meticulous work in graphics.

Bohdan S. Wynar
John Phillip Immroth

TABLE OF CONTENTS

6-UNIFORM TITLES

7-DESCRIPTIVE CATALOGING

8-SERIALS

9-CATALOGING OF NONBOOK MATERIALS

10-CLASSIFICATION

11—DEWEY DECIMAL CLASSIFICATION

12—LIBRARY OF CONGRESS CLASSIFICATION

13—OTHER GENERAL CLASSIFICATION SYSTEMS

14—SUBJECT HEADINGS

15–LIBRARY OF CONGRESS SUBJECT HEADINGS

16–SEARS LIST OF SUBJECT HEADINGS

17–CENTRALIZED SERVICES AND CATALOGING ROUTINES

1 INTRODUCTION TO CATALOGING

INTRODUCTION

The purposes of this chapter are to introduce the student to the basic concepts of cataloging and to provide him with a preliminary discussion of descriptive cataloging. Initially this chapter defines the terms "catalog," "cataloging," and "entry." The next section, characteristics of a catalog, describes the differences between library catalogs and bibliographies and/or indexes. The physical formats and characteristic qualities of book catalogs and card catalogs are compared. This is followed by an examination of the concept of the unit card, with two examples: a set of cards using current spacing and punctuation and a set of cards following the old practices. These two sets are included in this first chapter to alert the student to the two different forms of spacing and punctuation. Current punctuation is based on International Standard Bibliographic Description (ISBD); it is discussed in detail in Chapter 2 of this text. The section on basic concepts of cataloging concludes with a discussion of three ways to arrange entries in a catalog. These three methods of arrangement are represented by the dictionary catalog, the divided catalog, and the classified catalog.

The second part of this chapter serves as a basic introduction to descriptive cataloging. After a definition of descriptive cataloging and an explanation of its purpose, there is a section on how to examine the parts of the book that are essential to a catalog description—that is, how to read a book technically. The title page and its component parts—the author, the title proper and its various forms, the edition, and the imprint (place of publication, name of the publisher, and date of publication)—are all defined and described. This is an extremely important section, since it contains many technical definitions that are needed for an understanding of descriptive cataloging rules. The next section discusses the form of the catalog card and its seven separate parts: heading, body of the entry, collation, series, notes, tracing, and call number. The last section of this first chapter is a preliminary introduction to the formats to be followed in typing catalog cards (indentions, ISBD spacing, ISBD punctuation, capitalization, abbreviations, and numerals). Also included here is a discussion of the form, spacing, and punctuation according to pre-ISBD format. This discussion will allow students to examine the differences between these two forms of cataloging, and it will also serve as basic material for those libraries that do not follow ISBD cataloging.

BASIC CONCEPTS

Definitions

In order to provide access to the holdings of a library an index or list of the materials in the collection must be maintained. In libraries the principal index or list of available books and other materials is called the catalog. Its prime purpose is to record the books and other materials that a user can find in that specific library.

A **catalog** is a list, arranged by alphabet, by number, or by subject, of books, maps, coins, stamps, recordings, or any other medium that comprises a collection. It is a list that records, describes, and indexes the holdings of a specific collection. The collection may be private or it may represent the resources of a museum or of a library. **Cataloging** is the process of preparing a catalog, or preparing entries for a catalog.

Why prepare catalogs? Catalogs are necessary whenever a collection grows too large to be remembered item for item. A small private library or a classroom library will have little need for a formal catalog; the user can recall each book by author, title, or subject. When such a collection becomes a little larger, an informal arrangement, such as grouping the books by subject categories, provides access to them. But when a collection becomes too large for such a simple approach, a formal record is necessary.

A collection of any sort large enough to be recorded, or cataloged, must always depend upon a system by which each item is primarily identified. In an art museum exhibition catalog the artist's name and the number assigned to his painting are of utmost importance. A catalog of phonograph records will be itemized by composer and often by performer. Ordinarily, a collection of books will be listed by author; if he is not known, the books will be listed by title or by any other information that will provide positive identification. This information is called an **entry**. It is the record of an item in a catalog. Its purpose is to identify, with a name, the item described. These entries then become an index to the collection. Thus, in the catalog the patron can find two important items of information: whether the library has the book he wants, and, if so, where it is located in the collection.

Characteristics of a Catalog

Certain characteristics and functions of library catalogs distinguish them from other different but closely related forms of library tools—bibliographies and indexes. A **bibliography**, in simple terms, lists the literature on one subject—not only books but sometimes also pamphlets, articles in periodicals, documents, or other material not revealed in the ordinary library catalog. It may list the works of a certain author, describing all editions of those works. In contrast, a **library catalog** lists, arranges, and describes the holdings of a specific library or collection. The main functions of a library catalog are to enable a patron to determine

1) whether the library contains a certain book,
2) which works by a particular author are in the collection,
3) which editions of a particular work the library has, and
4) what materials the library has on a particular subject.

The rules for making catalog entries are, in general, standard rules that have national and, to a large extent, international acceptance. On the other hand, descriptive bibliographical practice follows a variety of codes for recording authors' names, for capitalization and punctuation, etc.; this is because the bibliographer's concern is not so much with choice and form of entry as with a critical appraisal of the history of the edition and the format of the work.

A library catalog frequently is described as an "index"; it may be more exact to say that a catalog leads the reader to a particular title in the collection, showing the user the location of the book, its physical description, and its subject content. (More detailed discussion of the problem of revealing the intellectual content of a book will be found in the chapter on subject headings.) An **index** exhibits the analyzed contents of a single book, of the books in a certain class or collection, or of one or more periodicals, reports, or documents. The purpose of an index is to show in what particular book, periodical, document, etc., and at what specific place the information on a certain topic or subject can be found.

Types of Catalog According to Format

Presently the library catalog exists in one of two physical formats: book catalog or card catalog. The **printed book** or **book catalog** is the oldest type known in the United States; it was used by many American libraries as the most common form of catalog until the late 1800s. For example, the report of the Bureau of Education in 1876 gives a list of 1,010 printed book catalogs, 382 of them published from 1870 to 1876. Because the book catalogs were rather expensive to produce and quickly became outdated, they were gradually replaced by the card catalogs. In a survey of 58 typical American libraries undertaken in 1893, 43 libraries had complete card catalogs and 13 had printed book catalogs with card supplements.[1] Thus, for many years book catalogs were out of favor in American libraries. It is only with today's modern, cheaper methods of printing and with the advent of automation for quicker cumulation that book catalogs are again becoming popular with certain types of libraries. An example of a book catalog produced by modern production techniques is the Library of Congress *Catalog of Books Represented by Library of Congress Printed Cards*, known since 1956 as the *National Union Catalog*. This catalog is published monthly, with quarterly, semiannual, annual, and quinquennial cumulations. The *National Union Catalog* is produced by photographic reduction of pre-existing catalog cards, hence it is a by-product of a card catalog. A similar technique is used by a number of commercial publishers (e.g., G. K. Hall), who reproduce card catalogs of certain libraries in a book catalog format.

Beginning in the 1950s, a new type of book catalog appeared, based on the use of computers. These **computer-produced catalogs**, which use machine-readable cataloging records, vary widely in format, typography, extent of bibliographical

---

[1] A good discussion of the historical development of cataloging practices is presented in an article written by Charles Martel, "Cataloging: 1876-1926," reprinted in *The Catalog and Cataloging*, edited by A. R. Rowland (Hamden, Conn., Shoe String Press, 1969), pp. 40-50.

detail, and pattern of updating. Their main drawback is still their tremendous cost; at this point only a very few large libraries can afford them. One of the best examples of a computer-produced catalog is the *Current Catalog* of the National Library of Medicine, started in 1966. It is published biweekly, with quarterly, semiannual, and annual cumulations.[2] Other examples are the New York Public Library catalogs and numerous county system catalogs.

The **card catalog** is the library catalog most often found in the United States. Each entry is prepared on a standard 7.5 x 12.5 cm. card (roughly 3 x 5 inches); these cards are then filed, usually in alphabetical order, in a tray.

A third form of catalog, which was maintained in some libraries in the United Kingdom, is the **sheaf catalog**. This catalog consists of entries prepared on oblong standardized slips of paper; the slips were inserted into a looseleaf binder so that entries could be easily added or removed. Examples of sheaf catalogs can still be found in some libraries.

Qualities of Catalog Format

An effective catalog in any format should possess certain qualities that will allow it to be easily consulted and maintained. If it is too difficult, too cumbersome, or too expensive, it is virtually useless. Hence the following comparative criteria exist for judging a catalog:

1) **It should be flexible.** A library's collection is dynamic and constantly changing. Since the catalog is a record of what is available in that library, entries should be added or removed as books are added to or discarded from the collection. The most flexible catalog is the card catalog; cards can be easily added to or removed from the trays whenever necessary. The book catalog is totally inflexible; once it has been printed it cannot admit additions or deletions except in supplements. On the other hand, a computer-produced catalog, representing bibliographical data in machine-readable form, is potentially even more flexible than the card catalog. Since the computer-produced catalog is still in an experimental stage, it is sufficient to say that its flexibility will depend on the library's access to the computer equipment necessary for its systematic and frequent updating.

2) **A catalog should be constructed so that all entries can be quickly and easily found.** This is primarily a matter of labeling. So far as the card catalog is concerned, the contents of each tray must be identified to the extent that a patron who wants to locate the works of Charles Dickens can find the Dickens entries easily. Labeling of each tray is essential; the patron must know exactly what part of the alphabet is contained in each one. Within the trays themselves there should be plentiful guide cards to identify coverage. Book catalogs are usually labeled on the spine, like encyclopedias. Often they have guides at the top of each page, indicating what entries are covered there.

3) **A catalog should be economically prepared and maintained.** The catalog that can be prepared most inexpensively and with greatest attention to currency has obvious advantages.

---

[2]The reader should consult some of the voluminous literature on this subject. One of the best summaries is provided in an article by George Piternick, "The Machine and Cataloging," in *Advances in Librarianship* (New York, Academic Press, 1970), pp. 1-35. For more recent developments in computer cataloging, see Chapter 17 of this textbook.

4) A catalog should be compact. It should not only take up the least possible amount of space, but it should also be easily removed for consultation and prolonged study if necessary. The book catalog is probably the most compact; the card catalog is the least compact and the least physically accessible in the sense that it cannot be removed for private study.

In summary, the following observations can be made concerning the two major types of catalog.

The book catalog is expensive to prepare unless numerous copies of the catalog are required; library systems that need multiple copies will find the book catalog less costly than the card catalog. Entries can be quickly found in the book catalog, and it is compact, easy to store, and easy to handle. However, it lacks flexibility.

Cards for the card catalog are easy to prepare and relatively inexpensive. The chief virtue of the card catalog is, of course, its flexibility. Though it is not compact and trays cannot ordinarily be removed for long intensive study, it should be remembered that many people can use it at the same time, as long as they do not need the same drawer.

The Unit Card

The Library of Congress did not begin to sell its standard printed catalog cards to libraries until 1901. Before that, individual libraries had to devise their own sets of cards to identify and describe the contents of each book. Duplicating machines were comparatively rudimentary and very expensive; therefore, the cataloger usually typed the card information or wrote it out in longhand. Obviously, under these conditions, it was costly to duplicate every necessary detail on each card in the set. For the sake of economy, only one card (the main entry card) was likely to carry complete bibliographic information. All other cards (secondary entry cards) were highly abbreviated.

When the Library of Congress decided to print cards and to sell them, it discovered that the most economical method was to print all cards of one set exactly alike. In this way it was not necessary to have one set for main entry and other sets for each other entry. This was the genesis of the **unit card** system of cataloging; encouraged by the development of duplicating machines, this system is now almost universal in American libraries.

The unit card system of providing multiple entries for a book is one in which a basic card, complete with all cataloging information, is used as a unit for identical duplication of all other necessary cards. After the reproduction of the unit card, all that is needed is the addition of appropriate added entries. This system has an important advantage for the patron: no matter what card he consults—author, title, or subject—he will find complete descriptive and bibliographical information for the book.

The main entry card is the basic catalog card; it is usually the author entry, and it gives all the information that identifies the work. It carries a record of all secondary entries under which the work is entered in the catalog. This record is called the **tracing**, and it is an essential part of the main entry card. The card set may have to be changed after it has been filed into the catalog or it may be necessary to remove it altogether. The set cannot be changed or removed unless all the cards of the set can be located. The tracing, usually found at the bottom of the main entry card or on the reverse of the card, gives this information.

Secondary entries, or **added entries**, are any entry other than the main entry. They may reflect joint authors, editors, illustrators, translators, titles, or subjects—any information that is sufficiently important or memorable that the patron might use it for searching. Obviously, the number of added entries will vary from book to book. There are usually at least four cards for every book: a main entry card (author), a shelflist card (for the library records), a title card (added entry), and a subject card (added entry). Often, however, added title entries are not made for such titles as *Works*, *Selected works*, and those that begin *A history of* ..., *A handbook of* ..., *How to* ... because these are not distinctive enough to warrant a separate entry. Also, some books do not need subject added entries (e.g., fiction). The topic of subject added entries is discussed in the chapter on subject headings. In addition to the usual four cards for each book, added entries for subject, joint authors, etc., will be typed as needed. Some books may require seven or eight added entry cards; some may need just one or none at all.

There are three basic types of library catalog entries: main entry and added entry (both of which are prepared by descriptive cataloging rules), and subject added entry (prepared by subject cataloging procedures). In most cases the **main entry** is the author entry. For example, a copy of *A New History of the United States* by William Miller will have as its main entry Miller, William, 1912- . The title, *A New History of the United States*, is an added entry. It describes the book by providing further identification apart from the author, whose name may not always be recalled. **United States—History** is a **subject added entry** for this book; it describes the intellectual content of the book. When this subject entry is filed with similar ones, it indicates one of many possible books on a single topic. It must be remembered that a patron may not know the author or title of a book on a certain subject. In such a case his only approach is to seek out information by subject.

Below is a transcription of the title page of a book for which two complete sets of cards are shown. The first set of cards shows current punctuation following ISBD; the second set of cards illustrates the previous practices.

**A NEW HISTORY
OF THE UNITED STATES**

by

William Miller, Ph.D.
Chairman of the History Department
Centre College

George Braziller, Inc.   New York

Second Edition

1961

ISBD Examples

**Main
entry**

Fig. 1.1

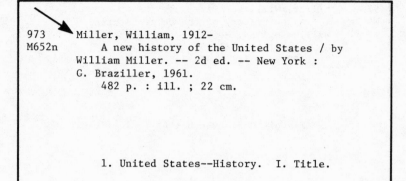

```
973      Miller, William, 1912-
M652n        A new history of the United States / by
         William Miller. -- 2d ed. -- New York :
         G. Braziller, 1961.
             482 p. : ill. ; 22 cm.




             1. United States--History.  I. Title.
```

The original unit card—i.e., the main entry card

(The following cards are all copies of this card with their appropriate added entries.)

Fig. 1.2

**Subject
added
entry**

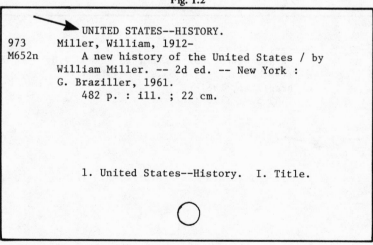

```
             UNITED STATES--HISTORY.
973      Miller, William, 1912-
M652n        A new history of the United States / by
         William Miller. -- 2d ed. -- New York :
         G. Braziller, 1961.
             482 p. : ill. ; 22 cm.



             1. United States--History.  I. Title.
```

Subject added to unit card

Fig. 1.3

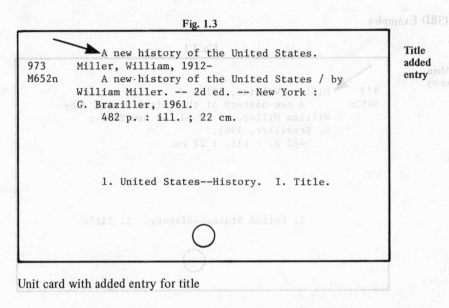

Unit card with added entry for title

On the shelflist used for the inventory record, librarians make notations on the card (depending on individual practice) indicating number of copies, price, accession number (if used), date when a copy was noted missing from the shelves, etc.

Fig. 1.4

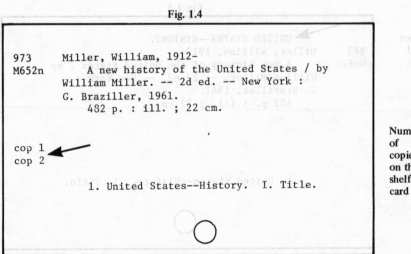

Unit card used as shelflist card

Pre-ISBD Examples

Fig. 1.5

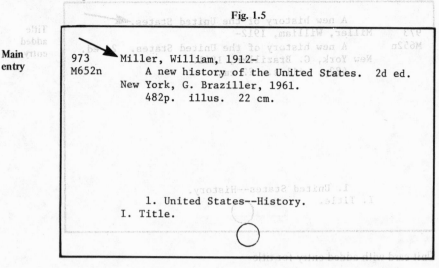

Main
entry

```
973     Miller, William, 1912-
M652n       A new history of the United States.   2d ed.
        New York, G. Braziller, 1961.
            482p.  illus.  22 cm.




            1. United States--History.
        I. Title.
```

The original unit card.

Fig. 1.6

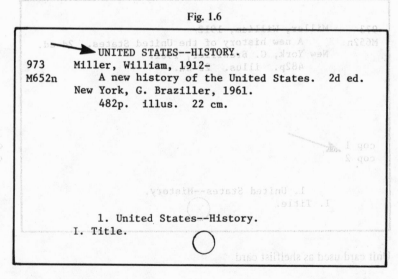

Subject
added
entry

```
        UNITED STATES--HISTORY.
973     Miller, William, 1912-
M652n       A new history of the United States.   2d ed.
        New York, G. Braziller, 1961.
            482p.  illus.  22 cm.




            1. United States--History.
        I. Title.
```

Subject added to unit card

Fig. 1.7

```
                A new history of the United States.  ◄──────
    973     Miller, William, 1912-                                   Title
    M652n        A new history of the United States.  2d ed.        added
             New York, G. Braziller, 1961.                          entry
                 482p.  illus.  22 cm.




                 1. United States--History.
             I. Title.
                              ◯
```

Unit card with added entry for title

Fig. 1.8

```
    973     Miller, William, 1912-
    M652n        A new history of the United States.  2d ed.
             New York, G. Braziller, 1961.
                 482p.  illus.  22 cm.



                                                                    Number
    cop 1  ◄──────                                   .              of
    cop 2                                                           copies

                 1. United States--History.
             I. Title.
                              ◯
```

Unit card used as shelflist card

Arrangement of Entries in a Catalog

A catalog must be arranged according to some definite plan. Depending on the subject and scope of the collection, many arrangements are possible. But no matter which one is used, it should cover the contents of the collection and guide the person who consults it to these contents.

Catalogs are ordinarily arranged according to one of three systems: dictionary, divided, or classed. The differences between them lie in the arrangement and filing of the entries.

Dictionary Catalogs

In the **dictionary** arrangement of entries, widely used in American libraries, all the entries—main, added, and subject—are combined, word by word, into one alphabetical file. This arrangement is said to be simple; undoubtedly it is, in the sense that only one file need be consulted. As the library grows, however, the dictionary arrangement becomes cumbersome and complex because all entries are interfiled. The problem becomes partly one of filing (do books by Charles Dickens, for example, file before those about him?) and partly one of dispersion. The subject of "industrial relations" has many aspects. How can all these aspects be located if they are entered under headings from "A" for "arbitration" to "W" for "wages"? Two primary justifications are offered in favor of the dictionary arrangement: most patrons seek material on one aspect of a subject rather than upon the broad subject itself, and the patron is provided with ample "see" and "see also" references, which direct him to other aspects of his subject.

Divided Catalogs

In the 1930s the realization that dictionary catalogs were becoming more and more complex led to a modification of the dictionary arrangement. The result was the **divided catalog**, which is in reality two catalogs: one for main and added entries other than subject; the other for subject entries only. The divided catalog permits a simpler filing scheme than does the dictionary catalog. Thus it is easier to consult, although the problem of scattered subjects still exists. There is a further complication implicit in this arrangement. The patron must determine whether he wants an author or title entry or a subject entry before he can know which part of the catalog he must check. When the divided approach is used, books about Dickens and books by Dickens are not filed together in the catalog. Patrons will need some guidance and education in this matter.

There are a few libraries that use other types of divided catalogs, such as the three-way divided catalog consisting of separate sections for author, title, and subject entries. Although this system may simplify the filing of cards, it can be even more confusing for a patron than the two-way divided catalog. In this arrangement, entries for books by Dickens will be filed under Dickens' name in the author catalog, the titles of his individual novels will be filed in the title catalog, and books about Dickens will be filed in the subject catalog.

Another type of two-way divided catalog is a name/title catalog and a topical subject catalog. In such a divided catalog names and titles that are used even as subject headings file in the name/title section. This type of divided catalog allows all the material by and about an author or a title to be filed together. Thus, to continue our previous example, books by and books about Dickens would be filed together in the same catalog. This system is potentially less confusing to the patron than any other form of divided catalog. In fact, the Library of Congress is considering adopting this type of divided catalog in place of its present dictionary catalog.

Classified Catalogs

The **classified catalog** has the longest history of all. Many American libraries used this form before they changed to the more popular dictionary form. It, too, is based upon some special system of classification. For example, the shelflist, a record of the holdings of a library arranged by classification number, is a classified catalog of a kind. It lacks only an alphabetical subject index to make it complete for this purpose. The major advantage of a classified catalog is that because it uses symbols or numbers it can keep up with changing terminology and thus be up to date. For efficient use it must have an alphabetical subject index. Perhaps its greatest disadvantage is that it is constructed on a particular classification scheme (even though this was an advantage as noted above). Since many patrons are not familiar with classification numbers, they would need special assistance when consulting the classified catalog. However, some fields—particularly the sciences— can make good use of such a catalog, inasmuch as science changes so rapidly. Since the classified catalog is flexible and can be easily updated, several large science and technology libraries provide this kind of index to their resources. Special libraries may, therefore, utilize them more and more in the future. A good example of a classified catalog is at the John Crerar Library in Chicago. This type of catalog arrangement will be discussed in greater detail in Chapter 14, Subject Headings.

DESCRIPTION OF MATERIAL
TO BE CATALOGED

Definition and Purpose of Descriptive Cataloging

Descriptive cataloging is that phase of the cataloging process which is concerned with the identification and description of a book and the recording of this information in the form of a cataloging entry. The term refers to the physical make-up of the book, without reference to its classification by subject or to the assignment of subject headings, both of which are the province of **subject cataloging**.

Identification and description are closely interrelated processes of descriptive cataloging; they are highly dependent upon each other. Identification consists of the choice of conventional elements, formulated by a set of rules, which catalogers use to describe a book. When the cataloger has properly identified these conventions, he must **describe** them on a catalog card in such a fashion that his description is unique and can be applied to no other book in the collection. What are the conventional elements that a cataloger tries to identify for the convenience of the patron? The majority of patrons will search for a specific book by author or title. This is universal. All catalogers, therefore, will ordinarily try to identify the author of the book and its title. In general, the **author** is the best known conventional element of identification and is the most important feature for this. The **title** is usually the second most memorable feature of the book. If the author is unknown, the book may be cataloged under title, which thus becomes the main entry. Even if the author is known and the book has been cataloged under his name, an added entry will be made for the title in most cases.

Many readers wish to identify a particular **edition** of a work when there has been more than one; therefore, additional information must be added to the author and title statements. A particular edition may be identified by the number of the edition (e.g., 5th edition), the name of the edition (e.g., Student edition), the name of the editor, the reviser, the illustrator, the translator, the author of an introduction, the publisher, the date of publication as well as the copyright date, or even the series of which the edition is a part. Even the size, the type of illustrations, or the number of pages or volumes may be helpful information for a reader seeking a specific edition of a work.

How to Read a Book Technically

In order to identify conventional elements of a book so that they can be described on a catalog card, it is necessary to know not only what to look for, but also how to look. Every cataloger must know how to **read a book technically**. Reading in this manner is scarcely the same as reading for information or for entertainment, when the entire text may be read at leisure. Obviously, the cataloger will have no time for reading of this sort. He must, therefore, learn to read technically. He must train himself to recognize quickly certain devices peculiar to books in general and to identify them in each book he handles. The obvious advantage of reading a book in this way is that the cataloger can quickly determine what the book is about, so that he can then pass this information on to the readers. The following discussion contains definitions useful to the cataloger in both descriptive cataloging and subject cataloging.

The first part of a book that the cataloger examines in detail is usually the **title page**. This page occurs very near the beginning of the book and contains the most complete bibliographic information about the book: the author's name, the fullest form of the book's title, the name and/or number of the book's edition, the name of the publisher, and the place and date of publication. In modern European language publications, the title page is usually a single, right-hand page. (A **leaf** is a sheet of paper that is bound into a book. A book is made up of leaves. Each leaf consists of two pages, a **recto** and a **verso**. A recto is a right-hand page of a book; the reverse of the recto—i.e., the other side of the leaf—is called the verso.) On the back of the title page is the **verso of the title page**, a page that often contains useful information for the cataloger.

The first element that the cataloger ordinarily notices on the title page is the **author**, whose name is usually the main entry. If the author is unfamiliar, the cataloger must try to find some information about him. For example, if the book is an imaginative work, he must know the author's nationality, since most classification schemes use the device of nationality to classify novels, drama, and poetry. This will be discussed in detail in Chapter 10 of this text. If the book is factual, it is helpful to know the author's academic background as an aid in identifying the kind of book he has written. Information about the author sometimes may be found on the title page, in the introduction, or on the dust jacket. The importance of correctly identifying the author cannot be over-emphasized. Rules for correct entry and aids for proper verification (biographical and bibliographical) are discussed as separate chapters.

The next most important cataloging element is the **title**. The **title page title**, which is generally the book's official title, is called the **title proper**; as such, it is used in all library records, in trade catalogs, and in bibliographies. It may or may not adequately describe the contents of the book. The title *A Short History of the United States* is self-evident, but Robert Lowell's title *The Mills of the Kavanaugh* needs an explanation. A glance through the text will reveal that it is a volume of poetry. This fact must be indicated on the catalog card.

The **subtitle** is a secondary title, often used to qualify the title proper. For example, the complete title of a book by critic and novelist Mary McCarthy is *On the Contrary: Articles of Belief, 1946-1961.* "Articles of Belief, 1946-1961" is the subtitle. It explains that the book consists of articles (i.e., essays) written during a specific period of time.

The **alternative title**, a form of subtitle usually introduced by "or," was widely used before the twentieth century. As in Gilbert and Sullivan's *Patience: or, Bunthorne's Bride*, it amplifies the title by telling the reader that "Patience," in this case, is a woman's name rather than the name of a specific virtue. Both subtitle and alternative title, if they exist, are on the title page.

The **parallel title** is the title proper written in another language or in another script. For instance, a bilingual book on snowmobiles in the Province of Quebec has its title proper in French, *La motoneige au Québec*, and its parallel title in English, *Snowmobiling in Quebec.*

Some books that have had changes in their titles in different editions or impressions may have both a current title proper and an original title. For example Anthony Burgess's study of James Joyce has the original title, *Here Comes Everybody*; the American edition has *Re Joyce* as its title proper on the title page. If at all possible, the cataloger should determine and note the original title of a work being cataloged.

The title proper and the other titles on the title page, however, are not the only possible ones.

Other titles exist, and each must be considered by the cataloger. He must note those that vary significantly from the title proper. In this fashion he can direct the patron who knows the work only by a variant title to the proper work desired. For example, Haydn's *Symphony 94 in G Major* is also known as the "Surprise Symphony"; many patrons would look for this popular form of the title instead of the title proper.

Many books carry a **cover title**. This is the title printed on the cover of the book, and it sometimes differs from the title proper.

The **binder's title** is lettered on the original spine of the book. If the title page or other title descriptions are lacking, the cataloger can use the binder's title or the cover title. He must be aware, however, that these are often not complete or accurate titles.

The **half title** is a brief title printed on a leaf directly preceding the title page. It generally repeats the title page title (sometimes in abbreviated form) or gives the name of the series to which the book belongs.

The half title, any added title pages, the verso of the title page, the cover title, and the binder's title make up a section of a book that catalogers call the **preliminaries**. Any of the preliminaries may be used to provide information not given on the chief title page.

The **caption title** is usually a brief title printed on the leaf directly preceding the text of the book.

The **head title** is the title given at the top of the first page of the text.

The **running title** is the title repeated at the top of each page or each alternate page of the book.

The **series title** indicates the series, if any, to which the book belongs. A series may be written by one author, as in Will Durant's *The Story of Civilization*, which consists of several uniform volumes. This is called an **author's series**. A series may also be issued by a publisher who commissions several authors to write one or more volumes on a specified subject. Such is the case with the Rinehart *Rivers of America* series of some thirty volumes. Or perhaps an author has submitted a mystery novel to Dodd, Mead who publish it as a part of the *Red Badge* series. In this instance the author was not commissioned to write the mystery. He simply submitted one through standard publishing channels and it happened to fit into a category established by the publisher. Both the *Rivers of America* and the *Red Badge* series are examples of different types of **publishers' series**.

The **monographic series** is a series that is usually issued with some regularity; each title in a monographic series is given a number, usually in chronological order. For many patrons, the name of the series and the number of a title in it are the important identifying elements. Patrons do not usually remember individual authors and titles but look for these under the series name. Thus, though author and title of an individual work are major identifying elements, the series title in a monographic series assumes a significant role.

Series information can be found on the title page, the half title page, or the dust jacket. The cataloger must always consider it as an element that will help a patron find the work he desires.

The **edition** of the book is usually stated on the title page, but it may appear instead on the verso or in the preface to the work. It is distinguished from a **printing** in that it indicates that certain specific changes—additions, deletions, modifications—have been made from the earlier versions of the text. On the other hand, a printing (or reprinting) usually means that more copies of the work were manufactured (without textual changes) in order to keep up with the demand for the book.

Editions may be named (e.g., "revised and enlarged," "abridged," "expurgated") or numbered (e.g., "5th edition"). Any of these edition statements indicates to the cataloger and the patron that some change in content or in form has been made. This information is very important to a scholar. To study the development of a poet, the literary scholar must have early and late editions of the poet's work. A physicist might want only the latest edition of a book on thermodynamics. More specific information concerning the verification of publication dates and of editions will be found in the chapter on descriptive cataloging.

Since the name of the publisher might indicate the type or quality of a work, this information might be important to the patron who must choose one book from several on a specific subject. If the publisher is noted for his excellence in a certain area—Skira in art; McGraw-Hill in technology—publisher information has some value to the patron. Place and date of publication are usually found on the title page and, by convention, are given a place in the catalog entry. Thus, the place, the name of the publisher, and the date of publication constitute the **imprint** of the work. This imprint is recorded in the catalog entry in a conventional order of place, publisher, date. If the name of the publisher or the place of publication is not known, the cataloger may need to list the name of the printer and the place of printing. If this information does not appear on the title page or the preliminaries, it might be found in a statement at the end of the book called the **colophon**. If the book is copyrighted, the **copyright date** and the holders of the copyright must be listed either on the title page or on the verso of the title page. This information might be important, especially in the case where the publication date (given on the title page) and the copyright date differ. If the date in the copyright statement is not the same as the date on the title page, both dates are given in the catalog entry.

To read a book technically, the cataloger must also be quick to identify other important and useful elements of a book. He will note **illustrative matter**. In children's books and collections of art reproductions, the kind and number of illustrations are significant. Diagrams and tables are very often as essential a feature of scientific and technological works as maps are of histories and geographies.

If there is a **preface**, the cataloger will read it because it will help him determine the author's plan or objective and thus provide a key to the subject matter of the book. The **introduction** and **foreword** are similar aids. The difference between these three elements is as follows: the foreword is a brief statement by a critic or colleague of the author, in which the author's views are amplified or explained. A preface, which is written by the author himself, usually delineates the author's objectives. An introduction contains material that the reader needs to know before he begins the book itself.

The **table of contents**, with its listing of topics, is a valuable indication of the scope of the work. The **index** is also a good source for determining subject content and special emphases.

Bibliographies, as a listing of sources consulted by the author, not only provide references for further study, but they serve as an aid in cataloging. They indicate the author's point of view. For the benefit of the patron, it is customary to note on the catalog entry bibliographies of any importance.

Another part of some books that can be very useful for subject cataloging is the book's **dust jacket** or wrapper. A brief summary of the book's contents may be printed on the front and back flaps of the dust jacket. Biographical information might also be included on the back of the dust jacket. Some books may have a different title on the dust jacket, occasionally a shortened form of the title proper.

Form of the Catalog Card

Uniformity is necessary in the form of the catalog card. If certain standards are followed throughout, patrons will universally recognize all the elements that make up the card. They will know, for example, that the imprint will always follow the rest of the body of the card and that the collation consists of certain items arranged in a specific order. This information then becomes readily identifiable.

Although various arrangements are possible, most libraries follow the Library of Congress system, simply because LC printed cards are extensively used. Sometimes it is not possible to use LC cards; they may not be available for certain books. Then the cataloger must devise a card very similar in form to that used by the Library of Congress. Doing this makes all the cards in the catalog as uniform as possible and therefore easy to consult.

Not all specific elements are present in every book, but all elements present must be recorded. Contemporary cataloging practice assumes that patrons are best served if these elements are recorded in the same order on all entries. For uniformity, which allows universal application, there is a generally accepted order to be followed when placing information about a book on a catalog card. This order is outlined below:

I.   HEADING
      A.   Author, *or*
      B.   Title, if author cannot be ascribed

II.   BODY OF THE ENTRY (first paragraph of the card)
      A.   Title and statement of authorship area
          1.   Title proper
          2.   Parallel title, subtitle, alternative title, or original title, if any
          3.   Author statement and joint authors, if any
          4.   Subsidiary authors, editor, translator, illustrator, abridger, etc., if any
      B.   Edition area
          1.   Named (i.e., enlarged and revised edition)
          2.   Numbered (i.e., 5th edition)
          3.   Combination of the above two (i.e., 5th enlarged and revised edition)
          4.   Author statement relating to particular edition (i.e., reviser, illustrator, etc.), if any
          5.   Illustration statement, if any
      C.   Imprint area
          1.   Place of publication
          2.   Name of publisher
          3.   Date of publication, including copyright date, if necessary
          4.   Place of printing if place of publication is unknown
          5.   Name of printer if name of publisher is unknown

III.) COLLATION AREA (second paragraph of the card)
    A.   Pagination or number of volumes
    B.   Illustrative material, if any
    C.   Size (height in centimeters)

IV.   SERIES AREA, if any (following the collation area as a continuation of the second paragraph of the card)

V.   NOTES AREA: To record necessary data that cannot be incorporated in above parts of the card. Each note is usually recorded in a separate area. The final note is the International Standard Book Number (ISBN).

VI.   TRACING
    A.   Subject headings
    B.   Added entries for joint authors, subsidiary authors, etc., or title
    C.   Series added entry

VII.   CALL NUMBER
    A.   Classification number
    B.   Author number (cutter) and work (title) mark

Fig. 1.9

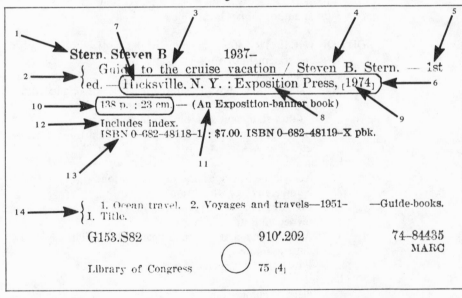

Stern. Steven B   1937–
   { Guide to the cruise vacation / Steven B. Stern. — 1st
   { ed. — Hicksville. N. Y. : Exposition Press, [1974]

138 p. : 23 cm.) — (An Exposition-banner book)
Includes index.
ISBN 0-682-48118-1 : $7.00. ISBN 0-682-48119-X pbk.

   { 1. Ocean travel. 2. Voyages and travels—1951–   —Guide-books.
   { I. Title.

G153.S82   910'.202   74-84435
                                                                  MARC

Library of Congress   75 [4]

[1] Heading: author's name	[8] Publisher
[2] Body of the entry	[9] Date of publication
[3] Title proper	[10] Collation
[4] Statement of authorship	[11] Series statement
[5] Edition statement	[12] Notes
[6] Imprint statement	[13] ISBN
[7] Place of publication	[14] Tracing

Typed Cards

The following instructions illustrate a simple and generally effective method of typing one's own catalog cards. The formalized rules may seem arbitrary, but they are essential for uniformity. Practice will make a typist proficient within a short time. Indention rules are given first. These are followed by detailed explanations of the typing rules (spacing, punctuation, capitalization, etc.) using ISBD format. Sample cards and detailed explanations for pre-ISBD rules begin on page 27.

Indentions

Most standard printed cards have the great advantage of more than one style and size of type to help differentiate between distinct items on the card. Lacking this advantage, typewritten cards must rely upon a standardized system (as follows) of spacing and punctuation for clarity.

Main entry begins nine spaces from the left margin of the card. This segment of nine spaces is called the **first indention**.

Second indention begins four typewriter spaces to the right of the main entry—or 13 spaces from the left margin. Second indention is used to align title, collation, notes, and tracing. Any of this information that is too long to be recorded on one line is brought back to first indention in standard paragraph form. All added entries begin at the second indention.

Occasionally there is need of a **third indention** (15 spaces from the left margin or six spaces to the right of the beginning of the main entry). This will occur in three instances:

1) When the author entry is too long to be contained on one line, the overflow is carried to third indention. (To use second indention in this case would be confusing because the title begins at second indention.)

2) When an added entry is too long for one line, the second line will carry over to third indention.

3) In the cataloging of one volume of a set that is in progress, the succeeding volumes must be allowed for. In this case the typist will space to third indention in the collation and type a "v." (lower case) for "volumes." When the set of books is complete, it then becomes a simple matter to type the completed number of volumes directly to the left of the "v."

Line Spacing

Main entry begins on the fourth line from the top of the card. A typewritten catalog card is single-spaced throughout, with the following exceptions:

1) Double-space before the beginning of a note or a statement of contents.

2) Begin the tracing at the bottom of the card, but above the hole.

1st indention: 9 spaces from left margin

2nd indention: 13 spaces from left margin

3rd indention: 15 spaces from left margin

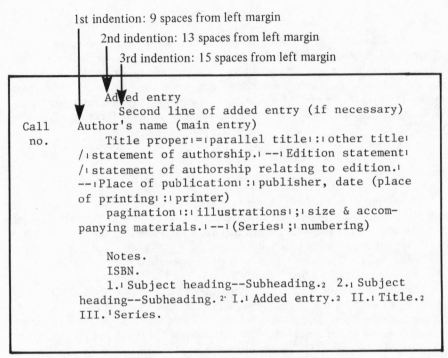

```
          Added entry
               Second line of added entry (if necessary)
Call      Author's name (main entry)
no.             Title proper₁=₁parallel title₁:₁other title₁
          /₁statement of authorship.₁ --₁Edition statement₁
          /₁statement of authorship relating to edition.₁
          --₁Place of publication₁ :₁publisher, date (place
          of printing₁ :₁printer)
               pagination₁:₁illustrations₁;₁size & accom-
          panying materials.₁ --₁(Series₁;₁numbering)

               Notes.
               ISBN.
               1.₁Subject heading--Subheading.₂  2.₁Subject
          heading--Subheading. ²· I.₁Added entry.₂  II.₁Title.₂
          III.¹Series.
```

Fig. 1.10—Sample form for typed card—ISBD format

Above is a sample form showing the location of information on a catalog card, indentions, spacing after punctuation, and vertical spacing between parts of the card. The small numbers "1" and "2" have been inserted to clarify the exact number of spaces to be used in each instance. Detailed instructions for spacing, punctuation, and capitalization (ISBD) are given on pages 21-27; the same instructions for pre-ISBD rules are given on pages 27-30.

The Library of Congress carries the **tracing** for the card set in paragraph form at the bottom of the card just above the hole (see example on page 21). For typed cards the tracings, instead of being placed on the front, may be typed on the back of the main entry card. This is particularly true when the tracings are long. In any case, the form, once established, should not vary. The subject headings are typed first in order of importance. If they are equally important, the order does not matter, except that biographical headings, or others in which the person is the subject, always come first. Each subject heading is preceded by an **arabic numeral**. Here again uniformity must be maintained, depending on the kind of heading established.

Those entries that bring out descriptive elements of a book rather than its subject are preceded by **roman numerals** and come after all subject entries. As part of the tracing, they follow a specific order: joint author, editor, translator, or any other individual person who has helped to create the work; corporate entries or sponsoring agencies such as societies, university departments, bureaus and the like; title; series.

Detailed rules and examples pertaining to the elements that make up the catalog card and the specifications for personal names will follow in succeeding parts on descriptive cataloging and rules for personal names.

Works entered under title are typed in the form called the **hanging indention**. The title begins at first indention and is continued at second indention. Collation and notes are indented as for all other cards. See sample below.

Fig. 1.11–Typed form for hanging indention

Title entry
 1st indention
 	
 2nd indention
	An Illustrated dictionary of geography / edited by R. Ogilvie Buchanan. -- London : Heinemann Educational, 1974.
	    [5], 242 p. : ill. (chiefly col.), col. maps ; 22 cm.
	
	    ISBN 0-435-34390-4
	
	    1. Physical geography--Dictionaries. 2. Geography--Dictionaries. I. Buchanan, Robert Ogilvie, 1894- ed.

ISBD Format

Spacing

1) **Author heading** begins on the fourth line from the top of the card.

2) **Single space the entries**, with the exception of a double space before beginning a note or statement of contents.

3) The **call number** begins on the fourth line from the top of the card. Indent the call number one space from the left edge of the card.

4) Leave **one space before and one space after**
   a) **Equal signs** used to indicate parallel titles:
      La motoneige au Québec = Snowmobiling in Quebec
   b) **Colons**:
      On the contrary : articles of belief, 1946-1961
      New York : Macmillan
      470 p. : ill.
   c) **Slashes** used to indicate the statement of authorship:
      Instrument pilot's guide / by L. W. Reithmaier
   d) **Dashes** used following the period that ends the title and statement of authorship, the edition area, and the collation area:
      by L. W. Reithmaier. – 2d ed. – Fallbrook, Calif.
      26 cm. – (Oxford in Asia university readings)

e) **Semicolon**

used to indicate different functions of subsidiary authorship:
by W. W. Helton ; photography, Woodward C.
Helton and James McKinney ; ill., Pete Dykes.

used to separate illustrative material from the size in the collation:
ill. ; 24 cm.

used to separate numbering from the series title:
Studies in Nigerian languages ; no. 1

f) The **ampersand** (&) used to separate accompanying materials from the size in the collation:
30 cm. & atlas

5) Leave **one space after**

a) Periods ending the title and statement of authorship area (see example in 4)d) above)

b) Periods ending the edition area (see example in 4)d) above)

c) Periods ending the collation area (see example in 4)d) above)

d) Commas separating publisher from date of publication:
Aero Publishers, 1975

e) Commas separating variations in dates in the imprint:
1958, 1960 printing
1965, t.p. 1970
1973, cover 1975

f) A mark of punctuation:
Williams, Alexander, tr.
Bliss, Henry Evelyn, 1870-1955
Tennyson, Alfred Tennyson, 1st baron

In stating volumes and pages, space before or after v. and before or after p.:
p. 238-287
247 p.
v. 11. p. 24-48

In stating height, space before cm.:
27 cm.

6) In imprint, omit space after a hyphen between two dates:
1870-1955.

7) Leave eight spaces after an initial in heading to complete a name:
Watson, R   James

Note: The peculiarities of ISBD spacing result from the dual use of punctuation marks: they can be used either as marks of punctuation or as marks of separation. The punctuation mark's function in a particular instance determines the spacing around it. The ISBD rules for punctuation and spacing are designed to simplify the conversion of bibliographic records to machine-readable form.

Punctuation

Punctuation in the catalog entry should follow as far as possible the current usage of the language concerned and the punctuation of the title page. The following examples are based on the new ISBD punctuation rules contained in Chapter 6, "Separately Published Monographs," *Anglo-American Cataloging Rules*, North American Text (Chicago: American Library Association, 1974). This chapter discusses more complex problems of punctuation and gives many additional examples.

1) Use **commas**
   a) Between the name of the publisher and the date of publication in the imprint area:
   Aero Publishers, 1975
   b) Between variations in dates in the imprint:
   1958, 1960 printing
   1965, t.p. 1970
   1973, cover 1975
   c) Between different pagination sections of a work:
   xxi, 259, 27 p., 15 leaves of plates
   d) To separate the surname and the forename.
   e) Following forenames, when words are added:
   Smith, Paul, ed.
   f) To separate date, number, place, or designation from the name or heading, unless a specific rule provides or indicates otherwise.

2) Use **semicolons**
   a) To indicate different functions of subsidiary authorship:
   by W. W. Helton ; photography, Woodward
   C. Helton and James McKinney ; ill., Pete Dykes. –
   b) Between illustrative material and the size in the collation area:
   ill. ; 24 cm.
   c) Between the title of a series and its numbering:
   (Studies in Nigerian languages ; no. 1)
   d) Between a series of titles from a work lacking a collective title:
   Romeo and Juliet ; King Lear ; Macbeth / by William Shakespeare. –
   e) Between two places of publication in the imprint:
   London ; New York :
   f) Between two separate places of publication and publishers:
   London : Oxford University Press ; Berkeley : University
   of California Press
   g) Between other series:
   1941-1943; 1944-1947.

   Note that there is no space **before** the semicolon in this case, since the semicolon serves as a mark of punctuation rather than a mark of separation.

3) Use **periods**
   a) At the end of the imprint area, unless the final mark of punctuation is a bracket:
   Oxford University Press, 1974.
   Aero Publishers, 1975 [c1974]

b) At the end of notes:
   Includes index.
   Cover title.
c) At the end of each entry in the tracing:
   1. Sociology.
   I. Title. II. Series.
d) Between a series of separate titles and authorship statements from a work lacking a collective title:
   Henry Esmond : a novel / by Thackeray. Bleak House : a novel / by Dickens
e) After abbreviations as indicated by the current usage of the language concerned:
   ill.
   ed.
f) Between subheadings of corporate author entry:
   United States. Antartic Projects Office.

4) Use **parentheses**
   a) To enclose a printer's imprint:
      (London : Wiggs)
   b) To enclose the series area:
      (Books that matter)
   c) To enclose the current name of a place of publication if the name has changed during publication of a work in several volumes:
      Christiania (Oslo) :
   d) To enclose explanations of folded leaves in the collation area:
      ill. (1 fold. in pocket) ; 27 cm.
   e) To enclose explanations of advertisements in the collation:
      158 p. (p. 149-158 advertisements) :
   f) For works in more than one volume with continuous pagination:
      3 v. (xix, 1269 p.) :
   g) For partially colored illustrative matter in the collation:
      ill. (some col.)
   h) For the collation of accompanying materials in the collation area:
      2 v. ; 32 cm. & atlas (159 leaves of plates : 25 col. maps ; 43 cm.). –
   i) For all theses that are not doctorates:
      Thesis (M.A.)–University of Denver.
   j) For supplied additions for certain corporate bodies:
      Graphica (Society)

5) Use **colons**
   a) Before subtitles:
      Human action : a treatise on economics
   b) Before alternative titles:
      Hans Brinker : or, The silver skates
   c) Between place of publication and the name of the publisher or place of printing and the name of the printer:
      New York : Macmillan

d) Between the pagination and illustrative material in the collation:
470 p. : ill.

e) Before explanatory additions to the title:
French rooster : [poem]. —

f) In imperfect copy notes:
Imperfect copy: all after p. 191 wanting.

Note that there is no space before the colon in this instance, since it is used as a mark of punctuation rather than a mark of separation.

g) For the separation of the name of a subseries from the name of the series:
(Series : Subseries ; number)
(Series ; number : Subseries ; number)

h) For any difference in title in the notes:
British ed. published under title:
Caption title:
Cover title:

i) For "at head of title" notes:
At head of title:

j) For bibliography notes:
Bibliography: p. 354-360.

k) For formal contents notes:
CONTENTS:

6) Use **period and dash**

a) After the title and statement of authorship area:
by L. W. Reithmaier. — 2d ed.

b) After the edition area:
2d ed. — Fallbrook, Calif. :

c) After the collation area:
26 cm. — (Oxford in Asia university readings)
In these three cases the format is period-space-hyphen-hyphen-space (the dash is represented by two hyphens on the typewriter).

d) For sequence in a contents note:
CONTENTS: Eisley, L.C. The ethic of the
group.—Seldes, G. Science and human values.
—Hurst, W. Law and the limits.
In this case, the format is period-hyphen-hyphen; there is no spacing before or after the dash.

7) **Dashes** are used in theses notes:
Thesis—Yale.
Note that no spacing is provided either before or after the dash.

8) **Slashes** are used before the authorship statement in both the title and statement of authorship area and the edition area:
Introduction to sociology / Paul Sites. —

9) **Equal signs** are used before parallel titles:
La motoneige au Québec = Snowmobiling in Quebec

10) **Ampersands** are used to separate accompanying materials from the size in the collation:

> 30 cm. & atlas

11) **Question marks** are used to denote
   a) Conjectural additions:
   > [Pittsburg? Calif.]
   > Pittsburg [Calif.?]
   b) Uncertain dates:
   > [1892?]
   > [189-?]
   > [18--?]

12) **Brackets** are used to show that the information enclosed has been supplied from a source other than the "primary source" according to the AACR. The primary sources of information vary according to the specified area of the card. These are discussed in Chapter 7, Rule 132B (p. 124) of this textbook.

13) **Omissions** of statements from title page, such as an unimportant part of a long title, are indicated by three dots:

The Dickens concordance, being a compendium of names and characters and principal places in all the works of Charles Dickens . . .

Capitalization

The rules for capitalization are those given in the United States Government Printing Office *Style Manual* (Rev. ed., 1973) with certain exceptions and additions. For the most part those codes follow general usage. One important exception is made, however, in that a title (in English) is written like an ordinary sentence; the first word is capitalized; e.g.,

> The will to live.
> Act one.

The capitalization of other words in the title is governed by ordinary rules for capitalization; e.g.,

> Across five Aprils.
> The Spirit of St. Louis.

The first word of every title quoted and every alternative title introduced by "or" or its equivalent is capitalized; e.g.,

> Selections from the Idylls of the king.
> Letters from the West: or, A caution to emigrants.

Abbreviations

Abbreviations are used except in the recording of titles. Abbreviations may be used in the body of the card, the series statement, the list of contents, or elsewhere in the entry. Some abbreviations may be used only for the heading, and single-letter abbreviations are not used to begin a note. Acceptable abbreviations are those listed in *Anglo-American Cataloging Rules*, Appendix III, and as modified in Appendix III of Chapter 6, "Separately Published Monographs" (p. 117). Do not use other abbreviations. When in doubt do *not* abbreviate.

1) Note that abbreviations are not used in recording titles.
2) The period is *not* used after the abbreviations 1st, 2d, 3d, 4th, etc.
3) Abbreviations are not used in quoted notes.

Numerals

Arabic numerals are substituted for roman except in the recording of the title or author statement, in the recording of pagination and references to pages, and in citing quoted matter.

Roman numerals are typed in capitals except those used in paging or page references and those appearing in lower case in the title or in quoted notes. Lower case numerals are used in paging or page references even if capitals appear in the work.

Inclusive numbers are given in full (e.g., p. 194-198). This means that century dates are repeated whether they designate the same century (1876-1889) or different centuries (1891-1912). The exception to this is that alternative dates give the second one as spoken (1802 or 3).

Pre-ISBD Cataloging Format

Fig. 1.12

```
Call      Author's name
 no.          Title, sub-title and/or alternative title,
          author statement (if necessary).² Edition
          statement. ⁴   Place, Publisher, Date.
              pagination² illus.² size ⁴ (Series
          statement)

              Notes as required; each note ordinarily
          forms a new paragraph.

              Tracings.
```

Sample form for a typed card. Note that small numbers have been inserted to indicate the exact spacing.

Just as in the first part of this chapter pre-ISBD examples were included to demonstrate the differences in these two forms of cataloging, examples of typing rules for pre-ISBD cataloging are given here. The student should note the major differences between ISBD and pre-ISBD formats. The importance of ISBD is discussed in Chapter 2. These pre-ISBD typing rules are included also for those libraries that have chosen *not* to follow ISBD format and that wish to retain the previous practices.

Spacing

1) **Main entry** begins on the fourth line from the top of the card.

2) **Single space the entries**, with the exception of a double space before beginning a note or statement of contents.

3) The **call number** begins on the fourth line from the top of the card. Indent the call number one space from the left edge of the card.

4) Leave **four spaces** between
   a) Edition and imprint
   b) Collation and series statement.

5) Leave **two spaces** between
   a) Pagination or number of volumes and illustrative material
   b) Title and edition
   c) Illustrative material and size.

6) **After punctuation**—as a rule, space once after a mark of punctuation.
   Williams, Alexander, tr.
   Bliss, Henry Evelyn, 1870-1955
   Tennyson, Alfred Tennyson, 1st baron.

   Exceptions to this rule are:

   In stating volumes and pages, omit space after v. and before and after p.:
   p.238-287.
   247p.
   v.11, p.24-48.
   In imprint, do not space after a comma or after the hyphen between two dates:
   1948,c1934
   1870-1955.

7) Leave eight spaces after an initial in heading to complete a name:
   Watson, R   James

Punctuation

Punctuation in the catalog entry should follow as far as possible the current usage of the language concerned. The following examples show usual practice in library catalogs.

1) Use **commas**
   a) Following a title before "by" and the author's name, when it is necessary to repeat the author's name:
      Adventures in contentment, by David Grayson.
   b) Before word or phrase in apposition with a name or term in a title:
      Alfred Nobel, dynamite king.
   c) To separate two or more series of volume numbers:
      v.1,3,10 printed in odd years.
   d) Between volume and date:
      v.2, Dec. 1953.
   e) To separate the surname and the forename.
   f) Following forenames, when words are affixed:
      Smith, Paul, ed.,
   g) To set off short phrases:
      Our earliest colonial settlements, their diversities of origin and later characteristics.
   h) To separate date, number, place, or designation from the name or heading, unless a specific rule provides or indicates otherwise.

2) Use **semicolons**
   a) Before a subtitle:
      Human action; a treatise on economics.
   b) Before an alternative title:
      Hans Brinker; or, The silver skates.
   c) To separate several works in one volume with titles on a common title page:
      The rivals; and The school for scandal.
   d) Between series:
      1941-43; 1944-47.

3) Use **periods**
   a) At the end of a title:
      Selected letters. Edited with an introd. by Diana Trilling.

      Exception: Use a comma, not a period, at the end of a title that is followed with "by," if the continuation repeats the author's name:
         Sam Bass and company, by Will C. Brown.
   b) At the end of the statement of edition or imprint, and of collation.
   c) Between subheadings of corporate author entry.
   d) After an author's name, except when dates of birth and death are included.
   e) After a subject heading at the head of a card.

4) Use **parentheses**
   a) To enclose the series statement:
   Kopf, Peter, 1832-
      Life adventures.   New York, Praeger,
   1900.
       92p.   31 cm.   (Books that matter)

5) Use **colons**
   a) To separate a statement of bibliography from the page citation:
   Bibliography: p.157-159.

6) Use the **period and dash**
   a) For sequence after a contents note:
      Contents.—The ethic of the group by
   L. C. Eisley.—Science and human values,
   by G. Seldes.—Law and the limits of
   individuality, by W. Hurst.

7) Avoid **double punctuation** as much as possible, especially the following double punctuation marks:
   a) Comma and dash
   b) Comma and parentheses
   c) Period and comma, except after abbreviations.

8) Use **brackets**
   a) To enclose any information in the body of the entry that is not found on the title page.

   Brackets are considered a mark of punctuation and, following the general rule of avoiding double punctuation, are not preceded or followed by commas, semicolons, or periods.

9) **Omissions** of statements from title page, such as an unimportant part of a long title, are indicated by three dots:

   The Dickens concordance, being a compendium of names and characters and principal places in all the works of Charles Dickens . . .

2 INTRODUCTION TO PRINCIPLES OF CATALOGING

INTRODUCTION

This chapter begins with a discussion of the purposes of catalogs. Cutter's objectives are presented and expanded for the modern catalog. The 1961 Paris Principles, which set an international standard for forms of headings in catalogs, are discussed in relation to the two basic purposes of a catalog: the finding list theory and the assembling of literary units theory. Following this is a brief history of the Cataloging Rules of the American Library Association, with specific comments on the 1908, 1941, and 1949 ALA Rules. The last section of this chapter deals with the current ALA Rules, the *Anglo-American Cataloging Rules*, 1967. In addition to discussing the general concept of the AACR, this section explains the various revisions, including the adoption of ISBD in revised Chapter 6, 1974, and the new rules for audiovisual media in revised Chapter 12, 1975. This section also introduces the student to the Library of Congress's policy of superimposition in relation to the AACR. The purpose of this chapter is to give the student an introduction to the theoretical and conceptual background for the current rules for descriptive cataloging, AACR 1967 and its revisions.

PURPOSES

The multiple-entry dictionary catalog, the standard form used in American libraries, records the holdings of a library in such a way as to offer the user a variety of approaches to the information he seeks. The objectives of this type of catalog as stated by Charles A. Cutter in his *Rules for a Dictionary Catalog* are still valid today, although modern practice indicates that they are incomplete. These objectives, first formulated in 1904, are as follows:

Objects

1) To enable a person to find a book when one of the following is known:
   a) The author
   b) The title
   c) The subject

2) To show what the library has
   d) By a given author
   e) On a given subject
   f) In a given kind of literature

3) To assist in the choice of a book
   g) As to the edition (bibliographically)
   h) As to its character (literary or topical).

Means

1) Author entry with the necessary references (for a and d)

2) Title entry or title reference (for b).

3) Subject entry, cross references, and classed subject table (for c and e)

4) Form entry and language entry (for f)

5) Edition and imprint, with notes when necessary (for g)

6) Notes (for h)[1]

Amplification of Cutter's Objects and Means

To conform to modern practice, the first objective needs to be rephrased as follows: To enable a person to find any literary creation whether issued in a print or non-print format. Cutter's first object is inadequate even for printed materials inasmuch as "book" does not unambiguously encompass "periodical," "serial," or "pamphlet." In addition, as stated, the objective makes no provision for audiovisual materials (e.g., "filmstrip," "tape recording").

Cutter's object "e" is too simplistic. Rephrased, it should read "on given and related subjects." It is clearly a prime function of a dictionary catalog to guide the user in the system of subject headings that any particular library may have adopted. Cutter's apparent assumption that the user always has a clearly formulated "given" subject in mind is contrary to all observation of catalog users.

Cutter's objectives remained the primary statement of catalog principles until 1961, when the International Federation of Library Associations at the Paris Conference approved the statement that the catalog should be an efficient instrument for ascertaining whether the library contains a particular book specified by:

1) a) its author and title, *or*
   b) if no author is named in the book, its title alone, *or*
   c) if author and title are inappropriate or insufficient for identification, a suitable substitute for the title,

---

[1] Charles A. Cutter, *Rules for a Dictionary Catalog*, 4th ed. (Washington, Government Printing Office, 1904), p. 12.

and

2) a) which works by a particular author *and*
   b) which editions of a particular work are in the library.[2]

These descriptions point out the dual functions that exist within the modern catalog causing it to be a finding list (see 1.a-c) for some purposes and an assembling device (see 2.a-b) for others. The catalog is a finding list in that it can provide the user with the necessary access to an individual item, whether the user approaches the item by author, title, or subject. In this sense the catalog is a finding list made up of specific individual pieces of information. A simple type of finding list would be a list of the titles of all the books in a collection. In fact, the white pages of the telephone directory may be considered as a typical finding list. In 1936, Julia Pettee pointed out the meaning of the finding list theory.

> The identification of the literary unit and the attribution of authorship in establishing the form of entry is so thoroughly ingrained in our catalogers, it may be a surprise to many to be told that these principles, in the long history of cataloging, are something very new and that they have not yet attained universal acceptance. The older working principle upon which all European rules have developed is that the catalog is a ready finding list for the particular book wanted, irrespective of its relation to any other book.[3]

A catalog constructed on this principle is efficient in showing whether or not a particular work by a certain author is in the collection. The deficiency is its failure to relate a particular work to other material—that is, it does not fulfill functions 2.a-b stated above. The assembling function provides means for bringing together in one place in a catalog all entries for like and closely related materials—e.g., for displaying together all the works of an author in the library collection. To achieve this, the assembling principle requires that the main entry for a work be in one "correct" form. Cataloging strictly from title page, which is sufficient for a finding list, would result in scattering rather than assembling related works. For example, the works of an author writing under more than one name or using various forms of a name would not have the same main entry and would be filed in several different places in the catalog. The library dictionary catalog represents an attempt to combine both the finding list and assembling device principles in construction and arrangement of entries. The advantage of utilizing both features in one catalog is obvious; at the same time, however, it results in a complex instrument, difficult to construct and often frustrating to use. The function of the main entry, the choosing of this entry and the form to follow must be viewed in this relationship to basic properties of the catalog.

---

[2] International Conference on Cataloguing Principles. Paris, 9th-18th October, 1961, *Report* (London, International Federation of Library Associations, 1963), p. 26.

[3] Julia Pettee, "Development of Authorship Entry and the Formulation of Authorship Rules as Found in the Anglo-American Code," *Library Quarterly* 6 (July 1936): 271.

Several solutions are used to deal with this problem. Main entries may be arranged according to the form of the author's name as it appears on the title page, in which case the assembling of all works of the same author is then achieved by using cross-references. The same approach may be used for titles. Main entries are arranged according to the titles of the particular works; assembling the various editions, translations, or literary forms of the same work is accomplished by using added entries.

The other method is to establish one "correct" form for an author's name, so that all publications by this author are automatically assembled in one place. Again, cross references are required to provide access to the form of name actually on the title page, or to variant forms widely known, for which some readers may search. In a similar manner, the main entry is chosen according to the original, best known, or some other accepted **uniform title**; the result of this is that all editions, translations, etc., of the same work are automatically assembled in one place. In this case, references or added entries are provided for titles of the work that vary from the chosen heading.

Thus, a basic decision to be made, one of cataloging policy for the library, is whether uniform headings are to be adopted or whether headings are to follow the form of name and title as these appear on the title page of each work. *The Anglo-American Cataloging Rules* provide guidance in this matter; as can be seen from a study of rules for form of entry, the AACR encourage use of the author's name as commonly known, choice of fewer title entries, and more uniform headings for certain entries. In either case, added entries and references of various types are essential if the objectives of the catalog are to be fulfilled. The AACR stress consistently that catalogers must consider added entries and references whenever a choice between two possible entries or forms of entry is necessary. The decision of how extensively to follow this practice is, of course, left to each individual library.

BRIEF HISTORY OF ALA CATALOGING RULES

Cataloging codes, which are basic principles and rules set down to guide catalogers, allow the expansion and development of a catalog within a fairly consistent and uniform framework. The present *Anglo-American Cataloging Rules* represent the influence of early British and American codes. Panizzi's British Museum *Rules for the Compiling of the Catalogue* (1841) was a major statement of principles underlying cataloging rules; as such, it exerted an influence on the American code. Cutter's *Rules for a Dictionary Catalog*, in its fourth edition at his death in 1903, presented the first complete set of rules for a dictionary catalog. The effect of these rules continued through LC *Rules on Printed Cards* (1903 through the 1930s), LC *Rules for Descriptive Cataloging* (1949), ALA *Rules* (1908, 1941, 1949), and the present AACR (published in 1967).

The ALA *Rules* of 1908 were the result of a seven-year study by a committee of ALA. In 1901 the Library of Congress began its printed card service, with the result that libraries became interested in ways to use LC cards with their own cards.

One of the important responsibilities of the committee was to formulate rules to encourage incorporation of LC printed cards into catalogs of other libraries. The committee attempted to reconcile the cataloging practices of LC with those of other research and scholarly libraries. The use of LC cards increased dramatically between 1908 and 1941; standardization of library catalogs progressed. However, the ALA *Rules* were not expanded during this 33-year period, drastically curtailing attempts of cataloging practice to stay in touch with cataloging done at the Library of Congress. In 1930 a subcommittee was appointed by ALA to begin work on a revision of cataloging rules, and the problems were outlined. Dissatisfaction with the 1908 code was expressed on the grounds of "omissions"; the basic rules were not in question. Expansion was required to meet the needs of large scholarly libraries or specialized collections.

> The preliminary edition, published in 1941, expanded the rules of 1908 to make more provision for special classes of material: serial publications, government documents, publications of religious bodies, anonymous classics, music and maps; to amplify existing rules to cover specific cases of frequent occurrence.[4]

The revised edition of 1949 states that

> the chief changes from the preliminary edition are a rearrangement of the material to emphasize the basic rules and subordinate their amplifications, and to make the sequence of rules logical as far as possible; reduction of the number of alternate rules; omission of rules for description; rewording to avoid repetition or to make the meaning clearer; and revision, where possible, of rules inconsistent with the general principles.[5]

The 1941 and 1949 rules were sharply criticized for being too elaborate and often arbitrary; emphasis had shifted from clearly defined principles to a collection of rules developed to fit specific cases rather than the conditions that the cases illustrated. Lubetzky commented that any logical approach to cataloging problems was blocked by the maze of arbitrary and repetitious rules and exceptions to rules.[6]

---

[4] *A.L.A. Cataloging Rules for Author and Title Entries* (Chicago, American Library Association, 1949), p. viii.

[5] Ibid., p. ix.

[6] Seymour Lubetzky, *Cataloging Rules and Principles: A Critique of the ALA Rules for Entry and a Proposed Design for Their Revision* (Washington, Processing Department, Library of Congress, 1953); also, by the same author, *Code of Cataloging Rules, Author, and Title; an Unfinished Draft . . . with an Explanatory Commentary by Paul Dunkin* (Washington, American Library Association, 1960).

ANGLO-AMERICAN CATALOGING RULES, 1967

The Catalog Code Revision Committee that prepared the 1967 *Anglo-American Cataloging Rules* realized that revision must be a complete reexamination of the principles and objectives of cataloging, not merely a revision of specific rules. First, the objectives of the catalog were agreed upon; it was further decided that certain general principles should be the basis for rules of entry and heading. These general principles of the new code are based on the "Statement of Principles" approved by 53 countries at the International Conference on Cataloguing Principles in Paris, October 1961. This important step toward international bibliographical standardization, among other things, encourages continuation and expansion of the "shared cataloging" project between the United States and other countries.

The AACR code is oriented toward large research libraries, although alternate rules are provided for use by non-research libraries when a general conflict is apparent. The rules are designed to satisfy the requirements of multiple-approach alphabetical catalogs in which uniform headings are used for particular persons and corporate bodies, or are related by references. Headings are more direct and provision is made for sufficient added entries and references to satisfy the various approaches readers might take to locate materials. The code incorporates rules for entry and heading, description, and cataloging of non-book material. An important shift occurred in the philosophy underlying the rules for entry: "The entry for a work is normally based on the statements that appear on the title page or any part of the work that is used as its substitute."[7] Statements on the cover, half title, verso of the title page, etc., are taken into account; information appearing only in the preface, introduction, or text is not considered unless the title page information is vague or incomplete. A basic change in the point of view of the AACR places different demands on the cataloger. Cataloging by types of authorship rather than types of works, by classes of names rather than classes of people, is a basic change that must be thoroughly comprehended. The cataloger must fully understand the general rules before attempting to use the code. The code provides ample specific rules to deal with aspects of a problem; however, even these specific rules are to be interpreted in context of relevant general rules.

The code distinguishes between choice of entry and form of entry. The section on choice of main entry brings together rules for works of personal authorship, unknown authorship, publications of corporate bodies and government agencies, and legal and religious publications. Choice of main entry is considered a question of determining authorship. Certain general principles are the basis of the rules for choice of entry, as follows:

1) Entry should be under author or principal author when one can be determined;

2) Entry should be under title in the case of works whose authorship is diffuse, indeterminate, or unknown.

Catalogers using the AACR will consult two places in the rules when preparing main entries; first, rules for choice of entry, and second, rules for form of

---

[7]*Anglo-American Cataloging Rules.* North American Text (Chicago, American Library Association, 1967), p. 9. (The AACR was issued in two editions: the North American text and the British text.)

entry. The first is a question of determining authorship—i.e., the person(s) or corporate body chiefly responsible for the intellectual or artistic content of a work. This may be a writer as a single author, joint authors, collaborators, editor, compiler, translator, composer or artist, etc. Rules for choice of entry prefer a personal or corporate name to a title in most cases. The actual construction of a main entry centers on a problem of name—the choice of a particular name and/or a particular form of that name, and the form in which that name is presented in the main entry. The introduction to the AACR states that the rules for form of entry of names are based on considerations of morphology, language, and customs as well as considerations of relationship to other headings, or dependence of the name on another name. Rules for form of entry are based on a general principle of using the form of name ordinarily used by a person or corporate body rather than the full name or official name as 1949 ALA rules directed. Following this general principle, entry for a person is under the name by which he is most commonly identified, whether this is his real name, assumed name, nickname, changed name, title of nobility, etc. This is in contrast to the ALA rules, where stress was placed on "real names" and full form—i.e., authoritative form of the name. The principle for entry of personal names is expanded by various specific rules, which require careful study. Pseudonyms are considered in specific rules but follow the general principle of entry under most commonly used form. However, the term "pseud." is not used in the heading or author statement in the body of the entry. The alternate rule for non-research libraries provides that each work of an author who uses several names may be entered under the name he uses in that particular work, with references to connect the various names used as main entries.

Other changes include use of the English forms of names instead of vernacular forms (e.g., Horace, not Horatius Flaccus, Quintus). Dates are added to a person's name if readily ascertainable, but they are not required except to distinguish between persons with the same name.

A very important area of change is in the form of entry for corporate bodies. The general rule follows the code principle of using the form of name that the body itself uses, except when the rules provide for entry: 1) under a higher body of which it is a part, or 2) under name of a government of which it is an agency. The rules of entry apply to all corporate names regardless of the nature of the organization. However, exceptions are stated exempting specified bodies of an institutional nature from the principle of entry under name, and these are entered under place as in the old rules. These exceptions are contrary to the Paris Principles and to earlier drafts of this code and the British text of AACR, but they were requested by the Association of Research Libraries. The request was based on the fact that many large research libraries, with thousands of entries of this nature in their catalogs, would be overburdened if they accepted the rule for entry of corporate bodies as originally stated. Critics of the code argue that by allowing an optional exception to the general rule the code is perpetuating a much criticized American practice. It is also pointed out that this inconsistent practice does not take advantage of the immediate prospects for further development of international bibliographic standards, nor does it respond to the user-convenience concept in practice or theory.[8] In 1974 this problem was largely resolved by dropping the

---

[8] Ron Taylor, "Corporate Authorship and Cultural Revolution," *Library Resources and Technical Services* 10 (Fall 1966): 451-454.

basic rule for entry under place (AACR 99) from the code. There is little doubt that the code now places cataloging on a more logical base; though it is not substantially a simplified code, it is a more comprehensible one, better suited for application to more situations.

In 1970 the AACR, North American text, was reprinted in a paperbound edition with a supplement of additions and changes from 1967 to 1969. Additions and changes to the code are regularly published in *Cataloging Service*, a bulletin from the Processing Department of the Library of Congress. It is presently a quarterly publication issued free by the LC Cataloging Distribution Service Division. Besides additions and changes to the code, the publication contains much additional information, including occasional issues devoted solely to cataloging decisions at the Library of Congress. These issues are particularly useful to the cataloger since they state the official LC interpretations and decisions relating to the application of AACR on LC printed cards. *Cataloging Service* also gives information on subject cataloging at the Library of Congress.

Since the publication of AACR, North American text, in 1967, at least 38 rules have been changed and three chapters totally revised. Four rules (3, 4, 11, and 98) have been completely rewritten and two rules (5 and 99) have been deleted. These changes reflect development toward the second edition of the AACR and the attempt to establish complete uniformity between the British and North American texts. Perhaps the most significant single change has been the application of standards of bibliographic description based on International Standard Bibliographic Description (ISBD) for descriptive cataloging of monographs, audiovisual media, and special instructional materials. In 1974 the revised Chapter 6 for separately published monographs (including photographic and other reproductions, formerly in Chapter 9) was published in a separate paperbound edition by the American Library Association; the following year, revised Chapter 12, for audiovisual media, was issued by the American Library Association. In addition, **ISBD(S)** (i.e., ISBD for serials) is being studied for possible adoption.

ISBD was developed from 1969 to 1974 by the Committee on Cataloging of the International Federation of Library Associations.

> The purpose of the ISBD(M) is to provide an internationally accepted framework for the representation of descriptive information in bibliographic records of monographic—i.e., non-serial—publications. It is designed to meet three requirements for the efficient international use of such records: first, that records produced in one country or by the users of one language can be easily understood in other countries and by the users of other languages; secondly, that the records produced in each country can be integrated into files or lists of various kinds containing also records from other countries; and thirdly, that records in written or printed form can be converted into machine-readable form with the minimum of editing.[9]

---

[9]International Federation of Library Associations. *ISBD(M): International Standard Bibliographic Description for Monographic Publications.* 1st standard ed. (London, IFLA Committee on Cataloging, 1974), p. vii.

ISBD facilitates the international exchange of bibliographic information by standardizing the elements to be used in the bibliographic description, assigning an order to these elements in the entry, and specifying a system of symbols to be used in punctuating these elements.

> ISBD requires that a publication be totally identified by the description. It is independent of the provisions for headings, main or added, and of the provisions for the use of uniform titles; these were internationally standardized by the Paris Principles.[10]

The application of ISBD to the descriptive cataloging rules of AACR has not resulted in any major changes in the elements to be included in the body of the entry, in the collation or in the notes sections on the catalog cards. The most significant change is the introduction of a system of formal and identifiable punctuation. The first stated purpose of ISBD is clearly met by cards cataloged according to the rules in revised Chapter 6. Because of the standard punctuation, a user unfamiliar with the language of the description can readily identify the elements of description. For example, the slash symbol indicates that the authorship statement is following. The period-space-dash-space following the authorship statement indicates that the authorship statement has concluded.

The other major change resulting from ISBD is the requirement that the authorship statement always be included in the body of the entry. This allows the body of the entry to perform the finding list function no matter what the main entry is. ISBD does then provide a *complete* bibliographic citation by itself. The previous rules in both the AACR and ALA codes allowed the authorship statement to be eliminated if it were already present in the main entry. Revised Chapter 6 does provide an alternative rule for omission of the authorship statement, but the Library of Congress has indicated that on its printed cards the authorship statement will appear in the body of the entry to conform to the basic rule and the principle of ISBD. It is this author's opinion that the present rule of automatic inclusion of the authorship statement is superior both for the internal integrity of the body of the entry and for economy of decision in the cataloging operation. While choice and form of entry may require professional judgment, descriptive cataloging using ISBD may now be a purely clerical operation.

Other improvements in revised Chapter 6 are found in the distinctions of the terms title proper, parallel title, alternative title, edition, and printing. The provisions for inclusion of place of printing and printer as well as generic titles for series and the indication of indexes in the notes are all improvements. In fact, the form of presentation, in general, in revised Chapter 6 is a major improvement for both catalogers and students. D. Whitney Coe, in a detailed comparison of the former Chapter 6 with the current one, says, "The opportunity has been taken for a careful examination of the code with the aim of providing both major change in certain rules as well as greater clarity in the wording of the text."[11]

---

[10]"International Standard Bibliographic Description," Library of Congress Processing Department, *Cataloging Service*, bulletin 105 (November 1972), p. 2.

[11]D. Whitney Coe, "A Cataloger's Guide to *AACR* Chapter 6, Separately Published Monographs, 1974," *Library Resources and Technical Services* 19 (Spring 1975): 120.

Finally, it may be restated that the AACR are a substantial departure from ALA rules in that a set of basic principles replaces rules based on specific cases or arbitrary rules and exceptions. The 1961 Paris principles are implemented by the rules for choice and form of entry, especially with the deletion of AACR 99 for entry under place. Revised Chapter 6 directly implements ISBD for monographs, and revised Chapter 12 extends these principles to audiovisual media. AACR and its revisions are now a direct reflection of international cataloging principles and practices.

Although the revised AACR now conform to these international principles, the vast majority of library catalogs contain many cards based on earlier rules for both entries and descriptions. In January of 1967 the Library of Congress announced its policy of **superimposition**.

This means that the rules for choice of entry will be applied only to works that are new to the Library and that the rules for headings will be applied only to persons and corporate bodies that are being established for the first time. New editions, etc., of works previously cataloged will be entered in the same way as the earlier editions (except for revised editions in which change of authorship is indicated). New works by previously established authors will appear under the same headings.[12]

Some libraries may choose to implement only selected sections of the AACR, and some libraries may be in the position to use all the rules. The administrative problems inherent in the application of these rules within a catalog whose entries are based on another set of rules is recognized as one requiring full and intensive study.[13] It is apparent that catalogers will need to be familiar with both sets of rules—or at least with the major differences between them as they apply to the catalogers' particular libraries. To assist beginning catalogers with this problem, Chapter 1 of this textbook contains a discussion and examples of the former rules for description.

It is hoped that the card samples in Chapters 3 through 9 will prove helpful in illustrating the basic rules. Needless to say, the complete AACR should be consulted for additional rules covering aspects of problems too detailed for inclusion in this text, for further explanation, definitions and references.

---

[12] Library of Congress Processing Department, *Cataloging Service*, bulletin 79 (January 1967), p. 1.

[13] Joseph A. Rosenthal, "The Administrative Implications of the New Rules," *Library Resources and Technical Services* 10 (Fall 1966): 437-444; "The New Rules in Action: A Symposium," *Library Resources and Technical Services* 13 (Winter 1969): 7-41. A detailed analysis of the code is also provided in *The Code and the Cataloger: Proceedings of the Colloquium on the Anglo-American Cataloging Rules* ... (Toronto, University of Toronto Press, 1969). For information on the new changes, see: Mary Ellen Soper, "Revision of Chapter 6, Anglo-American Cataloging Rules, a Review," *PNLA Quarterly* 39 (Winter 1975): 13-20; and Doris Hayashikawa, Mary V. Kuder, and Leila M. Payne, "Coping with Catalog Code Revision," *Texas Library Journal* 51 (Summer 1975): 74-76; of particular importance is Elizabeth L. Tate, "Descriptive Cataloger's Guide to the Revised Rules of Description," *Library of Congress Information Bulletin* 33 (August 2, 1974): A162-A166. An index to revised Chapter 6 has been compiled by Judith Hopkins, School of Library Science, University of Michigan, Ann Arbor, Michigan, June 1975.

3 CHOICE OF ENTRY RULES

INTRODUCTION

The rules in this chapter deal basically with the choice of entry and not the form of entry. Choice of entry means choosing the name of the author or the title of the work for the heading or main entry; this is done after an examination of the title page of a work. In addition, many of these rules require the choice of specific added entries. This chapter covers basic choice of entry for single authorship, shared authorship, collections and works produced under editorial direction, and serials. Additional rules cover works with authorship of mixed character, corporate authorship, and related and dependent works. The next to the last section of rules deals with works whose entries require a prescribed form of subheading such as laws, constitutions, treaties, sacred works, and liturgical works. Basic rules for added entries make up the last section of this chapter. The rules covered in this chapter deal only with basic or general instances; for more complex problems and special cases the student should consult the AACR, Chapter 1. Card examples are used in this text to allow the student to see not only the choice of entry for our examples but also the form of entry and the added entries in the tracing. The following chapters deal with these specific forms. In addition, the student should note that all of the following examples follow ISBD(M) according to AACR, revised Chapter 6, and Library of Congress practice.

BASIC RULES

Rule 1. Works of single authorship

1A. "Enter a work, a collection of works, or selections from works by one author under the person or corporate body that is the author, whether named in the work or not." Authorship is defined in AACR (p. 9, footnote 2) as follows: "By 'author' is meant the person or corporate body chiefly responsible for the creation of the intellectual or artistic content of a work. Thus composers, artists, photographers, etc., are the 'authors' of the works they create; chess-players are the 'authors' of their recorded games; etc. The term 'author' also embraces an editor or compiler who has primary responsibility for the content of a work, e.g. the compiler of a bibliography." It does not matter whether the author's name appears in the work or not. If the author is known the work is entered under his name.

See Chapter 4, Form of Entry Headings for Persons, and Chapter 5, Form of Entry Headings for Corporate Bodies, for the form of entry for these names.

Title Page

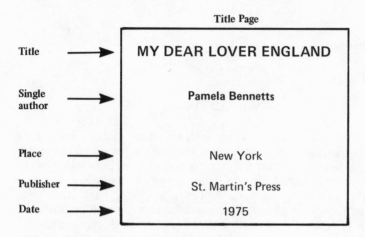

This title page may be used as an example of Rule 1A, a work of single authorship. The choice of main entry should be the single author, Pamela Bennetts. Note the form of this name on the following card example, Fig. 3.1.

Fig. 3.1

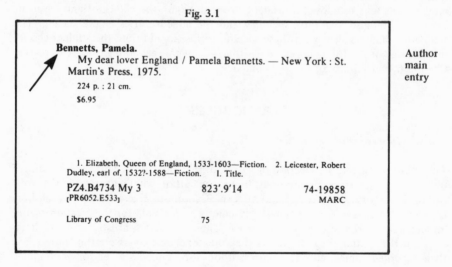

Rule 1A. A work of single authorship.

1B. When a publication erroneously or fictitiously attributes authorship to someone who is not the author, enter it under the actual author if possible and make an added entry under the attributed author if such an individual is a real person.

Fig. 3.2

Actual
author
as
main
entry

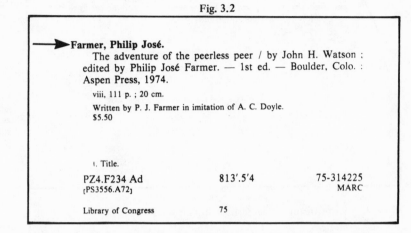

Farmer, Philip José.
   The adventure of the peerless peer / by John H. Watson ;
   edited by Philip José Farmer. — 1st ed. — Boulder, Colo. :
   Aspen Press, 1974.

   viii, 111 p. ; 20 cm.

   Written by P. J. Farmer in imitation of A. C. Doyle.
   $5.50

   ı. Title.

   PZ4.F234 Ad   813'.5'4   75-314225
   [PS3556.A72]   MARC

   Library of Congress   75

Rule 1B. Entry under the real author rather than the attributed author.

Note: No added entry is made for the attributed author, John H. Watson, since he is a fictional character created by A. C. Doyle in his series of detective stories about Sherlock Holmes and Dr. Watson.

Rule 2. Works of unknown or uncertain authorship, or by unnamed groups

   Enter under title the work of unknown or uncertain authorship. Always make an added entry under a person to whom authorship is attributed. **Note:** The body of the entry is generally presented in the form of a "hanging indention."

Title Page

Title

Subtitle

Unknown
author

Place

Publisher

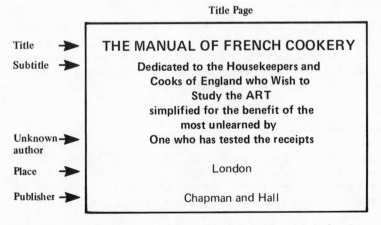

THE MANUAL OF FRENCH COOKERY

**Dedicated to the Housekeepers and
Cooks of England who Wish to
Study the ART
simplified for the benefit of the
most unlearned by
One who has tested the receipts**

London

Chapman and Hall

This title page is used as an example of Rule 2, works of unknown authorship. Since the author is not known, the choice of entry is the title: *The Manual of French Cookery*. See Fig. 3.3.

Fig. 3.3

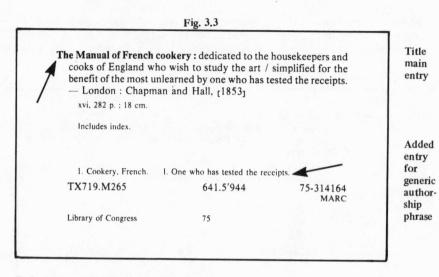

The Manual of French cookery : dedicated to the housekeepers and cooks of England who wish to study the art / simplified for the benefit of the most unlearned by one who has tested the receipts.
— London : Chapman and Hall, [1853]

xvi, 282 p. : 18 cm.

Includes index.

1. Cookery, French.   1. One who has tested the receipts.

TX719.M265   641.5'944   75-314164
                                                 MARC

Library of Congress   75

Title main entry

Added entry for generic authorship phrase

Rule 2. A work of unknown authorship entered under title.

Rule 3. Works of shared authorship[1]

This rule applies to situations when more than one author is responsible for the intellectual content of a work. Note the following categories:

1. "Works produced by the joint collaboration of two or more authors"—in which the contribution of each is not a separate and distinct part of the whole.

2. "Works for which different authors have prepared separate contributions, e.g., composite works, series of addresses, lectures, etc. . . ."

3. "Works consisting of an exchange between different persons, e.g., correspondence, debates, etc."

This rule also applies to cases of shared responsibility among editors, compilers, translators, etc. For special types of collaboration between artist or author of text, refer to Rule 8A; reporter or person reported, Rule 13; and writer or nominal author, Rule 16. Works of shared authorship will require a number of added entries. The general principles for making added entries are listed in Rule 33.

3A. Principal author indicated

Enter a work of shared authorship under the principal author if one is indicated by wording or typography. Make added entries under the other authors involved, if there are not more than two. Always make an added entry under the author, other than the principal author, whose name appears first on the title page. See Fig. 3.4.

---

[1]This rule has been revised from AACR 1967. The full revision is listed in *Cataloging Service*, bulletin 112 (Winter 1975): 1-5.

Title Page

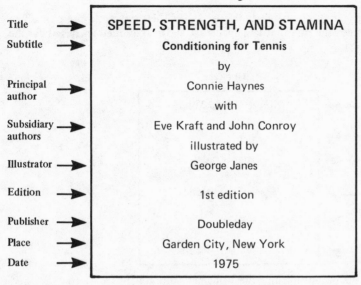

Since the principal author, Connie Haynes, is indicated on the title page of this work by the wording of the subsidiary authorship statement, the choice of main entry is the principal author. See Fig. 3.4.

Fig. 3.4

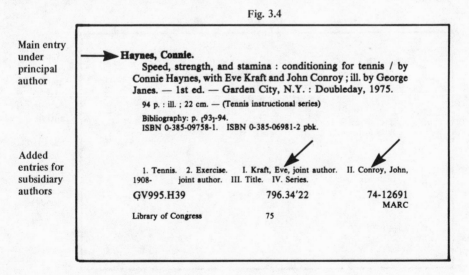

Rule 3A. Principal author indicated.

3B1. Principal author not indicated

If the principal author is not indicated and if there are not more than three authors, enter under the one that is named first and make added entries under the others. See Fig. 3.5.

Title Page

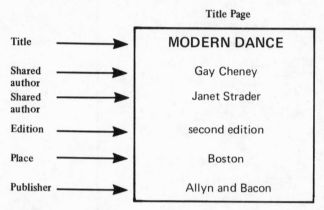

Title ⟶	**MODERN DANCE**
Shared author ⟶	Gay Cheney
Shared author ⟶	Janet Strader
Edition ⟶	second edition
Place ⟶	Boston
Publisher ⟶	Allyn and Bacon

In this case of shared authorship, the principal author is not indicated; further, there are not more than three authors listed (i.e., two in this example), so the choice of main entry is the first named author. See Fig. 3.5. If there had been more than three authors on the title page, the choice of entry would have been the title. See Fig. 3.6.

Fig. 3.5

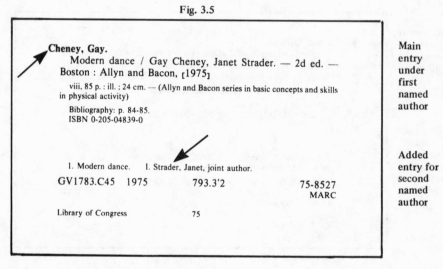

Cheney, Gay.
    Modern dance / Gay Cheney, Janet Strader. — 2d ed. — Boston : Allyn and Bacon, ₁1975₎
        viii, 85 p. : ill. ; 24 cm. — (Allyn and Bacon series in basic concepts and skills in physical activity)
        Bibliography: p. 84-85.
        ISBN 0-205-04839-0

    1. Modern dance.   1. Strader, Janet, joint author.
    GV1783.C45   1975   793.3'2   75-8527
                                                          MARC
    Library of Congress   75

Main entry under first named author

Added entry for second named author

Rule 3B. Principal author not indicated.

3B2. If principal author is not indicated and there are more than three authors, enter work under its title and make an added entry under the author named first on the title page. See Fig. 3.6.

Note: If the work is produced under the direction of an editor named on the title page, apply Rule 4.

Fig. 3.6

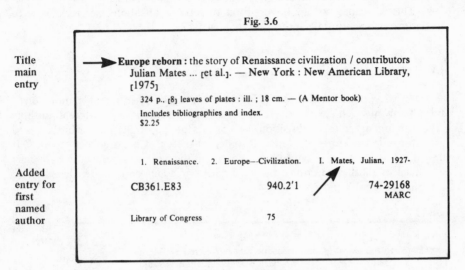

Title
main
entry

Added
entry for
first
named
author

Rule 3B2. Principal author not indicated with entry under title.

3C. Joint pseudonyms

3C1. "If collaborating authors consistently use a joint pseudonym instead of their real individual names, enter under the pseudonym and refer to it from their real names." (See Rule 121B1 for making a "pseudonym-and-title" reference for each work of an author that is so entered.)

Fig. 3.7

Main entry
under joint
pseudonym

Rule 3C1. Joint pseudonyms

Note: Ellery Queen is the joint pseudonym of Frederic Dannay and Manfred Bennington Lee and will require explanatory references to Queen from Dannay and Lee.

Rule 4. Collections, and works produced under editorial direction[2]

"Preliminary note. Many works containing material by more than one author are collections of works not written specifically for the same occasion or for the publication in hand, or are extracts from such works, brought together by a compiler, or are works produced under the direction of an editor."

This rule does not apply to editors of serial publications (see Rule 6) or to entries involving corporate authorship (see Rule 17).

4A. With collective title

"If a work is a collection of independent works by different authors, or of extracts from such works, or consists of contributions by different authors produced under editorial direction, or consists partly of such contributions and partly of independent works, enter it under its title, if it has a collective title." If the editor or compiler is named prominently on the work or is known to have been so named in another edition of the work, make an added entry under the editor or compiler. (Figs. 3.8 and 3.9)

Fig. 3.8

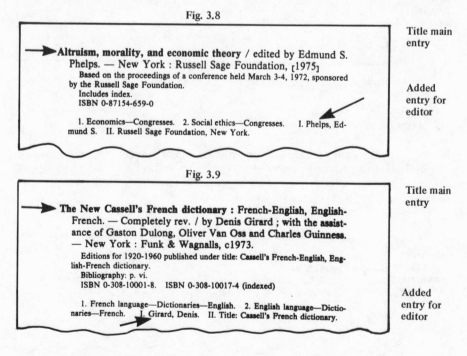

Fig. 3.8

Altruism, morality, and economic theory / edited by Edmund S. Phelps. — New York : Russell Sage Foundation, [1975]
Based on the proceedings of a conference held March 3-4, 1972, sponsored by the Russell Sage Foundation.
Includes index.
ISBN 0-87154-659-0

1. Economics—Congresses. 2. Social ethics—Congresses. I. Phelps, Edmund S. II. Russell Sage Foundation, New York.

Title main entry

Added entry for editor

Fig. 3.9

The New Cassell's French dictionary : French-English, English-French. — Completely rev. / by Denis Girard ; with the assistance of Gaston Dulong, Oliver Van Oss and Charles Guinness. — New York : Funk & Wagnalls, c1973.
Editions for 1920-1960 published under title: Cassell's French-English, English-French dictionary.
Bibliography: p. vi.
ISBN 0-308-10001-8. ISBN 0-308-10017-4 (indexed)

1. French language—Dictionaries—English. 2. English language—Dictionaries—French. I. Girard, Denis. II. Title: Cassell's French dictionary.

Title main entry

Added entry for editor

Rule 4A. Collections and works produced under editorial direction with collective titles. Added entries are made for the first-named editors.

[2]This rule has been revised from AACR 1967 and combined with Rule 5. The full revision is listed in *Cataloging Service*, bulletin 112 (Winter 1975): 5-8.

4B. Without collective title

"If a collection, or a work produced under editorial direction, lacks a collective title, enter it under the heading appropriate to the first work named on the title page, or, if there is no collective title page, under the heading appropriate to the first work in the collection. Make an added entry under the compiler or editor if he is named prominently. Make added entries under the other works or authors included if appropriate under the criteria given in A above." (Fig. 3.10)

Fig. 3.10

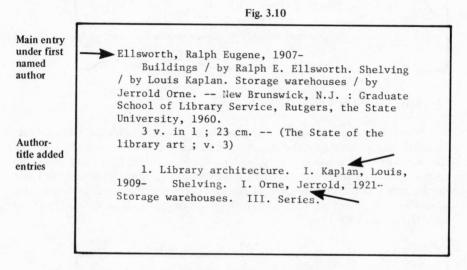

Main entry under first named author

Author-title added entries

```
Ellsworth, Ralph Eugene, 1907-
     Buildings / by Ralph E. Ellsworth. Shelving
/ by Louis Kaplan. Storage warehouses / by
Jerrold Orne. -- New Brunswick, N.J. : Graduate
School of Library Service, Rutgers, the State
University, 1960.
     3 v. in 1 ; 23 cm. -- (The State of the
library art ; v. 3)

     1. Library architecture.  I. Kaplan, Louis,
1909-   Shelving.  I. Orne, Jerrold, 1921--
Storage warehouses.  III. Series.
```

Rule 4B. Collections without a collective title.

Rule 6. Serials[3]

A serial is a publication issued in successive parts, at regular or irregular intervals, and intended to continue indefinitely. Serials include both periodicals and non-periodicals. A periodical is a serial that has a distinctive title, that is issued more frequently than once a year, and that generally has articles by several contributors. Non-periodicals are all other forms of serials, such as memoirs of societies, transactions, proceedings, yearbooks, indexes, directories, almanacs, annuals, etc. The following rules bring together both periodicals and non-periodicals; rules for serials also apply to the series added entries that are made for monographs in a series. It should be noted that a serial that changes title, author, or name of issuing body will have a separate entry for the issues appearing after the change. (See Rule 6D.)

---

[3] It is highly likely that this rule will be revised in the second edition of AACR, if not before. In 1975 the ALA Catalog Code Revision Committee recommended to the editors of AACR 2 that a rule specifying the entry of all serials under title should be developed. This potential revision would be in harmony with ISBD(S) and ISDS as discussed in Chapter 8 of this textbook.

6A. Serials not issued by a corporate body and not of personal authorship

Entry is under title. See Fig. 3.11.

Fig. 3.11

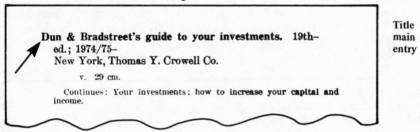

Dun & Bradstreet's guide to your investments. 19th–
ed.; 1974/75–
New York, Thomas Y. Crowell Co.

v. 29 cm.

Continues: Your investments; how to increase your capital and income.

Title
main
entry

6B. Serials issued by a corporate body

"Enter a periodical, monographic series, or a serially published bibliography, index, directory, biographical dictionary, almanac, or yearbook, issued by or under the authority of a corporate body, under its title with an added entry under the corporate body. *Exception*: If the title (exclusive of the subtitle) includes the name or the abbreviation of the name of the corporate body, or consists solely of a generic term that requires the name of the body for adequate identification of the serial, enter under the body."

Fig. 3.12

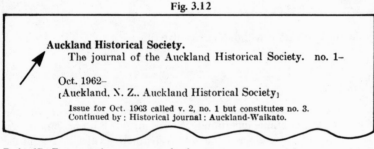

Auckland Historical Society.
 The journal of the Auckland Historical Society. no. 1–

Oct. 1962–
 [Auckland, N. Z.. Auckland Historical Society]

Issue for Oct. 1963 called v. 2, no. 1 but constitutes no. 3.
Continued by: Historical journal: Auckland-Waikato.

Main
entry
under
corporate
body

Rule 6B. Entry under corporate body.

WORKS WITH AUTHORSHIP OF MIXED CHARACTER

In many works the authorship is divided in responsibility. This occurs when different persons or bodies have contributed to the intellectual or artistic content performing different kinds of functions, e.g., writing, adapting, illustrating, translating, etc. Determination of main entry depends to a large extent on the relative importance of such contributions. The rules that follow prescribe the choice between several alternatives.

Rule 7. Adapter or original author

7A. "Enter an adaptation or other rewriting of a work in a different literary style (e.g., a paraphrase, epitome, version for children) or in a different literary form (e.g., a dramatization, novelization, versification) under the person who did the adapting or rewriting, if known; otherwise under its title. Make the appropriate added entry for the original work." See Fig. 3.13.

Fig. 3.13

Adapter as main entry

Original author as author-title added entry

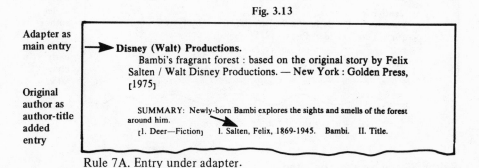

Rule 7A. Entry under adapter.

Rule 8. Artist or author of text

8A. Collaborative work

"Enter a work that is or appears to be a work of collaboration between an artist and the author of the text under the one who is named first on the title page unless the other's name is given greater prominence by wording or typography. In case of doubt, prefer entry under the author of the text. Make an added entry under the one not given main entry." (Cf. Rule 260 for individual pictorial works.) See Fig. 3.14.

Fig. 3.14

Main entry under artist named first on title page

Added entry for author

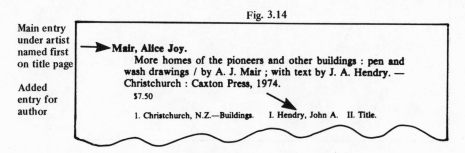

Rule 8A. Collaborative work entered under artist.

8B. Illustrated work

"Enter a work for which an artist has provided illustrations under the author of the text. Make an added entry under the illustrator of the work according to the provisions of 33F." See Fig. 3.15.

Fig. 3.15

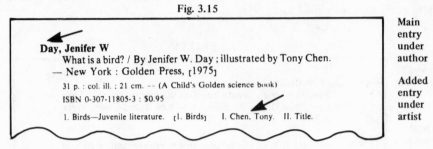

Main
entry
under
author

Added
entry
under
artist

Rule 8B. Illustrated work entered under author.

Rule 9. Biographer/critic or author

9A. "Enter a publication consisting of a work or a group of works of an author accompanied by or interwoven with biographical or critical material by another person, under the latter if he is represented as author. Make an author-title added entry under the author whose work is published with the biographical or critical material. In case of doubt enter under the person whose name appears first." See Fig. 3.16.

Fig. 3.16

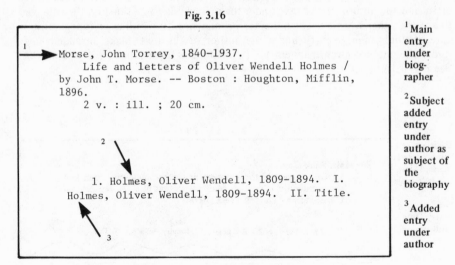

[1] Main
entry
under
biog-
rapher

[2] Subject
added
entry
under
author as
subject of
the
biography

[3] Added
entry
under
author

Rule 9. Biographical work entered under biographer.

9B. "If the one who is responsible for the biographical or critical material is represented as editor, enter under the author of the work and make an added entry under the editor." See Fig. 3.17.

Fig. 3.17

Main
entry
under
author

Added
entry under
editor

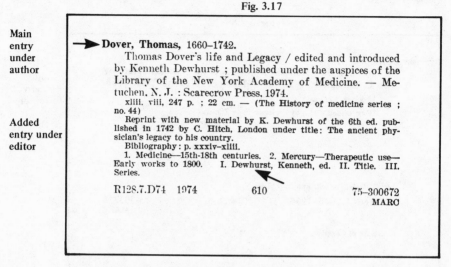

Rule 9B. Edited biographical work.

Rule 14. Reviser or original author

14A. "In general, enter an edition that has been revised, enlarged, abridged, condensed, etc., by another person, under the original author, with an added entry under the other person." See Fig. 3.18.

Fig. 3.18

Main
entry
under
original
author

Added
entry under
reviser

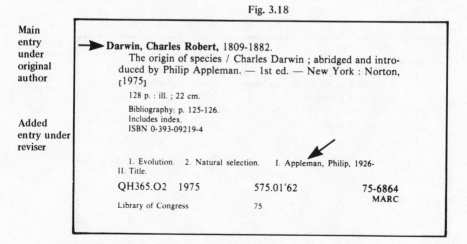

Rule 14A. Revised work entered under original author.

14B. "If the title page of the new edition clearly indicates that the work is no longer that of the original author, however, enter it under the new author. Make an author-title added entry under, or an explanatory reference from, the heading for the earlier work." See Fig. 3.19.

Fig. 3.19

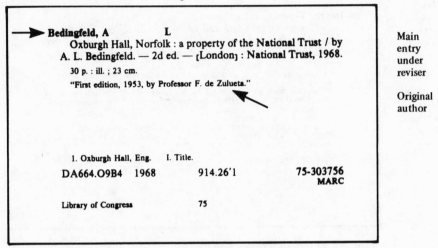

Rule 14B. Revised work entered under reviser.

Rule 15. Translator or author

15A. "Enter a translation of a work under the author of the original work." Make an added entry under a translator if such an entry may be needed as an approach to the publication (see Rule 33E).

Fig. 3.20

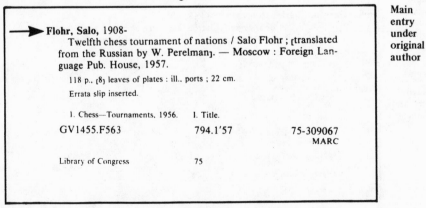

Rule 15A. Translation entered under original author.

CORPORATE AUTHORSHIP

Rule 17. Corporate author or personal author

"This rule applies to works issued by or bearing the authority of a corporate body, but with authorship or editorship specifically and prominently attributed to one or more persons, either by name or by official title."

17A. Works of Corporate authorship

17A1. "Enter under the corporate body, with an added entry under the personal author or the one named first, a work that is by its nature necessarily the expression of the corporate thought or activity of the body. Such works include official records and reports, and statements, studies, and other communications dealing with the policies, operations, or management of the body." See Fig. 3.21.

Fig. 3.21

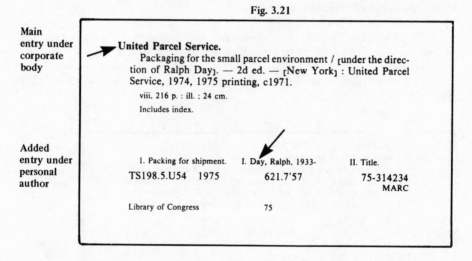

Main entry under corporate body

United Parcel Service.
 Packaging for the small parcel environment / ₁under the direction of Ralph Day₁. — 2d ed. — ₁New York₁ : United Parcel Service, 1974, 1975 printing, c1971.
  viii, 216 p. : ill. : 24 cm.
  Includes index.

Added entry under personal author

1. Packing for shipment.   I. Day, Ralph, 1933-   II. Title.
TS198.5.U54 1975   621.7'57   75-314234
                   MARC

Library of Congress   75

Rule 17A1. Official study entered under corporate body.

Excluded from 17A1 are: "Single reports . . . that are made by officers or other employees and that embody the results of scholarly investigation or scientific research . . . unless written by more than three persons, none of whom is represented as the principal author. All reports and studies prepared by consultants engaged for the particular purpose are excluded."

17A2. "Enter under the corporate body a work, other than a formal history, describing the body, its functions, procedures, facilities, resources, etc., or an inventory, catalog, directory of personnel, list of members, etc." See Fig. 3.22.

Fig. 3.22

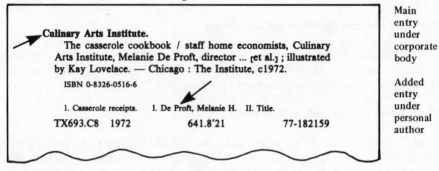

Main
entry
under
corporate
body

Added
entry
under
personal
author

Rule 17A2. Work describing corporate resources.

17B. Works not of corporate authorship

"If the work would not be entered under corporate body under the provisions of A above or if there is doubt as to whether it would, enter it under the heading under which it would be entered if no corporate body were involved. Make an added entry under the body unless it functions solely as publisher." See Fig. 3.23.

Fig. 3.23

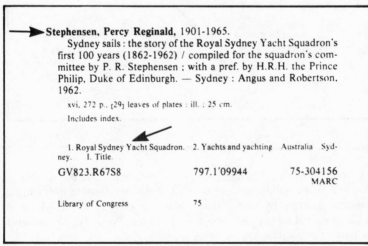

Main
entry
under
personal
author

Subject
added
entry for
corporate
body

Rule 17B. Work not of corporate authorship entered under the personal author, since this is a history.

17C. Works by chiefs of state, heads of governments, etc.

17C1. Official communications

"Enter an official communication (e.g., a message to a legislature or governing body, a proclamation, an executive order that does not come within the provisions of 20A) issued by a chief of state, a head of government, or a head of an international intergovernmental body under the corporate heading for the office which he holds (see 80)." See Fig. 3.24. In case of doubt as to the official character of a communication, enter it according to Rule 17C2 below.

Fig. 3.24

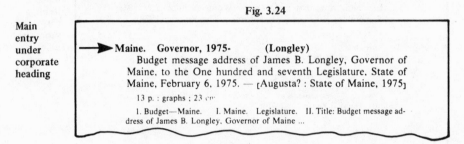

Main entry under corporate heading

> **Maine. Governor, 1975- (Longley)**
>   Budget message address of James B. Longley, Governor of Maine, to the One hundred and seventh Legislature, State of Maine, February 6, 1975. — ₍Augusta? : State of Maine, 1975₎
>   13 p. : graphs ; 23 cm
>   1. Budget—Maine.   I. Maine.   Legislature.   II. Title: Budget message address of James B. Longley, Governor of Maine ...

Rule 17C1. Official communication entered under corporate heading.

17C2. Other speeches and writings

"Treat any other speech or writing of such a person as a work of personal authorship." See Fig. 3.25.

Fig. 3.25

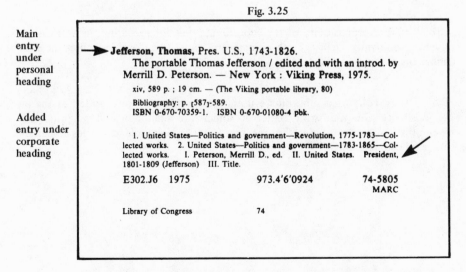

Main entry under personal heading

Added entry under corporate heading

> **Jefferson, Thomas, Pres. U.S., 1743-1826.**
>   The portable Thomas Jefferson / edited and with an introd. by Merrill D. Peterson. — New York : Viking Press, 1975.
>   xiv, 589 p. ; 19 cm. — (The Viking portable library, 80)
>   Bibliography: p. ₍587₎-589.
>   ISBN 0-670-70359-1.   ISBN 0-670-01080-4 pbk.
>   1. United States—Politics and government—Revolution, 1775-1783—Collected works.   2. United States—Politics and government—1783-1865—Collected works.   I. Peterson, Merrill D., ed.   II. United States.   President, 1801-1809 (Jefferson)   III. Title.
>   E302.J6   1975   973.4'6'0924   74-5805
>   MARC
>   Library of Congress   74

Rule 17C2. Other speeches entered under personal heading.

Rule 18. Corporate body or subordinate unit

18A. "Enter a work specifically and prominently attributed to a subordinate unit of a corporate body under the heading for the subordinate unit unless the unit simply acts as the information or publication agent for the parent body." See Fig. 3.26.

Fig. 3.26

➤**Ontario. Women's Bureau.**
     Law and the woman in Ontario / Women's Bureau, Ministry
of Labour. — Rev. ₍ed.₎. — Toronto : The Bureau, 1974.
       19 p. : ill. ; 23 cm.   C•••
       Cover title.
       1967 ed. written by Jo-Ann Poglitsch.

       1. Women—Legal status, laws, etc.—Ontario.   I. Poglitsch, Jo-Ann. Law
and the woman in Ontario. II. Title.
                   346'.713'013   75-311489
                                         MARC

     Library of Congress   75

(margin note:) Main entry under heading for subordinate unit

Rule 18A. Subordinate unit responsible for work.

Note: The Women's Bureau is a subordinate unit of the Ministry of Labour.

18B. "If the responsibility of the subordinate unit for preparing the work is not stated prominently, or if the subordinate unit cannot be identified, enter the work under the parent body."

18C. "If two or three subordinate units are prominently represented as sharing responsibility for the work, enter it under the one indicated as principally responsible; otherwise under the one first named. Make added entries under the other subordinate units."

RELATED AND DEPENDENT WORKS

Rule 19. Related works

This rule includes continuations, supplements, indexes, concordances, manuals, sequels, scenarios, choreographies, librettos, special numbers of serials, etc. **Note:** for adaptations, see Rule 7; for revisions, Rule 14; and for translations, Rule 15.

19A. Works with dependent titles

"Enter a work that has a title that is indistinctive and dependent on the title of another work under the same author and/or title as the work to which it is related . . ." (see also Rule 155).

19A1. "Auxiliary works the use of which is dependent on one particular edition of the main work (e.g., certain indexes, manuals, etc.)." See Fig. 3.27.

Fig. 3.27

Main work

Dependent work

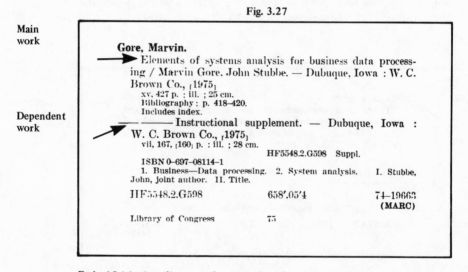

Gore, Marvin.
Elements of systems analysis for business data processing / Marvin Gore, John Stubbe. — Dubuque, Iowa : W. C. Brown Co., ₁1975₁
xv, 427 p. : ill. ; 25 cm.
Bibliography : p. 418–420.
Includes index.
————— Instructional supplement. — Dubuque, Iowa : W. C. Brown Co., ₁1975₁
vii, 167, ₁160₁ p. : ill. ; 28 cm.
HF5548.2.G598   Suppl.
ISBN 0–697–08114–1
1. Business—Data processing.   2. System analysis.   I. Stubbe, John, joint author.   II. Title.

HF5548.2.G598   658'.05'4   74–19663
                                                      (MARC)
Library of Congress   75

Rule 19A1. Auxiliary work entered under main work.

19A2. "Supplements that are continuations of the main work, except for a supplement by a different author that takes the form of an independent work."

19B. Other related works

"Enter any other related work under its own author and/or title according to the general rules. Make an added entry under the author and title or under the title of the work to which it is related." See Figs. 3.28 and 3.29.

Fig. 3.28

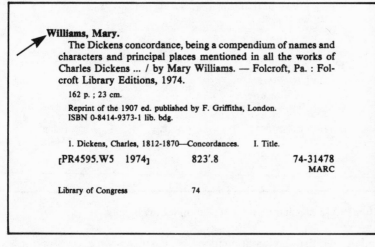

Cruickshank, William M
    Education of exceptional children and youth / editors, William M. Cruickshank, G. Orville Johnson. — 3d ed. — Englewood Cliffs, N.J. : Prentice-Hall, ₍1975₎

    xii, 708 p. ; 25 cm.

    Companion volume to W. M. Cruickshank's Psychology of exceptional children and youth.
    Includes bibliographies and index.
    ISBN 0-13-240382-X

    1. Exceptional children—Education.   I. Johnson, George Orville, 1915- joint author. II. Title.

LC3951.C7 1975   371.9   75-11⁻7
                                           MARC

Library of Congress   75

Note for companion volume

Rule 19B. Other related works. No added entry is necessary for the work in the case of a companion volume by the same author.

Fig. 3.29

Williams, Mary.
    The Dickens concordance, being a compendium of names and characters and principal places mentioned in all the works of Charles Dickens ... / by Mary Williams. — Folcroft, Pa. : Folcroft Library Editions, 1974.

    162 p. ; 23 cm.

    Reprint of the 1907 ed. published by F. Griffiths, London.
    ISBN 0-8414-9373-1 lib. bdg.

    1. Dickens, Charles, 1812-1870—Concordances.   I. Title.

₍PR4595.W5 1974₎   823'.8   74-31478
                                            MARC

Library of Congress   74

Entry under compiler of the concordance

Rule 19B. Other related works, including concordances.

SPECIAL RULES: WORKS WITH FORM SUBHEADINGS

Rule 20. Laws, etc.

20A. Laws governing one jurisdiction

Enter modern laws governing one jurisdiction under the heading consisting of the name of the jurisdiction governed by the law, followed by the appropriate subheadings. "If the jurisdiction is a country, state, city-state, province, or equivalent jurisdiction, use the subheading *Laws, statutes, etc.* [Fig. 3.30]. If it is a local jurisdiction (e.g., a county or municipal jurisdiction), use the subheading *Ordinances, local laws, etc.*, except that in the case of local jurisdictions within the British Commonwealth of Nations the subheading *Laws, by-laws, etc.* is used instead."

Fig. 3.30

[1] Name of jurisdiction

[2] Form sub-heading

[3] Uniform title, see Rule 101D, Chapter 6 of this text

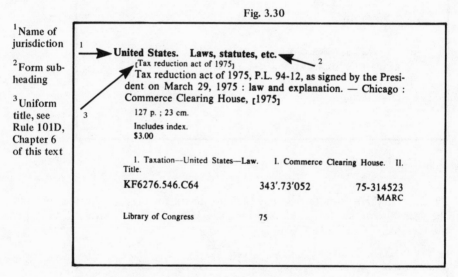

United States. Laws, statutes, etc.
[Tax reduction act of 1975]
Tax reduction act of 1975, P.L. 94-12, as signed by the President on March 29, 1975 : law and explanation. — Chicago : Commerce Clearing House, [1975]

127 p. ; 23 cm.

Includes index.
$3.00

I. Taxation—United States—Law.   I. Commerce Clearing House.   II. Title.

KF6276.546.C64   343'.73'052   75-314523
                                                      MARC

Library of Congress   75

Rule 20A. Laws governing a single jurisdiction.

Rule 22. Constitutions and charters

22A. Political jurisdictions

22A1. "Enter a constitution or charter of a political jurisdiction under that jurisdiction, followed by the subheading *Constitution* or *Charter*, as appropriate." See Fig. 3.31.

Fig. 3.31

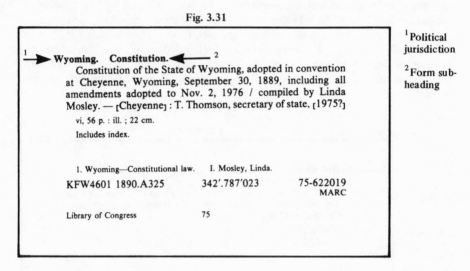

Rule 22A. Entry for constitution.

22A2. "If there is more than one such document for the same jurisdiction, add the year of adoption to the heading for each. If a collection is involved, however, use the general term alone." See Fig. 3.32.

Fig. 3.32

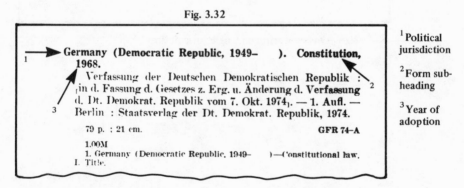

Rule 22A2. Entry for the 1968 German Democratic Republic Constitution.

Rule 25. Treaties, intergovernmental agreements, etc.

Treaties involving two countries are entered under an established form heading consisting of

1) name of one of the countries,
2) the form subheading Treaties, etc.,
3) name of the other country,
4) date of the treaty.

Added entries are made in the same form with the second named country listed first. See Fig. 3.33.

Refer to Rules 25A-F for details relating to multilateral treaties, agreements, concordats, protocols, etc., and collections of treaties.

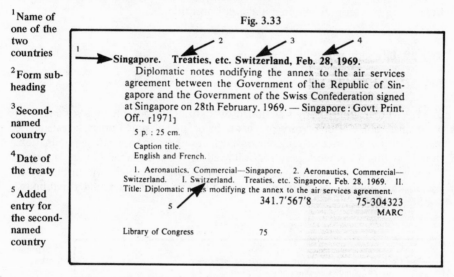

¹Name of one of the two countries

²Form subheading

³Second-named country

⁴Date of the treaty

⁵Added entry for the second-named country

Fig. 3.33

> Singapore.   Treaties, etc. Switzerland, Feb. 28, 1969.
>   Diplomatic notes nodifying the annex to the air services agreement between the Government of the Republic of Singapore and the Government of the Swiss Confederation signed at Singapore on 28th February. 1969. — Singapore : Govt. Print. Off., ₍1971₎
>   5 p. : 25 cm.
>
>   Caption title.
>   English and French.
>
>   1. Aeronautics. Commercial—Singapore.   2. Aeronautics. Commercial—Switzerland.   I. Switzerland.   Treaties. etc. Singapore. Feb. 28, 1969.   II. Title: Diplomatic notes modifying the annex to the air services agreement.
>   341.7′567′8   75-304323
>   MARC
>
> Library of Congress   75

Rule 25. Treaty involving two countries.

Peace treaties are entered under a uniform heading consisting of the name by which a treaty is known and the date, instead of under the signatories or under the name of the conference at which the treaty was signed. Example: Treaty of Paris, 1783, instead of Gr. Brit. Treaties, etc., 1760-1820 (George II).

Rule 27. Sacred scriptures

27A. "Enter a sacred scripture accepted as divine revelation by a religious group under uniform title (see 108-118). Make a *see also* reference from the name of any person that is associated with the revelation of such a work, except for the parts of the Bible."

Fig. 3.34

```
 ↘
   Suttapiṭaka. English. Selections.
        Some sayings of the Buddha, according to the Pali canon /
     translated ₍from the Pali₎ by F. L. Woodward ; with an introduc-
     tion by Christmas Humphreys. — Jubilee ed. — London : Bud-
     dhist Society, 1974.
        xxii, 249 p. ; 21 cm.                          GB74-00419
        £1.50


        I. Woodward, Frank Lee, 1870 or 71-1952, tr.   II. Humphreys, Christmas,
     1901-        III. Vinayapiṭaka. English. Selections. 1974.   IV. Title.
```

Uniform
title

Rule 27. Sacred scripture entered under uniform title.

Rule 29. Liturgical works

29A. General Rule

29A1. "Enter an officially sanctioned or traditionally accepted text of a religious observance, book of obligatory prayers to be offered at stated times, or calendar or manual of performance of religious observances under the specific denominational church to which the work pertains, followed by the subheading *Liturgy and ritual*. If the work is special to the use of a particular corporate body within the church, e.g., diocese, monastery, or religious order, make an added entry under that body." See Fig. 3.35.

Fig. 3.35

```
1
   ▶ Catholic Church.   Liturgy and ritual. ◀──── 2
        ₍Rite of ordination. English₎
           The ordination of deacons, priests, and bishops : provisional
     3   text prepared by the International Committee on English in the
        Liturgy, approved for interim use by the Bishops' Committee on
        the Liturgy, National Conference of Catholic Bishops, and con-
        firmed by the Apostolic See. — Washington : National Confer-
        ence of Catholic Bishops, Bishops' Committee on the Liturgy,
        1969.
           51 p. ; 28 cm.
           At head of title: The Roman pontifical; restored by decree of the Second

                          (Continued on next card)
                                            75-306712
                                                 MARC
                 75
```

[1] Corporate
heading
for
specific
church

[2] Form sub-
heading

[3] Uniform
title

Rule 29. Liturgical works.

ADDED ENTRIES

Rule 33. Added entries

The preceding rules have indicated the added entries required in typical circumstances to supplement the main entry by providing additional bibliographical access to materials represented in the catalog. In general, added entries are suggested to provide access to other names of persons or titles under which a work may be known and under which catalog users might reasonably search. Persons, corporate bodies, and works related to the work at hand are considered, providing these are openly stated in the work. It is a matter of local library policy to establish certain administrative procedures to make all required added entries, which in turn must be related to the extent of the collection, the needs it serves, and some economic considerations. The following general rule states principles for making added entries. See Figs. 3.36 through 3.38.

33A. General rule

"Make an added entry under any person or corporate body associated with the publication if it is believed that some catalog users might reasonably consider the person or body to be primarily responsible for it. Added entries are particularly important whenever the main entry is under a corporate body, under a special heading denoting the form of the material, or under title."

33N. Series

"Make an added entry under the series for each separately cataloged work (adding after the title the numerical designation of the work as part of the series if it is numbered) if it can be reasonably assumed that the work might be cited as part of the series or if the series might be reasonably cataloged as a collected set. The decision should be influenced by the importance of the series." Added entries are not made for series titles that are publishers' series or that do not have a subject limitation.

33P. Titles

Make a title added entry for every work of known authorship that is published anonymously, for any title other than the main title (cover title, etc.) by which the work is likely to be known, and for all other works, with the following exceptions: titles that are incomplete or meaningless without the author's name (e.g., Reports, Memoirs, etc.); long titles that are involved and nondistinctive unless entered under corporate headings or headings that include subheadings; titles that are essentially the same as the main entry heading; titles consisting solely of the name of a real person, except when they are works of imagination; and, in a dictionary catalog, titles that are identical with a subject heading, if the subject heading as used has no subdivision.

Summarization of specific rules for collaborators, editors, related persons and bodies, etc., will be found in AACR pp. 70-72.

Fig. 3.36

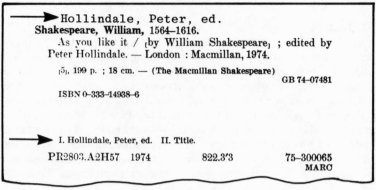

→ Hollindale, Peter, ed.
Shakespeare, William, 1564–1616.
  As you like it / ₍by William Shakespeare₎ ; edited by
Peter Hollindale. — London : Macmillan, 1974.

  ₍5₎, 199 p. ; 18 cm. — **(The Macmillan Shakespeare)**
  GB 74–07481

  ISBN 0–333–14938–6

→ I. Hollindale, Peter, ed. II. Title.
  PR2803.A2H57 1974   822.3′3   75–300065
                                               MARC

Added
entry for
editor

Fig. 3.37

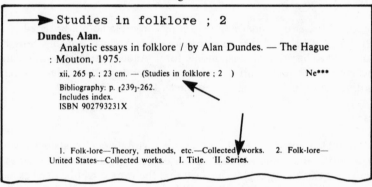

→ Studies in folklore ; 2
Dundes, Alan.
  Analytic essays in folklore / by Alan Dundes. — The Hague
: Mouton, 1975.

  xii, 265 p. ; 23 cm. — (Studies in folklore ; 2)   Ne***

  Bibliography: p. ₍239₎-262.
  Includes index.
  ISBN 902793231X

  1. Folk-lore—Theory, methods, etc.—Collected works. 2. Folk-lore—
United States—Collected works. I. Title. II. Series.

Added
entry for
series

Fig. 3.38

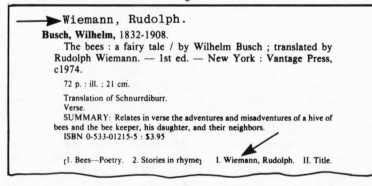

→ Wiemann, Rudolph.
Busch, Wilhelm, 1832-1908.
  The bees : a fairy tale / by Wilhelm Busch ; translated by
Rudolph Wiemann. — 1st ed. — New York : Vantage Press,
c1974.

  72 p. : ill. ; 21 cm.

  Translation of Schnurrdiburr.
  Verse.
  SUMMARY: Relates in verse the adventures and misadventures of a hive of
bees and the bee keeper, his daughter, and their neighbors.
  ISBN 0-533-01215-5 : $3.95

  ₍1. Bees—Poetry. 2. Stories in rhyme₎ I. Wiemann, Rudolph. II. Title.

Added
entry for
trans-
lator

Note: Fig. 3.38 follows the Library of Congress practice (as of mid-1975)
of deleting any designation of function in the heading except for joint
author.

4 FORM OF ENTRY HEADINGS FOR PERSONS

INTRODUCTION

The previous chapter dealt with choice of entry, while this chapter and the next two chapters will present rules for the form of entry headings and the form of added entries. After the decision has been made as to what is to be the main entry or heading and what are to be added entries, it must be determined how those entries are to be displayed or written on the card. Choice of entry rules deal with who or what is to be the entry; form of entry rules deal with how an entry is to be written or recorded.

Most entries in American library catalogs consist of the form of a personal name author, with the author's name entered under the surname, followed by forenames (like the white pages of a telephone directory). However, as the following rules for headings for persons show, there are certain complexities that must be considered in a library catalog. Rules—i.e., principles and practices—must be followed consistently for those authors known by more than one name. There are many possible instances when an author may be known and/or even write under more than one name. Some authors deliberately disguise their real names and write under a pseudonym or pen name—such as Charles Lutwidge Dodgson, who wrote his children's fantasies under the pseudonym of Lewis Carroll. Some authors consistently write under initialized forenames (e.g., H. G. Wells). Some authors, such as Bernard Shaw, consistently omit one of their forenames. If an author's original name is written in a non-roman alphabet, different romanization systems may create different spelling of the name (such as Chekhov, Chekov, or Tchekhov). A married woman has two possible surnames—her maiden surname and her husband's surname. Further compound surnames—i.e., surnames consisting of two or more parts—create problems. Granville-Barker is an example of a compound, hyphenated English surname. Prefixes to surnames create another type of compound surname. De Gaulle and von Goethe are examples of surnames with prefixes; O'Brien and MacPherson are other examples. Individuals who are members of nobility may have two names—a titled name and a common surname (such as Lord Byron, George Gordon). Certain individuals are known under their bynames or forenames rather than their surnames; these include royalty (Elizabeth II), saints (Joan of Arc), popes (Paul VI), and individuals in ancient and medieval periods prior to the development of surnames (Horace). Bynames or forenames often exist in different forms in different languages (such as Horace in English, but Horatius in

Latin). The purpose of this chapter is to demonstrate the general rules used to resolve all of these problems. For more complicated problems of personal names, the student should carefully examine AACR, Chapter 2.

BASIC RULES

As was indicated in Chapter 2, the general principle for the entry of names is to follow the form customarily used by a person. Thus, the basic rule for entry of a person is to use "the name by which he is commonly identified whether it be his real name, assumed name, nickname, title of nobility or other appellation." In general, for a personal author this means entry under the form of name found in most of his writings or commonly found in reference sources. The same principle is applied to pseudonyms. Please note that the Library of Congress does not plan to change many of the already established forms of headings; consequently, some of the following rules might not always be consistent with the practice of the Library of Congress.

Rule 40. Basic rule

"Enter a person under the name by which he is commonly identified, whether it is his real name, assumed name, nickname, title of nobility, or other appellation. The form of name of an author, editor, translator, etc., is ordinarily determined from the way it appears in his works issued in his language." See Fig. 4.1.

Fig. 4.1

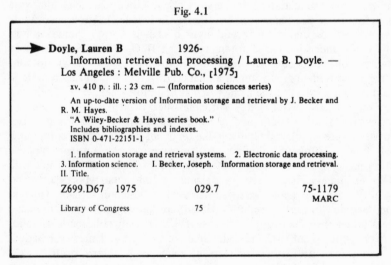

Rule 40. Entry under the name by which a person is commonly identified.

CHOICE AND FORM OF NAME

Rule 41. Choice among different names—General rule

"Enter an author who is not commonly identified in his works by one particular name according to the following order of preference: 1) under the name by which he is generally identified in reference sources; 2) under the name by which he is most frequently identified in his works; 3) under the latest name he has used." See Fig. 4.2.

Fig. 4.2

Latest
name
used

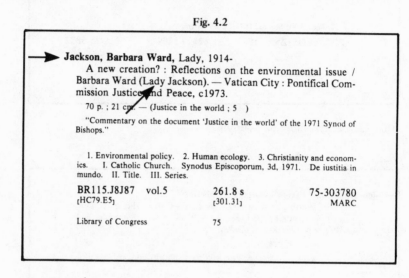

Jackson, Barbara Ward, Lady, 1914-
  A new creation? : Reflections on the environmental issue /
Barbara Ward (Lady Jackson). — Vatican City : Pontifical Com-
mission Justice and Peace, c1973.

  70 p. ; 21 cm. — (Justice in the world ; 5   )

  "Commentary on the document 'Justice in the world' of the 1971 Synod of Bishops."

  1. Environmental policy.   2. Human ecology.   3. Christianity and economics.   I. Catholic Church.   Synodus Episcoporum, 3d, 1971.   De iustitia in
mundo.   II. Title.   III. Series.

BR115.J8J87 vol.5	261.8 s	75-303780
[HC79.E5]	[301.31]	MARC
Library of Congress	75	

Refer from[1] : Ward, Barbara
Maiden name used in writings before author's marriage.

Rule 41. Entry under latest name used.

Rule 42. Pseudonyms

42A. "If all the works of an author appear only under one pseudonym, enter him under the pseudonym." See Fig. 4.3.

42B. "If the works of an author appear under several pseudonyms or under his real name and one or more pseudonyms, enter him under the name by which he is primarily identified in modern editions of his works and in reference sources. In case of doubt, prefer the real name." See Fig. 4.4.

---

[1] For examples of references, see Chapter 6 of this text, pp. 119-121.

Fig. 4.3

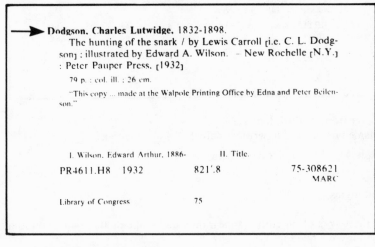

> ➤ **Ford, Ford Madox,** 1873-1939.
>   **It was the nightingale** / Ford Madox Ford. — New York :
> Octagon Books, 1975, c1933.
>   381 p. ; 24 cm.
>   Autobiography.
>   Reprint of the ed. published by Lippincott, Philadelphia.
>   Includes index.
>   ISBN 0-374-92782-0
>
>
>   1. Ford, Ford Madox, 1873-1939—Biography.   I. Title.
>   PR6011.O53Z55   1975   828'.9'1209   75-5832
>   [B]   MARC
>
>   Library of Congress   75

Entry
under
pseudonym

Rule 42A. Entry under pseudonym.

Fig. 4.4

> ➤ **Dodgson, Charles Lutwidge,** 1832-1898.
>   The hunting of the snark / by Lewis Carroll [i.e. C. L. Dodg-
> son] : illustrated by Edward A. Wilson. – New Rochelle [N.Y.]
> : Peter Pauper Press. [1932]
>   79 p. : col. ill. ; 26 cm.
>   "This copy ... made at the Walpole Printing Office by Edna and Peter Beilen-
> son."
>
>
>   I. Wilson, Edward Arthur, 1886-   II. Title.
>   PR4611.H8   1932   821'.8   75-308621
>   MARC
>
>   Library of Congress   75

Entry
under
real
name

Rule 42B. Entry under real name.

The application of this rule will require the following "see" reference to connect the names:

> Carroll, Lewis
>   see his real name: Dodgson, Charles Lutwidge

Rule 43. Fullness of name

43A. "If the forms of name appearing in the works of an author vary in fullness, use the fullest form that has appeared in a prominent position (e.g., on a title page, half title, or cover), except that a rarely used initial of an unused or non-existent forename, or a forename used by the author only on his dissertation, is normally ignored."

> Hamilton, John Peter
>> Predominant form: John P. Hamilton
>> Occasional form: J. P. Hamilton
>> Rare form: "Bud" Hamilton

43B. "If the fullest form of the name as indicated above includes one or more forenames represented only by initials, spell out the forenames if necessary to distinguish two or more persons. Always spell out a first forename represented by an initial if the surname is a common one. Refer from the form of name customarily used by the author if the first forename in the heading is one which he has not customarily used." See Figs. 4.5 and 4.6.

Fig. 4.5

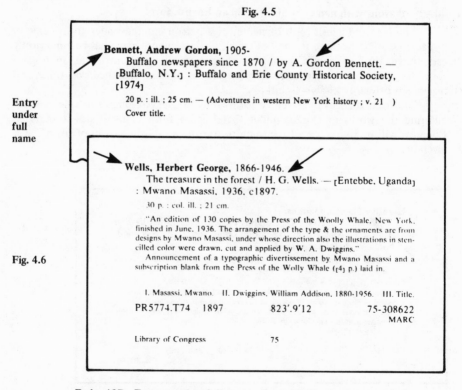

Entry under full name

Fig. 4.6

Rule 43B. Entry under full name for initialized names with common surnames. Refer from Wells, H. G.

Rule 44. Language

44A. Names in the Roman alphabet

"If a name is found in different language forms, prefer the one that has become most firmly established in reference sources.

>   Grotius, Hugo
>   Refer from: Groot, Hugo de

If no one form is firmly established in reference sources, follow the instructions below.

44A1. Authors writing in Latin

Prefer the Latin form of name for authors who wrote in Latin and who flourished before, or principally before, 1400.

>   Guilelmus Arvernus, Bp. of Paris, d. 1249
>   Refer from Guillaume d'Auvergne

For later writers prefer the vernacular form."

44A3. Persons with names established in an English form

"Prefer the English form of name for a person entered under given name or byname (see 49) or for a Roman of classical times, whose name has become firmly established through common usage in English-speaking countries in an English form, as is sometimes the case with persons of ancient and medieval times and others not primarily known as authors."

This rule changes many entry forms now in use. Although this rule calls for entering the works of Horace under that English form of name, the Library of Congress will in all likelihood continue to use the established form of his name as given below:

Fig. 4.7

```
┌──────────────────────────────────────────────────────────────────┬─────────────┐
│ Horatius Flaccus, Quintus.                                         │ LC practice,│
│      ͟ s art of poetry / Q. Horatius Flaccus ; Englished by Ben     │ not AACR    │
│ Jonson. — Amsterdam : Theatrum Orbis Terrarum ; Norwood,           │             │
│ N.J. : W. J. Johnson, 1974.                                        │             │
│      138 p., [1] leaf of plates ; 16 cm. — (The English experience, its record in early │
│   printed books published in facsimile ; no. 670   )               │             │
│      "S.T.C. no. 13798."                                           │             │
│      Photoreprint of 4 works printed by J. Okes, for J. Benson, London, 1640: Q. │
│   Horatius Flaccus: His art of poetry; of Execration against vulcan, by B. Jonson; │
│   of The masque of the gypsies, by B. Jonson, and of Epigrams to severall noble │
│   personages in this kingdome, by B. Jonson.                       │             │
│      ISBN 9022106705                                               │             │
│                                                                    │             │
│                        (Continued on next card)                   │             │
│                                              74-80190              │             │
│                                              MARC                  │             │
└──────────────────────────────────────────────────────────────────┴─────────────┘
```

Fig. 4.7 represents LC practice. Refer from Horace. This is not an example of Rule 44A3.

44B. Names not in the Roman alphabet

Names that must be romanized or transliterated present many problems. These problems are considered in detail in AACR 44B. Many libraries may choose to follow the form already established by the Library of Congress.

44B1. Choice between existing and systematic romanization

"If a romanized form of a name not written in the roman alphabet is found in English-language reference sources or, in the case of an author, in his works, choose the form to be used in the heading according to the following order of preference:

a. Use the form preferred by the person whenever it is known.
b. Use the form appearing in any work (other than a dissertation) that an author has written in English or any work in English that he has edited or translated.
c. Use the form found in the Authorized version of the Bible for the names of Biblical characters.
d. Use the form appearing in any work of an author published 1) in an English-speaking country, 2) in any country or territory formerly or presently under British rule if his language is other than Arabic or Chinese, or 3) in Israel (as first choice) or in any other country if his language is Hebrew or Yiddish.

Exception: Use the systematic romanization for a person whose name is written in the Cyrillic alphabet and is entered under surname." See Fig. 4.8.

Skriabin, Aleksandr Nikolaevich
   Refer from: Scriabin, Alexander

Fig. 4.8

Systematic
romaniza-
tion
	➤ **Skriabin, Aleksandr Nikolaevich,** 1872–1915.
	  [Études, piano, op. 8]
	   12 [i. e. Zwölf] Etüden für Klavier, op. 8 = 12 studies for piano / Alexander Skrjabin ; hrsg. von Günter Philipp. — Leipzig : Edition Peters, [1973] c1966.
	
	   47 p. ; 30 cm.
	
	   "Edition Peters Nr. 9287a."
	   Pref. in German, French, and English.
	   "Revisionsbericht" : p. [48]
	   Label beneath imprint reads: C. F. Peters, Frankfurt, London, New York.
	
	   1. Piano music.
	
	M25.S 75–764933
	Library of Congress 75 M

Rule 44B. **Exception**: Use of systematic romanization for person whose name is written in the Cyrillic alphabet.

ENTRY OF NAME

Surnames

"If the name by which a person is identified consists of several elements, it is necessary to determine which of these is to be the first or entry element. This element is normally that part of the name or title by which a person is entered or would be entered in alphabetical lists in his language. When a person's preference is known to be different from normal usage, however, his personal preference is observed." The following rules discuss problems of entry under surname, including compound surnames, titles of nobility, entries of Roman names, and entries under phrase. Only a brief summary of these problems will be provided here.

Rule 46. Entry under surname

"Enter a person whose name contains a surname and who is not known to be primarily identified by some other name, under the surname followed by the other parts of his name in the form and fullness he commonly uses." (See AACR 43-45.) "If he uses in his works only his surname or his surname and a term of address, complete his name from reference sources."

46B. Compound surnames

These rules are used for entry of persons known to have compound surnames (i.e., surnames made up of two or more proper names) and persons whose names appear to be compound names. Refer from those elements not chosen.

46B1. Preferred or established form known

"Enter a person with a compound surname under the element of his surname by which he prefers to be entered, or, if this is unknown, under the element by which he is listed in reference sources, preferably those in his own language." See Fig. 4.9.

Fig. 4.9

```
      Lloyd George, David, Earl Lloyd
         George, 1863-1945.
         War memoirs of David Lloyd George.
   -- Boston : Little, Brown, 1933-1937.
      6 v. : ill. ; 24 cm.


      1. European war, 1914-1918.   I. Title.
```

Entry under first part of compound surname

Rule 46B1. Preferred or established form of compound name.
Refer from: George, David Lloyd. George is his correct paternal surname.

46B2. Hyphenated surnames

"If the elements of the surname are hyphenated, either regularly or occasionally, enter under the first." See Fig. 4.10.

Fig. 4.10

Hyphenated
surname

> ➤ **Holt-White, William Edward Braddon,** 1878-
>   The man who dreamed right / by W. Holt White. — London
>   ; New York : M. Kennerley, 1911, c1910.
>   314 p. ; 18 cm. — (Mitchell Kennerley's railroad novels)
>
>
>   I. Title.
>   PR6015.O48M35   1911   823'.9'12   75-313446
>   MARC

Rule 46B2. Entry under hyphenated surname.
Refer from: White, William Holt.

46B3. Other cases of compound surnames

"In other cases of names known to be compound surnames the entry element is determined by normal usage in the language of the person involved, as indicated below."

46B3a. Persons other than married women

"Compound surnames, other than those of married women, are entered under the first element unless the bearer's language is Portuguese. If his language is Portuguese, entry is under the last element." See Fig. 4.11.

Fig. 4.11

Entry
under first
element of
compound
name

> ➤ **Flores Araoz, José.**
>   Catálogo formado por José Flores Araoz para la Exposición de Pinturas Francisco Laso inaugurada el 6 de diciembre de 1937 con una charla por José Antonio de Lavalle. — Lima : Sociedad Entre Nous, [1937?]
>   [77] p. : 17 ill. ; 25 cm.
>   Cover title: Catálogo de la Exposición Francisco Laso.
>   1. Laso, Francisco, 1823–1869.   I. Laso, Francisco, 1823–1869.
>   II. Title: Catálogo formado por José Flores Araoz ...   III. Title:
>   Catálogo de la Exposición Francisco Laso.

Rule 46B3. Entry under first element of compound Spanish name.

46B3b. Married women

"Names of married women that include both the maiden surname and the husband's surname are entered under the husband's surname unless the woman's language is Czech, Hungarian, Italian, or Spanish. In these cases entry is under the first surname, regardless of its derivation."

Fig. 4.12

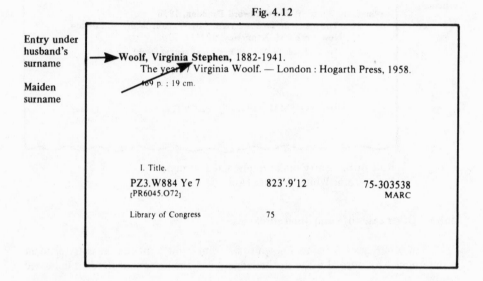

Entry under
husband's
surname

Maiden
surname

Woolf, Virginia Stephen, 1882-1941.
    The year / Virginia Woolf. — London : Hogarth Press, 1958.
    469 p. ; 19 cm.

I. Title.

PZ3.W884 Ye 7   823'.9'12   75-303538
₍PR6045.O72₎   MARC

Library of Congress   75

Rule 46B3. Entry under husband's surname.

Note: Stephen is the maiden surname. Formerly the Library of Congress would have placed this part of the entry in parentheses. This practice is no longer followed.

46E. Surnames with separately written prefixes

46E1. Articles and prepositions

"Enter a surname that includes a separately written prefix consisting of an article, a preposition, or a combination of the two, under the element most commonly used as entry element in alphabetical listings in the person's language."

The AACR contain many specific examples of names in different languages. Only the most basic of those rules are cited here.

English. Enter under the prefix. See Figs. 4.13 and 4.14.

Fig. 4.13

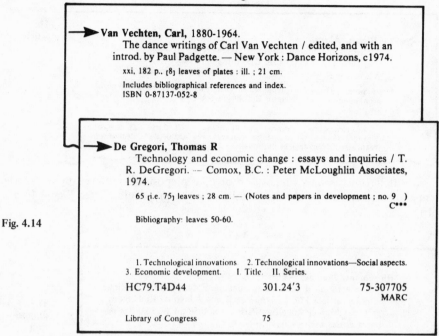

Fig. 4.14

Van Vechten, Carl, 1880-1964.
    The dance writings of Carl Van Vechten / edited, and with an
introd. by Paul Padgette. — New York : Dance Horizons, c1974.
    xxi, 182 p., [8] leaves of plates : ill. ; 21 cm.
    Includes bibliographical references and index.
    ISBN 0-87137-052-8

De Gregori, Thomas R
    Technology and economic change : essays and inquiries / T.
R. DeGregori. — Comox, B.C. : Peter McLoughlin Associates,
1974.
    65 [i.e. 75] leaves ; 28 cm. — (Notes and papers in development ; no. 9)
                                                         C•••
    Bibliography: leaves 50-60.

    1. Technological innovations 2. Technological innovations—Social aspects.
3. Economic development.   I. Title. II. Series.
    HC79.T4D44   301.24′3   75-307705
                                                         MARC
    Library of Congress   75

Dutch and Flemish. Enter under the part of the name following the prefix. If
prefix is *ver*, enter under the prefix. See Fig. 4.15.

Fig. 4.15

The
prefix

Dam, H   van.
    Theory of gravity / R. van Dam. — Nijmegen : University of
Nijmegen, Institute for Theoretical Physics, 1974.
    134 p. ; 30 cm.   Ne•••
    fl5.00

    1. Gravitation.   I. Title.
    QC178.D35   531′.14   75-312796
                                                         MARC
    Library of Congress   75

French. "If the prefix consists of an article or of a contraction of an article and a preposition, enter under the prefix." See Fig. 4.16.

Fig. 4.16

Le Bihan, Alain.
   Francs-maçons et ateliers parisiens de la Grande Loge de France au XVIIIe [i. e. dix-huitième] siècle : 1760–1795 / Alain Le Bihan. — Paris : Bibliothèque nationale, 1973.

   509 p. ; 24 cm. — (Mémoires et documents - Commission d'histoire économique et sociale de la Révolution française ; 28)   F 74–14151

   1. Freemasons. France. Grand orient.   I. Title.   II. Series : France. Commission d'histoire économique et sociale de la Révolution française. Mémoires et documents ; 28.

The article

"If it consists of a preposition or of a preposition followed by an article, enter under the part of the name following the preposition." See Figs. 4.17 and 4.18.

Fig. 4.17

Richemont, Jean de.
   L'intégration du droit communautaire dans l'ordre juridique interne : article 177 du Traité de Rome / Jean de Richemont ; préf. par Marcel Ancel. — Paris : Librairie du Journal des notaires et des avocats, [1975]

   vii, 149 p. ; 25 cm.   F***

The preposition

La Fontaine, Jean de, 1621-1695.
   Fables / La Fontaine ; préface et commentaires de Pierre Clarac. — Paris : le Livre de poche, 1972.

   xx, 395 p. ; 17 cm. — (Le Livre de poche classique ; 1198)   F73-6711
   4.30F

   I. Clarac, Pierre, 1894-

   PQ1808.A1   1972   841'.4   75-505608
                                                     MARC

   Library of Congress   75

[1] The article

[2] The preposition

Fig. 4.18

German. "If the prefix consists of an article or of a contraction of a preposition and an article, enter under the prefix, e.g.,

Zur Linde, Otto

If it consists of a preposition or a preposition followed by an article, enter under the part of the name following the prefix." See Fig. 4.19.

Fig. 4.19

The preposition

> **Weizsäcker, Carl Christian von.**
> Modern capital theory and the concept of exploitation / Carl Christian von Weizsäcker. — Rheda : Inst. f. Math. Wirtschaftsforschung an d. Univ. Bielefeld, 1972.
>
> 38 leaves ; 30 cm. — (Working papers - Institute of Mathematical Economics; Nr. 2)   GFR74-B5
>
> Includes bibliographical references.
>
> 1. Capital.   2. Capitalism.   3. Economic development.   I Title   II Series: Bielefeld.   Institut für Mathematische Wirtschaftsforschung.   Arbeiten aus dem Institut für Mathematische Wirtschaftsforschung ;   Nr. 2. 2.
>
> **HB501.W473**   332'.041   75-504767
>   MARC
>
> Library of Congress   75

Italian. "In general, enter under the prefix." See Fig. 4.20.

Fig. 4.20

The prefix

> **De Filippo, Peppino.**
> La lettera di mammà : farsa in due parti / Peppino De Filippo. — Napoli : Marotta, 1973.
>
> 74 p. ; 22 cm.   It 74–July
>
> "Tratta da Farse e commedie."
>
> I. Title.
>
> PQ4864.E324L4   75–530524
>
> Library of Congress   75

Spanish. "Enter under the part of the name following the prefix, except that if the prefix consists of an article only, enter under the article." See Fig. 4.21.

Fig. 4.21

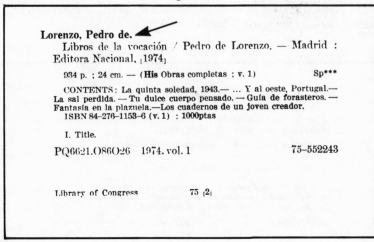

Preposition
as
prefix

Lorenzo, Pedro de.
  Libros de la vocación / Pedro de Lorenzo. — Madrid : Editora Nacional, ₁1974₎

  934 p. ; 24 cm. — (**His** Obras completas ; v. 1)   Sp***

  CONTENTS: La quinta soledad, 1943.— ... Y al oeste, Portugal.— La sal perdida. — Tu dulce cuerpo pensado. — Guía de forasteros. — Fantasía en la plazuela.—Los cuadernos de un joven creador.
  ISBN 84–276–1153–6 (v. 1) : 1000ptas

  I. Title.

  PQ6621.O86O26   1974. vol. 1   75–552243

  Library of Congress   75 ₍2₎

46E2. Other prefixes

"In general, if the prefix is other than an article, preposition, or combination of the two enter under the prefix." See Fig. 4.22.

Fig. 4.22

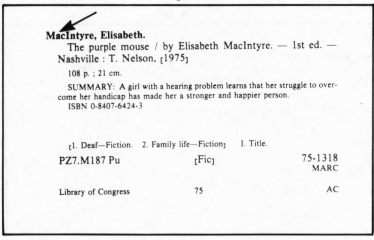

Entry
under
prefix

MacIntyre, Elisabeth.
  The purple mouse / by Elisabeth MacIntyre. — 1st ed. — Nashville : T. Nelson, ₁1975₎

  108 p. ; 21 cm.

  SUMMARY: A girl with a hearing problem learns that her struggle to over-come her handicap has made her a stronger and happier person.
  ISBN 0-8407-6424-3

  ₁1. Deaf—Fiction. 2. Family life—Fiction₎ I. Title.
  PZ7.M187 Pu   ₁Fic₎   75-1318
                                                   MARC

  Library of Congress   75   AC

Rule 46E2. Entry under the prefix. "Mac" is an attributive prefix.

46G. Titles of nobility, honor, address, etc., added to the name

46G1. Titles of nobility

"Add the title of nobility in the vernacular to the name of a nobleman who is not entered under his title and make appropriate references." See Fig. 4.23.

Fig. 4.23

Common name	**Bacon, Francis,** Viscount St. Albans, 1561-1626.
Title in nobility	Sylva sylvarvm; or A naturall historie. Published after the author's death, by William Rawley. The 3d ed. London. Printed by J. H[aviland] for W. Lee, 1631.
	258, 46, 43-44 p 29 cm.
	STC 1171.
	"New Atlantis": 46, 43-44 p.
	1. Natural history Pre-Linnean works. I. Rawley, William, 1588?-1667

46G2. British titles of honor

"Add before the forenames the terms of honor *Sir, Dame, Lord*, or *Lady*, used in conjunction with the names of British baronets and knights; dames of the Order of the British Empire and the Royal Victorian Order; younger sons of dukes and marquesses; and the daughters of dukes, marquesses, and earls." See Fig. 4.24. "Add after the forenames titles of rank, *bart.* or *Lady*, in the cases of a baronet and of the wife of a baronet or knight who is not entitled to the prefixed title of 'Lady' by virtue of her father's rank."

Note: It is current LC practice to place *all* titles after the forenames rather than before.

Fig. 4.24

Term of honor for knightage	**Younghusband, Francis Edward,** Sir. 1863-1942.
	The heart of a continent : a narrative of travels in Manchuria. across the Gobi Desert, through the Himalayas, the Pamirs, and Chitral, 1884-1894 / by Frank E. Younghusband. — New York : Scribner, 1896.
	xvii, 409 p., [18] leaves of plates : ill. 4 maps (1 fold. in pocket) ; 24 cm.
	Includes index.
	1. Asia, Central Description and travel. 2. Pamir—Description and travel. 3. Manchuria Description and travel. I. Title.

Fig. 4.25

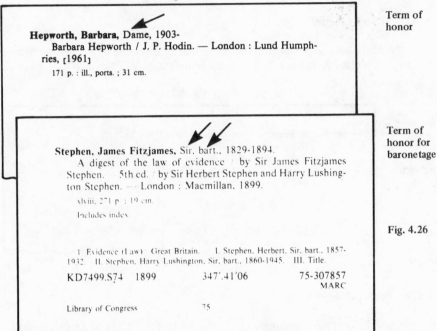

Term of
honor

Hepworth, Barbara, Dame, 1903-
 Barbara Hepworth / J. P. Hodin. — London : Lund Humph-
ries, ₁1961₎

 171 p. : ill., ports. ; 31 cm.

Term of
honor for
baronetage

Stephen, James Fitzjames, Sir. bart., 1829-1894.
 A digest of the law of evidence by Sir James Fitzjames
Stephen. 5th ed. by Sir Herbert Stephen and Harry Lushing-
ton Stephen. — London : Macmillan, 1899.

 xlviii, 271 p. ; 19 cm.

 Includes index.

Fig. 4.26

 1 Evidence (Law) Great Britain. I. Stephen, Herbert, Sir, bart., 1857-
1932. II. Stephen, Harry Lushington, Sir, bart., 1860-1945. III. Title.

KD7499.S74   1899   347'.41'06   75-307857
                                                       MARC

 Library of Congress   75

46G3. Terms of address of married women

If a married woman is identified only by her husband's name, include the
approach term of address. The cataloger should attempt to determine a married
woman's forenames if possible.

Note: The example below follows current LC practice of adding all titles of address
after forenames.

Fig. 4.27

Husband's
name

Term of
address

  Bruce, William, Mrs.
 Some intermarriages of some old Springfield, Ohio, families /
compiled by Mrs. Wm. Ultes, Jr., as dictated by her mother, Mrs.
Wm. Bruce. — ₁Springfield? Ohio : s.n.₎, 1967.

 1 sheet : geneal. table ; 44 x 59 cm. fold to 29 x 22 cm.

 1. Bruce family. 2. Cummings family. 3. Ultes family. I. Ultes, William,
Mrs. II. Title.

Rule 47. Entry under title of nobility

47A. "Enter under the proper name in the title of nobility (including a courtesy title) 1) an author who uses his title rather than his surname in his works and 2) any other person who is generally so listed in those reference sources that do not list noblemen either all under title or all under surname. The entry word is followed by the personal names in direct order, except for forenames that are not used, and by the term of rank in the vernacular." See Fig. 4.28.

Fig. 4.28

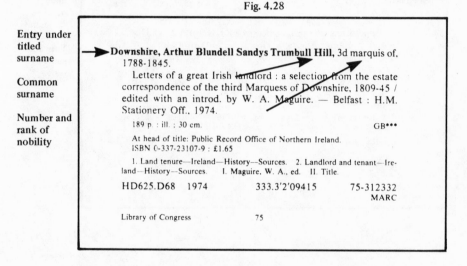

Entry under titled surname

Common surname

Number and rank of nobility

> **Downshire, Arthur Blundell Sandys Trumbull Hill,** 3d marquis of, 1788-1845.
>   Letters of a great Irish landlord : a selection from the estate correspondence of the third Marquess of Downshire, 1809-45 / edited with an introd. by W. A. Maguire. — Belfast : H.M. Stationery Off., 1974.
>   189 p. : ill. ; 30 cm.   GB•••
>   At head of title: Public Record Office of Northern Ireland.
>   ISBN 0-337-23107-9 : £1.65
>   1. Land tenure—Ireland—History—Sources.   2. Landlord and tenant—Ireland—History—Sources.   I. Maguire, W. A., ed.   II. Title.
>
> HD625.D68   1974   333.3'2'09415   75-312332
>   MARC
>
> Library of Congress   75

Rule 47A. Entry under titled surname, not common surname.

Bynames

Rule 49. Entry under given name or byname (epithet, sobriquet)

49A. General rules

49A1. "Enter a person whose name does not include a surname and who is not primarily identified by a title of nobility under the part of his name by which he is primarily identified in reference sources, normally the first of the names that he uses. Include any bynames that appear as integral parts of his name in these sources."

For example: John the Baptist

49B. Royalty

49B1. "Add the title in English (unless there is no satisfactory English equivalent) and the name of the state or people governed after the name of a monarch." See Fig. 4.29.

Fig. 4.29

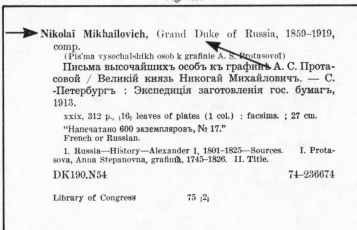

Entry
under
royal
forename

Title and
name of
state

49C. Saints

49C1. "Add the word *Saint* after the name of a Christian saint unless the person was an emperor, king, or pope, in which case he is identified only as such (see B and D)." See Fig. 4.30.

Fig. 4.30

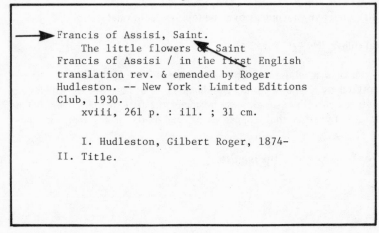

Entry
under
byname

Designation
"Saint"

Refer from: Francesco d'Assis, Saint.

49D. Popes

"Add the appropriate designation, in English, after the pontifical name assumed by a pope or antipope. For those of the same name add after the name the Roman numeral by which each is identified." See Fig. 4.31.

Fig. 4.31

Pontifical name

Designation "Pope"

```
     Pius XII, Pope, 1876-1958.
          Pio XII e l'umana sofferenza. -- Ed.
     Italiana del magistero di Pio XII sul
     dolore / a cura di D. Bertetto. -- Roma :
     Edizioni Paoline, 1961.
          874 p. ; 19 cm. -- (Biblioteca di cultura
     religiosa)



          1. Suffering--Collected works.  I. Ber-
     tetto, Domenico, ed.  II. Title.
```

Rule 50. Entry of Roman names

"Enter a Roman of classical times under the part of his name most commonly used as entry element in reference sources." See Fig. 4.32. "In case of doubt, enter under the first of his names."

Fig. 4.32

Entry under common Roman name

Seneca, Lucius Annaeus.
     The woorke of the excellent philosopher Lucius Annaeus Seneca / Seneca. — Amsterdam : Theatrum Orbis Terrarum ; Norwood, N.J. : W. J. Johnson, 1974.

120 [i.e. 240] p. ; 21 cm. — (The English experience, its record in early printed books published in facsimile ; no. 694)

Translation of De beneficiis.
Cover title: Woorke of Lucius Seneca.
Photoreprint ed.
Includes original t.p.: The woorke of the excellent philosopher Lucius Annaeus Seneca concerning benefyting, that is too say the dooing, receyving, and requyting of good turnes. Translated out of Latin by Arthur Golding. Imprinted

(Continued on next card)

74-80233
MARC
75

ADDITIONS TO NAMES

It should be noted that AACR stress the use of dates with a person's name if such dates are *readily* ascertainable at the time of cataloging, but they are not required except to distinguish between persons with the same name. Other means of distinguishing such persons (if dates are not available) are used only if they regularly appear in reference sources or author statement.

Rule 52. Dates

"Add the years of a person's birth and death as the last element of the heading if they are readily ascertainable at the time the heading is established. If the person's name is the same as that of another person whose name has already been established as a heading, make every reasonable effort to provide dates for both. When identical names are not involved, approximate dates should be avoided if it is likely that exact dates will be available in the future."

Fig. 4.33

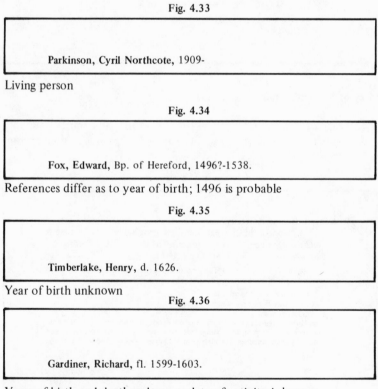

Parkinson, Cyril Northcote, 1909-

Living person

Fig. 4.34

Fox, Edward, Bp. of Hereford, 1496?-1538.

References differ as to year of birth; 1496 is probable

Fig. 4.35

Timberlake, Henry, d. 1626.

Year of birth unknown

Fig. 4.36

Gardiner, Richard, fl. 1599-1603.

Years of birth and death unknown; date of activity is known.
Not generally used for twentieth century.

Other means of distinguishing between authors with the same names are shown in Figs. 4.37 and 4.38.

Fig. 4.37

> **Smith, John,** of Mountague Close, Southwark.

Place added to distinguish from others of same name.

Fig. 4.38

> **Fischer, John,** 1910 (Apr. 27)-

Day, month, and year of birth added to distinguish from others of same name.

Rule 53. Distinguishing terms

53A. "If distinguishing dates are not available and the name would be otherwise insufficiently identified or distinguished from other names used as headings in the catalog, add a term of address, the title of a position or office, the initials of an academic degree or denoting membership in an organization, etc., that appears with the name in author statements or in reference sources." See Figs. 4.39 and 4.40.

Fig. 4.39

> **Chapman, William H**   M.A. ◄——
>   Introduction to practical phonetics / by William H. Chapman.
> — 3rd ed. — High Wycombe : Summer Institute of Linguistics,
> 1973 ₍i.e. 1974₎
>   ₍9₎. 89 p. : ill. ; 26 cm. — (Introduction to practical linguistics)
>   GB74-25852
>
>   ISBN 0-9503654-0-8 : £0.75

Fig. 4.40

> **Edwards, Jan,** Librarian. ◄——
>   A select bibliography on the poverty datum line in South
> Africa / compiled by Jan Edwards and Dudley Horner. —
> Johannesburg : South African Institute of Race Relations. 1974.
>   22 p. ; 30 cm.   SA•••

5 FORM OF ENTRY HEADINGS FOR CORPORATE BODIES

INTRODUCTION

As defined in the AACR, " . . . a corporate body is any organization or group of persons that is identified by a name and that acts or may act as an entity. Corporate bodies cover a broad range of categories of which the following are typical: associations, institutions, business firms, non-profit enterprises, governments, specific agencies of government, and conferences.

"Since commercial publishers typically do not bear the responsibility for the intellectual or artistic content of the works they publish, they are normally out of consideration when the term 'corporate body' is used in these rules. The following types of firms, however, when functioning as producers as well as publishers of the information in their works, are included by this term: publishers of legal, business, or financial services, city directories, guide-books, maps and atlases."

The general rule for entry of a corporate body follows the form of name that the body itself uses except when the rules specify entry under a higher body of which it is a part or under place. The AACR recommend use of the name that the corporate body generally uses (including conventional names), which in some cases may not be the official name. A similar principle is also followed for entry of personal names. Subordinate bodies whose names do not imply subordination will be entered directly under their own names. Furthermore, when the name of the corporate body changes, a new heading will appear under that name with cross-references to various names that will remain in use. The following rules and samples cover only the most important problems of corporate entry.

BASIC RULE

Rule 60. Basic rule

"Enter a corporate body directly under its name except when the rules that follow provide for entering it under a higher body of which it is a part, or under the name of the government of which it is an agency." See Fig. 5.1.

Fig. 5.1

Entry under
name of
corporate
body

▶**Lithuanian American Community.**
     The violations of human rights in Soviet occupied Lithuania
: a report for 1973 / prepared by Lithuanian American Community, inc. — Glenside, Pa. : The Community. 1974.

   112 p. ; 25 cm.

   Includes bibliographical references.

   1. Civil rights—Lithuania.   I. Title.

                        323.4′0947′5   75-303972
                                                MARC

Rule 60. Corporate body entered directly under its name.

CHOICE AND FORM OF NAME

Rule 61.   General rule

"When the name of a corporate body found in reference sources varies from that used by the body on the publications of which it is author, publisher, or sponsor, the latter form is preferred." (If there are no variations, the basic Rule 60 may be followed.)

Rule 62.   Variant forms in the publication

"If variant forms of the name are found in the body's own publications, use the name as it appears in formal presentations (as at the head of the title, in the imprint, and in formal author statements)." Choose a brief form of name if it is found in formal presentations and is adequate for cataloging purposes, otherwise choose official form of name wherever found. See Fig. 5.2.

Fig. 5.2

Entry under
brief form

▶**Dumbarton Oaks.**
     Dictionary catalogue of the Byzantine collection of the Dum-
barton Oaks Research Library, Washington, D.C. — Boston : G.
K. Hall, 1975.

   12 v. ; 37 cm.

   At head of title: Harvard University.
   ISBN 0-8161-1150-2

   1. Byzantine Empire - Civilization—Bibliography—Catalogs.   2. Dumbarton Oaks.

   Z6207.B9D85   1975   016.9495   75-314103

Rule 62. Use of the brief form of a corporate name.
Refer from: Harvard University. Dumbarton Oaks Research Library.
            Dumbarton Oaks Research Library.

Rule 63. Conventional name

63A. "When a body is frequently identified by a conventional form of name in the reference sources in its own language, prefer this conventional name to the official name and other forms used in its publications." See Fig. 5.3.

Fig. 5.3

➤**Bury St. Edmunds Abbey.**
    The customary of the Benedictine Abbey of Bury St.
    Edmunds in Suffolk : (from Harleian MS. 1005 in the
    British Museum) / edited by Antonia Gransden. — ₁London₁ : Henry Bradshaw Society. 1973.
        xlii, 142 p. : 23 cm. — (₁Publications₁ - Henry Bradshaw Society ;
    v. 99)   GB***
        Latin text with introd. and notes in English.
        Bibliography: p. xi–xiii.
        Includes index.

Entry
under
conven-
tional
name

63B. "When the name of a body of ancient origin or one that is international in character [i.e., diplomatic conferences, religious bodies] has become firmly established in English language usage under an English form, enter it under this form, regardless of the forms that may appear on its publications." See Figs. 5.4 and 5.5.

Fig. 5.4

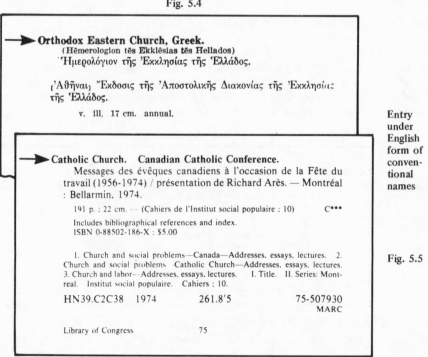

➤**Orthodox Eastern Church, Greek.**
    (Hēmerologion tēs Ekklēsias tēs Hellados)
    ʽΗμερολόγιον τῆς Ἐκκλησίας τῆς Ἑλλάδος.

    ₁Ἀθῆναι₁ Ἔκδοσις τῆς Ἀποστολικῆς Διακονίας τῆς Ἐκκλησίας
    τῆς Ἑλλάδος.

        v. ill, 17 cm. annual.

Entry
under
English
form of
conven-
tional
names

➤**Catholic Church.   Canadian Catholic Conference.**
    Messages des évêques canadiens à l'occasion de la Fête du
    travail (1956-1974) / présentation de Richard Arès. — Montréal
    : Bellarmin, 1974.
        191 p. ; 22 cm. — (Cahiers de l'Institut social populaire ; 10)   C***
        Includes bibliographical references and index.
        ISBN 0-88502-186-X : $5.00

        1. Church and social problems—Canada—Addresses, essays, lectures.   2.
    Church and social problems Catholic Church—Addresses, essays, lectures.
    3. Church and labor—Addresses, essays, lectures.   I. Title.   II. Series: Mont-
    real. Institut social populaire. Cahiers ; 10.

    HN39.C2C38   1974   261.8′5   75-507930
                                                      MARC

    Library of Congress   75

Fig. 5.5

Rule 64. Language

"If the name appears in different languages, prefer the form in the official language. **Note:** A form of name in a language suitable to the users of the catalog may be preferred to the form that would result from the application of these rules if the latter is in a language that is not one in which the library normally collects materials." See Fig. 5.6.

Fig. 5.6

Corporate name entered under official language

> **Fotografía Industrial S.A.**
> All Mallorca / Technical Department of F.I.S.A. — 1. éd. —
> Barcelona : Editorial Escudo de Oro, 1971.
>
> 123 p. : col. ill. ; 25 cm. -- **(Its All Spain ; 4)**   Sp72-Nov.
>
> Translation of Toda Mallorca.
> 225ptas
>
>
> 1. Majorca —Description and travel—Views.   I. Title.
>
> DP302.B27F6713   914.6'75   75-306690
>   MARC
>
> Library of Congress   *75

64B. Romanization

64B1. "If the language that is used is one that is not normally written in the Roman alphabet, romanize the name for the purpose of the heading by the application of the appropriate transliteration or romanization system adopted for library purposes." See Fig. 5.7.

Fig. 5.7

Corporate name entered under transliterated form

> **Akademiia nauk SSSR.**
> Noctilucent clouds : optical properties / Academy of Sciences
> of the U.S.S.R., Soviet Geophysical Committee, and Institute of
> Physics and Astronomy of the Academy of Sciences of the Es-
> tonian S.S.R. — Tallinn : The Academy, 1973.
>
> 116 p. : ill. ; 23 cm.   USSR***
>
> English or Russian.
> Includes bibliographies.
> 0.64-ub
>
> 1. Noctilucent clouds—Addresses, essays, lectures.   I. Akademiia nauk
> SSSR. Mezhduvedomstvennyĭ geofizicheskiĭ komitet.   II. Eesti NSV Tea-
> duste Akadeemia. Füüsika ja Astronoomia Instituut. III. Title.
>
> QC976.N6A4   1973   75-308616
>   MARC
>
> Library of Congress

Rule 65.   Additions to names

"When two bodies have the same name or names so closely similar that they are likely to be confused, they are distinguished by adding a word or phrase to the name of each."

65A.   Local place names

"Add the name of the place in which the body is located [or name of place generally associated with the body] if the same name has been used by another body in a different location." See Fig. 5.8.

Fig. 5.8

Good Housekeeping Institute, London.
 Good Housekeeping freezer recipes / compiled by Good Housekeeping Institute ; ₍edited by Gill Edden ; photographs by Stephen Baker₎. — London : Ebury Press, 1974.

 256 p., ₍12₎ p. of plates : ill. (some col.) ; 26 cm.   GB74-13024

 Includes index.
 ISBN 0-85223-051-6 : £2.95

 1. Food, Frozen. 2. Cookery. I. Edden, Gill, ed. II. Title.
 TX828.G66 1974   641.5′55   75-309029

Local place name to distinguish corporate body

65B.   Names of countries, states, provinces, etc.

65B1.   "Add the name of the country, state, province, etc., in parentheses, instead of the local place name if the name has been used by different bodies that have a character that is national, state, provincial, etc." See Fig. 5.9.

Fig. 5.9

Socialist Party (India).
 The Hyderabad problem : the next step ; foreword by Jaya-prakash Narayan. — Bombay : Issued by Hyderabad Struggle Committee, Socialist Party, 1948.

 iii, 96, vii p. : 2 fold. maps ; 22 cm.

 1. Hyderabad, India (State)—Politics and government. I. Title.
 DS485.H9S63 1948   320.9′54′8404   75-307890
                   MARC

Name of country added

Note: If the addition of place does not sufficiently distinguish between bodies, add in parentheses the year of founding, inclusive years of existence, or a suitable general term of identification or qualification. See Figs. 5.10 and 5.11.

Fig. 5.10

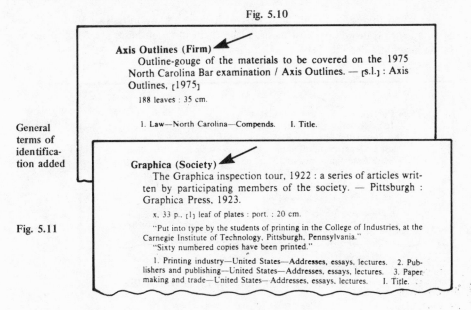

General terms of identification added

Axis Outlines (Firm)
  Outline-gouge of the materials to be covered on the 1975 North Carolina Bar examination / Axis Outlines. — ₁s.l.₁ : Axis Outlines, ₁1975₁

  188 leaves : 35 cm.

  1. Law—North Carolina—Compends.   I. Title.

Fig. 5.11

Graphica (Society)
  The Graphica inspection tour, 1922 : a series of articles written by participating members of the society. — Pittsburgh : Graphica Press, 1923.

  x, 33 p., ₁1₁ leaf of plates : port. ; 20 cm.

  "Put into type by the students of printing in the College of Industries, at the Carnegie Institute of Technology, Pittsburgh, Pennsylvania."
  "Sixty numbered copies have been printed."

  1. Printing industry—United States—Addresses, essays, lectures.   2. Publishers and publishing—United States—Addresses, essays, lectures.   3. Paper making and trade—United States—Addresses, essays, lectures.   I. Title.

Rule 66.   Omissions from names

66A.   Initial articles

"Omit initial articles unless required for reasons of clarity or grammar." See Figs. 5.12 (article required) and 5.13 (article omitted).

Fig. 5.12

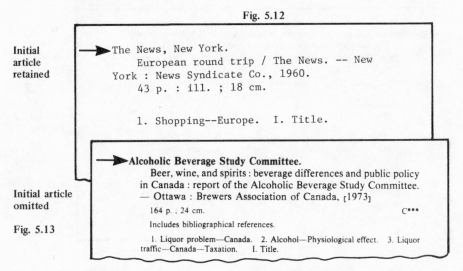

Initial article retained

The News, New York.
    European round trip / The News. -- New York : News Syndicate Co., 1960.
    43 p. : ill. ; 18 cm.

    1. Shopping--Europe.   I. Title.

Initial article omitted

Fig. 5.13

Alcoholic Beverage Study Committee.
  Beer, wine, and spirits : beverage differences and public policy in Canada : report of the Alcoholic Beverage Study Committee. — Ottawa : Brewers Association of Canada, ₁1973₁
  164 p. ; 24 cm.   C***
  Includes bibliographical references.

  1. Liquor problem—Canada.   2. Alcohol—Physiological effect.   3. Liquor traffic—Canada—Taxation.   I. Title.

Rule 67. Modifications of names

67A. Initials and abbreviations of forenames

"When the corporate name begins with one or more initials or abbreviations of forenames followed by a surname, place them in parentheses after the surname in the heading." See Fig. 5.14.

Fig. 5.14

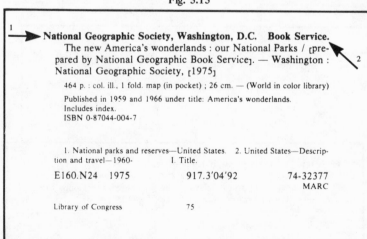

Van Poollen (H. K.) and Associates.
    In place volumetric determination of reservoir fluids, Sadlerochit Formation, Prudhoe Bay Field : report prepared for State of Alaska, Department of Natural Resources / by H. K. van Poollen and Associates, inc., and State of Alaska Division of Oil and Gas. — ₍Juneau₎ : State of Alaska, Dept. of Natural Resources, Division of Oil and Gas, 1974.

    xix, 41, ₍96₎ p., ₍25₎ fold. leaves of plates : ill. ; 28 cm.

    1. Petroleum—Geology—Alaska—North Slope. 2. Oil reservoir engineering. I. Alaska. Division of Oil and Gas. II. Alaska. Dept. of Natural Resources. III. Title: In place volumetric determination of reservoir fluids ...

Initials of
forenames

SUBORDINATE AND RELATED BODIES

Rule 69. Bodies with names implying subordination

    Enter a subordinate body as a subheading under a higher body if the name of the subordinate body loses its distinctive character when used without the name of the higher body. See Figs. 5.15 and 5.16.

Fig. 5.15

1
National Geographic Society, Washington, D.C. Book Service.
    The new America's wonderlands : our National Parks / ₍prepared by National Geographic Book Service₎. — Washington :   2
National Geographic Society, ₍1975₎

    464 p. : col. ill., 1 fold. map (in pocket) ; 26 cm. — (World in color library)

    Published in 1959 and 1966 under title: America's wonderlands.
    Includes index.
    ISBN 0-87044-004-7

    1. National parks and reserves—United States. 2. United States—Description and travel—1960-   I. Title.

E160.N24   1975   917.3'04'92   74-32377
                                       MARC

Library of Congress   75

[1] Higher body as main entry

[2] Subordinate body as subheading

Fig. 5.16

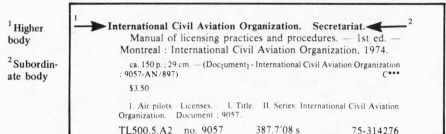

¹ Higher
body

² Subordin-
ate body

69A. Direct or indirect subheading

"Enter a body treated subordinately as a subheading of the lowest element in the hierarchy above it that may be independently entered. Omit intervening elements in the hierarchy that are not essential to clarify the function of the smaller body as an element of the larger one." See the example below.

Heading: American Library Association. Copying
             Methods Section. Library Standards for
             Microfilm Committee.

Hierarchy: American Library Association
             Resources and Technical Services Division
             Copying Methods Section
             Library Standards for Microfilm Committee

Fig. 5.17

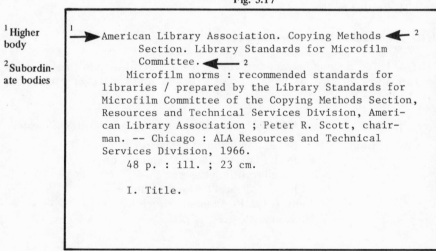

¹ Higher
body

² Subordin-
ate bodies

Rule 70. Other subordinate bodies

70A. Enter a subordinate body directly under its own name if its name does not require the application of Rule 69.

Heading: World Health Assembly

Refer from: World Health Organization. Assembly
                  World Health Organization. World Health Assembly

Fig. 5.18

```
World Health Assembly.
     International sanitary regulations adopted
by the fourth World Health Assembly in 1951, and
amended by the Eighth, Ninth, Thirteenth, Six-
teenth, and Eighteenth World Health Assembly in
1955, 1956, 1960, 1963, and 1965. -- 3d ed. --
Geneva : World Health Organization, 1966.
     121 p. : ill., maps ; 25 cm.



     1. Public health laws, International.
I. Title.
```

Subordin-
ate body
as main
entry

Rule 71. Related bodies

71B. Joint committees, commissions, etc.

71B1. "Enter a joint committee, commission or other unit made up of representatives of two or more corporate bodies under its own name." See Fig. 5.19.

Heading: Joint ARC/MRC Committee on Food and Nutrition Research.

Refer from: Great Britain. Agricultural Research
                      Council. Joint ARC/MRC Committee on
                      Food and Nutrition Research.
                  Great Britain. Medical Research Council.
                      Joint ARC/MRC Committee on Food and
                      Nutrition Research.

Fig. 5.19

Joint
committee
as main
entry

➤**Joint ARC/MRC Committee on Food and Nutrition Research.**
Food and nutrition research : report of the ARC/MRC com-
mittee. — London : H.M. Stationery Off. ; New York : Elsevier
Scientific Pub. Co., 1974.

xv, 211 p. ; 25 cm.   GB***

At head of title: Agricultural Research Council. Medical Research Council.
Includes index.
ISBN 0-444-99871-3 (Elsevier) : £3.80

1. Nutrition—Research.   2. Food research.   I. Title.

GEOGRAPHIC NAMES

"The basic sources for standard forms of geographic names for American libraries are the publications of the U.S. Board on Geographic Names and its predecessors, the Board on Geographical Names (1934-1947), and the Geographic Board (1890-1934). The principal sources for foreign names are the *Gazetteers* of the present Board. The principal source for domestic names is the *Sixth Report* (1933) of the U.S. Geographic Board as supplemented and amended by the *Decisions* of the Board on Geographical Names and the *Decisions on names in the United States* of the present Board. It should be noted that all decisions of these boards are confined to current forms of geographic names." Care should be taken not to confuse the geographic name of the country with the political name of that same country.

Rule 72. Language

72A. "Prefer the English form of a geographic name if there is one in general use, e.g., Austria not Österreich."

72B. "If there is no English form in general use, prefer the form in the official language of the country, e.g., Buenos Aires."

Rule 73. Additions

"Add the name of a larger geographical entity in which the place is located except in the case of 1) states of the United States and provinces of Canada and 2) other non-local places when the place in question is clearly the place of that name that is best known to users of the catalog."

Example: Formosa, Argentina

For local place names in the United States or Canada add the name of the state or province. See Fig. 5.20.

Example: New York, N.Y.

This example is a revision in the AACR from the previous form of New York (City), which is no longer correct.

Fig. 5.20

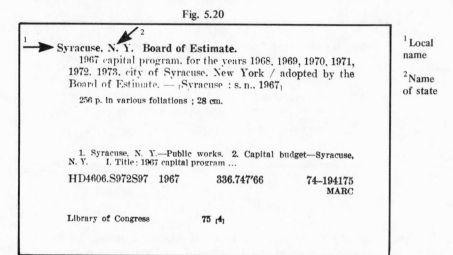

¹ Local name

² Name of state

```
1 ──►  Syracuse, N. Y.   Board of Estimate.
           1967 capital program, for the years 1968, 1969, 1970, 1971,
        1972, 1973, city of Syracuse, New York / adopted by the
        Board of Estimate. — ₍Syracuse : s. n., 1967₎
           256 p. in various foliations ; 28 cm.



           1. Syracuse, N. Y.—Public works.  2. Capital budget—Syracuse,
        N. Y.    I. Title : 1967 capital program ...

        HD4606.S972S97   1967        336.747′66        74–194175
                                                         MARC

           Library of Congress          75 ₍4₎
```

GOVERNMENTS

Government publications follow principles similar to those established for other corporate bodies. There are two basic principles for entry of governmental agencies. Those agencies that are directly involved in legislative, judicial, or executive functions of the government are entered under their political jurisdiction (e.g., departments of executive branch, courts, legislative organs, etc.). Secondly, all other governmental organizations are entered under their own name if possible. Typical of this second category are governmental organizations engaged in scientific or cultural activities. As a result of these changes many governmental organizations will now be entered directly under their names (e.g., National Agricultural Library, not United States. National Agricultural Library). There is also a tendency to omit intervening elements in the hierarchy that are not essential to clarify the function of a subordinate agency. As a result more governmental agencies that are subordinate to other governmental bodies will be entered directly under the government rather than under the higher agency of which they are a part.

Rule 75. General rule

"Use the conventional name (see 72-74) of a country, province, state, county, municipality, or other political jurisdiction as the heading for its government, unless the official name of the government is in more common use." See examples below.

Massachusetts, not Commonwealth of Massachusetts

France, not République Française

Rule 77. Distinguishing governments with the same name

77A1. When different political or administrative units have the same conventional name and cannot be satisfactorily distinguished, add in parentheses an appropriate designation for non-municipal governments. See Fig. 5.21.

Fig. 5.21

Distinguish-
ing term
added to
name of
state

> **New York (State). Legislative Commission on Expenditure Re-**
> **view.**
> State aid to libraries : program audit 4.1.74, March 4, 1974 /
> Legislative Commission on Expenditure Review. — Albany :
> The Commission, [1974]
>
> 12. iv. 82 p. : ill. ; 28 cm.
>
> At head of title: The Legislature, State of New York.
> Cover title.
> Includes bibliographical references.
>
> 1. Libraries and state —New York (State)   I. Title.

77A2. "If the type of jurisdiction does not provide a satisfactory distinction, add whatever other words or phrases are appropriate in the particular case." See Figs. 5.22 and 5.23.

Fig. 5.22

Distinguish-
ing terms
based on
political
names and
dates

> **Germany (Federal Republic, 1949–   ). Laws, statutes,**
> **etc.**
> Realkreditgesetze : in neuer Fassung 1974 ; Textsamm-
> lung mit Einl., Regierungsbegründung, Bericht d. Wirt-
> schafts- u. d. Finanzausschusses, vergleichender Übersicht
> u. Anm. / hrsg. von Klaus Hammer. — Frankfurt (am
> Main) : Knapp, 1974.

Fig. 5.23

> **Russia   (1923-   U.S.S.R.).   Ministerstvo**
> **zdravookhraneniĩa.**
> The training and utilization of feldshers in the USSR : a review
> / prepared by the Ministry of Health of the USSR for the World
> Health Organization. — Geneva : World Health Organization,
> 1974.
>
> 52 p. ; 22 cm. — (Public health papers ; no. 56)   Sw•••
> ISBN 9241300566 : 5.00F
>
> 1. Paramedical education—Russia.   2. Physicians' assistants--Russia.   3.
> Public health personnel—Russia.   I. World Health Organization.   II. Title.
> III. Series: World Health Organization.   Public health papers ; no. 56.
>
> R847.R87   1974   610.69′53′0947   75-312823
>   MARC
>
> Library of Congress   75

GOVERNMENT BODIES AND OFFICIALS

"The general principle underlying the following rule is that agencies through which the basic legislative, judicial, and executive functions of government are exercised should be entered as subheadings for the government; other bodies created or controlled by the government should be entered, if possible, under their own names."

Rule 78. General rule

78A. "Enter a corporate body created or controlled by a government under the general rules for corporate bodies, i.e., 60-68, regardless of its official nature (except for necessary references) or of whether or not it is subordinate to an agency of government, if it is one of the following types." See Figs. 5.24-5.30.

Fig. 5.24

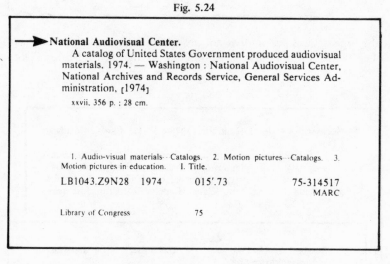

National Audiovisual Center.
    A catalog of United States Government produced audiovisual materials. 1974. — Washington : National Audiovisual Center, National Archives and Records Service, General Services Administration, ₁1974₁
    xxvii, 356 p. ; 28 cm.

Type 1

    1. Audio-visual materials--Catalogs. 2. Motion pictures--Catalogs. 3. Motion pictures in education.   I. Title.

LB1043.Z9N28   1974   015'.73   75-314517
                                                        MARC

Library of Congress   75

78A.—Type 1. Organizations engaged in commercial, cultural, or scientific activities, or the promotion of such activities.

Fig. 5.25

Type 2

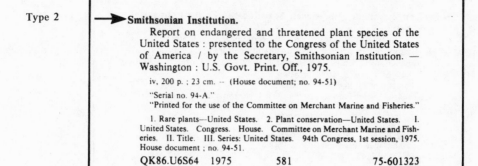

Smithsonian Institution.
　　　Report on endangered and threatened plant species of the
United States : presented to the Congress of the United States
of America / by the Secretary, Smithsonian Institution. —
Washington : U.S. Govt. Print. Off., 1975.

　　　iv, 200 p. ; 23 cm. -- (House document; no. 94-51)

　　　"Serial no. 94-A."
　　　"Printed for the use of the Committee on Merchant Marine and Fisheries."

　　　1. Rare plants—United States.　2. Plant conservation—United States.　　I.
United States.　Congress.　House.　Committee on Merchant Marine and Fish-
eries.　II. Title.　III. Series: United States.　94th Congress, 1st session, 1975.
House document ; no. 94-51.

QK86.U6S64　　1975　　　　　　581　　　　　　　　75-601323
　　　　　　　　　　　　　　　　　　　　　　　　　　　　　　　MARC

Library of Congress　　　　　　　75

78A.–Type 2. Institutions (typically with their own physical plant).

Fig. 5.26

Type 3

Yellowstone National Park.
　　　Wonderful Yellowstone. -- Yellowstone
Park, Wyo. : Yellowstone National Park, 1967.
　　　18 p. : ill. ; 24 cm.

　　　1. Yellowstone National Park--Guide books.
2. Wyoming--Description and travel.　I. Title.

78A.–Type 3. Installations and parks.

Fig. 5.27

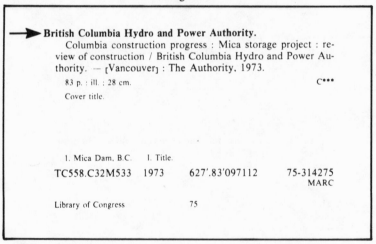

United Nations Educational, Scientific and Cultural Organization.
     Inventaire illustré d'œuvres démembrées célèbres dans la peinture européenne : avec un chapitre sur les tombeaux démembrés dans la sculpture française / ₍publié par l'₎ Unesco. — Paris : Unesco, 1973, 1974 printing.
     221 p. : ill. ; 30 cm.   F 74-10272
     Issued also in English under title: An illustrated inventory of famous dismembered works of art: European painting.
     Includes bibliographical references.
     ISBN 9232010399
     1. Paintings - Europe—Mutilation, defacement, etc.   2. Sculpture - France --Mutilation, defacement, etc.   I. Title.
     ND450.U47   1974a   759.94   75-506112
                                                   MARC

Library of Congress   75

Type 4

78A.–Type 4. Bodies created by intergovernmental agreement.

Fig. 5.28

British Columbia Hydro and Power Authority.
     Columbia construction progress : Mica storage project : review of construction / British Columbia Hydro and Power Authority. — ₍Vancouver₎ : The Authority, 1973.
     83 p. : ill. ; 28 cm.   C***
     Cover title.

     1. Mica Dam, B.C.   I. Title.
     TC558.C32M533   1973   627'.83'097112   75-314275
                                                   MARC

Library of Congress   75

Type 5

78A.–Type 5. Authorities and trusts for the operation of utilities and industries.

Fig. 5.29

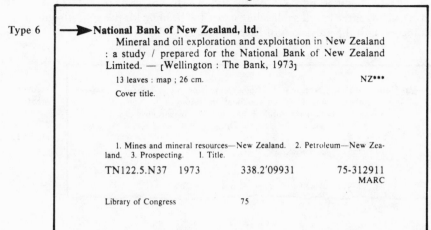

Type 6

National Bank of New Zealand, ltd.
Mineral and oil exploration and exploitation in New Zealand
: a study / prepared for the National Bank of New Zealand
Limited. — [Wellington : The Bank, 1973]

13 leaves : map ; 26 cm.   NZ•••

Cover title.

1. Mines and mineral resources—New Zealand.   2. Petroleum—New Zealand.   3. Prospecting.   I. Title.

TN122.5.N37   1973   338.2′09931   75-312911
                                                          MARC

Library of Congress   75

78A.—Type 6. Banks, corporations, manufacturing plants, farms, and
similar specific enterprises.

Fig. 5.30

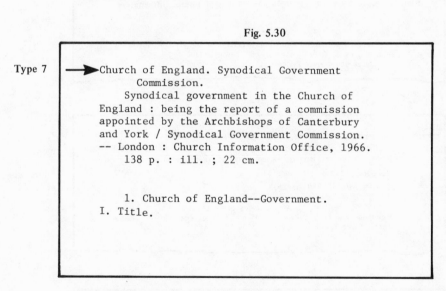

Type 7

Church of England. Synodical Government
        Commission.
    Synodical government in the Church of
England : being the report of a commission
appointed by the Archbishops of Canterbury
and York / Synodical Government Commission.
-- London : Church Information Office, 1966.
    138 p. : ill. ; 22 cm.

    1. Church of England--Government.
I. Title.

78A.—Type 7. Established churches.

78B. If the body is not one of the types listed in 78A, or if there is doubt that it is one, enter it as a subheading under the heading for the government and in accordance with the provisions of Rules 79-86.

Fig. 5.31

United States.   National Advisory Council on Adult Education.
A target population in adult education : report of the National Advisory Council on Adult Education. — Washington : The Council : for sale by the Supt. of Docs., U.S. Govt. Print. Off., 1974.

viii, 157 p. : ill., graphs, maps ; 26 cm.

Includes bibliographical references.
$2.35

1. Adult education—United States—Statistics.   I. Title.

¹Government

²Subordinate body

Fig. 5.32

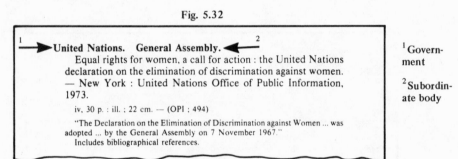

United Nations.   General Assembly.
Equal rights for women, a call for action : the United Nations declaration on the elimination of discrimination against women. — New York : United Nations Office of Public Information, 1973.

iv, 30 p. : ill. ; 22 cm. — (OPI ; 494)

"The Declaration on the Elimination of Discrimination against Women ... was adopted ... by the General Assembly on 7 November 1967."
Includes bibliographical references.

¹Government

²Subordinate body

Fig. 5.33

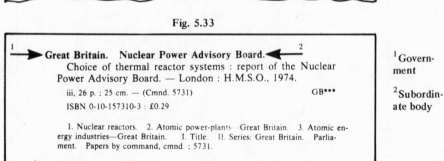

Great Britain.   Nuclear Power Advisory Board.
Choice of thermal reactor systems : report of the Nuclear Power Advisory Board. — London : H.M.S.O., 1974.

iii, 26 p. ; 25 cm. — (Cmnd. 5731)   GB•••
ISBN 0-10-157310-3 : £0.29

1. Nuclear reactors.   2. Atomic power-plants—Great Britain.   3. Atomic energy industries—Great Britain.   I. Title.   II. Series: Great Britain.   Parliament.   Papers by command, cmnd. ; 5731.

¹Government

²Subordinate body

Fig. 5.34

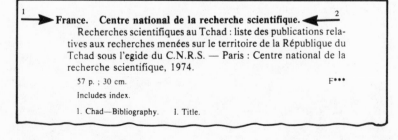

France.   Centre national de la recherche scientifique.
Recherches scientifiques au Tchad : liste des publications relatives aux recherches menées sur le territoire de la République du Tchad sous l'egide du C.N.R.S. — Paris : Centre national de la recherche scientifique, 1974.

57 p. ; 30 cm.   F•••
Includes index.

1. Chad—Bibliography.   I. Title.

¹Government

²Subordinate body

Rule 79. Subordinate agencies and units

79A. Direct subheading

"If a government body that is to be entered under the name of the government according to 78B above is subordinate to another such body, treat it as a direct subheading under the name of the government if its name has not been or is not likely to be used by another body in the same jurisdiction." See Fig. 5.35.

Fig. 5.35

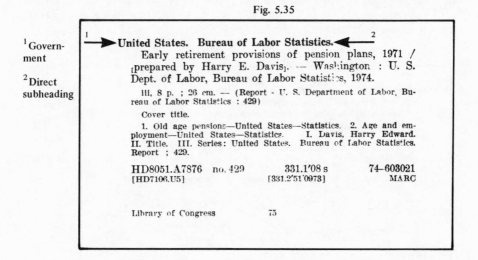

¹Government

²Direct subheading

Refer from: United States.Dept. of Labor. Bureau of Labor Statistics.

79B. Indirect subheading

"If the name of the body does not meet the above conditions or if there is doubt that it does, treat it as a subheading under the lowest element of the hierarchy that can be entered directly under the name of the government, omitting any intervening unit in the hierarchy that is not or is not likely to be essential to distinguish bodies with the same name or to identify the body." See Fig. 5.36.

Fig. 5.36

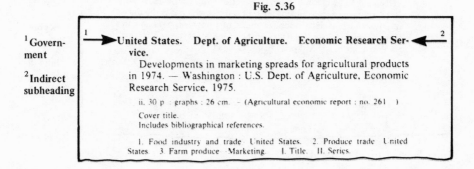

¹Government

²Indirect subheading

Rule 80. Government officials

80A. Chiefs of state, etc.

80A1. "The heading for a sovereign, president, other chief of state, or governor, in his official capacity (see 17C1), consists of the title of his office in English, unless there is no proper equivalent for the vernacular term, followed by the inclusive years of his reign or incumbency and, in parentheses, by his name in brief form in the language used for the heading for the person—all as subheading under the name of the government. If the title varies with the incumbent (e.g., 'King' and 'Queen') use a common designation of the office (e.g., 'Sovereign')." See Fig. 5.37.

Fig. 5.37

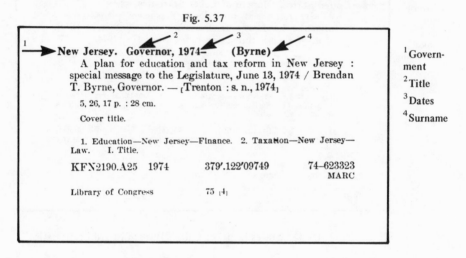

Rule 81. Legislative bodies

81A. "If a legislature has more than one chamber, enter each as a subheading under the legislature." See Figs. 5.38 and 5.39.

Fig. 5.38

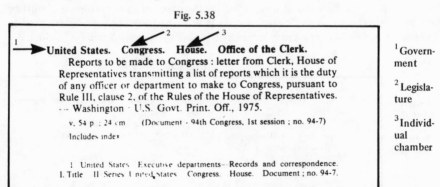

Refer from: United States. House.

If a legislature has only one chamber, enter it under the subheading legislature.

Fig. 5.39

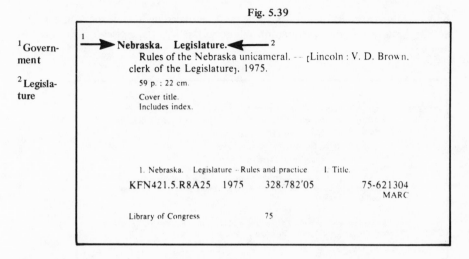

81B. "Enter committees and other subordinate units as subheadings under the legislature or of a particular chamber." See Fig. 5.40.

Fig. 5.40

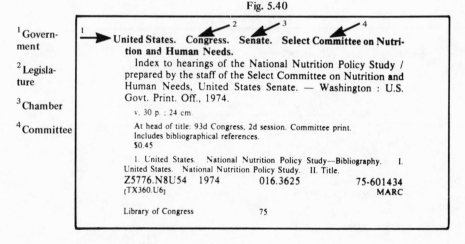

81C. "If successive legislatures are numbered consecutively, include the number and the year or years whenever the heading is for a particular legislature as a whole or for one of its chambers as a whole. If in such cases numbered sessions are also involved, give the session and its number, following the name and number of the legislature, and add the year or years of the session." Examples below:

United States. 87th Congress, 1961-1962.

United States. 87th Congress, 2d session, 1962. House.

Rule 83. Courts

83A. "Enter a court under its name as a subheading under the name of the country, state, or other jurisdiction whose authority it exercises." See Figs. 5.41 and 5.42.

Fig. 5.41

┌───┐

1
➤**Missouri. Supreme Court.**◀── 2

Vernon's annotated Missouri rules : Supreme Court rules. —
St. Paul : West Pub. Co., ₍1975-

v.   : forms ; 27 cm.

"Kept to date through cumulative pocket parts."
Includes bibliographical references and index.
CONTENTS: ₍1₎ Rules 1 to 26: The Missouri Bar and judiciary. Rules of
criminal procedure.—₍2₎ Rules 27 to 40: Rules of criminal procedure. Municipal
and traffic court rules.

1. Court rules—Missouri. 2. Criminal procedure—Missouri. 3. Civil procedure—Missouri. I. West Publishing Co., St. Paul. II. Title.

KFM8329.A2   1975b   347'.778'0355   75-315476
MARC

Library of Congress   75

└───┘

[1] Government

[2] Name of court

Fig. 5.42

┌───┐

1
➤**Massachusetts. Courts.**◀── 2

Massachusetts rules of court, 1975, with amendments to Nov.
15, 1974. -- St. Paul : West Pub. Co., ₍1975₎

xxix, 893 p. ; 25 cm.

"Text of the rules for all the Massachusetts courts and for the Appellate Tax
Board and the Industrial Accident Board. Also included are the local, bank-
ruptcy and magistrates rules for the United States District Court and the rules
for the United States Court of Appeals for the United States Court of Appeals
for the First Circuit."

1. Court rules Massachusetts.   I. Massachusetts. Appellate Tax Board.
II. Massachusetts. Industrial Accident Board. III. United States. Court of
Appeals for the First Circuit. IV. United States. District Court. Massa-
chusetts. V. Title.

KFM2929.A2   1975   347'.744'05   75-315486
MARC

Library of Congress   75

└───┘

[1] Government

[2] Form subheading used for more than one court

Rule 84. Armed forces

"Enter each of the principal services of the armed forces of a government as a direct subheading under the name of the government. Enter a component branch, command, district, or military unit, large or small, as a direct subheading under the heading for the service unless its name begins with the name of the service or with an adjective derived from that name; in either of the latter cases enter it as a direct subheading under the name of the government. Note that military installations and institutions are treated under 78A." See Fig. 5.43.

Fig. 5.43

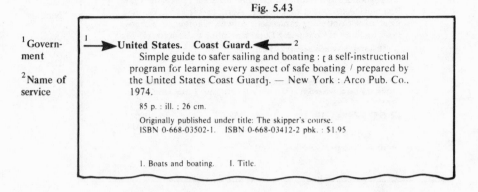

¹Govern-
ment

²Name of
service

> United States. Coast Guard. ◄─── 2
>
> Simple guide to safer sailing and boating : [a self-instructional program for learning every aspect of safe boating / prepared by the United States Coast Guard]. — New York : Arco Pub. Co., 1974.
>
> 85 p. : ill. : 26 cm.
>
> Originally published under title: The skipper's course.
> ISBN 0-668-03502-1. ISBN 0-668-03412-2 pbk. : $1.95
>
> 1. Boats and boating. I. Title.

CONFERENCES, CONGRESSES, MEETINGS, ETC.

"These rules apply to meetings of persons, either as individuals or as representatives of various bodies, for the purpose of studying, discussing, or acting on a particular topic or on various topics of common interest."

Rule 87. General rule

"Enter a conference, congress, or other meeting under its name, followed in many instances by one or more of the following elements: number, place, date." See Figs. 5.44 and 5.45.

Fig. 5.44

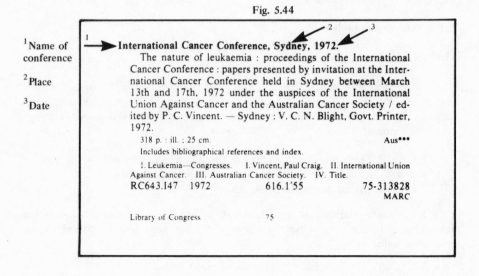

¹Name of
conference

²Place

³Date

> International Cancer Conference, Sydney, 1972.
>
> The nature of leukaemia : proceedings of the International Cancer Conference : papers presented by invitation at the International Cancer Conference held in Sydney between March 13th and 17th, 1972 under the auspices of the International Union Against Cancer and the Australian Cancer Society / edited by P. C. Vincent. — Sydney : V. C. N. Blight, Govt. Printer, 1972.
>
> 318 p. : ill. : 25 cm.   Aus•••
> Includes bibliographical references and index.
>
> !. Leukemia—Congresses. I. Vincent, Paul Craig. II. International Union Against Cancer. III. Australian Cancer Society. IV. Title.
> RC643.I47 1972   616.1'55   75-313828
>   MARC
>
> Library of Congress   75

Fig. 5.45

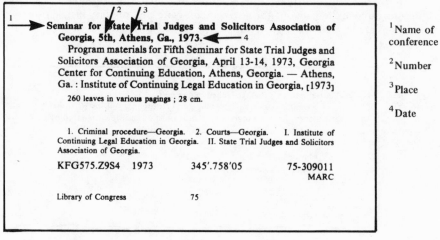

Seminar for State Trial Judges and Solicitors Association of
Georgia, 5th, Athens, Ga., 1973. ◄——— 4
    Program materials for Fifth Seminar for State Trial Judges and
Solicitors Association of Georgia, April 13-14, 1973, Georgia
Center for Continuing Education, Athens, Georgia. — Athens,
Ga. : Institute of Continuing Legal Education in Georgia, ₍1973₎
    260 leaves in various pagings ; 28 cm.

    1. Criminal procedure—Georgia. 2. Courts—Georgia. I. Institute of
Continuing Legal Education in Georgia. II. State Trial Judges and Solicitors
Association of Georgia.

KFG575.Z9S4   1973   345'.758'05   75-309011
                                                    MARC

Library of Congress   75

[1] Name of conference

[2] Number

[3] Place

[4] Date

RELIGIOUS BODIES AND OFFICIALS

Religious bodies are entered according to the general rules for corporate bodies except as these are modified by special provisions in Rules 92-98.

    Example: Philadelphia Baptist Association.
                   Catholic Church.
                   Council of Nicaea, 1st, 325- .

Rule 93. Patriarchates, dioceses, etc.

93B. Subordinate bodies

93B1. General rule

"Except as provided in 3 below [for units changed during Reformation from Catholic to Protestant], enter dioceses, provinces, and other subordinate units of religious bodies having jurisdiction within geographical districts as subheadings under the name of the body."

    Example: Evangelical and Reformed Church. Reading Synod.

93B2. Catholic patriarchates, dioceses, etc.

Enter under Catholic Church followed by the English form of name for a patriarchate, diocese, etc. Give the name of the see according to provisions for geographic names.

    Example: Catholic Church. Diocese of Harrisburg, Pa.

Rule 95. Administrative offices of the Catholic Church

95A. Pope

"The heading for a Pope in his capacity as Supreme Pontiff consists of the word *Pope* as subheading under the heading for the church, followed first by the inclusive years of his reign and then, in parentheses, by his pontifical name in its catalog entry form. Correlate such headings with the corresponding personal name headings by suitable references." See 17C for additional instructions. **Note:** English form of name is preferred.

    Example: Catholic Church. Pope, 1227-1241 (Gregory IX)

    not   Catholic Church. Pope, 1227-1241 (Gregorius IX)

Rule 96. Religious orders and societies

96A. "Enter a religious order or society under the name by which it is best known." See Figs. 5.46 and 5.47.

Fig. 5.46

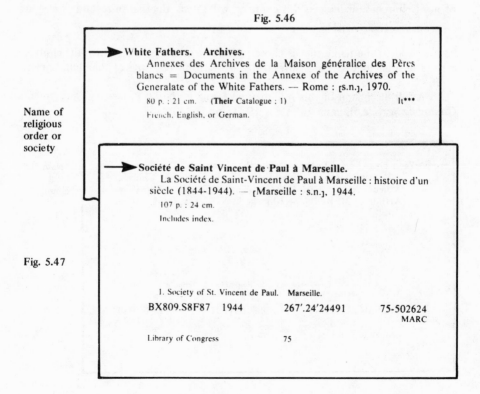

▶White Fathers. Archives.
    Annexes des Archives de la Maison généralice des Pères blancs = Documents in the Annexe of the Archives of the Generalate of the White Fathers. — Rome : [s.n.], 1970.
      80 p. : 21 cm.   **(Their** Catalogue ; 1)   lt***
      French. English, or German.

Name of
religious
order or
society

▶Société de Saint Vincent de Paul à Marseille.
    La Société de Saint-Vincent de Paul à Marseille : histoire d'un siècle (1844-1944). — [Marseille : s.n.], 1944.
      107 p. : 24 cm.
      Includes index.

Fig. 5.47

    1. Society of St. Vincent de Paul.   Marseille.
BX809.S8F87   1944   267'.24'24491   75-502624
                                           MARC

    Library of Congress   75

Rule 98. Local churches, etc.

98A. General rule

"Enter a local church, cathedral, monastery, convent, abbey, temple, mosque, or the like, in accordance with general rules 60-64. If, however, variant forms of the name of the body appear in formal presentations in the body's own publications, enter under the predominant form. If no one form predominates, choose a form according to the following order of preference:

1.   A name beginning with, or consisting of, the name of the person, persons, object, place, or event to which the church, etc., is dedicated or after which it is named;

2.   a name beginning with a generic word or phrase descriptive of a type of church, etc.;

3.   a name beginning with the name of the location in which the church, etc., is situated."

Note: This is one of the major revisions in AACR. Originally, AACR called for entry under the name of the place for local churches. This revision allows such entry only as the third alternative; this will probably be rarely used, since the names of most churches, at least in this country, will satisfy the first or second provision.

98B. "Add to the name that is chosen the name of the place in which the church, etc., is located unless this is sufficiently clear from the name of the church, etc., itself."

A full discussion of this rule may be found in the LC Processing Department *Cataloging Service*, bulletin 109 (May 1974), pp. 3-4.

Fig. 5.48

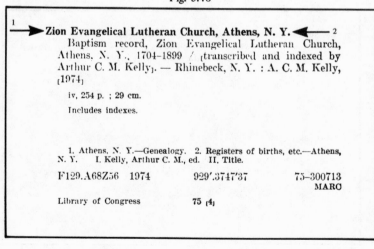

1
➤ **Zion Evangelical Lutheran Church, Athens, N. Y.** ◄──── 2
Baptism record, Zion Evangelical Lutheran Church, Athens, N. Y., 1704-1899 / ₁transcribed and indexed by Arthur C. M. Kelly₁. — Rhinebeck, N. Y. : A. C. M. Kelly, ₁1974₁

iv, 254 p. ; 29 cm.

Includes indexes.

1. Athens, N. Y.—Genealogy.   2. Registers of births, etc.—Athens, N. Y.   I. Kelly, Arthur C. M., ed.   II. Title.

F129.A68Z56   1974   929'.374737   75-300713
                                                                    MARC

Library of Congress   75 ₁4₁

[1] Name of local church

[2] Place

Fig. 5.49

[1] Place

[2] Name of
local
church

1

Salem, Mass.   First Church. ← 2

The records of the First Church in Salem, Massachusetts,
1629-1736 / edited by Richard D. Pierce ; introd. by Robert E.
Moody. — Salem, Mass. : Essex Institute, 1974.

xxvi, 421 p. ; 25 cm.

On spine: The First Church in Salem : records, 1629-1736.
Includes bibliographical references and indexes.
ISBN 0-88389-050-X

1. Salem, Mass.—Genealogy.   2. Church records and registers—Salem,
Mass.   I. Pierce, Richard Donald, 1915-1973.

F74.S1S173   1974   929'.3744'5   73-93302
                                                            MARC

Library of Congress   75

Example of entry under place, since First Church does not meet priority
one or two of Rule 98A.

6 UNIFORM TITLES

INTRODUCTION

When a work has appeared under more than one title, a uniform or conventional title mày be used for cataloging purposes in order to bring all editions of the work together. Uniform titles are used for sacred scriptures, creeds, liturgical works, and anonymous classics. "Bible" is a very common example of a uniform title in library catalogs; similarly, editions of the Mother Goose verses are assembled under the uniform title "Mother Goose." In these cases the uniform titles represent main entry headings. There are other instances when the uniform title is bracketed and placed between the main entry and the body of the card, as in the case of music (see Chapter 9), laws, liturgical works, and translations. AACR, Chapter 4, contains many further suggestions for extending these rules to other instances. The Library of Congress, however, on its printed cards uses uniform titles consistently only in those instances listed above, so libraries that apply these rules fully must also assume responsibility for revising many LC printed cards. The purpose of this chapter is to introduce the student to the more common forms of uniform titles. The explanation of uniform titles is followed by a section on the forms of necessary cross references in a library catalog. These examples relate to all the rules of entry covered in this and the two previous chapters.

UNIFORM TITLES

Rule 101D. Titles of laws

On the line following the form subheading for laws ("Laws, statutes, etc."), the uniform title for the law may be placed in brackets. The language of the law is indicated if it is a translation or if the law is written in more than one language. See Fig. 6.1.

Fig. 6.1

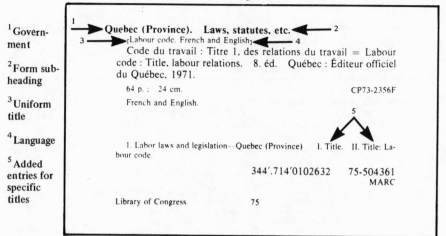

¹Govern-
ment

²Form sub-
heading

³Uniform
title

⁴Language

⁵Added
entries for
specific
titles

Rule 102. Works written before 1501

102A. General rule

"Prefer the title, in the original language, by which a work written before 1501 has become identified in reference sources. If evidence in reference sources is insufficient or inconclusive, prefer the title most frequently used in modern editions, early editions, or manuscript copies, in the order given." See Figs. 6.2 and 6.3.

Fig. 6.2

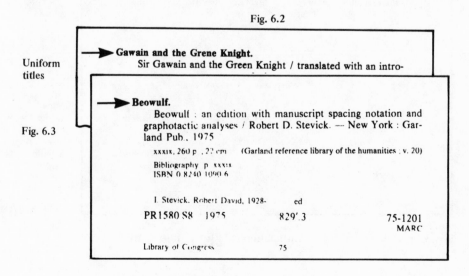

102C2. Anonymous works not written in the Roman alphabet

Prefer the title in English for works not written in the Roman alphabet. Indicate the language as a subheading of the title.

Fig. 6.4

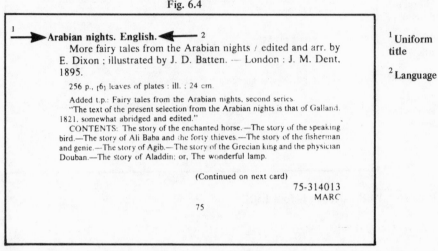

Fig. 6.4a

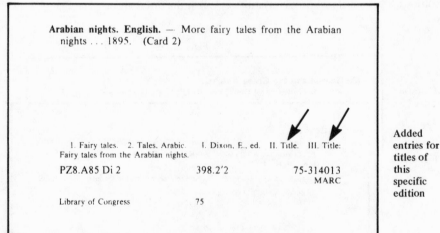

Fig. 6.4a is an example of a continuation card for a uniform title.

Rule 105. Translations

On the line between the heading and body of the card, place in brackets the uniform title of the translation (followed by a period-space) and the language of the translation. Note that this rule is applied by the Library of Congress only in certain cases. See Fig. 6.5.

Fig. 6.5

[1] Uniform title

[2] Language

[3] Author-title added entry

[4] Added entries for titles of this specific edition

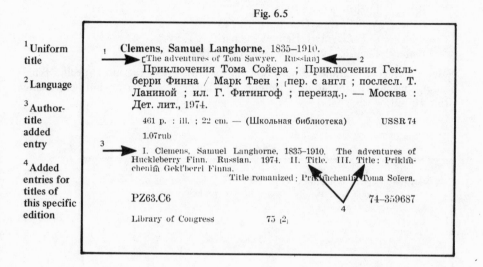

Clemens, Samuel Langhorne, 1835–1910.
[The adventures of Tom Sawyer. Russian]
Приключения Тома Сойера ; Приключения Гекльберри Финна / Марк Твен ; [пер. с англ ; послесл. Т. Ланиной ; ил. Г. Фитингоф ; переизд.]. — Москва : Дет. лит., 1974.

461 p. : ill. ; 22 cm. — (Школьная библиотека)   USSR 74

1.07rub

I. Clemens, Samuel Langhorne, 1835–1910. The adventures of Huckleberry Finn. Russian. 1974. II. Title. III. Title: Prikliucheniia Gekl'berri Finna.
Title romanized: Prikliucheniia Toma Soĭera.

PZ63.C6   74–359687

Library of Congress   75 [2]

Rule 108. General rule for the Bible

"Use the uniform title Bible for the Bible and any of its parts. Add to the heading the designation of a part, the language of the text, the name of the version, translator, or reviser, and the year of the edition."

Rule 109. Parts of the Bible

109A. Testaments and books

"Designate the Old Testament as *O.T.* and the New Testament as *N.T.* Treat the titles of individual books that are part of the Protestant canon as subheadings under the appropriate testament, using the brief citation form of the Authorized version. Follow the Authorized version also for the numbering of books, chapters, and verses. Use Arabic numerals for books, Roman numerals for chapters, and Arabic numerals for verses." Examples are:

Bible.   *N.T. Gospels . . .*
Bible.   *O.T. Historical books . . .*
Bible.   *O.T. Genesis XII, 1–XXV, 11 . . .*
Bible.   *N.T. 1 Corinthians . . .*

Bible.   [parts] [language] [versions] [selections] [date]
Bible.   English. Knox. 1956.
Bible.   *N.T.* English. Goodspeed. 1943.
Bible.   *O.T. Leviticus.* Hebrew. Samaritan. 1959.
Bible.   English. Authorized. Selections. 1947.

Note: Enter combinations of selections or excerpts under the most specific Bible heading and insert subheading Selections after language and version but before date (Rule 109E3).

Fig. 6.6

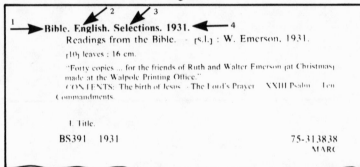

Bible. English. Selections. 1931.
Readings from the Bible. — [s.l.] : W. Emerson, 1931.
[10] leaves ; 16 cm.
"Forty copies ... for the friends of Ruth and Walter Emerson [at Christmas] made at the Walpole Printing Office."
CONTENTS: The birth of Jesus — The Lord's Prayer — XXIII Psalm — Ten Commandments.

1. Title.
BS391   1931   75-313838
                                                MARC

[1] Uniform title
[2] Language
[3] Selections
[4] Date

Fig. 6.7

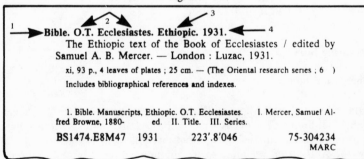

Bible. O.T. Ecclesiastes. Ethiopic. 1931.
The Ethiopic text of the Book of Ecclesiastes / edited by Samuel A. B. Mercer. — London : Luzac, 1931.
xi, 93 p., 4 leaves of plates ; 25 cm. — (The Oriental research series ; 6)
Includes bibliographical references and indexes.

1. Bible. Manuscripts, Ethiopic. O.T. Ecclesiastes.   I. Mercer, Samuel Alfred Browne, 1880-   ed. II. Title. III. Series.
BS1474.E8M47   1931   223'.8'046   75-304234
                                                MARC

[1] Uniform title
[2] Parts
[3] Language
[4] Date

Rule 119. Liturgical works

Liturgical works are entered under the proper heading for the denominational church to which the work pertains, followed by the subheading "Liturgy and ritual." AACR recommend the omission of uniform title whenever correct title is uncertain.

119A. Form and language of title

"Prefer a brief title in the language of the liturgy unless the name of the body under which the liturgical work is entered is given in English; in this case prefer a well established brief title in English when there is one." See Fig. 6.8.

Fig. 6.8

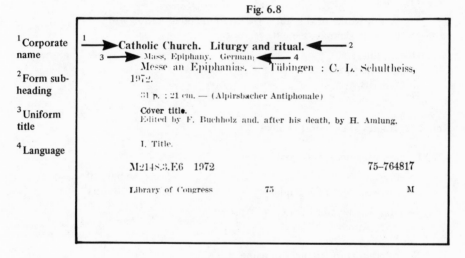

REFERENCES

"See" references must be made to direct the user from a name or form of name or title of a work not chosen for entry to the name or form of name selected. "See also" references guide the user to other headings that display related material. Explanatory references provide detailed information about the scope of a particular heading or method of entry—e.g., acronyms, changes in name of corporate body, surnames with prefixes, etc. Cf. Rules 120-126.

Rule 121. Names of persons

121A1a. See references. Different names

Refer from a name used by the author or found in reference sources that is different from the one used in the heading.

    Thibault, Anatole
        see France, Anatole, 1844-1924.

    Sklodowska, Marie
        see Curie, Marie, 1867-1934.

121A2. See references. Different forms of the name

Refer from different forms of the name.

Ruth, George Herman
    see Ruth, Babe, 1895-1948.

Homerus
    see Homer.

Wellesley, Arthur, 1st Duke of Wellington
    see Wellington, Arthur Wellesley, 1st Duke of, 1769-1852.

121B. Explanatory references

These references are needed for effective use of the headings.

Lee, Manfred

    For works of this author written in collaboration with
    Frederic Dannay, see entries under:

Queen, Ellery
Queen, Ellery, Jr.
Ross, Barnaby

Rule 122. Names of corporate bodies

122A1. See references. Different names.

Quakers
    see Society of Friends.

Jesus, Society of
    see Jesuits.

General Aniline and Film Corp. Ansco
    see Ansco

See references for changes in name

National Tuberculosis Association

    For works issued under its earlier name
see

National Association for the Study and Prevention of Tuberculosis.

122B. See also references

Treaty of Versailles, 1919

    see also Paris Peace Conference, 1919.

122C. Explanatory references

United Nations. Missions.
    Delegations, missions, etc. from member nations to the United Nations
and to its subordinate units are entered under the name of the nation
followed by the name of the delegation, mission, etc., e.g.

United States. Mission to the United Nations.
Uruguay. Delegación en las Naciones Unidas.

Rule 124. Uniform titles

124A1. See references. Different titles or variants of the title

> Use for works entered under title.
>
>> Song of Roland
>>> see Chanson de Roland. English
>
> For works entered under author, use **author-title reference.**
>
>> Maugham, W. Somerset, 1874-1965
>>
>>> Then and now
>>>> see his Fools and their folly.

7 DESCRIPTIVE CATALOGING

INTRODUCTION

The rules and examples in this chapter are based on AACR, Chapter 6, 1974. Chapter 2 of this text provides the background for using ISBD for these rules. The general rules for spacing and punctuation, and the basic definitions needed for descriptive cataloging, are presented in Chapter 1 of this text. The present chapter covers only the more general rules for descriptive cataloging. The reader should carefully examine AACR, revised Chapter 6, for more complex problems and for detailed examples of punctuation.

GENERAL RULES

Rule 130. Organization of the description

The body of the entry is the first paragraph after the heading. It includes the basic descriptive elements, in the following order: title and statement of authorship area, edition area, and imprint area.

The second paragraph of the card consists of the collation area and the series area.

The third and succeeding paragraphs contain the notes area, the ISBN area, and the tracing. See Fig. 7.1.

Fig. 7.1

1 → **Sheridan, Mary Dorothy Spinster.**

2 → The handicapped child and his home / Mary D. Sheridan ; illustrations by Tom S. Graves. — Revised [ed.]. — London : National Children's Home, 1973.

3 → 91 p. : ill. ; 23 cm. — (National Children's Home convocation lecture ; 1965)
GB74-24639

4 → ISBN 0-900984-18-X : £0.50

5 → 1. Handicapped children. 2. Parent and child. I. Title. II. Series: London. National Children's Home. Convocation lecture ; 1965.

HQ784.H3S47 1973 362.7'8'40941 75-309578
MARC

[1] Heading
[2] Body of the entry
[3] Collation and series areas
[4] ISBN note
[5] Tracing

Note: The body of the main entry under title or of the entry of an anonymous work is generally presented as a "hanging indention," with the first line of the body of the entry occupying the position of the heading. See Fig. 7.2. For a discussion of the form of hanging indention, see page 21 and Fig. 1.11.

Fig. 7.2–Example of Hanging Indention

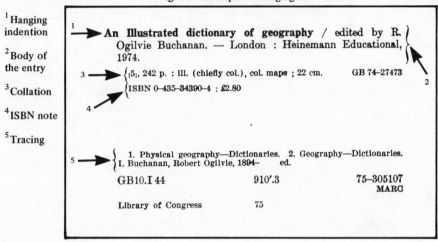

¹ Hanging indention

² Body of the entry

³ Collation

⁴ ISBN note

⁵ Tracing

Rule 131. Punctuation

A general discussion of punctuation is included in Chapter 1 of this text; a detailed discussion is provided under the individual rules in AACR, revised Chapter 6. The following is a general summary in the form of a schematic illustration of the punctuation rules.

Fig. 7.2a–Example of Punctuation

```
      Title proper = parallel title : other title
/ statement of authorship. -- Edition statement
/ statement of authorship relating to edition. --
Place of publication : publisher, date (place of
printing : printer)
      pagination : illustrations ; size & accom-
panying materials. -- (Series ; numbering)

      Notes.
      ISBN.

      Tracing.
```

Rule 132. Source of description

132A. Elements in the body of the entry and the series statement are taken from the work itself. The collation is the cataloger's description of the work stated in standard bibliographical terms. Other elements added to describe or identify the work may be taken from the work, taken from other bibliographic sources, or phrased by the cataloger, whichever method provides the clearest statement.

132B. Primary sources for each area of the description are:

"Area	Primary source of information
Title and statement of authorship	Title page, or if there is no title page, the source from within the publication that is used as its substitute (see 133B1)
Edition statement and statement of authorship relating to the edition	Title page, preliminaries,[1] and colophon
Imprint	Title page, preliminaries,[1] and colophon
Series statement	Series title page, title page, half title, cover, anywhere else in the publication
ISBN	Anywhere in the publication or in data supplied by the publisher and accompanying the book."

Rule 133. Relationship of the title page to the description of a work

133A. General rules

133A1. "The title page together with data from other primary sources (see 132B) serves as the basis of the description to be presented in the areas that precede the collation." Any information that must be supplied by the cataloger from a source other than the appropriate primary source (132B) is enclosed in brackets. For example, if the imprint information must be supplied from a source other than the title page, the preliminaries, or the colophon, that information must be placed in brackets, as Fig. 7.3 shows.

---

[1] Preliminaries are the half title, any added title pages, the verso of the title page, the cover title, the binder's title, and the spine. All of these terms are defined in Chapter 1 of this text as well as in the glossary.

Fig. 7.3

¹Supplied
compiler

²Supplied
imprint

Fischer, David C
    Northwest G. F. Mutual Insurance Company, Eureka, South
Dakota, 75th anniversary, 1897-1972 / ₍compiled by David C.
Fischer₎. — Eureka : ₍Northwest G. F. Mutual Insurance Co.,
1972₎

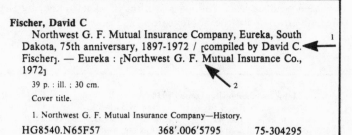

39 p. : ill. ; 30 cm.

Cover title.

1. Northwest G. F. Mutual Insurance Company—History.

HG8540.N65F57   368'.006'5795   75-304295

    Additions are given in the language of the title page, except that the abbreviations "etc." and "i.e." and "et al." are used. See Fig. 7.4.

Fig. 7.4

Abbrevia-
tion, "i.e."

Pompey, Sherman Lee.
    The 1860 census records of Jackson and Kannebec ₍i.e. Kana-
bec₎ Counties, Minnesota / Sherman Lee Pompey. — Independence, Calif. : Historical and Genealogical Pub. Co., c1965.

₍6₎ leaves ; 28 cm.

Cover title.

1. Jackson, County, Minn.—Census, 1860.   2. Kanabec Co., Minn.— Census, 1860.   I. Title.

F612.J2P65   929'.3776'235   75-303742

    "If an addition is conjectural, it is so indicated by a question mark." See Fig. 7.5.

Fig. 7.5

Rands, Minnie Frost, 1889-
    Frost family genealogy : genealogy of William Frost's son,
Ebenezer Frost, Sr. by his wives, Sarah Fairchild and Elizabeth
Wilson / compiled by his great-granddaughter, Minnie Frost
Rands. — ₍Washington? D.C.₎ : Rands, ₍1974?₎

¹Place con-
jectural, as
indicated by
use of "?"

²Date
conjectural

20 leaves : 19 geneal. tables ; 28 cm.

Cover title.   1
Chiefly tables.
Photoreproduction of holograph.

1. Frost family.   I. Title.

CS71.F939   1974   929'.2'0973   75-303758
                                                MARC

Library of Congress   75

"If a statement that is transcribed from the title page is inaccurate, it is recorded as it appears, followed (within brackets) either by the word 'sic' for an obvious error or by the abbreviation 'i.e.' and the correction." See Figs. 7.6 and 7.7.

Fig. 7.6

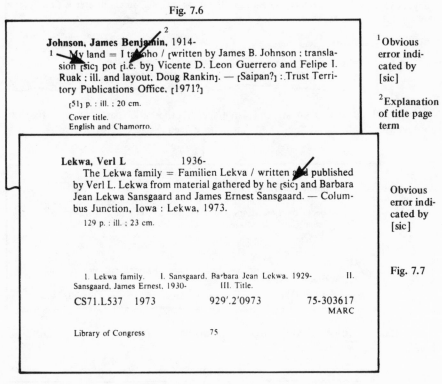

Johnson, James Benjamin, 1914-
My land = I tano ho / [written by James B. Johnson : translation [sic] pot [i.e. by] Vicente D. Leon Guerrero and Felipe I. Ruak : ill. and layout, Doug Rankin]. — [Saipan?] : Trust Territory Publications Office. [1971?]

[51] p. : ill. ; 20 cm.

Cover title.
English and Chamorro.

[1] Obvious error indicated by [sic]

[2] Explanation of title page term

Lekwa, Verl L   1936-
The Lekwa family = Familien Lekva / written and published by Verl L. Lekwa from material gathered by he [sic] and Barbara Jean Lekwa Sansgaard and James Ernest Sansgaard. — Columbus Junction, Iowa : Lekwa, 1973.

129 p. : ill. ; 23 cm.

Obvious error indicated by [sic]

1. Lekwa family.   I. Sansgaard. Barbara Jean Lekwa. 1929-   II. Sansgaard. James Ernest. 1930-   III. Title.

CS71.L537   1973   929'.2'0973   75-303617
                                             MARC

Library of Congress   75

Fig. 7.7

133B. Works without title pages

A work published without a title page is cataloged from some other part of the work. The part of the work supplying the most complete information is used as a substitute, whether this is cover title, half-title, etc. The fact that a substitute for the title page has been used is stated on the card, usually as one of the first notes. See Fig. 7.8.

Fig. 7.8

Ontario.   Ministerial Committee on the Teaching of French.
Report of the Ministerial Committee on the Teaching of French. — Ontario : Ministry of Education, [1974]
59 p. ; 30 cm.   C***
Cover title.
Bibliography: p. 57-58.

1. French language—Study and teaching—Ontario.

PC2068.O57O53   1974   440'.7'10713   75-310443

Source of title page substitute

133C2d.   Facsimile and reprint editions

In the case of facsimile editions and reprint editions that have both an original title page and a new title page, the new title page is to be preferred as the primary source for descriptive cataloging. Variant or different information on the original title page will be transcribed as one of the notes. See Fig. 7.9.

Fig. 7.9

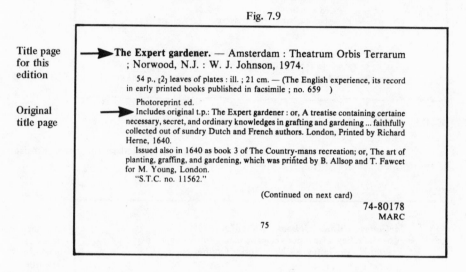

Title page for this edition

The Expert gardener. — Amsterdam : Theatrum Orbis Terrarum ; Norwood, N.J. : W. J. Johnson, 1974.

54 p., ₂₂₎ leaves of plates : ill. ; 21 cm. — (The English experience, its record in early printed books published in facsimile ; no. 659   )

Original title page

Photoreprint ed.
Includes original t.p.: The Expert gardener : or, A treatise containing certaine necessary, secret, and ordinary knowledges in grafting and gardening ... faithfully collected out of sundry Dutch and French authors. London, Printed by Richard Herne, 1640.
Issued also in 1640 as book 3 of The Country-mans recreation; or, The art of planting, graffing, and gardening, which was printed by B. Allsop and T. Fawcet for M. Young, London.
"S.T.C. no. 11562."

(Continued on next card)

74-80178
MARC

75

Rule 134. Title and statement of authorship area

134B.   Transcription of the title proper

134B1.   General rule

"The title proper is transcribed exactly as to order, wording, spelling, accentuation, and other diacritical marks (if possible), but not necessarily as to punctuation and capitalization."

134B2.   Abridgment

"Long titles are abridged if this can be done without loss of essential information. The first words of the title are always included. . . . All omissions from the title are indicated by the mark of omission" (i.e., three dots). See Fig. 7.10.

Fig. 7.10

The Universal cyclopædia of law : a practical compendium of legal information, comprising nearly 14,000 statements of the law ... with a full appendix of forms / edited by W. W. Thornton. — 2d rev. ed. — Northport, N.Y. : E. Thompson, c1885.	Abridged subtitle

2 v. (xxii, 1485 p.) ; 24 cm.

LC copy replaced by microfilm.
Includes bibliographical references and indexes.

1. Law—United States.   I. Thornton, William Wheeler, 1851-1932.

[KF154.U55 1885]   348'.73'6   75-313092
Microfilm   60079 KF   MARC

134B3. Author's name in title

If the author's name or the publisher's name is included in the title, it must be transcribed as part of the title proper. See Fig. 7.11.

Fig. 7.11

McGuffey, William Holmes, 1800-1873. ➤McGuffey's New third eclectic reader for young learners / by Wm. H. McGuffey. — New York : Gordon Press, 1974.	Author's name as part of the title

242 p. : ill. ; 24 cm.

Reprint of the 1885 ed. published by American Book Co., New York, issued in series: Eclectic educational series.
ISBN 0-87968-142-X

1. Readers—1870-1950.   I. Series: Eclectic educational series.

PE1117.M274   1974   428'.6   73-22832
                                                       MARC

Library of Congress   74

134B4. Additions

134B4a. "Additions may be made to the title in the language of the title if it needs explanation and if brief statements to clarify it can be taken from the work itself." See Fig. 7.12.

Fig. 7.12

Addition
to title

Pearson, Carol Lynn.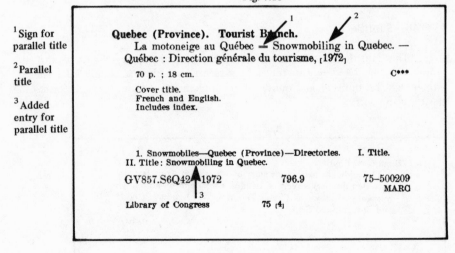
    Beginnings : ₍poems₎ / by Carol Lynn Pearson ; illustrated by
Trevor Southey. — Garden City, N.Y. : Doubleday, 1975.
c1967.

    63 p. : ill. ; 24 cm.
    ISBN 0-385-07711-4 : $3.95

    I. Title.

    PS3566.E227B4   1975   811'.5'4   74-28894
                                                        MARC

134C. Transcription of parallel titles, other titles and other title information

134C1. Parallel titles

134C1a. If there are no more than two parallel titles on the title page, both are recorded. (See Fig. 7.13.) For the transcription of more than two parallel titles or of parallel titles in Chinese, Japanese, or Korean characters, see AACR 134C1b-c. Original titles appearing on the title page of a later edition with a changed title are to be treated as parallel titles.

Fig. 7.13

¹Sign for
parallel title

²Parallel
title

³Added
entry for
parallel title

Quebec (Province). Tourist Branch.
    La motoneige au Québec = Snowmobiling in Quebec. —
Québec : Direction générale du tourisme, ₍1972₎

    70 p. ; 18 cm.   C•••

    Cover title.
    French and English.
    Includes index.

    1. Snowmobiles—Quebec (Province)—Directories.   I. Title.
    II. Title: Snowmobiling in Quebec.

    GV857.S6Q42 1972   796.9   75-500209
                                                    MARC

    Library of Congress   75 ₍4₎

134C4. Other titles and other title information

134C4a. Alternative title

"An alternative title is always transcribed in the catalog entry because the book may be referred to by it and because another edition may be published with the alternative title as the title proper." See Fig. 7.14. Note the capitalization and punctuation of the examples.

Fig. 7.14

Wollstonecraft, Mary, 1759-1797.
    Maria : or, The wrongs of woman / by Mary Wollstonecraft : with an introd. by Moira Ferguson. — New York : Norton, [1975]

    154 p. : 20 cm. — (The Norton library, N761)

    Reprint, with a new introd., of the 1798 ed. published for J. Johnson, London, as v. 1 of the Posthumous works of the author of A vindication of the rights of woman. i. e. M. Wollstonecraft.
    Includes bibliographical references.
    ISBN 0-393-08713-1.   ISBN 0-393-00761-8 pbk.

    I. Title. II. Title: The wrongs of woman.

PZ3.W8362 Mai 5   823'.6   74-30341
[PR5841.W8]   MARC

Library of Congress   74

Alternative title — (points to Wollstonecraft, Mary, 1759-1797.)

Added entry for distinctive alternative title — (points to II. Title: The wrongs of woman.)

134C4b. Subtitle

"The subtitle is transcribed in the entry in the same manner as the title proper (see Fig. 7.15), except that a long subtitle which is separable from the title proper may be omitted and quoted in a supplementary note, if this increases the clarity of the entry."

Fig. 7.15

Thompson, Phyllis.
    The midnight patrol : the story of a Salvation Army lass who patrolled the dark streets of London's west end on a midnight mission of mercy / by Phyllis Thompson. — London : Hodder and Stoughton, 1974.

    155 p. : 21 cm.   GB75-03381

    Bibliography: p. 157.
    ISBN 0-340-17896-5 : £2.10

    1. Prostitution—London. 2. Scott, Mary. 3. Salvation Army. I. Title.

HQ358.L8T46   362.8   75-309571
                                             MARC

Subtitle — (points to the story of a Salvation Army lass)

134D. Statement of authorship

"The statement of authorship includes, in addition to the names of the authors, personal or corporate, the statement of the names of subsidiary authors, e.g., editors, translators, writers of prefaces, illustrators."

134D1. The statement of authorship is given following the title proper, parallel title, other titles, and other title information. It is introduced by the slash mark. If the authorship statement is taken from any source other than the title page (e.g., cover title), it is enclosed in brackets. See Fig. 7.16.

Fig. 7.16

Statement of authorship	**Ewers, Dorothy Wood,** 1910- ↙ Ben Oliel and Seeley / ₁Dorothy Wood Ewers₁. — ₁Crete? Ill.₁ : Ewers. ₁1966₁ ca. 200 p. : 30 cm. 1. Ben-Oliel family. 2. Seeley family. I. Title. CS71.B4643 1966 929'.2'0973 75-308534 MARC

"If a word or phrase occurring in conjunction with a statement of authorship is indicative of the author's function rather than of the content of the publication, it is treated as part of the statement of authorship." This includes such phrases as "compiled by," "edited by," "modernized by," "abridged by," etc. See Fig. 7.17.

Fig. 7.17

Statement of authorship	**Cameron, Kenneth Walter,** 1908– ed. Response to transcendental Concord : the last decades of the era of Emerson, Thoreau, and the Concord School as recorded in newspapers / edited by Kenneth Walter Cameron. — Hartford : Transcendental Books, ₁1974₁ 359 leaves : ill. ; 29 cm. 1. Concord School of Philosophy. 2. Transcendentalism (New England) I. Title. B905.C298 141'.3'0974 75–300669 MARC Library of Congress 75 ₁4₁

134D5. "When several authors including subsidiary authors are recorded, the order is that indicated by the sequence on, or the typography of, the title page. Names of several persons performing the same function in relation to the work are separated by commas; names of persons performing different functions are separated by a space-semicolon-space even though joined by linking words." See Fig. 7.18.

Fig. 7.18

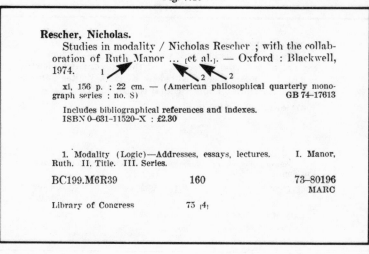

134D7. "If there are more than three authors or more than three subsidiary authors performing the same function in the author statement, all after the first named are omitted. The omission is indicated by the mark of omission (. . .) and the phrase 'et al.,' the latter enclosed in brackets." See Fig. 7.19.

Fig. 7.19

Rescher, Nicholas.
 Studies in modality / Nicholas Rescher ; with the collaboration of Ruth Manor ... [et al.]. — Oxford : Blackwell, 1974. 1

 xi, 156 p. : 22 cm. — (American philosophical quarterly monograph series : no. 8)   GB 74–17613

 Includes bibliographical references and indexes.
 ISBN 0–631–11520–X : £2.30

 1. Modality (Logic)—Addresses, essays, lectures.   I. Manor, Ruth. II. Title. III. Series.

 BC199.M6R39   160   73–80196
   MARC

 Library of Congress   75 [4]

[1] First named author of a group of more than three subsidiary authors

[2] Mark of omission and [et al.]

134D8. Omissions from the author statement

134D8a. "Titles and abbreviations of titles of address, honor, and distinction (but not of nobility), initials of societies, etc., are generally omitted from the author statement. Exception is made as follows:

    1) If the title is necessary grammatically.
    2) If the omission of the title leaves only the author's surname.
    3) If the title is necessary for the identification of the author.
    4) If the title explains the relationship of a personal author to the corporate author used as the heading for the work."

See Fig. 7.20.

Fig. 7.20

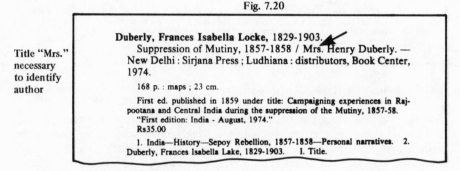

Title "Mrs." necessary to identify author

Duberly, Frances Isabella Locke, 1829-1903.
    Suppression of Mutiny, 1857-1858 / Mrs. Henry Duberly. — New Delhi : Sirjana Press ; Ludhiana : distributors, Book Center, 1974.

    168 p. : maps ; 23 cm.

    First ed. published in 1859 under title: Campaigning experiences in Rajpootana and Central India during the suppression of the Mutiny, 1857-58.
    "First edition: India - August, 1974."
    Rs35.00

    1. India—History—Sepoy Rebellion, 1857-1858—Personal narratives. 2. Duberly, Frances Isabella Lake, 1829-1903. I. Title.

139D9. Additions to the author statement

139D9a. "If necessary for intelligibility, a word or phrase in the language of the title is added to express what is shown on the title page by arrangement, or to clarify an ambiguous or misleading statement, except that a preposition is not added to connect the author's name to the title elements nor is a conjunction added before the last name if two or three names are recorded." See Fig. 7.21.

Fig. 7.21

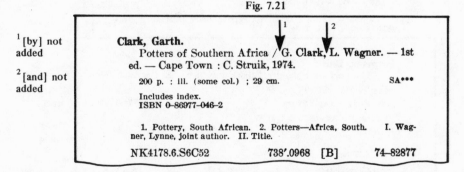

¹ [by] not added

² [and] not added

Clark, Garth.
    Potters of Southern Africa / G. Clark, L. Wagner. — 1st ed. — Cape Town : C. Struik, 1974.

    200 p. : ill. (some col.) ; 29 cm.   SA•••

    Includes index.
    ISBN 0-86977-046-2

    1. Pottery, South African. 2. Potters—Africa, South. I. Wagner, Lynne, joint author. II. Title.

    NK4178.6.S6C52   738'.0968 [B]   74-82877

In the above example neither the preposition "by" nor the conjunction "and" is added on the catalog card. This rule represents a change in practice; previously, both of these words would have been added (in brackets) to the above example.

Fig. 7.22 demonstrates a correct addition to the author statement. It adds the term "[catalogue compiled]" to explain the author's exact relationship to the work.

Fig. 7.22

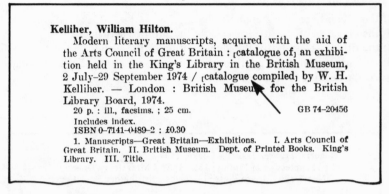

Kelliher, William Hilton.
    Modern literary manuscripts, acquired with the aid of the Arts Council of Great Britain : ₍catalogue of₎ an exhibition held in the King's Library in the British Museum, 2 July–29 September 1974 / ₍catalogue compiled₎ by W. H. Kelliher. — London : British Museum for the British Library Board, 1974.
    20 p. : ill., facsims. ; 25 cm.   GB 74–20456
    Includes index.
    ISBN 0–7141–0489–2 : £0.30
    1. Manuscripts—Great Britain—Exhibitions.   I. Arts Council of Great Britain. II. British Museum. Dept. of Printed Books. King's Library. III. Title.

Necessary addition

134D9.   Indication of pseudonymous authors

134D9b.   "If it is not apparent that the name in a personal author statement refers to the same person as that represented by the main entry heading, the name in the heading, preceded by the abbreviation 'i.e.,' is added in brackets after the name in the author statement in direct form and with forenames abbreviated to initials." See Figs. 7.23 and 7.24.

Fig. 7.23

Marreco, Anne Acland-Troyte, 1912–¹
    The Corsican ladies / Alice Acland ₍i. e. A. A.-T. Marreco₎.² — London : P. Davies, 1974.
    ₍5₎, 185 p. ; 23 cm.   GB 74–29054
    ISBN 0–432–00410–6 : £2.50
    1. Abrantès, Laure Saint-Martin Permon Junot, Duchesse d', 1784–1838—Fiction.   I. Title.

¹ Pseudonym

² Real name

Pargeter, Edith.
    The horn of Roland / Ellis Peters ₍i. e. E. Pargeter₎.¹ ² — London : Macmillan, 1974.
    160 p. : map ; 21 cm.   GB 74–11839
    ISBN 0–333–16675–2 : £1.95

    I. Title.

    PZ3.P2163Hn   823'.9'12   75–300097
    [PR6031.A49]   MARC
    Library of Congress   75 ₍4₎

¹ Pseudonym

² Real name

Fig. 7.24

Rule 135. Edition area

135A. "An edition statement in a work and any statements of authorship relating only to the particular edition of the work are always included in the catalog entry. Statements relating to the impression or printing are included only in the case of items having particular bibliographical importance or when the impression or printing has been corrected or otherwise revised."

The word "edition" and its foreign equivalents are to be abbreviated. This is true also of other terms, like "enlarged" or "revised," used in edition statements. A useful list of abbreviations is given in AACR, Appendix 3, pp. 358-366; modifications can be found on p. 117 of revised Chapter 6. For examples of edition statement, see Figs. 7.25 and 7.26.

Fig. 7.25

Edition
with
abbrevia-
tions

> **Murr, Alfred,** 1898-
>   Export/import traffic management and forwarding / by Al-
> fred Murr. — 3d ed., rev. and enl. — Cambridge, Md. : Cornell
> Maritime Press, 1974.
>   ix, 603 p. : forms ; 24 cm.
>   Bibliography: p. 594-595.
>   Includes index.
>   ISBN 0-87033-023-3 : $14.00
>
>   1. Freight forwarders. 2. Shipment of goods.   I. Title.
>
>   HE5999.A3M8   1974   380.5'2   75-313371
>   MARC
>
>   Library of Congress   75

Fig. 7.26

Edition
with foreign
abbrevia-
tions

> **Trotignon, Pierre.**
>   Heidegger / Pierre Trotignon. — 2. éd. revue et corr. —
> [Paris] : Presses universitaires de France, 1974, c1965.
>   128 p. ; 18 cm. — (Collection SUP : Philosophes)   F***
>   Bibliography : p. [124]-126.
>
>   1. Heidegger, Martin, 1889-
>
>   B3279.H49T7 1974   193   74-196679
>   MARC
>   Library of Congress   75 [4]

135D. "The edition statement is followed by a statement of any authors relating to the edition in hand, but not to all editions of the work. Such authors include the reviser, the illustrator, and the writer of the preface of the particular edition." See Fig. 7.27.

Fig. 7.27

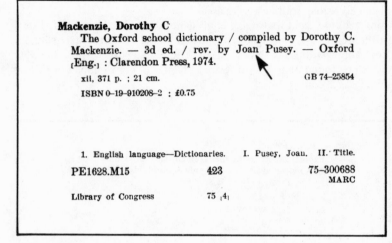

Mackenzie, Dorothy C
    The Oxford school dictionary / compiled by Dorothy C. Mackenzie. — 3d ed. / rev. by Joan Pusey. — Oxford ₍Eng.₎ : Clarendon Press, 1974.

    xii, 371 p. ; 21 cm.   GB 74–25854

    ISBN 0–19–910208–2 : £0.75

Statement of author-ship in edition area

1. English language—Dictionaries.   I. Pusey, Joan.   II. Title.

PE1628.M15   423   75–300688
                                          MARC

Library of Congress   75 ₍4₎

135F. Illustration statement

An illustration statement appearing on the title page, in the preliminaries, or in the colophon is included if the name of the illustrator is given, or if the statement indicates that the author illustrated the work. If the illustrator's name does not appear on the title page, in the preliminaries, or on the colophon, the statement of illustrative matter is included in the body of the entry only "if it adds an important characterization of the material that cannot be shown in the collation; e.g., the number of illustrations in a work containing many unnumbered illustrations or the kind of illustrations (such as woodcuts or engravings.)" See Figs. 7.28 and 7.29.

Fig. 7.28

Illustration
statement
as part of
authorship
statement

Paul, Leslie Allen, 1905-
    Traveller on sacred ground / by Leslie Paul ; illustrated by the
author's own photographs. — London : Hodder and Stoughton,
1963.
    160 p., ₍12₎ leaves of plates : ill. ; 23 cm.

    1. Palestine—Description and travel.   2. Paul. Leslie Allen. 1905-
I. Title.

DS107.4.P33   915.694'045   75-304224
                                              MARC

Library of Congress   75

Fig. 7.29

Separate
illustration
statement

```
Rubin, William Stanley.
     Dada and surrealist art / William
S. Rubin. -- With 851 ill. including 60
hand-mounted colour plates. -- London :
Thames & Hudson, 1969.
     525 p. : ill.(some col.) ; 31 cm.

     Bibliography: p. 492-512.

     1. Dadaism. 2. Surrealism.
I. Title.
```

Rule 136. Imprint area

136A. Order and source of elements

The imprint area consists of the place of publication, the name of the publisher, the date of publication and/or the copyright date, and in some cases the place of printing and the name of the printer. The normal order of the imprint is place, publisher, and date. If the place of printing and the name of the printer are included, they follow the date. The imprint is often most important in identifying particular editions of a work. "Imprint data taken from a source other than the title page, the preliminaries, or the colophon are enclosed in brackets." See Fig. 7.30.

Fig. 7.30

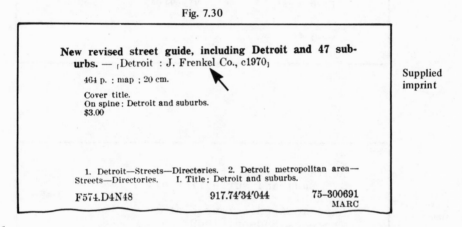

"If the original imprint data in the work are covered by a label bearing different imprint data, the data so covered are recorded if legible; the imprint data on the label are recorded in a note." See Fig. 7.31.

Fig. 7.31

Golzen, Godfrey, 1930-
    Introducing VAT : the simplified guide to value added tax /
Godfrey Golzen. — London : Kogan Page, 1973. ◄—   Original
                                          imprint
    61 p. : ill. ; 16 cm.   GB•••

    Label mounted on t.p.: Available from: International Publications Service
Collings, Inc., New York, N.Y.   Imprint
    ISBN 0-85038-047-2 : £2.45.   ISBN 0-85038-046-4 pbk.   on label

    1. Value-added tax—Great Britain.   I. Title.   II. Title: The simplified guide
to value added tax.

    HJ5715.G7G63   336.2'71   75-308993
                                                     MARC

136C. Works with more than one place and publisher

136C1. "A work that gives indication of being published in several places by one publisher or by several publishers, is generally described in the catalog entry by an imprint consisting of the first named place of publication and the corresponding publisher."

136C3. "If a city in the country of the cataloging agency, with or without a corresponding publisher, is named in a secondary position in a work containing a foreign imprint, that information is included in addition to the foreign imprint." See Figs. 7.32 and 7.33.

Fig. 7.32

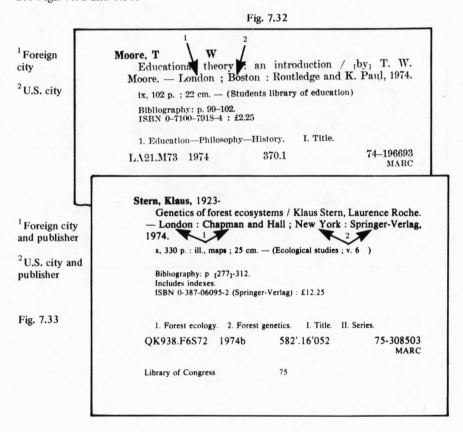

[1] Foreign city

[2] U.S. city

Moore, T   W
    Educational theory : an introduction / [by] T. W. Moore. — London ; Boston : Routledge and K. Paul, 1974.
    ix, 102 p. ; 22 cm. — (Students library of education)
    Bibliography: p. 99–102.
    ISBN 0–7100–7918–4 : £2.25

    1. Education—Philosophy—History.   I. Title.
    LA21.M73 1974   370.1   74–196693
                                            MARC

[1] Foreign city and publisher

[2] U.S. city and publisher

Fig. 7.33

Stern, Klaus, 1923-
    Genetics of forest ecosystems / Klaus Stern, Laurence Roche. — London : Chapman and Hall ; New York : Springer-Verlag, 1974.
    x, 330 p. : ill., maps ; 25 cm. — (Ecological studies ; v. 6   )
    Bibliography: p [277]-312.
    Includes indexes.
    ISBN 0-387-06095-2 (Springer-Verlag) : £12.25

    1. Forest ecology. 2. Forest genetics.   I. Title. II. Series.
    QK938.F6S72 1974b   582'.16'052   75-308503
                                                     MARC

    Library of Congress   75

136D. Photographically reproduced reprint and facsimile editions with only the original title page

If a reprint or facsimile edition contains only the original title page, the reprint publisher's imprint should be used in the imprint area. (If there is both an original title page and reprint title page, use the reprint title page. See Rule 133C2d.) The reprint publisher's imprint may appear on the original title page, on the verso of the title page, elsewhere in the preliminaries, or in the colophon; if it must be supplied from any other source, it must be placed in brackets. The original imprint is not to be included in the imprint area but should be given as a note. See Fig. 7.34.

Fig. 7.34

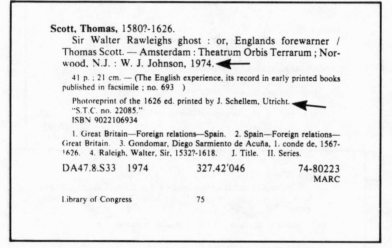

Scott, Thomas, 1580?-1626.
    Sir Walter Rawleighs ghost : or, Englands forewarner / Thomas Scott. — Amsterdam : Theatrum Orbis Terrarum ; Norwood, N.J. : W. J. Johnson, 1974. ◄——

    41 p. ; 21 cm. — (The English experience, its record in early printed books published in facsimile ; no. 693)

    Photoreprint of the 1626 ed. printed by J. Schellem, Utricht. ◄——
    "S.T.C. no. 22085."
    ISBN 9022106934

    1. Great Britain—Foreign relations—Spain. 2. Spain—Foreign relations—Great Britain. 3. Gondomar, Diego Sarmiento de Acuña, 1. conde de, 1567-1626. 4. Raleigh, Walter, Sir, 1532?-1618. J. Title. II. Series.

DA47.8.S33   1974   327.42'046   74-80223
                                                   MARC

Library of Congress   75

Reprinter's imprint

Original imprint

Rule 137. Place of publication

"The place of publication is the place in which the offices of the publisher are located."

137A. Place unknown

"If the place of publication is unknown, the probable place of publication is given, enclosed in brackets. The probable place may be the editorial office, the seat of the institution, or the headquarters of the society publishing the work. If the probable place of publication cannot be determined, the place is represented by the abbreviation 's.1.' (*sine loco*) enclosed in brackets." See Fig. 7.35.

Fig. 7.35

Place
unknown

Elzner, Jonnie Ross, 1910-
   Relighting lamplights of Lampasas County, Texas / by Jonnie
Elzner. — ₁s.l.₁ : Hill Country, 1974.
   v, 331 p. : ill. ; 24 cm.

   1. Lampass Co., Tex.   I. Title.
F392.L38E42   976.4′513   75-314060
                                                  MARC

Note: The use of the abbreviation "s.l." conforms with ISBD abbreviations; the
abbreviation "n.p." is no longer used.

137B. Additions to place names

   "The place of publication is followed by its country, state, or similar
designation if it is necessary to identify the place or to distinguish it from another
place of the same name. Abbreviations are used for most such designations." See
Figs. 7.36 and 7.37.

Fig. 7.36

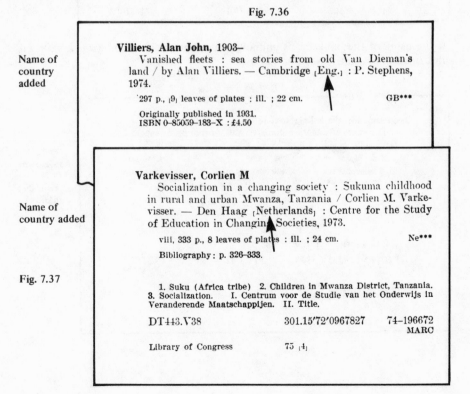

Name of
country
added

Villiers, Alan John, 1903–
   Vanished fleets : sea stories from old Van Dieman's
land / by Alan Villiers. — Cambridge ₁Eng.₁ : P. Stephens,
1974.
   297 p., ₁9₁ leaves of plates : ill. ; 22 cm.   GB***

   Originally published in 1931.
   ISBN 0-85059-183-X : £4.50

Name of
country added

Varkevisser, Corlien M
   Socialization in a changing society : Sukuma childhood
in rural and urban Mwanza, Tanzania / Corlien M. Varkevisser. — Den Haag ₁Netherlands₁ : Centre for the Study
of Education in Changing Societies, 1973.
   viii, 333 p., 8 leaves of plates : ill. ; 24 cm.   Ne***

   Bibliography : p. 326–333.

Fig. 7.37

   1. Suku (Africa tribe) 2. Children in Mwanza District, Tanzania.
3. Socialization.   I. Centrum voor de Studie van het Onderwijs in
Veranderende Maatschappijen. II. Title.

DT443.V38   301.15′72′0967827   74–196672
                                            MARC

Library of Congress   75 ₁4₁

Rule 138. Publisher

138A. General rule

"The publisher statement appearing on a work is abridged as much as possible without loss of intelligibility or identification of the publisher at the international level. Unnecessary parts of the statement are omitted, abbreviations are employed, and names known to be forenames are represented by initials or, in the case of well-known publishers, omitted." See Fig. 7.38.

Fig. 7.38

Michael, George, 1919–
    The basic book of antiques / by George Michael. — New
York : Arco Pub. Co., [1974]

    viii, 293 p. : ill. ; 27 cm.

    Bibliography: p. 281–284.
    Includes index.
    ISBN 0–668–03433–5 : $10.00

Publisher's name abbreviated

    1. Art objects—Collectors and collecting.   I. Title.

    NK1125.M46   745.1'075   74–77072

"If the name of the publisher is unknown, the abbreviation 's.n.' (*sine nomine*) is substituted in brackets." See Fig. 7.39.

Fig. 7.39

Jamieson, Elizabeth Leighton, 1892-
    The story of Lanark / prepared and written by Elizabeth L.
Jamieson. — [s.l. : s.n.], c1974.

    86 p. : ill. ; 25 cm.   2   C74-5063-X

    "Reprint of an historical souvenir originally published in connection with the
centenary of Lanark Village."

[1] Place unknown

[2] Publisher unknown

    1. Lanark, Ont.   I. Title.

    F1059.5.L32J35   1974   971.3'82   75-315963
                                                             MARC

    Library of Congress   75

138B.   Essential parts of the publisher statement

The AACR specify several situations in which there is information deemed necessary for the intelligibility of the publisher statement. The examples in Figs. 7.40 through 7.43 illustrate common cases.

Fig. 7.40

Published
for . . .
by . . .

Noyes, Richard, 1923–
    At the edge of megalopolis : a history of Salem, N. H., 1900–1974 ₁Noyes, Turner₁. — Canaan, N. H. : Published for the Town of Salem, N. H., by Phoenix Pub., c1974.

xiv, 397 p. : ill. ; 28 cm.

Includes indexes.
ISBN 0–914016–11–3 : $12.00

1. Salem, N. H.—History. 2. Salem, N. H.—Biography.
I. Turner, Howard E., 1901– joint author. II. Title.

F44.S14N69   974.2′6   74–21031
                                         MARC

Library of Congress   75

Fig. 7.41

Avail-
able
from . . .

Emmings, Steven D
    Minnesota : historical data on fuels and electricity / Steven Emmings. — ₁Minneapolis₁ : Minnesota Energy Project ; St. Paul : ₁available from the State Planning Agency₁, 1974.

iv, 208 p. : ill. ; 28 cm.

Tables.
"MEP-74-18."
Includes index.

1. Power resources—Minnesota—Statistics. 2. Electric utilities—Minnesota
—Statistics. 3. Power resources—Minnesota—Transportation—Statistics 4. Energy consumption—Minnesota—Statistics. I. Minnesota Energy Project. II. Minnesota. State Planning Agency. III. Title: Minnesota : Historical data on fuels and electricity.

HD9502.U53M63   333.7   75-621944
                                         MARC

Library of Congress   75

Fig. 7.42

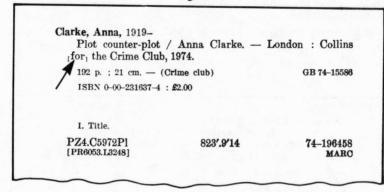

Clarke, Anna, 1919–
    Plot counter-plot / Anna Clarke. — London : Collins
[for] the Crime Club, 1974.
    192 p. ; 21 cm. — (Crime club)   GB 74–15586
    ISBN 0–00–231637–4 : £2.00

    I. Title.
    PZ4.C5972Pl   823'.9'14   74–196458
    [PR6053.L3248]   MARC

Necessary
supplied
preposi-
tion

Fig. 7.43

Pointer, Dennis Dale.
    The National labor relations act : a guidebook for health care
facility administrators / Dennis D. Pointer and Norman
Metzger. — New York : Spectrum Publications : distributed by
Halsted Press, [1975]
    272 p. : 24 cm. - (Health systems management)
    Includes bibliographical references and index.
    ISBN 0-470-69146-8

    1. Health facilities—Law and legislation—United States. 2. Labor laws and
legislation - United States.   I. Metzger, Norman, 1924-   joint author.
II. Title.
    KF3580.H4P6   344'.73'041   74-34375

Distribu-
tor
indicated

138C. Unnecessary parts of the publisher statement

138C1. "The following parts are generally considered unnecessary:

a) the phrases 'published by,' 'published for,' and the word 'publisher,' and their equivalents in other languages, when the name of a single firm is given in the work,

b) words showing that the publisher is also the printer, bookseller, or distributor,

c) the initial article, except when necessary for clarity,

d) the phrases 'and company,' 'and sons,' etc., and their foreign equivalents,

e) terms meaning 'incorporated' or 'limited' and abbreviations." A detailed list is provided in AACR, revised Chapter 6, p. 41.

138D. Publisher as author

"When the publisher (person or corporate body) is the author of the work, and the name appears in the title and statement of authorship area, the name may be given in abbreviated form in the imprint. In the case of a corporate body the abbreviation may be the initialism of the body or, if there is no widely used initialism and the usage of the language permits, the abbreviation may consist of the generic word in the name preceded by the definite article." See Figs. 7.44 through 7.46.

Fig. 7.44

Shortened
name

United States.   Commission on Civil Rights.
Equal opportunity in suburbia : a report of the United States Commission on Civil Rights. — Washington : The Commission, 1974.

v, 72 p. : ill. ; 26 cm.

Includes bibliographical references.

1. Discrimination in housing—United States.   2. Suburbs—United States. I. Title.

Fig. 7.45

Shortened
name

Bombay (State).   Political and Services Dept.
Second five-year plan, 1956-57 to 1960-61 of the new Bombay State : provisional statement showing the list of schemes in the various areas of the State, 26th November 1956. — [Bombay] : The Dept., 1956.

48 p. ; 34 cm.

Cover title.

1. Bombay (State)—Economic policy.   I. Title.

HC437.B6B67   1956b   75-313300

Fig. 7.46

Surname
only

Quant, Carol Wilkinson.
Equal higher education / Carol Wilkinson Quant. — Raleigh, N. C. : Quant, c1974.

91 p. ; 21 cm.

ISBN 0-915304-01-5

1. Education, Higher—United States.   I. Title.

LA227.3.Q36   378.73   74-29347

"Brackets are not required provided some form of the name appears on the title page, in the preliminaries, or in the colophon." But if the authorship statement has been placed in brackets, so must the abbreviated form of the publisher be placed in brackets. See Fig. 7.47.

Fig. 7.47

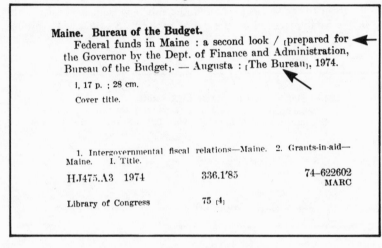

Maine. Bureau of the Budget.
    Federal funds in Maine : a second look / ₍prepared for ←   Author-
the Governor by the Dept. of Finance and Administration,   ship state-
Bureau of the Budget₎. — Augusta : ₍The Bureau₎, 1974.   ment

    I, 17 p. ; 28 cm.

    Cover title.   Shortened
                                                name
                                                placed in
                                                brackets

    1. Intergovernmental fiscal relations—Maine. 2. Grants-in-aid—
Maine.   I. Title.

    HJ475.A3   1974   336.1'85   74–622602
                                                            MARC

    Library of Congress   75 ₍4₎

Rule 139. Date

139A. General rule

"The date is the year of publication of the first impression of the edition. In the case of a reprint by another publisher, the date is the year of publication of the first impression of the reprint edition. . . . If there is no evidence to the contrary, either in the publication or elsewhere, the date on the title page is taken to be the date of the edition. The date may be followed by the date of a later impression, qualified by the word 'printing,' if there is a difference and if it is important to identify a later impression as such, e.g., because it contains textual variations." See Fig. 7.48.

Fig. 7.48

Opie, Iona Archibald.
    Children's games in street and playground : chasing,
catching, seeking, hunting, racing, duelling, exerting, dar-
ing, guessing, acting, pretending / by Iona and Peter
Opie. — Oxford : Clarendon Press, 1969, 1970 printing. ←   Printing
    xxvi, 371 p. : ill. ; 24 cm.   GB***   date

    Includes bibliographical references and index.
    ISBN 0-19-827210-3 : £2.50

    1. Games—History.   2. Games—Great Britain.   I. Opie, Peter,
joint author. II. Title.

The date on the title page is always recorded, even if it is known to be incorrect. The correct date is then added, with the abbreviation "i.e." preceding the correct date. If this date does not appear in the preliminaries or the colophon, the date and the abbreviation "i.e." are placed in brackets. See Fig. 7.49.

Fig. 7.49

¹Imprint
date on
title page

²Corrected
imprint
date

New industrial polymers : a symposium sponsored by the Division of Organic Coatings and Plastics Chemistry at the 167th meeting of the American Chemical Society, Los Angeles, Calif.. April 1–2, 1974 / Rudolph D. Deanin, editor. — Washington : American Chemical Society, 1972 ₁i. e. 1974₁

x. 179 p. : ill. ; 24 cm. — (ACS symposium series ; 4)

Includes bibliographical references and index.

ISBN 0-8412-0229-X

1. Plastics—Congresses. 2. Polymers and polymerization—Congresses. I. Deanin, Rudolph D., ed. II. American Chemical Society. Division of Organic Coatings and Plastics Chemistry. III. Series: American Chemical Society. ACS symposium series ; 4.

TP110.3.N47   668.4   74–26794
                                              MARC

Library of Congress   75 ₁4₁

"If the date on the title page is the date of a later impression, it is given following the publication date, qualified to show its position on the publication." See Fig. 7.50.

Fig. 7.50

¹Original
date

²Later
impression

Quinn, Gerald Dennis.
The rebellion of 1914-15 : a bibliography / compiled by Gerald Dennis Quinn. — ₁Cape Town₁ : University of Cape Town Libraries, 1959, t.p. 1974. ◄━ 2

x. 22 p. : 23 cm ◄━ (Bibliographical series - University of Cape Town Libraries) 1   SA•••

"Presented in partial fulfilment of the requirements for the Higher Certificate and Diploma in Librarianship, 1957."

Includes indexes.

ISBN 0-7992-0129-4

1. Africa, South—History—Rebellion, 1914-1915—Bibliography. I. Title. II. Series: Cape Town. University of Cape Town. Library. Bibliographical series.

Z3608.A5Q5   1974   016.96805   75-314136
₁DT779.5₁   MARC

Library of Congress   75

"If the publication date of the first impression of the edition cannot be ascertained, the copyright date, preceded by a "c," or the date of the impression in hand, in that order of preference, or both, are given." See Fig. 7.51.

Fig. 7.51

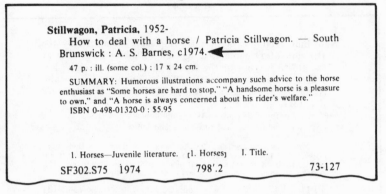

Copyright
date

139B. Multiple volume works

If the work is in more than one volume and the publication dates vary, the inclusive dates are given in the imprint area.

For example: 1959-1962

Fig. 7.52

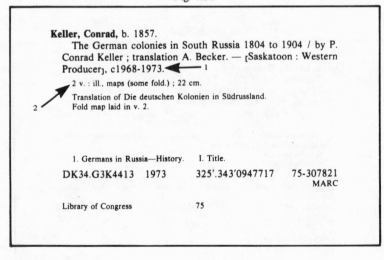

[1] Inclusive
dates

[2] Two-
volume
work

139F. Date uncertain

If there is no publication date given in the book and the exact date cannot be ascertained by bibliographic research, an approximate date is supplied. See Figs. 7.53 and 7.54. See also the examples in AACR, revised Chapter 6, p. 46.

Note: To show approximate date, use [ca. 1937].

Fig. 7.53

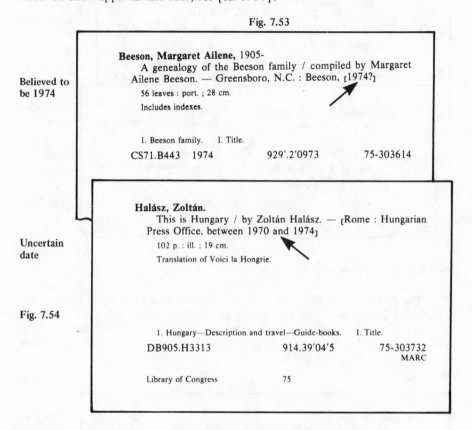

Beeson, Margaret Ailene, 1905-
    A genealogy of the Beeson family / compiled by Margaret
Ailene Beeson. — Greensboro, N.C. : Beeson, [1974?]
    56 leaves : port. ; 28 cm.
    Includes indexes.

Believed to be 1974

    1. Beeson family.   I. Title.
    CS71.B443   1974   929'.2'0973   75-303614

Halász, Zoltán.
    This is Hungary / by Zoltán Halász. — [Rome : Hungarian
Press Office, between 1970 and 1974]
    102 p. : ill. : 19 cm.
    Translation of Voici la Hongrie.

Uncertain date

Fig. 7.54

    1. Hungary—Description and travel—Guide-books.   I. Title.
    DB905.H3313   914.39'04'5   75-303732
                                                    MARC

    Library of Congress   75

139G. Copyright date

"If the date in the copyright statement is not the same as the date of publication of the first impression of the edition, both dates are given. If there is more than one copyright date in a work, the latest date is chosen, except that copyright dates applying to only a part of a work and renewal dates are ignored." The copyright date is always preceded by a "c" and is not usually placed in brackets. The copyright date will be placed in brackets only if it does not appear on the title page, in the preliminaries, or on the colophon; most copyright laws require the copyright date to be placed on the title page or the verso of the title page, so it would be unusual for it to be placed in brackets. See Figs. 7.55 and 7.56.

Fig. 7.55

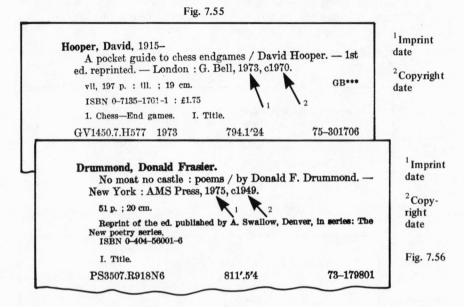

Rule 140. Printer's imprint

The printer's imprint consists of the place of printing and the name of the printer. "If the place of publication and the name of the publisher are unknown, the place of printing and the name of the printer are given if they appear in the work." The printer's imprint follows the date in the imprint area and is enclosed in parentheses. See Figs. 7.57 and 7.58.

Fig. 7.57

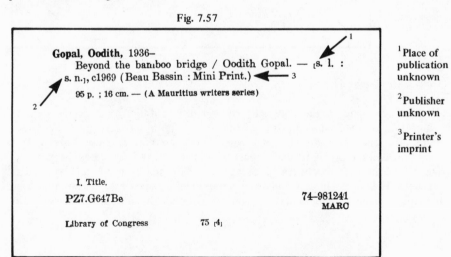

Fig. 7.58

Murphy, Marion Emerson.
The ancestry and descendants of Marion Simon Garrison of Morgantown, West Virginia, and allied families—Ammons, Kendrick, Metz, Murphy, Tripp / by Marion Emerson Murphy. — [s. l. : s. n.], 1973 (San Diego, Calif. : Murphy)

Printer's imprint

x, 83 p. : geneal. tables ; 25 cm.

"Privately printed."
Bibliography : p. 79.
Includes index.

1. Garrison family.   I. Title: The ancestry and descendants of Marion Simon Garrison ...

CS71.G2422   1973   929'.2'0973   75-315326
MARC

Library of Congress   75

Rule 141. Collation area

"The collation is the cataloger's description of the physical work and consists of a statement of the extent of the work in pages, volumes, or volumes and pages, the important illustrative matter, the size, and accompanying materials, if any."

141B.   Extent of text in one volume

141B1.   General rules

"In describing the extent of a work that is complete in one volume, the terminology suggested by the work is followed as far as possible. That is, a work with leaves printed on both sides is described in terms of pages, one with the leaves printed on only one side, in terms of leaves. A work which has numbered pages and unnumbered leaves is described only in terms of pages, one that has numbered leaves and unnumbered pages is described only in terms of leaves." See Fig. 7.59 and the examples at the top of page 152.

Fig. 7.59

Bisbee, M   J
Two brothers in the Pennsylvania Triangle : a biographical encyclopedia of the descendants of Reuben Bisbee, born 1776, Massachusetts / M. J. Bisbee. — Erie, Pa. : Bisbee, 1974.

Number of leaves

iii, 62 leaves : 28 cm.

"Cousin chart": [2] p. inserted.
Number 33 of 100 copies printed.
Includes bibliographical references and indexes.

1. Bisbee family.   I. Title.

Examples:

92p.	leaves printed on both sides
62 leaves	leaves printed only on one side
[34] leaves, [5] p.	unnumbered leaves and unnumbered pages
ix, 289 p.	last numbered page in roman numerals sequence and in arabic numerals sequence

If the form of pagination changes without being consecutive, the last *numbered* page of each section is recorded:

xii, [63] , 128, vi, 247 p.

If it is necessary to refer in a supplementary note to unnumbered pages that would not otherwise be covered by the collation, the collation is elaborated to include the unnumbered group of pages; enclose unnumbered pages in brackets. See Fig. 7.60.

Examples:

94, [2] p.
Bibliography: p. 93-[96]

Fig. 7.60

Symonds, Robert Wemyss, 1889-1958.
A book of English clocks / by R. W. Symonds. — Rev. ed. —
London : Penguin Books, 1950.
79, ₁1₁, 64 p. : ill. ; 19 cm. -- (The King Penguin books ; 28)
First ed. published in 1947 under title: A history of English clocks.
Bibliography: p. ₁80₁ ◀—— 2

1

1. Clocks and watches - Great Britain.   2. Clocks and watch making—Great Britian.   I. Title.

TS543.G7S93   1950   75-308750
                                              MARC

Library of Congress   75

[1] Unnumbered page indicated

[2] Note refers to unnumbered page

141B1d. "The number of leaves of plates is given at the end of the sequences of pagination, whether the plates are found together in the publication or are distributed throughout the work, or even if there is only one plate, such as a frontispiece." A **plate** is defined by AACR, revised Chapter 6, (Glossary, p. 115) as "A leaf containing illustrative matter, with or without text, that does not form a part of the numeration of the pages or leaves of text. It is not an integral part of a gathering. Plates may be distributed throughout the publication or gathered together; they may be numbered or unnumbered. A plate is usually, though not always, made of a different type of paper from that used in the rest of the publication." The numeral indicating the quantity of unnumbered plates is enclosed in brackets. See Figs. 7.61 and 7.62.

Fig. 7.61

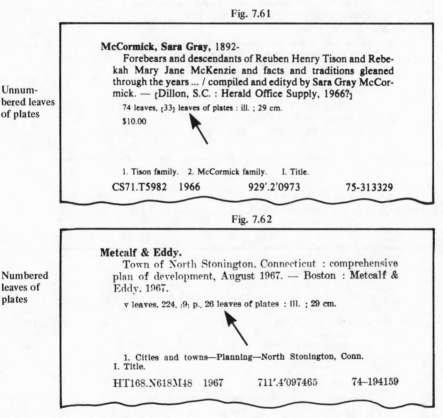

Unnumbered leaves of plates

McCormick, Sara Gray, 1892-
    Forebears and descendants of Reuben Henry Tison and Rebekah Mary Jane McKenzie and facts and traditions gleaned through the years ... / compiled and edityd by Sara Gray McCormick. — [Dillon, S.C. : Herald Office Supply, 1966?]
    74 leaves, [33] leaves of plates : ill. ; 29 cm.
    $10.00

    1. Tison family.   2. McCormick family.   I. Title.
    CS71.T5982   1966   929'.2'0973   75-313329

Fig. 7.62

Numbered leaves of plates

Metcalf & Eddy.
    Town of North Stonington, Connecticut : comprehensive plan of development, August 1967. — Boston : Metcalf & Eddy, 1967.
    v leaves, 224, [9] p., 26 leaves of plates : ill. ; 29 cm.

    1. Cities and towns—Planning—North Stonington, Conn.
    I. Title.
    HT168.N618M48   1967   711'.4'097465   74-194159

If the last numbered page or leaf does not represent the total number of pages or leaves in the work or section, a correction may be shown:

last page incorrectly numbered; 227 [i.e. 272] p.

141B2. Unpaged works

"If a work in one volume printed without pagination or foliation contains 100 pages or leaves or less, they are counted and the number is enclosed in brackets." **Note**: "The count begins with the first printed page and ends with the last printed page, exclusive of advertising matter; intermediate blank pages and leaves are counted." See Fig. 7.63.

Fig. 7.63

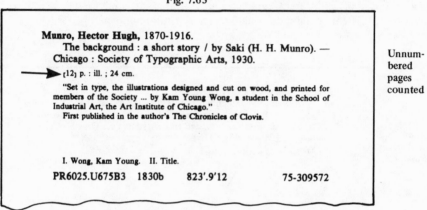

Munro, Hector Hugh, 1870-1916.
  The background : a short story / by Saki (H. H. Munro). —
Chicago : Society of Typographic Arts, 1930.
  [12] p. : ill. ; 24 cm.

    "Set in type, the illustrations designed and cut on wood, and printed for
  members of the Society ... by Kam Young Wong, a student in the School of
  Industrial Art, the Art Institute of Chicago."
  First published in the author's The Chronicles of Clovis.

  I. Wong, Kam Young. II. Title.
PR6025.U675B3   1830b   823'.9'12   75-309572

Unnumbered pages counted

"If the work contains more than 100 pages or leaves, they may be counted or approximated to the nearest multiple of 50." See Fig. 7.64.

Fig. 7.64

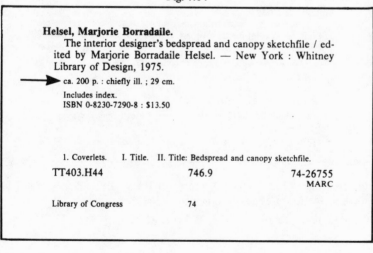

Helsel, Marjorie Borradaile.
  The interior designer's bedspread and canopy sketchfile / ed-
ited by Marjorie Borradaile Helsel. — New York : Whitney
Library of Design, 1975.
  ca. 200 p. : chiefly ill. ; 29 cm.
  Includes index.
  ISBN 0-8230-7290-8 : $13.50

  1. Coverlets.   I. Title.   II. Title: Bedspread and canopy sketchfile.
TT403.H44   746.9   74-26755
                                                  MARC

Library of Congress   74

Unnumbered pages approximated

141B3. Complicated or irregular paging

141B3a. "If a publication contains no more than three numbered main sections accompanied by lesser variously numbered or unnumbered sections, the number of pages or leaves in each of the main sections is recorded and the total number of the remaining variously numbered and unnumbered sections is added in brackets." See Fig. 7.65.

Fig. 7.65

Two separate numbering sections

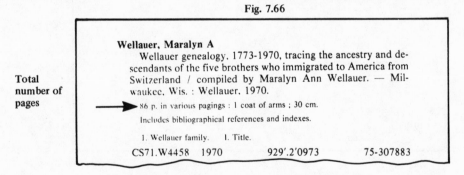

> **Gasson, Harold.**
> Firing days : reminiscences of a Great Western fireman / by Harold Gasson. — Oxford : Oxford Publishing Co., 1973.
> ▸ ₍6₎, 113 p., ₍32₎ p. of plates : ill., facsims., map, ports. ; 23 cm.
> GB 74–05573
> ISBN 0–902888–25–0 : £1.90
>
> 1. Locomotives—Great Britain—History. 2. Great Western Railway (Great Britain)—History. 3. Locomotive firemen—Great Britain—Correspondence, reminiscences, etc. I. Title.

141B3b. "If a publication contains more than three numbered main sections, the numbers on the last numbered page or leaf of each section are added and the total is given followed by the words 'in various pagings' or 'in various foliations'." See Figs. 7.66 and 7.67.

Fig. 7.66

Total number of pages

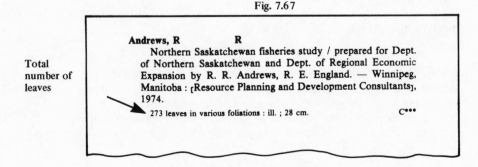

> **Wellauer, Maralyn A**
> Wellauer genealogy. 1773-1970, tracing the ancestry and descendants of the five brothers who immigrated to America from Switzerland / compiled by Maralyn Ann Wellauer. — Milwaukee, Wis. : Wellauer, 1970.
> ▸ 86 p. in various pagings : 1 coat of arms ; 30 cm.
> Includes bibliographical references and indexes.
>
> 1. Wellauer family. I. Title.
> CS71.W4458 1970   929'.2'0973   75-307883

Fig. 7.67

Total number of leaves

> **Andrews, R   R**
> Northern Saskatchewan fisheries study / prepared for Dept. of Northern Saskatchewan and Dept. of Regional Economic Expansion by R. R. Andrews, R. E. England. — Winnipeg, Manitoba : ₍Resource Planning and Development Consultants₎, 1974.
> ▸ 273 leaves in various foliations : ill. ; 28 cm.   C•••

141C. Extent of text in more than one volume

141C1. "The number of bibliographical volumes or parts of a work in more than one volume is shown in the collation":

> 4 v.

"If this number differs from the number of physical volumes, both are stated, the bibliographical volumes first":

> 6 v. in 3

141C2. "If the work is paged continuously, the pagination is indicated, in parentheses, following the number of volumes, according to the rule for indicating the pagination of a work that is complete in one volume. Separately paged preliminary matter in volumes after the first is ignored unless it is important." See below and Fig. 7.68.

> 2 v. (xxi, 689 p.)

Fig. 7.68

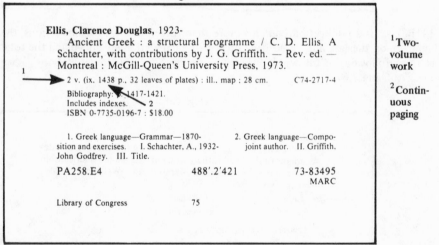

Ellis, Clarence Douglas, 1923-
　　　Ancient Greek : a structural programme / C. D. Ellis. A Schachter, with contributions by J. G. Griffith. — Rev. ed. — Montreal : McGill-Queen's University Press, 1973.

1 ➤ 2 v. (ix. 1438 p., 32 leaves of plates) : ill.. map : 28 cm.　　C74-2717-4

　　Bibliography: p. 1417-1421.
　　Includes indexes. ＼ 2
　　ISBN 0-7735-0196-7 : $18.00

　　　1. Greek language—Grammar—1870- 　　2. Greek language—Composition and exercises.　　I. Schachter, A., 1932-　　joint author.　　II. Griffith, John Godfrey.　　III. Title.

PA258.E4　　　　　　　488'.2'421　　　　　　73-83495
　　　　　　　　　　　　　　　　　　　　　　　　　　　MARC

Library of Congress　　　　　　75

[1] Two-volume work

[2] Continuous paging

141D. Illustrative matter

141D1. General rule

"Brief mention of the illustrative matter in a work comprises the second part of the collation statement. The abbreviation 'ill.,' for illustrations, is used to describe all types of illustrative matter unless particular types in the work are considered important enough to be specifically designated. When particular types are important, they are designated by the following terms in alphabetical order: coats of arms, diagrams, facsimiles, forms, genealogical tables, graphs, maps, music, plans, portraits (or group portraits, but not both), samples. When both illustrations and one or more particular types of illustrative matter are included, the abbreviation 'ill.' is given first." See Figs. 7.69 and 7.70. Note that tables are no longer listed in the collation but are treated as a note. See Fig. 7.5.

Fig. 7.69

Illustrations

Patton, Janice.
    The exodus of the Japanese / Janice Patton. — Toronto : McClelland and Stewart, 1973.
    47 p. : ill., ports. ; 21 cm.   C74-8056-3
    On cover: Stories from the Pierre Berton Show.
    Based on P. Berton's television interviews with H. Nobuoka and C. Tanaka.
    ISBN 0-7710-1379-5

    1. World War, 1939-1945—Evacuation of civilians. 2. Japanese in Canada.
    I. Berton, Pierre, 1920-   II. Nobuoka, Harry. III. Tanaka, George. IV.
    The Pierre Berton show (Television program). V. Title.
    D801.C3P37   940.54'72'71   75-314135

Particular
types of
illustrations
identified

Fig. 7.70

Armstrong, Jack Roy.
    A history of Sussex / J. R. Armstrong — 3d ed. / cartography by J. Broughton and Roy Mole`; drawings by Caroline Lockwood. — Chichester : Phillimore, 1974.
    176 p., [24] p. of plates, 1 leaf of plate : ill. (incl. 2 col.), coats of arms, maps, plans ; 26 cm. — (The Darwen county history series)
                                                        GB 74-19765
    Bibliography: p. 168–171.
    Includes index.
    ISBN 0–85033–185–4 : £3.95

    1. Sussex, Eng.—History. 2. Sussex, Eng.—Maps.   I. Title.
    DA670.S98A7 1974   942.2'5   74–196636
                                                        MARC
    Library of Congress   75 [4]

141D2. Colored illustrative matter

"Important illustrative matter that is printed with ink in two or more colors (counting black as a color), or some of which is so printed, is described as colored." See Figs. 7.71 and 7.72.

Fig. 7.71

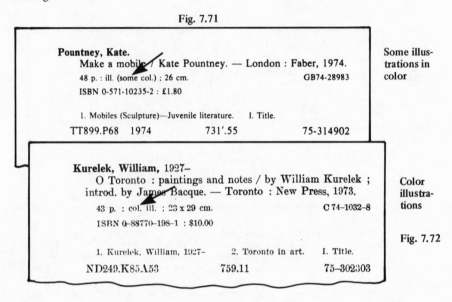

Pountney, Kate.
    Make a mobile / Kate Pountney. — London : Faber, 1974.
    48 p. : ill. (some col.) ; 26 cm.   GB74-28983
    ISBN 0-571-10235-2 : £1.80

    1. Mobiles (Sculpture)—Juvenile literature.   I. Title.
    TT899.P68   1974   731'.55   75-314902

Some illustrations in color

Kurelek, William, 1927–
    O Toronto : paintings and notes / by William Kurelek ; introd. by James Bacque. — Toronto : New Press, 1973.
    43 p. : col. ill. ; 23 x 29 cm.   C 74-1032-8
    ISBN 0-88770-198-1 : $10.00

    1. Kurelek, William, 1927–   2. Toronto in art.   I. Title.
    ND249.K85A53   759.11   75-302303

Color illustrations

Fig. 7.72

141D7. Illustrations with little or no text

"If the work consists entirely or chiefly of illustrations, this fact is noted in the illustration statement." See Figs. 7.73 and 7.74.

Fig. 7.73

Gordon, Maggie.
    Alphabets and images : inspiration from letterforms / Maggie Gordon. — New York : Scribner, [1975] c1974.
    96 p. : chiefly ill. ; 21 cm.
    ISBN 0-684-14083-7 : $7.95

    1. Lettering.   2. Letters in art.   I. Title.

Entire work is mostly illustrations

Joint Passive Resistance Council of Natal and Transvaal.
    How we live : an album of photographs showing the living conditions of the Indian people in South Africa / compiled by the Joint Passive Resistance Council of Natal and Transvaal. — Durban, S.A. : The Council, [195-].
    [39] leaves : all ill. ; 24 x 30 cm.
    Cover title.

    1. East Indians in South Africa—Pictorial works.   2. Africa, South—Social conditions—Pictorial works.   I. Title.

Entire work is illustrations

Fig. 7.74

141E. Size

"The size of the work is included in the catalog entry as an aid in finding the work on the shelves and as an aid to the user of the catalog in selecting a desirable edition. It also serves the reader who wishes to borrow the work through interlibrary loan or who wishes to order a photocopy of the work or a part of it." It is also a valuable figure for libraries with a separate storage area for oversized books.

141E1. "The height of the work is given in centimeters, exact to within one centimeter, fractions of a centimeter being counted as a full centimeter."

141E2. "The width of the work is also specified if it is less than half the height or if it is greater than the height. The height is given first, in the following form: 20 x 8 cm. or 20 x 32 cm." See Figs. 7.75 and 7.76.

Fig. 7.75

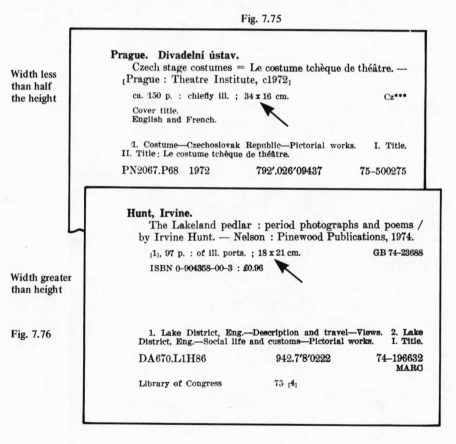

Width less than half the height

Prague. Divadelní ústav.
Czech stage costumes = Le costume tchèque de théâtre. — ₍Prague : Theatre Institute, c1972₎
ca. 150 p. : chiefly ill. ; 34 x 16 cm.   Cz***
Cover title.
English and French.

1. Costume—Czechoslovak Republic—Pictorial works. I. Title.
II. Title: Le costume tchèque de théâtre.
PN2067.P68 1972   792'.026'09437   75-500275

Hunt, Irvine.
The Lakeland pedlar : period photographs and poems / by Irvine Hunt. — Nelson : Pinewood Publications, 1974.
₍1₎, 97 p. : of ill. ports. ; 18 x 21 cm.   GB 74-23688
ISBN 0-904358-00-3 : £0.96

Width greater than height

Fig. 7.76

1. Lake District, Eng.—Description and travel—Views. 2. Lake District, Eng.—Social life and customs—Pictorial works. I. Title.
DA670.L1H86   942.7'8'0222   74-196632
MARC
Library of Congress   75 ₍4₎

141F. Accompanying materials

Accompanying materials include answer books, teacher's manuals, atlases, portfolios of plates, slides, and phonodiscs. These materials are typically placed in pockets on the back or front cover of the work being cataloged. Their description makes up the fourth element of the collation area.

141F1. "Accompanying material is described in terms of a word or phrase indicating the nature of the material." See Fig. 7.77.

Fig. 7.77

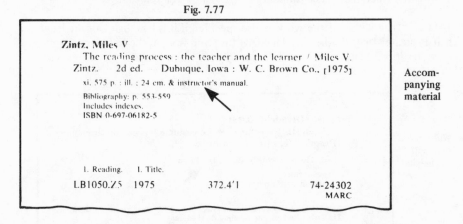

141F2. "If further description is desired, as in the case of atlases and portfolios of plates, a statement of the extent of the publication and of the illustrative material it contains is given within parentheses after the characterizing term." See Fig. 7.78.

Fig. 7.78

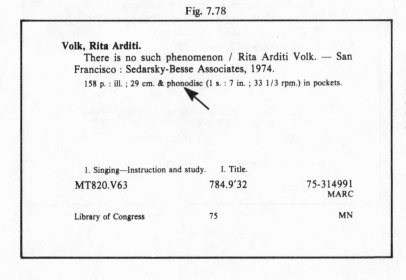

Rule 142. Series area

142A. General rules

142A1. "A series statement, i.e., a statement of the collective title under which a work is issued as one of its parts, is transcribed enclosed in parentheses. If the statement or any part of it does not appear anywhere in the work being cataloged, and is supplied from another source (as when it has been inadvertently omitted from the work), the part is supplied, enclosed in brackets. If the entire series statement is supplied, it is enclosed in brackets within parentheses. . . .

"The series statement on the work may include, in addition to the title of the series (in one or more languages), the name of a personal or corporate author or authors or of an editor or editors, and the number of the volume if the series consists of consecutively numbered volumes or parts. The series area generally includes all of this information except the names of editors." See Fig. 7.1.

"When a series has been assigned an International Standard Serial Number (ISSN), the ISSN is given as found in the publication after the title of the series and its numbering or after the title of the subseries and its numbering, preceded by a space and the letters ISSN." See Fig. 7.79.

Fig. 7.79

^{1} Series title

^{2} Series number

^{3} ISSN

Marsh, Leonard Charles, 1905-
    Report on social security for Canada / Leonard Marsh ; with a new introd. by the author ; and a pref. by Michael Bliss. — Toronto ; Buffalo : University of Toronto Press, [1975]
    xxxi, 330 p. ; 23 cm. — (The Social history of Canada ; 24 ISSN 0085-6207)
    Includes bibliographical references and index.
    ISBN 0-8020-2168-9 : $15.00.   ISBN 0-8020/6250-4 pbk. : $5.50

    1. Social security—Canada.   I. Title.   II. Series: The Social history of Canada ; 24.

HD7129.M3   1975   368.4'00971   74-82286
                                                              MARC

Library of Congress   74

142E. Author in series statement

142E1. "If the title of a series is the title of a multi-volume monograph and the author of the series is the same as the author of the individual part being cataloged, the appropriate possessive pronoun is substituted for the author's name, unless the name is integrated with the series title." See Figs. 7.80 through 7.82.

Fig. 7.80

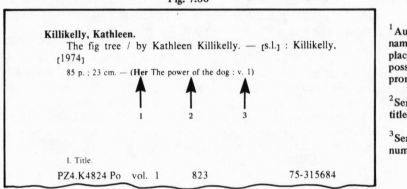

> **Killikelly, Kathleen.**
>   The fig tree / by Kathleen Killikelly. — ⌐s.l.⌐ : Killikelly,
> ⌐1974⌐
>   85 p. ; 23 cm. — **(Her** The power of the dog : v. 1)
>
>   1   2   3
>
>   I. Title.
>   PZ4.K4824 Po   vol. 1   823   75-315684

[1] Author's name replaced by possessive pronoun

[2] Series title

[3] Series number

Fig. 7.81

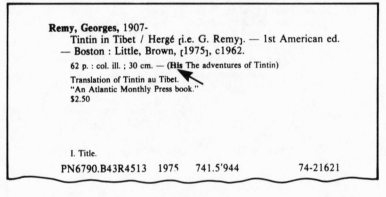

> **Remy, Georges,** 1907-
>   Tintin in Tibet / Hergé ⌐i.e. G. Remy⌐. — 1st American ed.
> — Boston : Little, Brown, ⌐1975⌐, c1962.
>   62 p. : col. ill. ; 30 cm. — **(His** The adventures of Tintin)
>   Translation of Tintin au Tibet.
>   "An Atlantic Monthly Press book."
> $2.50
>
>   I. Title.
>   PN6790.B43R4513   1975   741.5'944   74-21621

Possessive pronoun

Fig. 7.82

> **Commerce Clearing House.**
>   Pension plan guide. — New York : Commerce Clearing
> House, ⌐1975⌐
>   4 v. ; 26 cm. — **(Its** Topical law reports)
>   Replaces 2d ed. of Pension plan guide and Plans and clauses.
>   Loose-leaf for updating.
>   Unnumbered v. 4 has special title: Plans and clauses.
>
>   1. Pension trusts--United States.   I. Title. II. Title: Plans and clauses.
>   KF3512.A6C64   344'.73'01252   75-313113

Possessive pronoun

142E3. "If the title of a series consisting solely of a generic term is the title of a serial, the generic term is followed by the author statement. The two elements are separated by a space-hyphen-space (-). The author statement is transcribed as it appears on the publication except that, if the statement includes a corporate hierarchy, those parts of the hierarchy (generally intermediate) which are not necessary for the identification of the author are omitted. The parts of the hierarchy which are recorded are separated by commas." See AACR, revised Chapter 6, p. 68 and Figs. 7.83 through 7.85.

Fig. 7.83

¹Generic title

²Authorship statement

The Cooper River environmental study / by Frank P. Nelson, editor. — Cayce : South Carolina Water Resources Commission, 1974. 1
164 p. : ill. ; 28 cm. — (Report - South Carolina Water Resources Commission ; no. 117) 2
On cover: State water plan.

1. Water quality—South Carolina—Cooper River. I. Nelson, Frank P. II. Series: South Carolina. Water Resources Commission. Report - South Carolina Water Resources Commission ; no. 117.

Fig. 7.84

Supplied generic title

Liu, Yüan-shen.
The current and the past of Lin Piao / Liu Yuen-sun ; translated from the Chinese by Robert Liang ; introd. by Thomas Robinson. — [Santa Monica : Rand Corp.], 1967.
58 p. ; 28 cm. — ([Paper] - Rand Corporation ; P-3671)
Translation of Lin Piao ti kuo ch'ü yü hsien tsai from Studies on Chinese communism (Fei ch'ing yen chiu), Jan. 31, 1967.
Cover title.
Includes bibliographical references.

I. Lin, Piao, 1908-1971. II. Title. III. Series: Rand Corporation. Paper : P-3671.

Fig. 7.85

Supplied generic title

Chaiken, Jan M
The impact of police activity on crime : robberies on the New York City subway system / Jan M. Chaiken, Michael W. Lawless, Keith A. Stevenson. — New York : New York City Rand Institute, 1974.
xv, 74 p. : ill. ; 28 cm. — ([Report] - Rand Corporation ; R-1424-NYC)
Includes bibliographical references.

1. Robbery—New York (City) 2. New York (City)—Police. 3. Subways —New York (City) I. Lawless, Michael W., joint author. II. Stevenson, Keith A., joint author. III. Title. IV. Series: Rand Corporation. Rand report : R-1424-NYC.

Rule 143. Notes area—general rules

143A. Many works require description beyond that presented in either the body of the entry or the collation. "This description may be combined with the formalized part of the entry or it may be added in the form of supplementary notes.

"Additional information may be incorporated in the formalized part of the entry only to the extent that the rules for the preparation of this part of the description provide. This limitation is necessary if the advantages of a formalized description are not to be lost.

"Notes amplify or qualify the formalized description, either when the rules do not permit the inclusion of the needed information in any form other than a note or when the incorporation of the information in the formalized description would be misleading, cumbersome, or inappropriate."

143B. Categories of notes

"In general, supplementary notes fall into two categories: 1) notes that contribute in a significant way to the identification of the work or the intelligibility of the catalog entry (e.g., a note explaining the relationship to the work of a person or a corporate body for whom a secondary entry is indicated) or that are essential for the reader who does not already have in hand the exact citation to the work he is seeking, and 2) notes that characterize the work and tell its bibliographic history. Most of the notes in the first category are indispensable, regardless of the inherent value of the work being cataloged. The others, in either category, will be supplied at the discretion of the cataloger who will be guided by bibliographic considerations peculiar to the work, its relative importance, and the availability and costs of obtaining certain information."

AACR 143-150 provide fixed forms for certain notes. Informal notes are used for any other data that need to be supplied. Fixed forms are not prescribed for informal notes but some of the most important principles are discussed in AACR.

143D. Order

Various considerations affect the order of notes. AACR recommend the following sequence:

1) Analytical note (see Rule 157).

2) Original title notes, including the original title of a translated work, the original title of a work with a changed title, and other variations in the original title.

3) Notes that refer to the elements in the formalized description in the following order: title proper, other titles and title information, authorship area, edition area, imprint area, collation area, and additional physical description.

4) Notes that provide bibliographical history (e.g., relationships to other editions of the same work).

5) Contents note (see Rule 148).

Rule 144. "At head of title" note

This note is generally a formal note that begins with the phrase "At head of title" and that is used for any information appearing in that position on the title page. Information noted in this fashion includes:

"a) Different form of author's name from that in the heading.
 b) Corporate body not chosen as author heading although named at head of title.
 c) Initials, seal or other insignia indicating the necessity for an added entry.
 d) Miscellaneous types of data not included in the body of the entry."

See Fig. 7.86.

Fig. 7.86

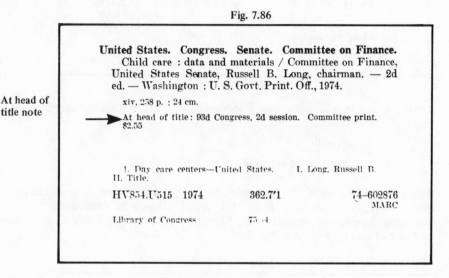

At head of
title note

United States. Congress. Senate. Committee on Finance.
Child care : data and materials / Committee on Finance, United States Senate, Russell B. Long, chairman. — 2d ed. — Washington : U. S. Govt. Print. Off., 1974.

xiv, 258 p. ; 24 cm.

At head of title: 93d Congress, 2d session. Committee print.
$2.55

1. Day care centers—United States.   I. Long, Russell B.
II. Title.

HV854.U515   1974   362.7'1   74-602876
                                                              MARC

Library of Congress   75 4

Rule 145. Notes of works bound together

145A. "If two or more distinct works, each with its own title page and paging, are issued together in one cover, or if several works issued independently are subsequently bound together, the entry for each work in the volume bears a note to show the presence of the other work or works." Each work in a bound-with is cataloged as a separate entry.

145B. If the works were originally issued together in one binding, the note begins:

Issued with

Issued with the author's

See Fig. 7.87 on page 166.

Fig. 7.87

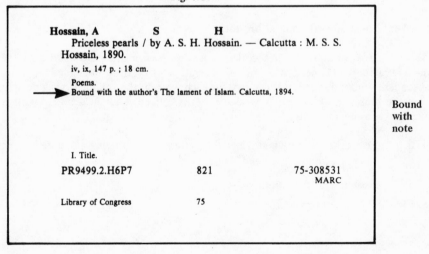

American dainties and how to prepare them / by an American
lady. — London : R. Jackson, [190-?]

    iv, 92 p. ; 19 cm.

    Cover title: American fancy groceries and recipes by an American lady for
170 dainty dishes.
    ▶Issued with 40 p. price list entitled: American fancy groceries imported by Rt.
Jackson & Co.
    Includes index.

    1. Cookery, American.   I. An American lady.   II. Title: American fancy
groceries and recipes by an American lady for 170 dainty dishes.

TX715.A51254   641.5'973   75-314153
                                                     MARC

Library of Congress   75

Issued
with
note

145D. If the works were issued independently and were subsequently bound
together, the note begins:

    Bound with

    Bound with the author's

145E. "The citation of the other work or works in the volume, to be added to the
above, takes the following form: the author's name in catalog entry order,
forenames represented by initials; brief title (the uniform title, if one is used); place
and date of publication." See Fig. 7.88.

Fig. 7.88

Hossain, A   S   H
    Priceless pearls / by A. S. H. Hossain. — Calcutta : M. S. S.
Hossain, 1890.

    iv, ix, 147 p. ; 18 cm.

    Poems.
    ▶Bound with the author's The lament of Islam. Calcutta, 1894.

    I. Title.

PR9499.2.H6P7   821   75-308531
                                               MARC

Library of Congress   75

Bound
with
note

Rule 146. Thesis note

146B. Designation of the thesis

146B1. "The English word 'thesis' is used to designate all theses. If the author was a candidate for a degree other than that of doctor, this fact is also shown." "The name of the institution to which the thesis was presented is named as briefly as possible" (Rule 146D). See Figs. 7.89 and 7.90.

Fig. 7.89

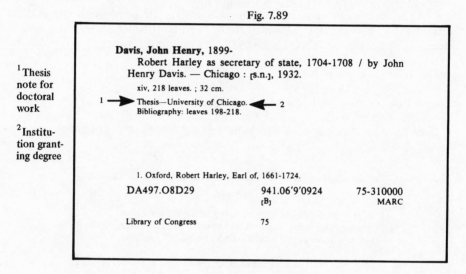

¹Thesis note for doctoral work

²Institution granting degree

Davis, John Henry, 1899-
    Robert Harley as secretary of state, 1704-1708 / by John Henry Davis. — Chicago : ₁s.n.₁, 1932.
    xiv, 218 leaves. ; 32 cm.
    1 ➤ Thesis—University of Chicago. ◄— 2
    Bibliography: leaves 198-218.

1. Oxford, Robert Harley, Earl of, 1661-1724.

DA497.O8D29   941.06′9′0924   75-310000
                         ₁B₁   MARC

Library of Congress   75

Fig. 7.90

¹Thesis note for M.A. degree

²Institution granting degree

Verwilghen, Albert Felix.
    The character of Mencius / by Albert Felix Verwilghen. — ₁Seattle : s.n.₁. 1964.
    xviii, 152 leaves ; 29 cm.
    1 ➤ Thesis (M.A.)—University of Washington. ◄— 2
    Bibliography: leaves ₁129₁-152.

1. Mencius.   I. Title.

B128.M35V39   181′.09′512   75-309041
                         ₁B₁   MARC

Library of Congress .   75

Rule 148. Contents notes

There are two types of contents notes: informal contents notes and formal contents notes. They are used if it is necessary to bring out important parts of the content of the work not mentioned in the title, or to give a fuller and more detailed description of the contents than the title supplies. "If an added entry is to be made for an item in the work, the presence of this item is specified in the contents note." Contents notes are made for works in several volumes, whether they are single works or collections of works by one or more authors.

In relation to other notes, the contents note is always the last note in the catalog entry. This is done for two reasons: because of its length and because in case of an open entry the contents note will have additions.

148A. Informal contents notes

Informal notes may be used for bibliographies, indexes, appendices, and other appended matter, such as errata slips. Figs. 7.91 through 7.94 show possible formats for informal contents notes. More detailed directions and examples appear in AACR, revised Chapter 6, p. 92.

Fig. 7.91

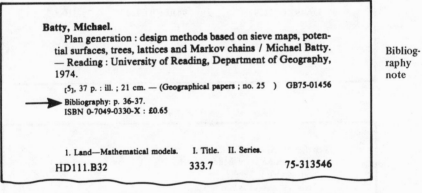

Fig. 7.92

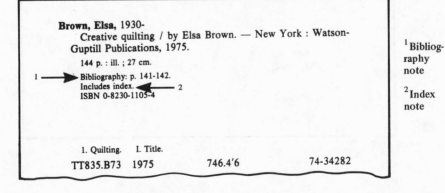

Fig. 7.93

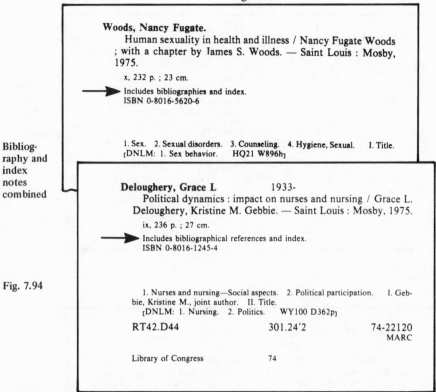

Bibliog-
raphy and
index
notes
combined

Fig. 7.94

148B. Formal contents notes

The formal contents are listed in the entry for collections of works by the same author (especially if they are on different subjects) or for collections of works by different authors. **Note:** If the collection contains the complete works of an author in one volume, the contents are not listed. The partial contents are noted if one or more selected items of the work need to be specified.

The items in the contents note are given in the order in which they appear in the work. In general, for works of one volume, the items in a contents paragraph are separated by a dash; for multi-volume works, the dash precedes the volume number, and items within the volumes are punctuated as separate sentences. Paging is in the contents paragraph only for bibliographies and for a particular item that occupies a disproportionately large section of the work. If paging is given, it is cited within parentheses. For more details as to the scope, position, and form of different kinds of contents notes consult Rule 148. See Figs. 7.95 through 7.98.

Fig. 7.95

Deihl, Edna Groff, 1881-1935.
    The three books and other big day stories : Aunt Este's little stories of big days / by Edna Groff Deihl. — Chicago : A. Whitman, [1925]
    125 p. : ill. ; 19 cm. — (A Just right book)
    ➤ CONTENTS: A story for Lincoln's birthday.—Prongy Fork's valentine.—The cherry tree that never grew up.—Why Robin Redbreast sings at Easter time.--The story Queen Moon heard.—Cornflower's message.—Jenny Pumpkin and the black witch.—The prince of the Kingdom of Thankful.—Strutty Gobler.—How the gnomes tried to stop Thanksgiving.—The star angel.—The story of Baby Gretel.—The three bells.

    1. Holidays – Juvenile fiction.   I. Title.   II. Series: Just right books.

PZ7.D367 Th   75-314449
                                             MARC

Library of Congress   75

Contents note for collection of works of one author

Fig. 7.96

---

²
Combat SF / edited by Gordon R. Dickson. — 1st ed. — Garden City, N.Y. : Doubleday, 1975.   ³
    ix, 204 p. ; 22 cm. (Doubleday science fiction)
¹ ➤ CONTENTS: Laumer, K. The last command.—Bova, B. & Lewis, M. R. Men of good will.—Hensley, J. The pair.—Drake, D. The butcher's bill.—Green, J. Single combat.—Anderson, P. The man who came early.—Saberhagen, F. Patron of the arts.—Haldeman, J. W. Time piece.—Dickson, G. R. Ricochet on Miza.—Harrison, H. No war, or battle's sound.—Pournelle, J. His truth goes marching on.—Wolfe, G. The HORARS of war.
    ISBN 0-385-04575-1

    1. Science fiction, American.   I. Dickson, Gordon R.   II. Title.

PZ1.C727   813'.0876   74-24486
[PS648.S3]   MARC

Library of Congress   75

¹ Contents note for collection of works by different authors

² First-named author

³ First-named title

Fig. 7.97

Churchill, Winston Leonard Spencer, Sir, 1874-1965.
    The collected works of Sir Winston Churchill. — Centenary
limited ed. — London : Library of Imperial History, 1973-

Contents
note for
multi-
volume
work

         v.   : ill. ; 24 cm.   GB•••
    CONTENTS: v. 1. My early life. My African journey.—v. 2. The story of the
Malakand field force.
    ISBN 0-903988-01-1 (v. 1)

    1. Churchill, Winston Leonard Spencer, Sir, 1874-1965.   2. Great Britain—
Politics and government—20th century—Collected works.   3. Great Britain—
Foreign relations—20th century—Collected works.

DA566.9.C5A2   1973   941.082′092′4   73-90444
                                                  MARC

    Library of Congress   75

Fig. 7.98

Mitchell, Loften.
    Voices of the Black theatre / by Loften Mitchell. — Clifton,
N.J. : J. T. White, [1975]
    ix, 238 p. : ill. ; 24 cm.

Partial
contents
note

    Contains taped individual recollections of Black theatrical figures with intro-
ductory essays and comments by L. Mitchell.
    Includes index.
    PARTIAL CONTENTS: The words of Eddie Hunter.—The words of Regina
M. Andrews.—The words of Dick Campbell.—The words of Abram Hill.—
Interlude: Paul Robeson.—The words of Frederick O'Neal.—The words of Vin-
nette Carroll.—The words of Ruby Dee.
    ISBN 0-88371-006-4
    1. Theater—United States.   2. Negro actors.   3. American drama--Negro
authors—History and criticism.   I. Title.

PN2286.M5   792′.028′0922   74-30081
                                                  MARC

    Library of Congress   74

Rule 149. International Standard Book Number (ISBN)

The International Standard Book Number appears immediately after the last item in the notes area. The letters "ISBN" precede the number, which is recorded as found in the publication. **Note**: "The Library of Congress will also record the price for current imprints whenever the information is available; in certain instances the type of binding will also be recorded." Price and binding are not part of the AACR, revised Chapter 6; inclusion of price and binding is optional in the ISBD principles. See Figs. 7.99 and 7.100.

Fig. 7.99

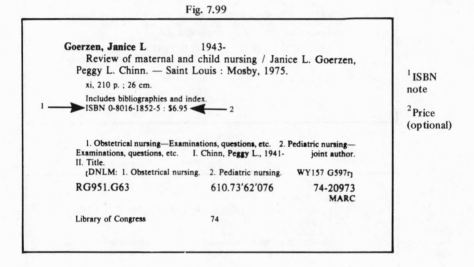

Goerzen, Janice L   1943-
    Review of maternal and child nursing / Janice L. Goerzen,
Peggy L. Chinn. — Saint Louis : Mosby, 1975.
    xi, 210 p. ; 26 cm.
    Includes bibliographies and index.
1 ——▶ISBN 0-8016-1852-5 : $6.95 ◀—— 2

    1. Obstetrical nursing—Examinations, questions, etc.   2. Pediatric nursing—
Examinations, questions, etc.   I. Chinn, Peggy L., 1941-   joint author.
II. Title.
    [DNLM: 1. Obstetrical nursing.   2. Pediatric nursing.   WY157 G597r]

RG951.G63   610.73′62′076   74-20973
                                            MARC

Library of Congress   74

¹ISBN note

²Price (optional)

Fig. 7.100

Duberman, Lucile, 1926-
    Gender and sex in society / by Lucile Duberman ; with chap-
ters by Helen Mayer Hacker and Warren T. Farrell. — New
York : Praeger, 1975.
    xii, 274 p. ; 22 cm.
    Bibliography: p. 253-268.
    Includes index.
1 ——▶ISBN 0-275-52110-9 : $7.50.   ISBN 0-275-85070-6 pbk.   2

    1. Sex role.   2. Socialization.   3. Feminism.   4. Interpersonal relations.
I. Title.
    [DNLM: 1. Psychology, Social.   2. Sex behavior.   BF692 D814g]

HQ1154.D79   301.41   73-10658
                                            MARC

Library of Congress   75

¹ISBN note

²ISBN for paper-back edition

Rule 150. "Title romanized" note

Any work whose title is in non-roman script may have a "title romanized" note. "The note begins with the words 'Title romanized,' followed by a colon and the title of the work in romanized form according to the approved system of romanization." The existence of a romanized form of the title is most valuable for filing. Fig. 7.101 is an example of this note.

Fig. 7.101

Title romanized note

> **Cervantes Saavedra, Miguel de,** 1547–1616.
> ₁Novelas ejemplares. Russian. Selections₁
> Английская испанка : новеллы / Мигель де Серван-
> тес ; пер. с исп. ₁и примеч.₁ Б. Кржевского ; стихи в
> пер. М. Лозинского ; ₁вступит. статья З. Плавскина ;
> ил. М. Беломлинский₁. — Ленинград : Худож. лит.,
> Ленингр. отд-ние, 1974.
> 251 p. : ill. ; 16 cm. — (Народная библиотека)   USSR 74
> Includes bibliographical references.
> CONTENTS: Rinkonete i Kortadil'o. — Angliĭskaı̐a ispanka. —
> Lit͡sent͡siat Vidriera.—Vysokorodnaı̐a sudomoĭka.
> 0.38rub
>   Title romanized: Angliĭskaı̐a ispanka.
>
> PQ6332.R8A6   1974   75-532669
>
> Library of Congress   *75

Although Fig. 7.101 shows this note in its traditional location as the last element on the card, the current practice of the Library of Congress is to place the romanized form of the title in parentheses between the heading and the body of the entry. See Fig. 7.102. If the work is entered under title, the romanized title, in parentheses, is printed above the body of the entry. See Fig. 7.103. Only when a uniform title is present (as in the case of Fig. 7.101) will the Library of Congress use the formal title romanized note.

Fig. 7.102

Romanized title

> **Melas, Leōn,** 1812–1879.
> (Ho Gerostathēs)
> Ὁ Γεροστάθης : ἤ, ᾽Αναμνήσεις τῆς παιδικῆς μου ἡλικίας :
> μεταφορὰ στὴ δημοτικὴ / Λέοντος Γ. Μελᾶ. – ᾽Αθήνα : Βιβλιο-
> πωλεῖον Δωδώνη Ε. Κ. Λάζος, 1973.
> 482 p., ₁16₁ leaves of plates : ill. ; 22 cm.
>
> I. Title. II. Title: Anamnēseis tēs paidikēs mou ēlikias.
> PA5610.M33G4   1973   75-528484

Fig. 7.103

─────►**(Klassifikatsiia korrespondentsii transporta)**
Классификация корреспонденции транспорта. — Москва : НКПС, 1924.

    214 p. : 22 cm.

    Includes bibliographical references and index.

    1. Transportation—Records and correspondence—Indexing.

HE151.K54 1924   75-529358

Library of Congress   75

Romanized title for hanging indention

Rule 151. Tracing

151A. The tracing appears after the ISBN area and before the title romanized note if one is present (see Fig. 7.101). "Subject headings are listed first, numbered consecutively with Arabic numerals, followed by the added entry headings numbered with Roman numerals. Added entry headings for persons are given first, followed by those for corporate bodies; within each category the headings are given in the order in which they appear in the entry. Author-title added entry headings are included in the appropriate category. Added entry headings for the title proper, titles other than the title proper, and for series follow in this order." The title proper is indicated by the word "Title" only. Other titles are indicated in full preceded by the word "Title." The title of the series is indicated by the word "Series," unless there is some necessary variation between the series statement and the series entry. See AACR, revised Chapter 6, page 99 for detailed examples of the series in the tracing; additional examples may be found in L.C. Processing Department, *Cataloging Service*, bulletin 114 (Summer 1975), p. 4.

Sample tracing

```
      1. Subject heading.  2. Subject heading.
   3. Subject heading.  I. Personal added entry.
  II. Personal added entry.  III. Corporate
  body added entry.  IV. Title.  V. Series.
```

SPECIAL RULES

Rule 155. Supplements, indexes, etc.

Some continuations, supplements, and indexes are so dependent upon the works to which they are related that they are best described by means of an addition to the catalog entry for the main work. (See Rule 19A.) If the supplements or indexes are minor in character, they may simply be noted informally. Cf. Rule 155B. See Fig. 7.104.

Fig. 7.104

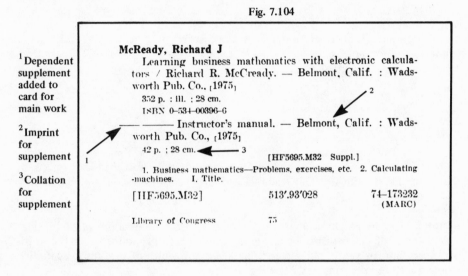

¹ Dependent supplement added to card for main work

² Imprint for supplement

³ Collation for supplement

McReady, Richard J
    Learning business mathematics with electronic calcula-
tors / Richard R. McCready. — Belmont, Calif. : Wads-
worth Pub. Co., [1975]
        352 p. : ill. ; 28 cm.
        ISBN 0-534-00396-6

————— Instructor's manual. — Belmont, Calif. : Wads-
worth Pub. Co., [1975]
        42 p. ; 28 cm.   3
                            [HF5695.M32 Suppl.]
        1. Business mathematics—Problems, exercises, etc. 2. Calculating
-machines.   I. Title.

    [HF5695.M32]   513'.93'028   74-173232
                                        (MARC)

    Library of Congress   75

Rule 156. Microform photoreproductions

The description for microform reproductions follows the description of the original if the description of the original can be determined from the reproduction or from a reliable source.

156A. Description of original

The original from which the microform is reproduced is described according to the general rules for cataloging monographs, serials, music, etc. If the collation, or some part of it, cannot be determined, it is omitted. The parts of collation that are known are, of course, included. Note in Fig. 7.105 that the size of the original is omitted.

156B. Description of reproduction

The microform is described as the first note following any notes that pertain to the original. The microform description note includes three elements:

156B1. "The general type of reproduction is described by one of the following terms: microfilm, microfiche, micro-opaque, photocopy (or other appropriate term), or, if the type is uncertain, photoreproduction." If the reproduction is a negative, this fact is indicated parenthetically.

> Microfilm (negative)
>
> Photocopy (negative)

If the physical form of the original is a typescript or a manuscript, this fact is indicated in this note. Examples:

> Microfiche of typescript.
>
> Microfilm (negative) of ms.

See Fig. 7.105.

156B2. "The organization, firm, or individual responsible for the reproduction, and the place and year in which the reproduction was made are given in conventional imprint order, if readily ascertainable, with prescribed punctuation." See Fig. 7.105.

156B3. Last is the physical description of the microreproduction, which includes the number of pieces (cards, sheets, reels, containers, etc.) and the size. "The width of microfilm is given in millimeters; the height and width of sheet microreproductions are given in centimeters." See Fig. 7.105.

Fig. 7.105

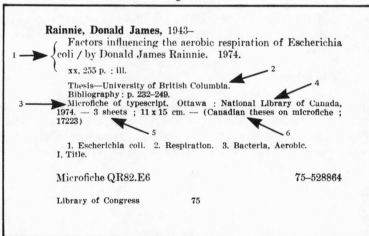

Rainnie, Donald James, 1943–
Factors influencing the aerobic respiration of Escherichia
coli / by Donald James Rainnie. 1974.
xx, 255 p. : ill.

Thesis—University of British Columbia.
Bibliography : p. 232–249.
Microfiche of typescript. Ottawa : National Library of Canada, 1974. — 3 sheets ; 11 x 15 cm. — (Canadian theses on microfiche ; 17223)

1. Escherichia coli. 2. Respiration. 3. Bacteria, Aerobic.
I. Title.

Microfiche QR82.E6   75–528864

Library of Congress   75

[1] Description of original
[2] Notes for original
[3] Type of reproduction
[4] Imprint
[5] Collation
[6] Series

If the microform is not based on a previous original edition, it is an original edition in microform. In that case, the physical description becomes the collation and the type of reproduction becomes the first note. See AACR, revised Chapter 6, p. 109.

Rule 157. Analytical entries

"Definition and scope: An analytical entry is an entry for a part of a work or series of works for which another, comprehensive, entry is made. The part analyzed may be a complete volume, bibliographically independent from the set of which it forms a part, or it may be a mere page or two which is inadequately described (either from the author or the subject approach) by the catalog entry for the work as a whole. If the part analyzed is an independent work, it is cataloged according to the rules for separately published monographs, with a series note indicating its relationship to the more comprehensive work."

It should be noted that analytical entries are made for parts of a monograph that would not normally appear in the body of the card (e.g., chapters, separate sections, etc.). Obviously, preparing these additional entries requires considerable time; quite often the effect of analytical entries is achieved by some other method, such as by making a series added entry for each item in the series. Usually the decision in this matter will depend on the administrative policy of an individual library and the local needs. In deciding whether or not analyticals are needed, certain general principles may be taken into consideration.

1) The availability of printed indexes, bibliographies, and abstracting services that will locate the material to be analyzed.

2) The availability of LC analyticals; in the case of certain university monographic series, for example, these should be ordered from the Library of Congress on a standing order basis.

3) The quantity and quality of material on the given subject already in the catalog.

4) The quantity of material by the same authors already in the catalog. The best example in this category is provided by the library's policy regarding books in sets that usually represent various types of collections or compilations of one or more authors—e.g., Harvard Classics or Harvard Shelf of Fiction. If the library has little material by an author, the need for analyticals may be greater.

5) The parts to be analyzed have a special significance for a given library (e.g., parts written by local noted authors, etc.).

6) The parts occupy the major portion of a given work.

The rules given below are limited to analytical entries for parts not bibliographically independent—i.e., parts without numbers to distinguish them from other parts of the more comprehensive work. These entries are commonly called "page" analyticals or "in" analyticals.

Rule 157A. Parts with special title pages and separate paging

A part that has its own title page and its own pagination results in the most complete analytical entry. In fact, the part might be treated as a separate, as a bound-with, if there were not a general or collective title page to preclude this possibility. A part with a special (i.e., separate) title page is prepared according to the rules for the body of the entry—the title and statement of authorship area, the edition area, and the imprint area. Secondly, since this part has its own separate paging, the collation area is developed as it would be for separately published monographs. "The first note shows the relationship of the part to the larger work. This 'analytical' note begins with the word 'In,' printed in boldface or underlined, and contains the following items, in this order: author's name and initials of forenames (for which may be substituted 'his,' 'her,' 'their,' or 'its,' printed in boldface or underlined, when the author is the same as that of the part analyzed), brief title, edition, place and date of publication of the larger work." See Fig. 7.106.

Fig. 7.106

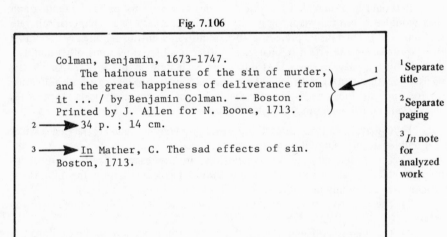

```
    Colman, Benjamin, 1673-1747.
        The hainous nature of the sin of murder,              1    ¹ Separate
    and the great happiness of deliverance from                        title
    it ... / by Benjamin Colman. -- Boston :
    Printed by J. Allen for N. Boone, 1713.                         ² Separate
2 ─────► 34 p. ; 14 cm.                                              paging

3 ─────► In Mather, C. The sad effects of sin.                   ³ In note
    Boston, 1713.                                                    for
                                                                     analyzed
                                                                     work
```

157B. Parts with separate title pages and continuous paging

"The collation of a part paged continuously with other matter in the same volume is omitted. Instead the analytical note contains, in addition to items specified in A above, the size of the volume, volume number (if any), inclusive pagination, and important illustrative matter." The preceding order is followed. See Fig. 7.107.

Fig. 7.107

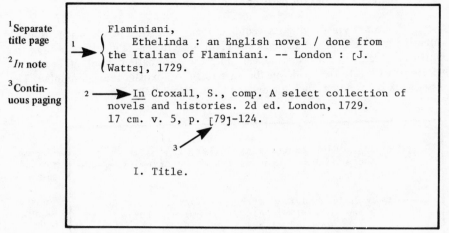

¹ Separate
title page

² *In* note

³ Contin-
uous paging

Flaminiani,
     Ethelinda : an English novel / done from
the Italian of Flaminiani. -- London : ₍J.
Watts₎, 1729.

    In Croxall, S., comp. A select collection of
novels and histories. 2d ed. London, 1729.
17 cm. v. 5, p. ₍79₎-124.

    I. Title.

157C. Parts without special title pages

"If the part to be analyzed does not have a special title page, the descriptive portion of the entry consists only of the title and statement of authorship area and the edition area if required, followed by the analytical note." The form of the analytical note is the same as in Rule 157B. See Fig. 7.108.

Fig. 7.108

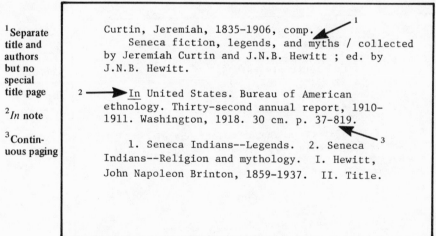

¹ Separate
title and
authors
but no
special
title page

² *In* note

³ Contin-
uous paging

Curtin, Jeremiah, 1835-1906, comp.
    Seneca fiction, legends, and myths / collected
by Jeremiah Curtin and J.N.B. Hewitt ; ed. by
J.N.B. Hewitt.

    In United States. Bureau of American
ethnology. Thirty-second annual report, 1910-
1911. Washington, 1918. 30 cm. p. 37-819.

    1. Seneca Indians--Legends. 2. Seneca
Indians--Religion and mythology. I. Hewitt,
John Napoleon Brinton, 1859-1937. II. Title.

157D. Analytical entries for parts of analyzed parts

"If an analytical entry is required for a part of a work which is itself cataloged by means of an analytical entry, the analytical note mentions both of the works in which the part is contained, since the information about either may be necessary to locate the work on the shelves and to explain the call number. The lesser work is given first, then the comprehensive work." See Fig. 7.109.

Fig. 7.109

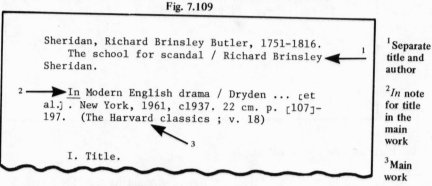

Sheridan, Richard Brinsley Butler, 1751-1816.
    The school for scandal / Richard Brinsley Sheridan.

In Modern English drama / Dryden ... [et al.]. New York, 1961, c1937. 22 cm. p. [107]-197. (The Harvard classics ; v. 18)

    I. Title.

[1] Separate title and author

[2] *In* note for title in the main work

[3] Main work

In order to prepare the particular analytical for Fig. 7.109, the cataloger must first have cataloged the entire set of the Harvard Classics (see Fig. 7.110 and 7.110a) and particularly v.18, Modern English drama (see Fig. 7.111).

Fig. 7.110

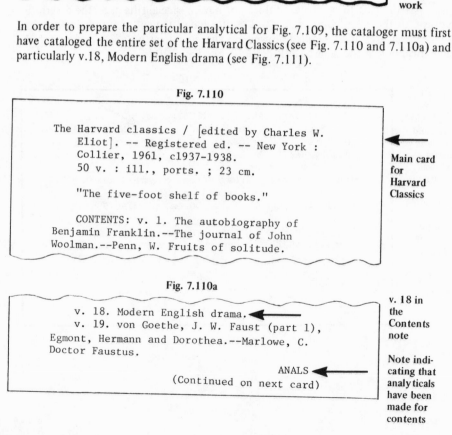

The Harvard classics / [edited by Charles W. Eliot]. -- Registered ed. -- New York : Collier, 1961, c1937-1938.
    50 v. : ill., ports. ; 23 cm.

    "The five-foot shelf of books."

    CONTENTS: v. 1. The autobiography of Benjamin Franklin.--The journal of John Woolman.--Penn, W. Fruits of solitude.

Main card for Harvard Classics

Fig. 7.110a

    v. 18. Modern English drama.
    v. 19. von Goethe, J. W. Faust (part 1), Egmont, Hermann and Dorothea.--Marlowe, C. Doctor Faustus.

                                    ANALS
                    (Continued on next card)

v. 18 in the Contents note

Note indicating that analyticals have been made for contents

Fig. 7.111

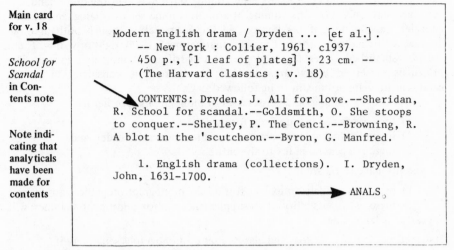

Main card for v. 18 →

School for Scandal in Contents note

Note indicating that analyticals have been made for contents

```
Modern English drama / Dryden ... [et al.] .
  -- New York : Collier, 1961, c1937.
  450 p., [1 leaf of plates] ; 23 cm. --
  (The Harvard classics ; v. 18)

  CONTENTS: Dryden, J. All for love.--Sheridan,
R. School for scandal.--Goldsmith, O. She stoops
to conquer.--Shelley, P. The Cenci.--Browning, R.
A blot in the 'scutcheon.--Byron, G. Manfred.

     1. English drama (collections).  I. Dryden,
John, 1631-1700.
                          ⟶ ANALS.
```

157E. Added entries as analytical entries

157E1. "If the catalog entry for a work includes (in title, contents, or other place) reference to a part for which analytical entry is required, an added entry may be made instead of a separate analytical entry." See Fig. 7.112.

Fig. 7.112

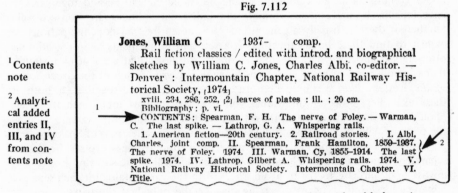

[1] Contents note

[2] Analytical added entries II, III, and IV from contents note

```
Jones, William C      1937-    comp.
     Rail fiction classics / edited with introd. and biographical
  sketches by William C. Jones, Charles Albi, co-editor. --
  Denver : Intermountain Chapter, National Railway His-
  torical Society, [1974]
     xviii, 234, 286, 252, [2] leaves of plates : ill. ; 20 cm.
     Bibliography: p. vi.
     CONTENTS: Spearman, F. H. The nerve of Foley. -- Warman,
  C. The last spike. -- Lathrop, G. A. Whispering rails.
     1. American fiction--20th century.  2. Railroad stories.    I. Albi,
  Charles, joint comp.  II. Spearman, Frank Hamilton, 1859-1937.
  The nerve of Foley.  1974.  III. Warman, Cy, 1855-1914.  The last
  spike.  1974.  IV. Lathrop, Gilbert A.  Whispering rails.  1974.  V.
  National Railway Historical Society. Intermountain Chapter.  VI.
  Title.
```

Note that added entries II, III, and IV are author-title added entries.

MONOGRAPHS IN COLLECTED SETS

The discussion that follows concerns a descriptive cataloging problem that is not specifically covered by AACR, revised Chapter 6. A publication issued in two or more volumes may be defined as a set. Usually, monographs in collected sets represent various types of collections or compilations by one or more authors. Many reference books are examples of monographs in collected sets. The number of physical volumes making up such a set may cause problems in cataloging and classification. If the works of a single author are collected in several volumes, the cataloger may be tempted to class each volume separately. On the other hand, the cataloger may only have one volume of a multi-volume set to catalog, and he may consider classing it as if the library had the entire set. Although both of these approaches are arguable, the fact remains that neither is really right or wrong. There are no established codes for cataloging and classifying monographs in sets. The principles presented below are provided merely for the consideration of the cataloger; they are not meant to be followed slavishly.

One usually catalogs and classes a set of monographs together if

1) they are issued in a uniform format,
2) the individual volumes are numbered in consecutive order, and
3) there is a general index to the entire set.

Two additional criteria are if

1) patrons are likely to expect to find the monographs together as a set, and
2) there is a possibility that supplements and/or additional volumes will appear at a later date.

However, one usually catalogs and classes a set of monographs separately if

1) not all the volumes of the set are in the library, nor are they likely to be added to the library's collection, and
2) each volume has a separate title, especially in the case of literary works.

Obviously, these two sets of principles are somewhat contradictory and demand individual application in actual practice. The following examples are designed to clarify these problems. First, it should be quite obvious that a set of books comprising an encyclopedia should be cataloged and classed together. An encyclopedia is uniform in format; the individual volumes are consecutively numbered; there is usually a general index to the entire encyclopedia; patrons do expect to find these books together as a set; and supplements and/or yearbooks often appear at a later date. Second, it similarly follows that a set of monographs that is a collection of great works (such as the *Harvard Classics* or the *Great Books of the Western World*) should be both cataloged and classed together. In both of these examples, however, individual volumes have one or more separate titles. Should the volumes in either of these two sets (both of which, for example, include the plays of William Shakespeare) be classed with other collections of Shakespeare's plays or not? Should the non-literary material in either of these two sets be classed separately in its appropriate location? Either choice will create some problems. It is unwise in either case to try to avoid a record in the card catalog for each separate bibliographical unit. The card catalog may be the only key the patron uses for discovering the library's holdings. See AACR 157D and Fig. 7.109 for one method of solving this particular problem. The use of analytical entries in the example for Rule 157D allows these sets of monographs to be cataloged and classed together while also providing separate entries for individual bibliographical units.

The collected or complete works of one author present another problem of monographs in sets. This is particularly apparent if the author writes in more than one discipline. For example, Will Durant's *Story of Civilization* may be cataloged together or separately. If this work is cataloged together as a set, the individual parts or volumes are listed in a contents note; and the set receives general subject added entries and a general subject classification number. See Fig. 7.113. On the other hand, if each of the parts of this work are cataloged separately, the relationship of each part to the main work is shown by a series note. This latter approach allows for a complete imprint, including the date for each part, and for separate specific subject added entries. See Fig. 7.114. Cataloging each part separately allows the cataloger to choose whether to classify each part separately or in the more general number. There are many advantages to the separate cataloging of parts—advantages in both descriptive and subject cataloging—but it must be remembered that this approach requires the production of more cards.

Fig. 7.113

Title of
entire set

```
Durant, William James, 1885-
    ──► The story of civilization / by Will Durant.
-- New York : Simon and Schuster, 1935-
       v. : ill., maps, ports. ; 28 cm.

     Includes bibliographies and indexes.
     CONTENTS. pt. 1. Our oriental heritage.--pt.
2. The life of Greece.--pt. 3. Caesar and Christ.
--pt. 4. The age of faith.--pt. 5. The
Renaissance.--pt. 6. The Reformation.
```

General
subject
added
entries

```
     1. Civilization.   2. World history.
I. Title.
```

Durant's *Story of Civilization* cataloged as a set using a contents note for the individual bibliographical units.

Fig. 7.114

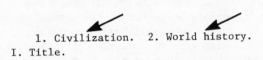

¹Title of
individual
volume

²Title of
set

³Specific
subject
added
entries

```
Durant, William James, 1885-
     1 ──► Caesar and Christ : a history of Roman
        civilization and of Christianity from their
        beginnings to A.D. 325 / by Will Durant. --
        New York : Simon and Schuster, 1944.
             751 p. : ill., maps, ports. ; 28 cm. -- (His
     2 ──► The story of civilization ; pt. 3)
           3 ──►             ◄── 3
             1. Rome--History.   2. Rome--Antiquities.
        3. Christianity.   4. Church history.   I. Title.
        II. Series.
```

One part of Durant's work cataloged as a separate bibliographical unit using a series note to relate to the collected set.

The advantage of the second example (Fig. 7.114) is that this method provides separate subject headings for each individual volume. The classification problems will be dealt with in Chapter 10 of this textbook.

8 SERIALS

INTRODUCTION

A **serial** is a publication issued in successive parts at regular or irregular intervals and intended to continue indefinitely. Serials include both periodicals and non-periodicals. A **periodical** may be defined as a serial that has a distinctive title and that is issued more frequently than twice a year, with each issue containing articles by several contributors. **Non-periodicals** are all other forms of serials, such as yearbooks, annuals, memoirs, transactions and proceedings of societies, and any series cataloged together instead of separately.

A clear distinction should be made between serials and monographs. A **monograph** represents a complete bibliographic unit; it may be issued in successive parts at regular or irregular intervals, but it is *not* intended to continue indefinitely. In most cases, of course, a monographic publication is completed in one volume. However, there are certain types of monographs that are often treated as serials by libraries because they are not complete in one volume. These include continuations of sets, provisional serials, and pseudo-serials. A **continuation of a set** is a non-serial—i.e., monographic—set in process of publication. The *Oxford History of English Literature* and the *Encyclopedia of Library and Information Science* are examples of continuations of sets. Neither publication is presently complete although many individual volumes have been issued. Such publications require a special order record—i.e., a standing order—for follow-up purposes; if such works are cataloged as sets (see Chapter 7, pp. 181-183), this creates problems of accurate records in the library's holdings record for the set. **Provisional serials** are those publications which are treated as serials while in the process of publication and as non-serials when complete. The justification for such treatment is often a particularly lengthy period of publication and/or a complicated numbering of individual issues. Either of the two previous examples of continuations of sets could be treated by individual libraries as provisional serials. A **pseudo-serial** is a frequently reissued and revised publication that is generally treated as a monographic work at first publication but that is often treated as a serial after numerous successive editions have appeared. Serial numbering may be taken from the edition number or from the date of publication. Examples of pseudo-serials are Sir John Bernard Burke's *Genealogical and Heraldic History of the Peerage* (commonly called Burke's *Peerage*) or the *Guide to Reference Books* edited successively by Alice Bertha Kroeger, Isadore Mudge, and Constance Winchell. Monographic treatment of a pseudo-serial requires individual descriptive cataloging for each new edition as well as additional added entries for previous editors or compilers. If a pseudo-serial is treated as a serial, the main entry is made under title instead of author and will require only one set of catalog cards.

In general, the principles for cataloging serials are the same as those for cataloging monographic publications. On the other hand, certain physical characteristics of serial publications (e.g., numerous changes in bibliographic descriptions, including changes of titles) necessitate some special rules. The aim of these special rules is to prepare an entry that will stand the longest time and will allow necessary changes to be made with a minimum of modification. If the serial is still being published or if the library has only part of the set and hopes to complete it, an **open entry** is prepared according to the rules that are presented in this chapter.

The descriptive cataloging of serials is generally more complex than that of monographs because of their greatly varied and possibly intricate bibliographic structure. On the other hand, classification and subject headings are likely to be somewhat more general, therefore simpler. Indeed, in many libraries, periodicals are not classified at all but are shelved alphabetically by main entry. The detail with which serials are described may vary widely from library to library. Some consider a highly analytic description essential, while others reduce serials cataloging to the entry and holdings statement, a method most suitable for computer-produced catalogs.

The serials cataloger is likely to be faced with the problem of describing a full set completely although he has at hand only a few volumes or current issues. The chief sources of additional information are the *Union List of Serials*, *New Serials Titles*, *British Union Catalogue of Periodicals*, and *Ulrich's International Periodicals Directory*, with its companion publication, *Irregular Serials and Annuals: An International Directory*.[1] Other important sources are the Library of Congress catalogs and national and trade bibliographies, as well as publishers' catalogs. *Titles in Series* is useful for its lists of titles in monographic series, especially those published by university presses.[2] In addition, a recent Library of Congress publication, *Monographic Series*, lists all monographs cataloged by the Library of Congress which appear as parts of series since 1974 as well as all revised cards regardless of the date of publication. This is a quarterly publication with annual cumulations.[3]

---

[1] *Union List of Serials in Libraries of the United States and Canada*, 3d ed. (New York, H. W. Wilson, 1965); coverage through 1949. *New Serials Titles: A Union List of Serials Commencing Publication after December 31, 1949* (Washington, Library of Congress, 1953-). *Ulrich's International Periodicals Directory 1969-70*, 13th ed. (New York, Bowker, 1969; suppls.). *Irregular Serials and Annuals: An International Directory* (New York, Bowker, 1967). *British Union Catalogue of Periodicals* (London, Butterworths, 1955-58; 4v.). *British Union Catalogue of Periodicals. New Periodical Titles* (London, Butterworths, 1964- ; quarterly).

[2] *Titles in Series: A Handbook for Librarians and Students* (Metuchen, N.J., Scarecrow Press, 1953-).

[3] Library of Congress, *Library of Congress Catalogs: Monographic Series* (Washington, 1974-).

The following rules, extracted from Chapter 7 of AACR, are the current rules for cataloging serials. Since 1971 the Library of Congress has, for the most part, followed these rules. LC serial cards prior to 1971 do not consistently follow AACR. Although these are the current rules for cataloging serials, they will be revised in the near future to conform with ISBD(S). Just as AACR Chapter 6 was revised for ISBD(M), so will Chapter 7 be revised; the revision will either appear as a separate publication or will be incorporated into the second edition of AACR. The revised rules will in all probability reflect **ISDS** (International Serials Data System), a network of national and international centers that develop and maintain registers of serial publications; this includes the assignment of ISSN's (International Standard Serial Number) and key titles. The Library of Congress is the national center for the United States. The international center is sponsored by Unesco's Unisist project in Paris.[4] Current Library of Congress practice in cataloging of serials attempts to harmonize ISDS requirements, AACR Chapter 7, and ISBD(S) as well as the appropriate sections of ISBD(M).[5] It should be noted that the special punctuation required by ISBD(S), similar to ISBD(M), has not yet been adopted by the Library of Congress and is not reflected in its current cataloging of serials, as the examples given below demonstrate.

DESCRIPTION

Rule 160. Variations from the cataloging of monographic publications

The main differences between the form of the catalog entry for a serial and that for a monograph may be summarized as follows:

160A. "A serial that changes its title or that is entered under a corporate body that changes its name during the course of publication is normally cataloged with a separate entry for each new title or new name of the corporate body. A note relates the new title to the serial it continues. See Figs. 8.1 through 8.14.

160B. "A serial publication in several volumes with varying bibliographical details is described from the latest volume, with the variations from that volume noted, whereas a monographic work in several volumes is cataloged from the first volume, with variations noted.

---

[4] International Centre for the Registration of Serial Publications, *Guidelines for ISDS* (Paris: United Nations Educational, Scientific and Cultural Organization, Unisist, International Serials Data System, 1973).

[5] For LC interpretations, see *Cataloging Service*, bulletin 112 (Winter 1975): 10-12 and bulletin 110 (Summer 1974): 3.

160C. "The subtitle is frequently omitted or presented in a supplementary note.

160D. "The author statement does not appear in the body of the entry; if needed, it is presented in a supplementary note.

160E. "The editor statement is given as a supplementary note instead of in the body of the entry, because the more prominent position following the title is devoted to the statement of 'holdings' and because, when editors change, the adding of that information is more convenient and economical if the editor statement has been given in a note.

160F. "The catalog entry for a serial publication should show which parts of it are in the library's collection or refer to another catalog such as the shelflist or a special record of serials.

160G. "An important feature for the characterization of a serial, and occasionally for its identification, is the frequency of its publication.

160H. "If the statement of holdings does not show the duration of publication, supplementary notes are essential to show it. This includes the facts of suspension and resumption of publication.

160J. "The fact that a serial is the organ of a society or other body is stated.

160K. "Serial publications frequently have special numbers that must be described."

Rule 161. Body of the entry: organization and source of data

161A. "The body of the entry consists of the following elements, in the order given here: title, subtitle (if required), volume designation and dates of the serial as published (or of the volumes held by the library), and imprint. The title and imprint are taken from a single source as far as possible. If the publication has no title page, the title is taken from the cover, caption, masthead, editorial pages, or other place, the order of preference being that of this listing. The source of the data is specified if it is not the title page, cover, caption, or masthead. However, if there is no title page or cover, and the caption or other titles differ, the source of the title used is specified and the other titles are noted.

161B. "The title page, or title page substitute, chosen as the basis of the catalog entry is that of the latest volume. Exception to this rule may be made in the case of a serial which has ceased publication, if an earlier title has continued for a much longer period of time than the later title. In such a case the title chosen for the body of the entry is the one that persisted the longest."

Rule 162. Recording of the title

162A. "A short title is generally used in cataloging serial publications if this makes it possible to disregard minor variations in the wording on various issues, especially if these occur in subtitles. Subtitles are omitted unless necessary for identification or for clarification of the scope of the publication. A long subtitle which is considered necessary may be presented in a note instead of following the title in the body of the entry." See Fig. 8.1.

Fig. 8.1

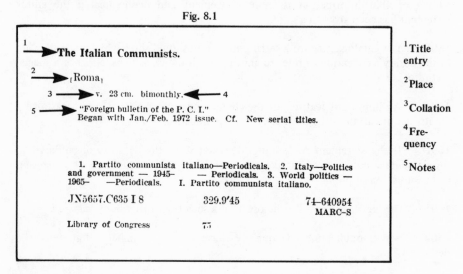

Rule 163. Holdings

163A. General rules

163A1. "The statement of the volumes 'held' by the library is given immediately after the title or subtitle in the catalog entry. If the work has ceased publication, this statement consists of the designation of the first and last volumes or parts, followed by the dates of the first and last volumes or parts."

v. 1-50; 1901-1950.

"If the library does not have all the volumes that have been published, the extent of the complete set is recorded, provided the information is available (the chief sources of this information are *New Serial Titles*, the *Union List of Serials*, and the *British Union Catalogue of Periodicals*). The volumes that are lacking are specified in a supplementary note." See Fig. 8.2.

Fig. 8.2

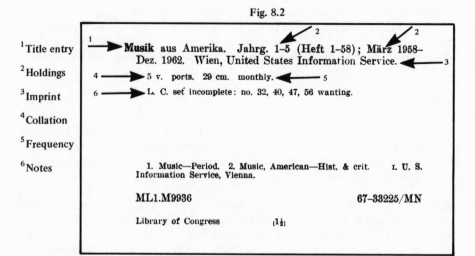

¹ Title entry

² Holdings

³ Imprint

⁴ Collation

⁵ Frequency

⁶ Notes

163A2. "If the work is still in progress of publication, the statement consists only of the data relating to the first issue." See Fig. 8.3.

Fig. 8.3–Work "in progress" v.1– summer 1973–

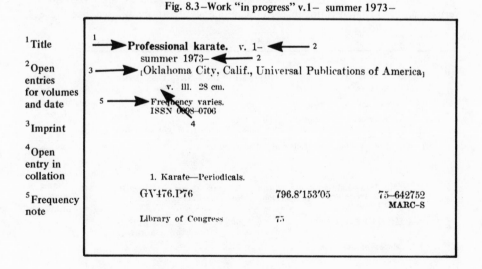

¹ Title

² Open entries for volumes and date

³ Imprint

⁴ Open entry in collation

⁵ Frequency note

Methods of showing holdings vary widely.⁶ It is common not to add a permanent note of volumes missing to the card set because of the possibility of

⁶ See Rosamond H. Danielson, "Serials Holdings Information Service in Research Libraries," *Library Resources and Technical Services* 10 (Summer 1966): 261-283.

completing the set; a penciled note is frequently used. Or, to facilitate adding volumes of titles "in progress" or filling gaps, check cards may be used, filed behind the main entry card or the shelflist card, or in another location. In any case, notes or references should direct the patron to the source of holdings information if it does not appear on all cards.

163B. Designation

163B1. "The statement of holdings is limited to volume designation for those publications that do not carry dates by which the parts are identified; volume designation may be a volume number, edition number, or other designation according to the usage of the publisher.

163B2. "The date may consist of the month, day, and year; month or season and year; or year alone, depending upon the frequency of publication and the usage of the publisher. If each issue of a serial bears both a date of publication and an indication of period covered by the contents, the latter is given in the holdings statement."

163C. Abbreviation and numerals

"Terms used in volume designations and for months are given in the vernacular, abbreviated if possible. Arabic numerals are normally used. See Fig. 8.4.

Fig. 8.4

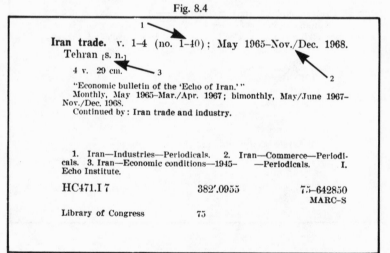

Iran trade. v. 1–4 (no. 1–40) : May 1965–Nov./Dec. 1968.
Tehran ₍s. n.₎

4 v. 29 cm. 3

"Economic bulletin of the 'Echo of Iran.' "
Monthly, May 1965–Mar./Apr. 1967; bimonthly, May/June 1967–Nov./Dec. 1968.
Continued by : Iran trade and industry.

1. Iran—Industries—Periodicals. 2. Iran—Commerce—Periodicals. 3. Iran—Economic conditions—1945– —Periodicals. I.
Echo Institute.

HC471.I 7   382'.0955   75–642850
                                                MARC-S

Library of Congress   75

[1] Whole numbers in parentheses

[2] Months abbreviated

[3] Name of publisher unknown

Note: Serials and other non-ISBD cataloging use ISBD abbreviations such as " [s.n.] " and "ill."

163D. Punctuation

163D1. "Volume, report, and edition numbers are separated from the dates by a semicolon. If there are two or more series of volume numbers, commas are used between volumes and dates, and semicolons between series. Whole numbers, i.e., the numbers of parts which continue from one volume to another, are enclosed in parentheses following the volume numbers." See Fig. 8.4.

163D2. "A diagonal line is used in recording the date of a report or other publication that covers either a year that is not a calendar year or a period of more than one year. A dash connects the dates of the first and the final issue." See Fig. 8.5.

Fig. 8.5

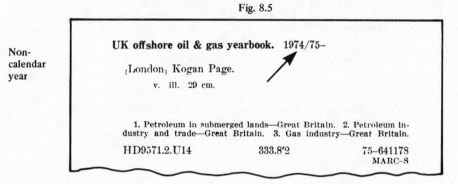

Non-
calendar
year

UK offshore oil & gas yearbook. 1974/75–

ₜLondonₗ Kogan Page.

v. ill. 29 cm.

1. Petroleum in submerged lands—Great Britain. 2. Petroleum industry and trade—Great Britain. 3. Gas industry—Great Britain.

HD9571.2.U14   333.8'2   75–641178
                                        MARC-S

Rule 164. Imprint

164A. General rules

164A1. "The imprint in the catalog entry for a serial publication is limited to the place of publication and the name of the publisher if dates are recorded in the statement of holdings following the title. If dates are not recorded in the statement of holdings, they are given in the imprint, as for monographs." The Library of Congress frequently uses an imprint date following the name of the publisher if that date differs significantly from the coverage date, for example in the case of reprint editions or of titles issued serially but providing retrospective coverage. The date may also be used in the imprint to emphasize that it does not show coverage, but rather the year of publication. See Fig. 8.6.

Fig. 8.6

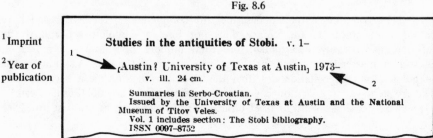

[1]Imprint

[2]Year of
publication

Studies in the antiquities of Stobi. v. 1–

ₜAustin? University of Texas at Austinₗ 1973–

v. ill. 24 cm.

Summaries in Serbo-Croatian.
Issued by the University of Texas at Austin and the National Museum of Titov Veles.
Vol. 1 includes section: The Stobi bibliography.
ISSN 0097-8752

164A2. "If the record of the final volume is not included in the statement of holdings, the imprint begins a new line in the catalog entry."

164B. Place of publication

"Changes in the place of publication that do not warrant specific description are indicated by the abbreviation 'etc.' following the place of publication." See Fig. 8.7.

Fig. 8.7

Ulysses S. Grant Association.
    Newsletter—Ulysses S. Grant Association. v. 1–10; Oct. 1963–July 1973. Carbondale, Ill., ₍etc.₎ Ulysses S. Grant Association.

    10 v. 28 cm. quarterly.
    ISSN 0041-6266.

    1. Grant Ulysses Simpson, Pres. U. S., 1822–1885—Periodicals.
    2. Ulysses S. Grant Association—Periodicals.

E672.U38a   973.8′2′0924   75–641965
                                         MARC-S

Library of Congress   75

[etc.]
indicating
more than
one place
of
publication

164C. Publisher

164C1. "If the name of the publisher is essentially the same as the title of the publication, as is often the case with periodicals, it is omitted from the imprint." See Fig. 8.1.

Rule 165. Collation

165A. General rule

"The collation statement describes the completed set for serials that have ceased publication. If the library does not have a complete set and if the information is easily ascertained, the total number of volumes is indicated. Illustrative matter is described for the set as a whole. If the serial is still in process of publication, the collation describes the set as it is at the time it is cataloged." The frequency of publication is given immediately after the collation if it can be expressed by a single word or brief phrase. If not, it appears as the first note. See Fig. 8.8.

Fig. 8.8

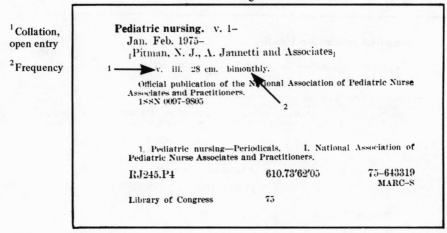

¹Collation, open entry

²Frequency

Pediatric nursing. v. 1–
Jan. Feb. 1975–
₍Pitman, N. J., A. Jannetti and Associates₎

1 ⟶ v. ill. 28 cm. bimonthly.
Official publication of the National Association of Pediatric Nurse
Associates and Practitioners.
ISSN 0097-9805
2

1. Pediatric nursing—Periodicals.   I. National Association of
Pediatric Nurse Associates and Practitioners.

RJ245.P4   610.73′62′05   75-643319
                                                   MARC-S

Library of Congress   75

Rule 167. Notes

167A. General rules

"Many of the supplementary notes necessary to the cataloging of serial publications are presented in a conventional style." The following figures indicate some typical notes. For further details, consult subsections in AACR 167. Also see *Cataloging Service*, bulletin 112 (Winter 1975): 12-13, for LC interpretations.

Fig. 8.9

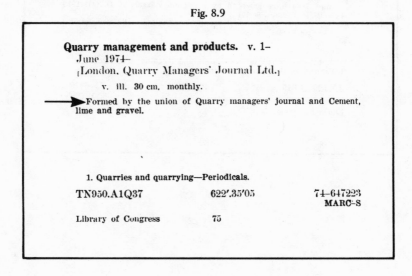

Merger
note

Quarry management and products. v. 1–
June 1974–
₍London, Quarry Managers' Journal Ltd.₎
v. ill. 30 cm. monthly.
⟶Formed by the union of Quarry managers' journal and Cement,
lime and gravel.

1. Quarries and quarrying—Periodicals.

TN950.A1Q37   622′.35′05   74-647223
                                                   MARC-S

Library of Congress   75

Fig. 8.10

Industrial information bulletin.

Canberra, Australian Government Publishing Service.

    v. 26 cm. monthly.

1 ——▶Continues : Australia. Dept. of Labour and National Service. Industrial Relations Division. Industrial information bulletin.
2 ——▶Vols. for 19   –73 issued by the Australian Dept. of Labour; 1974–   by the Australian Dept. of Labor and Immigration.

     1. Arbitration, Industrial—Australia—Cases.   I. Australia. Dept. of Labour. II. Australia. Dept. of Labor and Immigration.

                344′.91′018914   75–641909
                                       MARC–S

Library of Congress   75

Continues note

Issuing agency note

Fig. 8.11

International studies newsletter.

  ₍Pittsburgh, International Studies Association₎

    v. 28 cm. monthly.   2

1 ——▶Began with Mar. 1974 issue. Cf. New serial titles. ◀——
      Mar. 1974 issue preceded by Preliminary issues A–D, fall 1973–Feb. 1974. Cf. New serial titles.
3 ——▶Supersedes : International Studies Association. ISA newsletter.
     ISSN 0007–8965
4 ◀

     1. International relations—Study and teaching—Periodicals.
I. International Studies Association.

JX1291.I 615   327′.07   75–641875
                                         MARC–S

Library of Congress   75

[1] Date of origin

[2] Source of information

[3] Supersedes note

[4] ISSN note

Fig. 8.12

Merger
note

Journal of fluids engineering. v. 95–
Mar. 1973–
ₗNew Yorkₗ American Society of Mechanical Engineers.

v. illus. 29 cm. quarterly.

➤With Journal of engineering materials and technology, supersedes
Journal of basic engineering, continuing its vol. numbering, and
called also Series I of the society's Transactions.
ISSN 0098-2202

1. Fluid mechanics—Periodicals. 2. Fluids—Periodicals.
I. American Society of Mechanical Engineers.

TA357.J66   620.1′06   74–644131
                                                        MARC-S

Library of Congress   75

Fig. 8.13

[1] Cover title
note

[2] Editors
note

Fodor's Japan and Korea. 1975–
New York, D. McKay Co.

1

v. ill. 21 cm.

Cover title, 1975–   : Fodor's Japan and S. Korea.
Editors: 1975–   E. Fodor and others.
ISSN 0098-1613

2

1. Japan — Description and travel — 1945–   — Guide-books. 2.
Korea—Description and travel—1953–   —Guide-books.   I. Fodor,
Eugene, 1905–   ed. II. Title: Fodor's Japan and S. Korea.

DS811.F6   915.2′04′4   75–643542
                                                        MARC-S

Library of Congress   75

Fig. 8.14

The U. S. factbook: the American almanac. 1975–

New York, Grosset & Dunlap.

    v. ill. 22 cm. annual.

1 ————▶ Continues: The American almanac; the U. S. book of facts, statistics & information.

2 ————▶ Commercial ed. of: U. S. Bureau of the Census. Statistical abstract of the United States.

     ISSN 0097-9589

    1. United States—Statistics—Periodicals.

HA202.A68   317.3   75-642066

                   MARC-S

Library of Congress   75

[1]Continues note

[2]Edition note

9 CATALOGING OF NONBOOK MATERIALS

INTRODUCTION

This chapter covers the *Anglo-American Cataloging Rules* for four distinct groups of nonbook materials: maps and atlases; audiovisual media and special instructional materials; printed music; and sound recordings. These nonbook materials represent only one category of the items that ·comprise the "special materials" group; special materials are not handled the same way as monographs are handled. Some of the other special materials categories are serials, pamphlets, rare books, government publications, archival material, and manuscripts as well as nonbook materials. Maps, atlases, globes, motion pictures, filmstrips, video-recordings, slides, transparencies, charts, dioramas, flash cards, games, kits, microscope slides, models, realia, printed music, sound recordings, pictures, and photographs are all considered to be forms of nonbook materials. Special materials may be both cataloged and classified if desired.

An administrative decision within each library determines whether to catalog and/or classify each of these special materials. It is not necessary to do complete descriptive cataloging and subject cataloging for all special materials. Libraries may catalog special materials but not classify them. Since most special materials can not be physically shelved with the corresponding monographic materials, a book classification system, which would shelve like materials together, is unnecessary. Some special materials may have special classification schemes (e.g., maps and printed music); some may use a simple accession or serial number (e.g., microfilms); some may be arranged alphabetically (e.g., periodicals); and some may be arranged by subject headings (e.g., pamphlets).

Some libraries provide separate catalogs for special materials. For example, all the sound recordings (i.e., phonograph records) may be listed in a separate card catalog. A visible index and a computer print-out for periodicals are other examples of separate catalogs for separate materials. Some libraries indicate nonbook materials by using different colored cards in the card catalog or by putting colored strips on the top of regular buff catalog cards. These cards are filed in the main card catalog, but their colors identify them as cards for nonbook materials.

Although the question of whether to catalog and classify nonbook materials must be answered by the administration of the particular library, it is nonetheless recommended that some form of cataloging control be maintained over these materials. If the librarian cannot easily remember the contents of the collection, then cataloging control is needed. If the library only has six maps, for instance, there is little need to catalog and/or classify them. Sixty maps, however, or even sixteen, may well need to be cataloged. The disadvantage of failing to catalog descriptively any special materials is that the patron must look somewhere other than in the main card catalog for the record of the material. It is strongly recommended that as many special materials as possible be cataloged descriptively and thus recorded in the main card catalog; a single main card catalog is preferable to separate catalogs for each different type of material.

This chapter is designed to demonstrate the general patterns for descriptive cataloging of the four types of nonbook materials indicated. Some nonbook materials require special adjustments of the standard descriptive cataloging practices for monographs (e.g., How many pages does a globe have? What is the height of a cassette recording?). On the other hand, the cataloging for two forms of nonbook materials is quite similar to that used for monographs: these are atlases and printed music. As the rules below will demonstrate, however, even these two forms require special revisions of the monographic rules—the collation for atlases requires special attention to the number of pages and plates as well as to the illustrative material, and printed music usually requires the consistent use of uniform titles. It should be noted that both atlases and printed music follow the general spacing and punctuation as given in AACR, revised Chapter 6, so these two nonbook forms do appear in ISBD(M) format. AACR, revised Chapter 12, provides a similar ISBD format for audiovisual media and special instructional material. Cataloging of maps, globes, and sound recordings does not presently use ISBD format for spacing or punctuation; it does, however, follow the new abbreviation forms found in revised Chapter 6.

The primary purpose of this chapter is to present the general rules from AACR for cataloging nonbook materials. An additional purpose is to provide the cataloger with information about certain other possible systems of cataloging nonbook materials.

Although the Library of Congress and the AACR have for some time provided national rules and practices for cataloging nonbook materials, these rules have not been followed by many libraries, for a variety of reasons. New media and new packaging of media have been developing more rapidly than have the rules and cataloging practices pertaining to them. Some libraries found AACR, Part III, "Non-Book Materials," to be too complicated, too sophisticated, or otherwise inappropriate for their collections. School libraries particularly sought simpler card formats, which could be used by children. In addition, commercial and centralized processing agencies produced nonbook catalog cards in a highly inconsistent, individual, and often incompatible fashion.[1] According to Hagler, the major reason for these problems is "not that we don't know our own minds, but that the material we are trying to catalog adequately is still in a state of flux as to its own indicia of identification. We are, by analogy, trying to catalog the book before the title page came into existence."[2] Another major problem has been the development

---

[1] Two recent and useful articles on this problem are Suzanne Massonneau's "Which Code for the Multimedia Catalog?" *School Media Quarterly* 2 (Winter 1974): 116-122; and Ronald Hagler's "The Development of Cataloging Rules for Nonbook Materials," *Library Resources and Technical Services* 19 (Summer 1975): 268-278.

[2] Hagler, "The Development of Cataloging Rules," p. 277.

and proliferation of local do-it-yourself cataloging methods for nonbook materials. Massonneau observes that

> the do-it-yourself cataloging methods which have been devised by librarians in the past are no longer adequate to cover the many types of materials and present stimulated usage. Furthermore, the impetus toward standardized cataloging which has been engendered by cooperative cataloging, centralized processing, and the MARC program is not compatible with do-it-yourself codes.[3]

In 1970, the Canadian Library Association attempted to resolve this problem and to provide for an integrated system of cataloging both book and nonbook materials. The Association published a preliminary edition of *Nonbook Materials: The Organization of Integrated Collections*, by Jean Riddle Weihs, Shirley Lewis, and Janet Macdonald in consultation with the Technical Services Committee of the Canadian School Library Association. This was followed by an expanded first edition in 1973, with the approval of a Joint Advisory Committee on Nonbook Materials made up of representatives from the American Library Association, the Association for Educational Communications and Technology, the Canadian Library Association, and the Educational Media Association of Canada.[4] *Nonbook Materials* includes specific rules for 19 different forms of media. It is designed to be used in place of parts of AACR, Part III, and to be consistent with the rules in Parts I and II of AACR. It does not reflect ISBD punctuation, since AACR, revised Chapter 6, did not appear until 1974, a year after the publication of *Nonbook Materials*, 1st ed. Besides general and specific rules for entry and description, *Nonbook Materials* includes sections on cataloging policy, references to materials not listed in the catalog, a glossary and list of abbreviations, and guidelines for storage, care, and handling of media. Because of its origin, *Nonbook Materials* is often called the "Canadian Rules." It includes many necessary examples of cards. Although the "Canadian Rules" have been widely accepted, in general the individual rules are not stated as precisely as are the AACR; many minor rules are not stated at all but are only shown in the examples. Title main entry is favored, but materials whose origins are with printed forms (books) are entered under the main entry for the books. The "Canadian Rules" are now serving as one source for the revision of AACR, Part III.

Two basic problems confront any compilation of rules for nonbook materials. One is choice of main entry, and the other is the definition of nonbook materials. Choice of main entry is a problem particularly for those nonbook materials that are representations of monographic materials (e.g., the sound recording of a play or the motion picture version of a novel). The examples included in this chapter demonstrate part of this problem. Although the sound recording of a play may represent a literal recital of the words of the play, a motion picture is in most cases

---

[3]Massonneau, "Which Code . . . ," p. 116.

[4]Jean Riddle Weihs, Shirley Lewis, and Janet Macdonald, *Nonbook Materials: The Organization of Integrated Collections*, 1st ed. (Ottawa, Canadian Library Association, 1973).

only based on the plot line of the novel and does not represent a literal recital of the printed words. In short, a motion picture version of a novel represents an adaptation of the novel to another form. Further, because the creative responsibility for a motion picture is usually very diffuse, most codes would recommend entry under title. Massonneau points out that since subject headings "may be the most important line of access for nonbook media, integration is impossible unless both the book and nonbook forms have the same title."[5]

The definition of nonbook materials varies from code to code. AACR, Part III, includes such book-like materials as manuscripts, atlases, and music. The "Canadian Rules" do not include these three forms, concentrating instead on media center materials. These media center materials, with the major exceptions of sound recordings and pictures, are included in the AACR, revised Chapter 12, entitled "Audiovisual Media and Special Instructional Materials."[6] This revised chapter, issued in 1975, uses an ISBD format; a discussion of revised Chapter 12 begins on page 210 of this textbook.

The following chart demonstrates how the media included in the "Canadian Rules" are dispersed in AACR.

Nonbook Materials	AACR
Audiorecords	Chapter 14, called Sound recordings
Charts	Chapter 12
Dioramas	Chapter 12
Filmstrips	Chapter 12
Flash cards	Chapter 12
Games	Chapter 12
Globes	Chapter 11
Kits	Chapter 12
Machine Readable Data Files	Currently being developed
Maps	Chapter 11
Microforms	Chapter 6
Microscope slides	Chapter 12
Models	Chapter 12
Motion pictures	Chapter 12
Pictures	Chapter 15
Realia	Chapter 12
Slides	Chapter 12 for sets, Chapter 15 for separates
Transparencies	Chapter 12
Videorecordings	Chapter 12

---

[5] Massonneau, "Which Code . . . ," p. 118.

[6] For a discussion of the background and development of this revised chapter, see B. R. Tucker's "A New Version of Chapter 12 of the *Anglo-American Cataloging Rules*," *Library Resources and Technical Services* 19 (Summer 1975): 260-267.

MAPS, ATLASES, ETC.

Introduction

There are basically two approaches to the cataloging of maps: one (of which the AACR are the primary example) calls for the main entry under the responsible body (personal or corporate); the other enters maps directly under geographic area and subject.[7] Three examples of the second approach are Samuel W. Boggs and Dorothy Cornwell Lewis, *The Classification and Cataloging of Maps and Atlases* (New York, Special Libraries Association, 1945); Special Libraries Association, Geography and Map Division, Committee on Map Cataloging, "Final Report," *Bulletin* 13 (October 1953): 19-24; and Roman Drazniowsky, *Cataloging and Filing Rules for Maps and Atlases in the Society's Collection*, rev. ed. (New York, American Geographical Society, 1969). *Nonbook Materials* calls for main entry under title, with an alternate method for main entry under geographic area.

Any elaborate discussion of this problem is outside the scope of an introductory text. We will discuss briefly, however, some of the essential points that support entry under geographical area and subject. One of the principal differences between maps and books is the primary identification of maps with area rather than with the author. Nearly all maps are published by corporate organizations and few maps, unlike books, are the responsibility of a personal author. Map users usually present their requests for a map of a particular area, with little concern for authorship of a map. The special subject information graphically presented on a map is the second item of significance to the user. Some special kind of record of the map's subject, other than a conventional subject heading, may be needed when the subject is specific and competes with area for the user's interest. Next, a map's date is of unusual significance; there is a need to record both the situation date and the publication date. Other features peculiar to a map for which there are no counterparts in a book are the scale and projection. Map titles, perhaps even more than book titles, are vague, incomplete, and misleading. The principal features shown on a map can best be described when information about area, date, and subject are used to supplement and clarify a vague title. Also, for pragmatic purposes the size is probably more important in cataloging of maps because it may directly influence the location of particular maps in a given collection.

Thus, contrary to the AACR, some methods of cataloging maps recommend the main entry under area or subject rather than under the author; in general, practices in individual libraries vary in this respect. It should be recognized, however, that most of these different methods are designed for a separate map library where cards are not interfiled with the rest of the collection. In fact, cataloging by a geographic area main entry approach is in contradiction to the basic principles and purposes of cataloging as stated in Chapter 2. Such a main entry combines subject cataloging and descriptive cataloging. The AACR approach

---

[7]Gail N. Neddermeyer, "Map Cataloging—An Introduction," *Drexel Library Quarterly* 9 (October 1973): 27-35; and Bill M. Woods, "Map Cataloging: Inventory and Prospect," *Library Resources and Technical Services* 3 (Fall 1959): 257-273. Both of these articles provide useful background reading on the problem.

maintains the basic catalog principles, which allows cards for maps to be interfiled in the library's main catalog.

The following figures provide three different examples of main entry by geographic area and one example of main entry by title.

Fig. 9.1–Boggs and Lewis Format

```
Call              Area, subject, date.
no.
          Title; author.  Edition.  Place, publisher,
     date.

          Scale.  Number of sheets, measurements.
     Projection.  Prime meridian.  Series note.


          Notes.




          Tracing.
```

Fig. 9.2–SLA, Geography and Map Division, Committee on Map Cataloging

```
Map
class.  Area.  Date.  Subject.  Scale.  Size.
no.
          Authority.
          Title.  Place of publication, publisher if
          other than authority, date of publication.

          Notes.

          Tracing.
```

Fig. 9.3—American Geographical Society

```
                                              Call
     Area, date.                              no.

        Title.

        Scale.
        Projection, if indicated.

        Author &/or publisher.
        Place of publication, date.
        Size.
        Notes.
```

Fig. 9.4—Weihs, *Nonbook Materials*

```
Call    Title (Map)
no.           Edition.  Producer or manufactor, date.

              Number of sheets.  Color.  Size.

           Scale.
           Prime meridian.
           Projection.
           Other notes.
```

Entry

Rule 210. General rule

"A map, a series or set of maps, an atlas, a relief model, or a globe is entered under the person or corporate body that is primarily responsible for its informational content. If the content has both geographic and subject aspects, the aspect that constitutes the principal feature of the work determines the rules of entry to be applied. If the subject aspect is the principal feature, the rules of entry for books and book-like materials are applied; if the geographic aspect is the principal feature, rule 211 is applied."

Rule 211. Non-subject maps, atlases, etc.

211A. Primary responsibility explicit

"A map, series or set of maps, or an atlas, etc., the content of which is mainly confined to geographic information, is entered under the person or corporate body that is explicitly indicated as primarily responsible for its geographic content. The appearance on a map of the phrase 'compiled by' or its equivalent in a foreign language is ordinarily understood to indicate primary responsibility. Likewise, the inclusion in the title of the name or part of the name of a corporate body, excluding a commercial firm other than a map publisher, is to be interpreted as indicating that body's primary responsibility. An added entry is made under any person or corporate body that has a significant share in the responsibility for the work." See Figs. 9.5 and 9.6.

Fig. 9.5

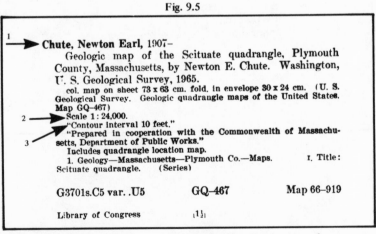

Note: Figs. 9.5 through 9.11 are referred to for illustration of more than one aspect of choice of entry or description of material. Also please note that sample cards for maps do not use ISBD punctuation, since ISBD for maps has not yet been adopted.

Fig. 9.6

<table>
<tr><td>Corporate
main entry</td><td>▶**Booth (R. C.) Enterprises, Harlan, Iowa.**
    The 1974 atlas of Adams County, Iowa. — Harlan, Iowa : R.
C. Booth Enterprises, ₍1974₎
    14 leaves : chiefly maps ; 46 cm.

    Blue line print.
    Cadastral maps of townships, scale ca. 1:32,000. ◀
    Corrected to Dec. 11, 1974.
    Previous editions (1963, 1971) also entered under Booth, cataloged with title:</td></tr>
</table>

<table>
<tr><td>Corporate
main entry</td><td>▶**Booth (R. C.) Enterprises, Harlan, Iowa.**
The 1974 atlas of Adams County, Iowa. — Harlan, Iowa : R.
C. Booth Enterprises, ₍1974₎

14 leaves : chiefly maps ; 46 cm.

Blue line print.
Cadastral maps of townships, scale ca. 1:32,000. ◀
Corrected to Dec. 11, 1974.
Previous editions (1963, 1971) also entered under Booth, cataloged with title:</td></tr>
<tr><td>Scale note</td><td>The ... atlas of Adams County, Iowa.

    1. Adams Co., Iowa—Maps. 2. Real property—Adams Co., Iowa—Maps.
I. Title.

   G1433.A3B6   1974   912'.777'76   75-307836
                                                       MARC

   Library of Congress   75   MAP</td></tr>
</table>

211B. Primary responsibility not explicit

"When the primary responsibility for a map, atlas, etc., is not explicit, the main entry is chosen according to the order of preference given below. Added entries are made under any persons or corporate bodies that have a significant share in the responsibility for the work."

1) The individual whose survey provided the basis for the cartography. See Figs. 9.5 and 9.8.

2) The cartographer. See Fig. 9.7.

3) The engraver, if known to be also a cartographer.

4) The corporate body, including a map publisher, that prepared the maps. See Figs. 9.9 through 9.11.

5) The title.

Fig. 9.7

<table>
<tr><td>Cartog-
rapher as
main entry</td><td>▶**Butler, Lowell.**
    A map of the marked historical sites of California. Com-
piled from the official registrations of the California State
Dept. of Natural Resources, by Phil Townsend Hanna and
William Webb. Cartography by Lowell Butler, drawings by
Gordon Brusstar, color by Harry Diamond. ₍Los Angeles₎
Automobile Club of Southern California, ᵉ1952.
    col. map on sheet 106 x 74 cm. fold. to 27 x 19 cm. ◀
    Scale ca. 1 : 1,300,000.
    Sites are numbered to correspond with descriptive list on verso.
    With insets of principal urban and historical areas.</td></tr>
<tr><td>Folded map</td><td>   1. California—Historical geography—Maps.   I. Hanna, Phil
Townsend, 1896–   II. Automobile Club of Southern California.
   G4361.S1 1952.B8   Map 52–1278</td></tr>
</table>

Description

Rule 212. Maps

212A. Title

212A1. "The title may be taken from any part of the face of the map. If two titles appear on the face of a map, the more appropriate one is selected, with the variant title recorded in a note." See Figs. 9.5 and 9.8 for added entries showing variant titles.

212A2. "The title for a composite set of maps is taken from latest sheet.

212A3. "If no title appears on the map, a title is supplied in brackets, preference being given to a) a title appearing on a portfolio, envelope, or other container, b) a title that has been used in reference sources to describe the same map, or c) the title of another edition of the map. If no satisfactory title is found, the name of the area shown may be used, in the form that appears on the map."

Fig. 9.8

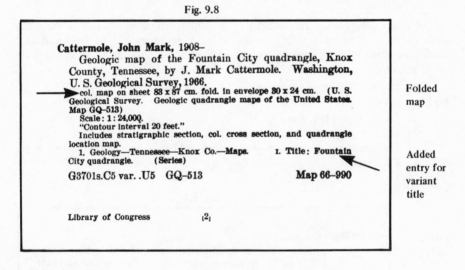

Cattermole, John Mark, 1908–
    Geologic map of the Fountain City quadrangle, Knox County, Tennessee, by J. Mark Cattermole. Washington, U. S. Geological Survey, 1966.
    col. map on sheet 83 x 87 cm. fold. in envelope 30 x 24 cm. (U. S. Geological Survey. Geologic quadrangle maps of the United States. Map GQ–513)
        Scale: 1 : 24,000.
        "Contour interval 20 feet."
        Includes stratigraphic section, col. cross section, and quadrangle location map.
        1. Geology—Tennessee—Knox Co.—Maps.   i. Title: Fountain City quadrangle.   (Series)

G3701s.C5 var. .U5   GQ–513   Map 66–990

Library of Congress   ⌊2⌋

Folded map

Added entry for variant title

212B. Collation

212B1. "The collation consists of the number of maps with a statement of size. For a single map on one sheet, the word 'map' or phrase 'col. map' is used. If, on the other hand, the work consists of a number of sheets, each of which has the characteristics of a complete map, it is described as a number of maps; e.g., '4 maps.'

212B2. "The size of the map (i.e., height followed by width) is given in centimeters, any fraction being counted as a full centimeter." See Figs. 9.5, 9.7, and 9.8.

212B4. "If a map is printed with an outer cover within which the map sheet is intended to be folded, or if the map sheet itself contains a panel or section designed to appear on the outside when the map is folded, the size of the map and the size of the sheet in folded form are both given." See Figs. 9.5, 9.7, and 9.8.

212C. Series statement

(See AACR 142) "If a map is part of more than one series, all series statements, each enclosed in its own set of parentheses, are given immediately following the collation. In choosing the series for the first position preference is given to the one that is more closely related to the heading."

212D. Scale

"If the statement of the scale of the map is inseparable from the title or subtitle, it is included in the body of the entry. Otherwise it is given in the first paragraph after the collation, in the style indicated" by examples 9.8 through 9.11. If the scale is calculated from the graphic scale, from the projection grid, or from other sources on the map, the fraction is qualified by the abbreviation "ca." If the representative fraction is computed arithmetically from a statement of approximate equivalence on the map, "ca." is also used. If the scale cannot be computed, or if a map is not drawn to scale, a note states this fact (e.g., "Scale not given" or "Not drawn to scale").

Fig. 9.9

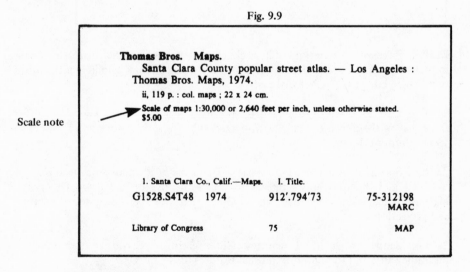

Scale note

Thomas Bros. Maps.
    Santa Clara County popular street atlas. — Los Angeles : Thomas Bros. Maps, 1974.
    ii, 119 p. : col. maps ; 22 x 24 cm.
    Scale of maps 1:30,000 or 2,640 feet per inch, unless otherwise stated.
    $5.00

    1. Santa Clara Co., Calif.—Maps.   I. Title.
    G1528.S4T48   1974   912'.794'73   75-312198
                                                       MARC

    Library of Congress   75   MAP

212E. Other supplementary notes

"Except for the scale note, and a second series statement (if any) which always follows it immediately, no definite order of notes can be prescribed. A logical sequence should be maintained as far as possible, but this need not be the same for every map. The following are the types of information frequently mentioned in supplementary notes and the approximate order of these notes in the catalog entry":

212E1. Holdings of composite sets.

212E2. Source of title and variant titles. See Fig. 9.10.

Fig. 9.10

Alexandria Drafting Company, Alexandria, Va.
  Fairfax County street and area designation atlas. — 1974 ed.
  — Alexandria, Va. : Alexandria Drafting Co., ₍1974₎

  36 p. : col. maps ; 36 cm.

  Cover title.
  Scale of maps 1:24,000 or 1" = 2000".
  Includes index.

Source
of title

  1. Fairfax Co., Va.—Maps.   I. Title.
  G1293.F2A4   1974   912'.755'291   75-311517
                                                  MARC

  Library of Congress   75   MAP

212E3. Physical description. Physical characteristics of the map (including imperfections and pecularities of the copy) are noted if they help in identification (e.g., "Blue line print," "Pictorial map").

212E4. Date of situation depicted by the map is noted if it is known to differ from that in the imprint—e.g., "Wells posted July 15, 1952; projection October 5, 1951." Imprint shows 1952.

212E5. Special cartographic information. The name of the map projection is given if stated and if sufficiently unusual to affect the use of the map. The prime meridian is named if other than that of Greenwich. See Fig. 9.8, notes of contour and projection.

212E6. Scope and cultural features. Notes given to clarify an indefinite or misleading title and to point out unusual features of the map.

212E7. Notes on authorship, including editors, engravers, etc.

212E8. Sources and bibliographical history. If it is known that a map has been based on a single source map, the source is noted.

212E9. Accompanying text.

212E10. Contents. A partial contents note is made to bring out important parts of a map, especially marginal or inset maps. See Figs. 9.5 and 9.7 for notes on insets, marginal data, sites, etc.

212E11. Pecularities of the copy being described.

Rule 215. Atlases

"The cataloging of atlases varies from general book cataloging practice in only two respects, as follows." (**Note**: Atlases use ISBD punctuation and spacing.)

215A. Collation

215A1. "To distinguish an atlas from a set of loose maps and to aid in identifying copies and distinguishing between editions, the collation given represents the pages or leaves of text and the number of maps, or the pages or leaves of maps (or a combination of these) according to the make-up of the atlas. If a separate section of numbered maps is also paged, the number of maps is ignored." See Fig. 9.11.

215A2. "Maps not forming a separate section are described in the same manner as maps in works that are not atlases." See Fig. 9.11.

215B. Scale

"If all the maps, except index maps, are of one or two scales, a supplementary note states the scale. This note is placed with notes on physical description." See Fig. 9.11.

Fig. 9.11

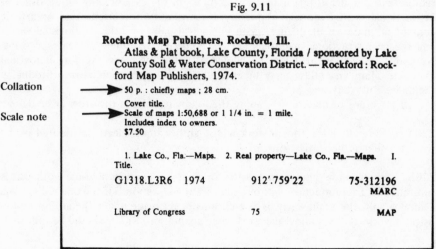

Collation

Scale note

> **Rockford Map Publishers, Rockford, Ill.**
>   Atlas & plat book, Lake County, Florida / sponsored by Lake County Soil & Water Conservation District. — Rockford : Rockford Map Publishers, 1974.
>   50 p. : chiefly maps ; 28 cm.
>   Cover title.
>   Scale of maps 1:50,688 or 1 1/4 in. = 1 mile.
>   Includes index to owners.
> $7.50
>
>   1. Lake Co., Fla.—Maps.   2. Real property—Lake Co., Fla.—Maps.   I. Title.
>   G1318.L3R6   1974   912'.759'22   75-312196
>   MARC
>
>   Library of Congress   75   MAP

AUDIOVISUAL MEDIA AND
SPECIAL INSTRUCTIONAL MATERIALS

Introduction

AACR 220-230 comprise the revised Chapter 12 of the AACR. This chapter formerly dealt only with cataloging of motion pictures and filmstrips. The revised Chapter 12, issued in 1975, has been expanded to include videorecordings, slides, and transparencies as well as instructional aids such as charts, dioramas, flash cards, games, kits, microscope slides, models, and realia. Other types of nonprint materials are covered in various AACR chapters: Chapter 6 for microform reproductions of books as well as for original editions in such a medium; Chapter 11 for maps, atlases, etc.; Chapter 14 for sound recordings; and Chapter 15 for pictures, designs, and similar two-dimensional representations. The rules for audiovisual media have been developed to parallel ISBD(M) as presented in revised Chapter 6; however, there are at this time no specific international standards for audiovisual media, so this entire chapter may be revised in the future, when an international standard bibliographic description for nonprint materials has been completed.

Entry

Rule 220. Main entry

The rules for entry of audiovisual media and instructional material supplement rather than replace the basic principles and rules in AACR, Chapter 1. Since the contribution by individual or corporate bodies to the intellectual or artistic content of the typical motion picture is diffuse, the "general principles" usually require entry under title for motion pictures. In the case of other audiovisual or instructional works for which primary responsibility for intellectual or artistic content is unknown or diffuse, main entry is usually by title. Audiovisual works and special instructional materials are not to be entered under commercial firms. Note this distinction between the choice of entry for maps and for audiovisual materials. Maps and atlases may be entered under the commercial firm producing them. See Rules 210 and 211.

For choice of main entry, apply the following rules in the order given below.

220A. "Enter under author a work whose authorship is clearly attributed in the work or other authoritative source."

220B. "Enter in the same manner as the original work any audiovisual work that is substantially a reproduction without significant adaptation." If the original work is a monograph, the main entry is not automatically made under the author of the original work. If the audiovisual work is an adaptation, Rule 7 should be followed.

220C. "Enter under title a work whose authorship is diffuse, indeterminate, or unknown."

Rule 221. Added entries

The following information can be mainly used for added entries. For additional possibilities consult AACR 33.

1) Author and title of a published work upon which a work is based or with which it is correlated.

2) The person or corporate body responsible for the production of the work.

3) The director of a theatrical motion picture if the director's name is important for the identification of the film.

Description

Rule 222. Organization of the description

Just as the descriptive part of the catalog entry for a monograph consists of six areas, the descriptive part of the catalog entry for audiovisual media and instructional materials also consists of six parallel or similar areas. These areas are:

1) the title, medium designator, and statement of responsibility area,
2) the edition area,
3) the release and publication area,
4) the physical description (or collation) area,
5) the series area, and
6) the notes area.

The title and statement of authorship area used for monographs is replaced here by the title, medium designator, and statement of responsibility area; the imprint area is replaced by the release and publication area; and the collation area is called the physical description area. The punctuation for each of these areas is very similar to the punctuation for monographs. Differences in punctuation will be cited below; more complex punctuation is discussed in AACR, revised Chapter 12.

Fig. 9.11a—Example Card for Title Entry

```
The title. [Medium designator] / statement of
   responsibility. -- Edition area. -- Location
   of releasing agent or publisher : releasing
   agent or publisher, date of release.

   Number of items, with running time : sound
and color ; dimensions & accompanying materials.
-- (Series name ; series number)

   Notes area
   SUMMARY note
   CONTENTS note

   Tracing
```

Rule 223. Source of the description

"The three primary sources of the description are listed below in the prescribed order of use:

1) the work itself, including the container when it is either an integral part of an item (e.g., a cassette) or its unifying part (e.g., the box of a kit or game),

2) accompanying material, e.g., manuals, guides, etc., issued with the item, and

3) the container, when it is not an integral part or unifying part of the item and therefore may be discarded."

When none of the primary sources contains the title or other data that can be used as the basis of the description, 1) the information may be supplied from any available source or 2) if no source is available, the cataloger must devise a title based on the content of the work. In either of these cases any information taken from a source other than a primary source is bracketed. Similarly, if the series statement is taken from a source other than a primary source, it must be bracketed.

Rule 225. Title/medium designator/statement of responsibility area

225A. Recording of the title

The title proper, other titles, and other title page information are transcribed exactly as they appear in the primary source except for punctuation and capitalization, which follow the rules for monographs. "The last element of title information is separate from the medium designator by a period-space (.)."

Example:

Rate of aging in mammals. [Chart]

225B. Medium designator

A generic term indicating the category of material to which the work belongs is always placed after all of the title information and enclosed in brackets. The most common medium designators are:

Chart
Diorama
Filmstrip
Flash card
Game
Kit
Microscope slide
Model
Motion picture
Realia

Slide (sets)
Transparency (sets)
Videorecording

Note: Sound recordings (phonorecords), individual slides, and pictures are not covered by these rules.

"The medium designator is separated from

a) the edition area or the release/publication area by a period-space-dash-space (. –)

Example:

Narcotics & dangerous drug abuse. [Chart] . – San Diego, Calif.

b) the statement of primary responsibility by a space-slash-space (/)."

Example:

Rate of aging in mammals. [Chart] / Alice Eberhart.

225C. Statement of responsibility

225C1. If a person or corporate body has been selected as main entry, transcribe the name as found in the work as a formal statement of responsibility. "If the main entry is not under such a person or body, transcribe such statements only if considered to be of primary significance in the identification of the work."

Examples:

National Geographic Society.
　　Indians of North America. [Filmstrip] / National
Geographic Society.

Oil : global weapon. [Filmstrip] / The New York Times,
　　Education Division.

225C2. If a production company or person responsible for the physical processes of production is stated in addition to the body or person primarily responsible for originating the work, name the production company or person second, with a phrase indicating the function. If no phrase is present, supply the bracketed words "[made by]" or their equivalent in the appropriate language. Follow the rules of punctuation of joint or subsidiary authorship for monographs (Rule 134D5).

Example:

Drilling and tapping cast steel. [Motion picture]
　　/ U.S. Office of education ; [made by] Emerson
　　Yorke Studio.

225C3. "If the only entity named is the publisher, manufacturer, etc., issuing the material, transcribe the name in the release/publication area (see 227), even though it might be conjectured that the person or body in question is also primarily responsible for conception, design, etc."

Example:

> Narcotics & dangerous drug abuse. [Chart] . – San
> Diego, Calif. : Winston Products for Education,
> 1968.

Rule 226. Edition area

The edition area is transcribed as found in the primary source and generally follows the rules for monographic edition areas. See Rule 135.

Rule 227. Release/publication area

227A. This area, which parallels the imprint area for monographs, consists of the location of releasing agent or publisher or other body responsible for issuing the work, and the date of the release or publication. The punctuation follows the rules for the imprint of monographic works: e.g., place-space-colon-space-name-comma-space-year-period. (See Rules 136-139.)

Example:

> Washington : The Office, 1942.
>
> New York : Doubleday, 1967.

227D. "For motion pictures and similar works, give also the year of production if it differs from the year of release or if the latter is unknown. Specify that the year is that of production by adding before it 'made' or the equivalent in the appropriate language, e.g., 1972, made 1960."

Example:

> Washington : U.S. Office of Education, 1948, made 1942.

Rule 228. Physical description area

228A. General rules

These rules are generally parallel to the style and punctuation of the collation area for monographs. The order of the physical description is 1) number of items with running time, 2) sound and color characteristics, and 3) dimensions. A fourth element is accompanying material, which may be recorded if a brief statement is adequate.

The number of items with running time is parallel to the pagination; the sound and color characteristics to the illustrative material; and the dimensions to the size. The punctuation follows directly the punctuation for a monographic collation:

> number of items with running time space-colon-space
> sound and color characteristics space-semicolon-space
> dimensions space-ampersand-space accompanying material;

or

> number of items with running time : sound and color
> characteristics ; dimensions & accompanying material

Example:

> 35 fr. : col. ; 35 mm.
>
> 3 models : col. ; 45x60 cm. & lesson plan.
>
> 1 cassette, 25 min. : sd., b&w ; super 8 mm.

This entire description area is separated from the series just as a monograph is, by a period-space-dash-space (. —).

228B. Charts, collation

"Give the number of charts, designating 'charts' or 'flipcharts,' indicate the presence or absence of color (using the abbreviations 'col.' or 'b&w'), and give their height and width." The dimensions are given in centimeters. The number of sheets is given for a flipchart.

Examples:

> 5 charts : col. ; 28x37 cm.
>
> 1 flipchart (42 sheets) : col. ; 59x42 cm. & teacher's guide.

228C. Dioramas, collation

These three-dimensional representations of scenes are described as the first note. Dioramas have no descriptive or collation area. Include in the note, as appropriate, the overall size in centimeters (height x length x depth) of the assembled display, the number of figures, the construction material, and the container.

Example:

> A display in color made of plastic; includes figures of a
> group of printers (4 pieces) and hand printing equipment (3 pieces)
> with an interior print-shop background; the assembled display
> measures 75x125x50 cm.

228D. Filmstrips, collation

The number of frames (or rolls), the presence or absence of color, and the width in millimeters is given for filmstrips. Accompanying materials may be the last element of the description. For the description of sound recordings in accompanying materials see Rule 252D. See revised Chapter 12, AACR 228D, for more complex problems with filmstrips and additional examples.

Examples:

18 fr. : b&w ; 35 mm. & cassette (4-track. mono. 2? min.) and guide.

48 double fr. : col. ; 35 mm. & disc (33 1/3 rpm. mono. 12 in 10 min.) and script.

5 rolls : col. ; 35 mm.

228E. Flash cards, collation

The descriptive area for flash cards is the same as that for charts, except that the term "cards" is used rather than "charts."

Example:

100 cards : b&w ; 13x4 cm.

228F. Games, collation

"If all the components of the game are in a container, give only the total number of 'pieces,' or use the phrase 'various pieces' if a count is impractical, followed by the phrase 'in container' and, within parentheses, the dimensions of the container (length x width x depth or length x width). If there is no container which holds all the components, enumerate them; the statement may include within parentheses details of physical description if such data can be stated succinctly."

Examples:

32 pieces in container (28x18x8 cm.)

various pieces in container (21x21x4 cm.)

1 board (30x30 cm.) and 32 pieces in container (28x18x6 cm.)

228G. Kits, collation

A kit consists of more than one medium packaged together and designed to be used as a single unit. If any one of the media is clearly the principal medium, catalog it under that medium and describe the other media as accompanying material. If the item is really a kit, describe the media contained in the package in alphabetical order by the form designator with the number of each media indicated and followed by the phrase "in container," and the dimensions of the container in parentheses in the same order as containers for games (228F).

Examples:

> 25 activity cards, 60 artifacts, 3 books, 3 filmstrips,
> 1 learning guide, 25 study prints (25 copies each), 2 sound
> recordings (tape cassettes), and 14 transparencies.

> 2 books (36 copies each), 1 sound recording (disc),
> 4 ditto masters, 4 posters, 35 student handbooks, and
> teacher's guide in container (37x4?x25 cm.)

Note: In the above examples the phrase "sound recording" is not a medium designator; "tape cassette" or "disc" is used as the alphabetizing element.

228H. Microscope slides, collation

"Give the number of 'slides' and indicate if they are stained."

Examples:

> 9 slides : stained.

> 25 slides : stained & manual.

228J. Models, collation

Models or three-dimensional representations of real things are described by listing the number of "models" or "mock-ups"; in addition, if the fact that a model is colored is deemed significant, it may be noted, or the color may be named; the dimensions may be given in centimeters.

Examples:

> 1 model : col. ; 34x8 cm.

> 2 models : red ; 30x21x6 cm.

228K. Motion pictures, collation

Motion pictures are described by 1) the number of "reels," "cartridges," or "cassettes," followed by the running time in minutes; 2) the presence or absence of a sound track (using the abbreviations "sd." or "si."), followed by the presence or absence of color; 3) the width of the film in millimeters with super 8 mm. specified as "super 8 mm."; and 4) any accompanying material. The punctuation is as follows:

> reels-comma-space-time-space-colon-sound-comma-
> space-color-space-semicolon-space-width-space-
> ampersand-space-accompanying material-period.

Examples:

> 1 reel, 13 min. : sd., col. ; 16 mm.

> 1 reel, 28 min. : si., b&w ; 16 mm.

> 1 cassette, 20 min. : sd., col. ; super 8 mm & guide.

228L. Realia, collation

Actual objects such as artifacts or specimens are cataloged as realia. They are described just as models are described, except that the collation names the actual object instead of using the term "model."

Example:

2 hand puppets : col. ; 36 cm.

228M. Slides, collation

Slides are described by 1) the number of "slides," "stereoscope slides," or "slides (glass)"; 2) the presence or absence of color; 3) the height and width in inches; and 4) any accompanying materials.

Examples:

60 slides : col. ; 2x2 in. & guide.

100 slides : b&w ; 2x2 in. & 4 cassettes (4-track. mono. 160 min.)

228N. Transparencies, collation

Transparencies are described by 1) the number of "transparencies" including in parentheses the exact number of "overlays"; 2) the presence or absence of color; 3) the height and width in centimeters including any mount; and 4) any accompanying material.

Examples:

15 transparencies (5 overlays) : b&w ; 25x30 cm.

8 transparencies : col. ; 23x28 cm. & lesson plan.

228O. Videorecordings, collation

The cataloging of videorecordings is similar to that of motion pictures: 1) the number of "reels," "cassettes," "cartridges," or "discs" is given, followed by running time in minutes; 2) sound and color characteristics are given in a form identical to that used for motion pictures, except that for a videorecording the format of a "disc" must have its revolutions-per-minute indicated as the first element of this part of the description; 3) the dimensions are given in inches either for the width of the tape or the diameter of the disc; and 4) any accompanying material is described.

Examples:

1 reel, 25 min. : si., b&w ; 1 in.

1 cassette, 22 min. : sd., col. ; 1/2 in. & guide.

1 disc, 5 min. : 1500 rpm., sd., b&w ; 9 in.

Rule 229. Series area

The rules for the series area of audiovisual media and special instructional materials are the same as the rules for the series area of monographic publications, Rule 142.

Example:

35 fr. : col. ; 35 mm. — (The world of economics series)

Rule 230. Notes area

Notes are used for audiovisual media and special instructional materials just as notes are used for monographs to expand or complete the description of the work being cataloged. See AACR revised Chapter 12, Rule 230, for detailed examples and complex problems. The following is only a brief summary of that important rule.

The order and some examples of notes follow:

230A. Earlier titles are recorded;

230B. The source of the title is given if the source used is neither the work itself nor the material accompanying it;

230C. Variations in title within the work are given;

230D. The physical description is extended if necessary; e.g.,

Loop film
Magnetic sound track.

230E. Accompanying materials are described if they have not already been adequately described in the collation;

230F. Works related to the work being cataloged are cited; e.g.,

Based on the motion picture of the same title.

230G. The country of original release of foreign motion pictures and filmstrips is given; e.g.,

First released in France.

230H. The intended users are indicated, if the work is designed for a particular group of users; e.g.,

For primary grades.

230J. The cast of a motion picture or similar work is listed using the caption "CAST:" and the names of featured players; e.g.,

CAST: Henry Fonda, James Cagney, William
Powell, Jack Lemmon, Betsy Palmer.

230K. The credits for a motion picture or similar work are listed using the caption "CREDITS:" and the positions and names of the individuals who have participated in the artistic or technical production of the work; e.g.,

> CREDITS: Producer, Leland Howard; directors,
> John Ford, Mervyn LeRoy; screenplay, Frank
> Nugget, Joshua Logan; music composer and
> conductor, Frank Waxman; film editor, Jack
> Murray.

230L. A brief, objective summary of the subject content is given as the next to the last note. This note is introduced by the caption "SUMMARY:" and is formulated according to the following guidelines:

"1) Be brief; in general avoid using more than about 50 words.

"2) Avoid promotional or evaluative phrases or even a tone suggestive of subjective judgment.

"3) Avoid repeating the title, subtitle, or information adequately expressed by them.

"4) Include statements of the purpose of the work, any abilities or knowledge it is intended to impart, and any particular group of users or narrowly defined age group it has been designed for.

"5) Include references to techniques used in the production when these are significant."

Example:

> SUMMARY: Close-up, slow-motion, and fast-motion
> photography is used in showing how animals move in water,
> on land, and in the air. Explains that an animal's movement
> helps it to acquire food, to find a home, to move from place
> to place, and to adapt to its environment.

230M. The last note is the contents note, which is also introduced by the caption "CONTENTS:"

Example:

> CONTENTS: The first Americans. 58 fr.—The eastern
> woodlands. 60 fr.—The Plains. 58 fr.—West of the shining
> mountains. 61 fr.—Indians today. 55 fr.

Examples of Selected Audiovisual Media

Fig. 9.12—Example of a Locally Produced Diorama

Medium designator

Phillips, John.
    The sixteenth century printer. ₁Diorama₁ /
John Phillips.

Descriptive note replaces collation

    A display in color made of plastic; includes
figures of a group of printers (4 pieces) and hand
printing equipment (3 pieces) with an interior print-
shop background; the assembled display measures
75x125x50 cm.
    Title on label attached to container.

    I. Title.

Fig. 9.13—Example of a Silent Filmstrip

Medium designator

The animals of farmboy Bill. ₁Filmstrip₁ /
    McGraw-Hill ; ₁made by₁ William P. Gottlieb Co.
    -- New York : McGraw-Hill, 1956.
    43 fr. : col. ; 35 mm. -- (Animal stories series)

    Eastman color.
    CREDITS: Educational consultant, Christine B.
Gilbert.
    SUMMARY: Captioned photographs are used in
introducing horses, cows, goats, pigs, and other
animals commonly found on a farm.

    1. Domestic animals. I. McGraw-Hill Book Co.

Fig. 9.14—Example of a Sound Filmstrip

A ducky decision. ⌈Filmstrip⌉. -- Burbank, Calif. :
    Cathedral Films, 1961.
    51 fr. : col. ; 35 mm. & disc (33 1/3 rpm.
mono. 15 min.) and study guide. -- (Tales of
Jiminy Cricket ; series 1)

    Based on the Walt Disney motion picture of
the same title.
    SUMMARY: Presents a story about a conflict
between Donald Duck and an ant in order to discuss
its application to Christian living.

    1. Christian life--Juvenile films. I. Cathedral
Films, Inc., Burbank, Calif. II. Series.

Accompany-
ing material
for a sound
filmstrip

Figures 9.15 and 9.16 have been taken from *Nonbook Materials* and converted to the ISBD style of AACR, revised Chapter 12.

Fig. 9.15—Example of a Kit

Rocks and minerals kit. ⌈Kit⌉ / Dept. of Mines and
    Technical Surveys. -- Made by National Film
    Board of Canada, ⌈1964?⌉
    1 chart, 3 filmstrips, 1 map, 5 pamphlets,
13 rocks and minerals, and teacher's guide.

    SUMMARY: Introduces elementary and secondary
students to Canadian mines, rocks and minerals.

    1. Mines and mineral resources--Canada.
2. Mineralogy--Canada. 3. Rocks.

Fig. 9.16–Example of a Model

```
Rosetta stone unit. ⌐Model⌐ / Consultant: Edward
     L. B. Terrace. -- Long Island, N.Y. : Alva
     Museum Replicas, 1965.
     1 model : black ; 30x23x5 cm. & teacher's manual
manual and student's activity sheet.

     1. Rosetta stone inscription.  I. Terrace,
Edward L        B
```

Fig. 9.17–Example of a Motion Picture

```
Wayward river. ⌐Motion picture⌐. -- Ottawa :
     National Film Board of Canada, 1962.
     1 reel, 11 min. : sd., b&w ; 16 mm.

     French version released under the title
La Chaudière.
     CREDITS: Producer, Tom Wilson; director, Ray
Garceau; commentary, Strowan Robertson; music,
Maurice Blackburn; photographer, François Séguillon.
     SUMMARY: Depicts life along the Chaudière, in
Beauce County, Quebec. Shows how this French-Canadian
area adapts to the winter changes in the river, when
the ice jams, and the villagers must move to the
upper floors of their homes.

     1. Chaudière River.  2. Beauce Co., Que.--Soc.
life & cust.  I. Canada. National Film Board.
```

Note: The cataloger should realize that material not covered by these specific media may be cataloged in an analogous fashion. The following is an example of how a jigsaw puzzle might be cataloged.

Fig. 9.18

```
Lord Howe on the Quarter Deck of the Queen Charlotte,
    June 1st, 1794. [Jigsaw puzzle]. -- Leeds :
John Waddington, c1970.
    ca. 500 pieces in container (32x26x5 cm.)

    Based on a painting by Mather Brown.
    Completed puzzle 38x55 cm.
    Only vertical sides in straight lines; hori-
zontal sides form wavy lines.
    SUMMARY: The picture shows a battle scene on the
deck of a British war ship during the Revolutionary
War. The officers are in full dress uniforms for
1787-1795 period.
```

Another type of special instructional material is a portfolio or packet of reproductions of documents. This type of special kit is handled by AACR as monographic material in revised Chapter 6. The following card is an example of this.

Fig. 9.19

Coxey's army / compiled by Henry I. Tragle. — ₍New York : Grossman Publishers, 1974₎

➤ 1 portfolio (₍33₎ pieces) : ill. ; 23 x 35 cm. — (Jackdaw : no. A19)

Contents brochure, 27 reproductions of documents and prints, and 5 explanatory broadsheets.
Includes bibliography.
ISBN 0-305-62096-7

1. Coxey, Jacob Sechler, 1854-1951. 2. Labor and laboring classes—United States—Sources. 3. Unemployed—United States—Sources. ₍1. Coxey, Jacob Sechler, 1854-1951. 2. Labor and laboring classes. 3. Unemployed₎ I. Tragle, Henry Irving. II. Series: Jackdaw (New York) ; no. A19.

HD8072.C79   331.1'37973   74-7306
                                          MARC

Library of Congress   75   AC

Note the collation

PRINTED MUSIC

Cataloging of music scores is very closely related to the cataloging of monographs. Rules for choice of entry apply, the composer being regarded as author except in special cases, as noted below. Perhaps the most notable difference in music cataloging is the frequent use of the uniform title, a title devised to bring together all editions of the same work regardless of the title-page title or language.

The following examples represent only a small portion of cataloging procedures for descriptive cataloging; they are greatly amplified in Chapter 13 of the AACR.

Entry

Rule 230. Musical works with authorship of mixed character

230A. General rule

"A musical work that also embodies the work of a poet, dramatist, scenarist, etc. (e.g., a song, opera, musical comedy, ballet), is entered under the composer. Author-title added entries are made under the other persons who share in the responsibility for the work as a whole if their work is fully represented in the edition being cataloged (as in a full score or piano-vocal score). If the non-musical part of such a work is based on another work, an explanatory reference is made from the author and title of the other work to the composer and title of the musical work."

> Title page: Promises, promises. Book by Neil
> Simon, based on the screenplay The Apartment
> by Billy Wilder and I.A.L. Diamon. Music by
> Burt Bacharach, Lyrics by Hal David.

Main entry under Bacharach.
Added entries (author-title) under Simon and David.

> Wilder, Billy, 1906—
> The apartment.

> For a musical composition based on this work *see*

> Bacharach, Burt F
> Promises, promises.

Rule 231. Arrangements, transcriptions, etc.

Preliminary note: "These rules apply to 'arrangements,' 'transcriptions,' 'versions,' 'settings,' etc., in which music for one medium of performance has been rewritten for another. They also apply to simplified versions, whether for the same or for a different medium. If, however, an arrangement is characterized by such expressions as 'freely transcribed,' 'based on,' etc., or if it is known that extensive new material has been introduced or that the harmony or musical style of the original work has been substantially altered, apply 232.

231A. "An arrangement or transcription of one or more works of a composer, or of parts of the same, is entered under the composer. An added entry is made under the name of the arranger or transcriber followed by the designation '*arr.*,' unless the arrangement was made by the composer himself."

> Title page: Duets for two clarinets, from the
> Duets for violin . . . [by Ignaz Joseph Pleyel]
> Arranged and edited by David Glazer.

> Main entry under Pleyel.
> Added entry under Glazer.

> Title page: Berceuse, from The Firebird by Igor
> Strawinsky, transcribed for string orchestra
> by Quinto Maganini.

> Main entry under Stravinskii.
> Added entry under Maganini.

Rule 232. Related music

232A. General rule

"A work that represents a distinct alteration of another work (e.g., a free transcription), a work that paraphrases parts of various works or the general style of another composer, or one that is merely based on other music (e.g., variations on a theme) is entered under its own composer."

> Title page: Mother Goose; concert suite for the
> piano by David W. Guion, based on the nursery
> tunes of J.W. Elliott.

> Main entry under Guion.
> Added entry under Elliott.

Title page: The naked Carmen, created, written,
        produced and arranged by John Corigliano and
        David A. Hess, adapted from Bizet's Carmen.

Main entry under Corigliano.
Added entry under Hess, joint composer.
Author-title added entry under Bizet, Carmen.

Uniform Titles

Uniform titles are frequently used in cataloging music because the same musical composition is often issued in numerous editions with variations in the language and the wording of the title pages. A uniform title may also be used whenever a filing device is needed for music entered under a person other than a composer, e.g., arranger. Composer-title cross references are made from forms of the title not used as uniform title, as may be advisable. The following examples are typical:

Beethoven, Ludwig van, 1770-1827.
    Battle of Vittoria
    see his
    Wellingtons Sieg.

Beethoven, Ludwig van, 1770-1827.
    Cantata on the death of Emperor Joseph II
    see his
    Kantate auf den Tod Kaiser Josephs II.

"In Library of Congress entries, the uniform title is enclosed in brackets and printed in eight-point type at title indention beneath the heading." The cataloger should be aware of the subject index at the back of the Library of Congress Music and Phonorecords Catalogs, which provide examples of uniform titles. Examples are also provided in *Code for Cataloging Music and Phonorecords.* [8]

In the selection and construction of uniform titles the most reliable bibliographical sources are consulted, such as thematic indexes, bibliographies, music encyclopedias, etc. Information given in the work cataloged is not used without an attempt at verification. The Library of Congress catalogs are certainly useful in constructing a uniform title, but only after the cataloger has identified the work in thematic or other musical sources.

Rules 233-237, which give the principles of construction of a uniform title for a single work or type of work, are not fully quoted here. The most basic type of uniform title is generally that of the first edition of the work, modified as stated in

---

[8] Music Library Association, *Code for Cataloging Music and Phonorecords* (Chicago, American Library Association, 1958). For general background, see also Olga Buth, "Scores and Recordings," *Library Trends* 23 (January 1975): 427-450.

Rules 233-234, with the choice of language dependent on the type of composition (Rule 235). The next element is the medium of performance, the instruments for which it was written (Rule 236); that is followed by further identifying elements to distinguish the work from other compositions by the same composer, generally the serial number, opus (or thematic index) number, and the key (Rule 237). Examples of such entries follow:

> **Bach, Johann Sebastian**, 1685-1750.
> [Die Kunst der Fuge]
> The Art of the fugue

> **Bach, Johann Sebastian**, 1685-1750.
> [Lobet den Herrn, alle Heiden, S. 230]
> Motet no. 6: Praise the Lord, all ye heathen
> (BWV 230)

> **Haydn, Joseph**, 1732-1809.
> [Quartet, strings, no. 83, op. 77, no. 2, F major]
> Quartet, op. 77, no. 2, in F major

> **Dvořák, Antonín**, 1841-1904.
> [Symphony, no. 8, op. 88, G major]
> From the new world: symphony no. 8 by Dvořák.

Uniform titles for collections, excerpts, arrangements, and adaptations are constructed basically to provide the most reasonable filing location (see Rules 239-242). For example:

> [Works, organ]
> [Works, organ. Selections]
> [Sonatas, piano]
> [Artaxerxes. The soldier tir'd]
> [Fantasiestücke, piano, op. 12. Traumes Wirren]
> [Quartets, strings, no. 8-13, op. 2]

> **Cowell, Henry**, 1897-1965.
> [Concerto brevis, accordion; arr.]
> Concerto brevis, for accordion and orchestra;
> Piano reduction by the composer.

Titles of works in the larger vocal forms (operas, oratorios, etc.) generally require additional modification because of the various versions in which they are likely to be issued (Rule 243). For example:

Puccini, Giacomo, 1858-1924.
[Manon Lescaut]

[Manon Lescaut. Piano-vocal score]

[Manon Lescaut. Libretto. English]

Fig. 9.20

¹Uniform
title

²Language

> Monteverdi, Claudio, 1567–1643.
> 1 ➤ L'Orfeo. Italian₁ ◄── 2
> L'Orfeo / Claudio Monteverdi ; nouvelle édition et restitution, Edward H. Tarr. — Paris : Éditions Costallat, ₁1974₁
> xxxviii p., score (120 p.) ; 37 cm.
> Opera.
> Italian libretto by A. Striggio, also printed as text with German, French, and English translations on p. x–xxxiii.
> 500 copies printed.
> Prefatory material in French, German, and English.
> 1. Operas—To 1800—Scores. I. Tarr, Edward H. II. Monteverdi, Claudio, 1567–1643. L'Orfeo. Libretto. English, French, German & Italian. 1974. III. Striggio, Alessandro, the younger. L'Orfeo. IV. Title.
>
> M1500.M78O7 1974 75-765042
>
> Library of Congress 75 M

Fig. 9.21

¹Uniform
title

²Languages

> Mozart, Johann Chrysostom Wolfgang Amadeus, 1756–1791.
> 1 ➤ ₁Don Giovanni. Libretto. English, French and Italian₁ ◄── 2
> Don Giovanni / libretto di Lorenz Da Ponte ; musica di Wolfgang Amadeus Mozart ; traduction mot à mot accent tonique par Marie-Thérèse Paquin. — Montréal : Les Presses de l'Université de Montréal, 1974.
> 232 p. ; 17 x 20 cm.
> Opera in 2 acts.
> Italian text with word-for-word and line-by-line renderings in English and French in middle column; English and French translations in outer columns.
> Introd. and synopsis in English and French.
> ISBN 0-8405-0244-3
> 1. Operas—To 1800—Librettos. I. Da Ponte, Lorenzo, 1749-1838.
> Don Giovanni. II. Pa-   quin, Marie Thérèse. III. Title.
>
> ML50.M939D52 1974 75-765062
>
> Library of Congress 75 MN

Description

Rule 244. Relationship of the title page to the description

244A. "Music title pages frequently do not have the distinctive character of title pages of literary works; the title page may have only a listing of some of the composer's works, or of works of the same type by other composers; the work in hand may appear as one of many items, usually briefly listed. In these cases another source having fuller information, such as the caption or cover, is more satisfactory as the basis of the description. In case of doubt, however, the title page is preferred."

244B. "Medium of performance, serial and opus numbers, and key are included after the transcription of the title if they appear on the title page or title page substitute, even though they may have been stated in the uniform title."

Rule 245. Imprint

Imprint in music is treated the same as for literary works, with the following qualifications: the publisher whose plate number appears on the work is always named; full imprint is given for music published in the United States through 1820 because these are rare publications, and complete transcription of the imprint (place, publisher, printer, addresses, price, etc.) may be necessary for identification of the work; and care should be taken in supplying a date on the basis of information found in Hofmeister[9] (see Rule 245C).

245D. Plate numbers and publishers' numbers

245D1. "For music which does not bear a publication, printing or copyright date, a plate number or publisher's number, if available, is added immediately after the supplied imprint date, for its value in identifying copies and comparing editions. The plate number appears at the foot of each page of most engraved music, and may also appear on the title page. If the number appears only on the title page, it is designated as the 'publisher's number.'

245D2. "The number is given without brackets. It is designated 'Pl. no.' or 'Pub. no.' and is copied exactly as it appears: letters, figures, and punctuation."

> New York: J. Fischer [1949] Pl. no. J. F. & B. 8478-50.

> Milan: Edizioni Suvini Zerboni [1950] Pl. no. S. 4623 Z.

> New York: E. Schuberth [1941] Pub. no. 5227.

---

[9]C. F. Whistling's *Handbuch der musikalischen Literatur* 3. Aufl. (Leipzig, Friedrich Hofmeister, 1845; 16 supplements, through 1943). See also *Bibliographie des Musikschriftums* (Leipzig, Frankfurt am Main: Hofmeister, 1936– ; frequency and publisher vary, now annual).

Rule 246. Collation

"Music which is not described as score and/or parts (such as music for a solo instrument, songs, hymnals, etc.) follows the rules for collation of other monographic or serial publications." See Fig. 9.22.

Fig. 9.22

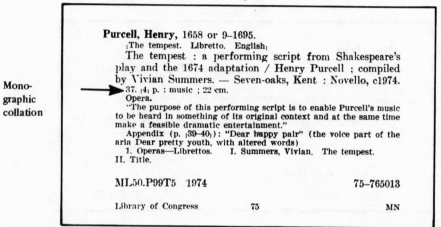

Mono-
graphic
collation

> **Purcell, Henry,** 1658 or 9-1695.
> ₍The tempest. Libretto. English₎
> The tempest : a performing script from Shakespeare's play and the 1674 adaptation / Henry Purcell ; compiled by Vivian Summers. — Seven-oaks, Kent : Novello, c1974.
> 37. ₍4₎ p. : music ; 22 cm.
> Opera.
> "The purpose of this performing script is to enable Purcell's music to be heard in something of its original context and at the same time make a feasible dramatic entertainment."
> Appendix (p. ₍39–40₎): "Dear happy pair" (the voice part of the aria Dear pretty youth, with altered words)
> 1. Operas—Librettos.   I. Summers, Vivian. The tempest.
> II. Title.
>
> ML50.P99T5 1974   75–765013
>
> Library of Congress   75   MN

246A. Works consisting of score only

"Scores are specified as such in the collation by the appropriate term, score, close score, condensed score, piano-conductor score, miniature score, piano-vocal score, etc. unless the term appears in the uniform title. Following the term for the score, the paging is stated within parentheses."

score (46 p.)

miniature score (93 p.)

Fig. 9.23

Score in
uniform
title

Score not
specified,
as it is in
uniform
title

> **Vivaldi, Antonio,** 1678–1741.
> ₍Magnificat. Piano-vocal score. Latin₎
> Magnificat : for four-part chorus of mixed voices, soprano, alto, tenor, and bass solos with piano or orchestra acc. / Antonio Vivaldi ; edited by Robert Stockton. — Valley Forge, Pa. : Music 70, ₍c1974₎
> 36 p. ; 27 cm.
> "First version."
> Edited from the holograph in the Biblioteca nazionale, Turin.
> $3.00
> 1. Choruses, Sacred (Mixed voices) with orchestra—To 1800—Vocal scores with piano. 2. Magnificat (Music)
>
> M2023.V63M255 1974   75–764818
> [M2079.L6]
>
> Library of Congress   75   M

246B. Works consisting of parts or score and parts

246B1. "Whenever the music cataloged consists of or includes musical parts for performance, this fact is shown in the collation by the word 'part(s)' preceded by the number if more than one." The Library of Congress omits the number of parts for the convenience of other libraries using the printed cards.

Fig. 9.24

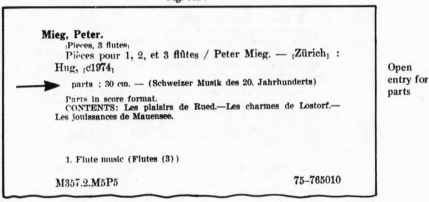

Mieg, Peter.
₍Pieces, 3 flutes₎
Pièces pour 1, 2, et 3 flûtes / Peter Mieg. — ₍Zürich₎ :
Hug, ₍c1974₎

     parts ; 30 cm. — (Schweizer Musik des 20. Jahrhunderts)

Parts in score format.
CONTENTS: Les plaisirs de Rued.—Les charmes de Lostorf.—Les jouissances de Mauensee.

1. Flute music (Flutes (3))

M357.2.M5P5   75–765010

Open entry for parts

246B2. "If the work consists of score and parts, the presence of parts is shown after the collation of the score, following the word 'and.' " See Figs. 9.25 and 9.26.

Fig. 9.25

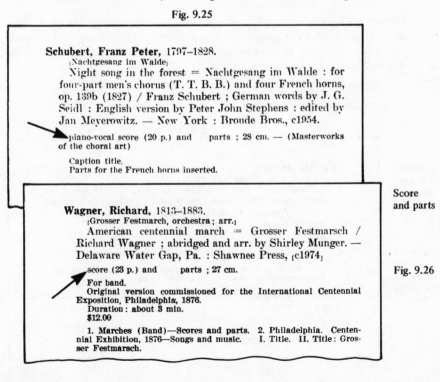

Schubert, Franz Peter, 1797–1828.
₍Nachtgesang im Walde₎
Night song in the forest = Nachtgesang im Walde : for four-part men's chorus (T. T. B. B.) and four French horns, op. 139b (1827) / Franz Schubert ; German words by J. G. Seidl : English version by Peter John Stephens : edited by Jan Meyerowitz. — New York : Broude Bros., c1954.
  piano-vocal score (20 p.) and   parts ; 28 cm. — (Masterworks of the choral art)
Caption title.
Parts for the French horns inserted.

Wagner, Richard, 1813–1883.
₍Grosser Festmarch, orchestra ; arr.₎
American centennial march = Grosser Festmarsch / Richard Wagner ; abridged and arr. by Shirley Munger. — Delaware Water Gap, Pa. : Shawnee Press, ₍c1974₎
  score (23 p.) and   parts ; 27 cm.
For band.
Original version commissioned for the International Centennial Exposition, Philadelphia, 1876.
Duration : about 3 min.
$12.00
1. Marches (Band)—Scores and parts. 2. Philadelphia. Centennial Exhibition, 1876—Songs and music.   I. Title. II. Title : Grosser Festmarsch.

Score and parts

Fig. 9.26

Rule 248. Notes

"Additional information necessary in the catalog entry may be given as notes. Notes referring to the title are given first, followed by those describing the music. Any other notes precede the final note, which is for contents." Species, medium of performance, language and other information on the text, and notation are specified in notes if the information does not appear in the uniform title or body of the card, or if it differs from normal (as "Plainsong notation"). Duration of performance may be stated and contents may be listed as briefly as possible. See Rules 248A through 248E.

Some typical examples are as follows:

Contents.–v. 1. Sonatas op. 2 to op. 28.–v. 2. Sonatas op. 31 to op. 111.

Contains a prelude, 16 fugues, and 11 interludes, for piano.

Includes thematic indexes.

Two melodies of the opera arranged for piano solo: [5] p. at end.

Duration: 28 min., 50 sec.

For soprano and bass voices, clarinet, trumpet, piano, and contrabass.

"To use this score as original sextet score, omit [double] bass [and] tutti, solo, divisi signs."

First performed at the Salzburg Music Festival, 1935.

Nos. 1-25, voice and lute (in tablature) and part for a bass instrument (inverted).

Nine airs are set to poems by Ben Jonson and one each to words by John Donne and Thomas Campion.

SOUND RECORDINGS

Introduction

Since there is at this time no ISBD for sound recordings, these rules do not reflect the distinctive ISBD punctuation; however, in mid-1975 all of the rules in Chapter 14 of AACR were revised extensively as noted in *Cataloging Service*, bulletin 115 (Fall 1975). Certain of these revisions make these rules more consistent with revised Chapter 12 of AACR. It should be noted, however, that these rules and their revisions provide no specific instructions for the description of the statement of authorship within the body of the entry. The name of Chapter 14 was changed from "Phonorecords" to "Sound Recordings"; other major changes are in the collation and order of notes.

The term **sound recording** is used to describe all types of aural media as specified in the introductory notes to Chapter 14 of the *Anglo-American Cataloging Rules*. The following excerpts from the rules apply primarily to the disc (commonly called the phonograph record); rules applying to other types of recordings (such as tapes, cylinders, sound film, etc.) should be consulted in Chapter 14. Catalog entry and description of sound recordings closely resemble those for printed material, with the addition of technical information to describe the item as being aural, rather than visual.

While the cataloging of records is generally standardized and closely related to cataloging of printed matter, classification or shelf order varies widely from library to library. There is no generally accepted classification scheme for aural materials. Records present particular problems of classification because of the extremely disparate materials that often appear on a single physical item. Several schemes for organizing records are documented in the literature.[10] The simplest methods of organization are those without classification by subject matter: shelving by catalog entry, size or physical form, or by accession number. Others are based broadly on existing classification systems, particularly Dewey with cutter numbers, or utilize methods devised by individual libraries. The system of organization adopted by any library should be based on the size and type of the record collection, the needs of the patrons, and the requirements of internal control.

Entry

Rule 250. Main entry

250A. Single works and excerpts

"The entry for a recording of a work is the same as the entry for the same material in its visual form. The applicable rules of entry for books and book-like materials and for music are followed."

Example:

Vivaldi, Antonio, 1678-1741.
    [Magnificat. Piano-vocal score. Latin] [Sound recording]

---

[10]Summarized in Mary Jane Sudler, "Organization of Recorded Sound," *Library Resources and Technical Services* 13 (Winter 1969): 93-98. Also see Dominique-René de Lerma, "Philosophy and Practice of Phonorecord Classification at Indiana University," *Library Resources and Technical Services* 13 (Winter 1969): 86-92. One specialized classification system for sound recordings is Caroline Saheb-Ettaba and Roger B. McFarland, *Alpha-Numeric System for Classification of Recordings* (City of Industry, Calif., Bro-Dart, 1969).

250B. Collections

250B1. With collective title

"Two or more works by different persons issued under a collective title are entered under the title."

Example:

Russian orchestral masterpieces. [Sound recording]

250B2. Without collective title

"Separate entries are made for each work when two or more works by different persons are issued together without a collective title."

Note that several types of added entries may be made (e.g., for performers, for performing groups, and for works not given the main entry). Refer to Rules 251A through 251D.

See selected examples, page 238 of this chapter.

Description

Rule 252. Processed recordings

This rule applies to recordings produced in multiple copies, which include most commercial recordings.

252A. Physical medium

"A statement of physical medium is provided in order to identify the item as nonprint material, and in many cases, in order to distinguish recordings from scores or printed texts of the work."

252A1. "For works with uniform titles, the generic medium designator 'Sound recording' is enclosed within a separate pair of brackets and added after the uniform title heading. In the case of recordings of the Bible, 'Sound recording' precedes the date."

Examples:

Ives, Charles Edward, 1874-1954.
[Works, orchestra. Selections] [Sound recording]

Bible. O.T. English. Authorized. Selections [Sound recording] 1965.

252A2. "For works without uniform titles, the generic medium designator 'Sound recording' is enclosed within brackets and inserted after all titles."

Examples:

> O'Neill, Eugene Gladstone, 1888-1953.
>   Ah, wilderness! [Sound recording]

> Russian orchestral masterpieces. [Sound recording]

252B. Transcription of title

"The title may be taken from a label or the cover of an album, a container, the rim of a cylinder, etc. By analogy with titles for visual media, titles on two or more sides of a disc may be treated as if they extended across confronting pages.

252C. Imprint

252C1. "If the publisher is known to be primarily a publisher of recordings, the imprint consists of the trade name of the publisher and the serial identification (set or individual item numbers) followed by a period and the date of release."

Examples:

> Decca DL 9674. [1968]

> Angel COLH-125. [1966]

252C2. "If the publisher is not known to be primarily a publisher of recordings, the imprint consists of the place, the name of the publisher, and the date of release. The serial identification is given following the date."

Example:

> New Haven, Conn.   Yale University School of Music
>   [1954]   YM 175.

252D. Collation

The collation of recordings varies for each class of physical media (discs, tapes, etc.) and may be supplemented by notes. Rules 252D2 through 252D7 should be consulted for media other than discs or tapes.

252D1. Disc

"The number of discs is given, followed by the speed (in revolutions per minute) and one of the following terms: 'mono.' (for monophonic), 'stereo.' (for stereophonic), or 'quad.' (for quadraphonic), with disc diameter added last."

Examples:

> 3 discs. 33 1/3 rpm. stereo. 12 in.

> 5 discs. 78 rpm. mono. 10 in.

> 1 disc. 33 1/3 rpm. quad. 12 in.

Note: This is a major change from the previous rules, which indicated number of sides rather than discs as well as indicating microgroove; e.g.,

> 6 s. 12 in. 33 1/3 rpm. microgroove. stereophonic.

"When separate works are issued together so that the physical extent of the particular work being cataloged is less than that of the whole grouping, express the fractional extent in the form 'on side 3 of 2 discs' (if the sides are numbered in one sequence) or 'on 1 side of 2 discs' (if there is no such whole numbering)."

252D3. Tape

252D3a. "For open-reel tape, the number of reels is given, followed by playing speed (in inches per second), the number of tracks, one of the three terms 'mono.,' 'stereo.,' 'quad.,' with reel diameter and tape width (if other than 1/4 in.) added last."

Example:

> 4 reels. 7 1/2 ips. 2-track. stereo. 14 in.

252D3b. "For tape in cassettes or cartridges, the number of cassettes or cartridges is given, followed by the number of tracks of the tape, the dimensions of the cassette (if other than 3 7/8 x 2 1/2 in.) or cartridge (if other than 5 1/4 x 7 7/8 in.), and one of the three terms 'mono.,' 'stereo.,' or 'quad.' "

Example:

> 1 cassette. 4-track. stereo.

252E. Series statement

"The form of the series statement follows that for visual materials."

252F. Notes

Notes are used to amplify the catalog entry for records in much the same way as for visual materials. The order of notes is specified in Rule 252F. Notes particularly relevant in the cataloging of records are those referring to source of title; participant, performer, and medium; edition recorded; details concerning the event; duration; contents; and "with" note listing works issued together when a separate entry has been made for each.

Rule 253 gives the rules for cataloging nonprocessed records, those that are not produced in multiple copies and that are frequently unique. The preliminary note suggests that "the entries are as brief as possible, giving all of the essential data without citation of source." Notes are used as for processed records and may supply additional identifying data as necessary. Most collections of oral history would presumably contain many nonprocessed items, and extremely detailed analyses of some items may be desirable.

Selected Examples

Fig. 9.27

Bach, Johann Sebastian, 1685-1750.
   [Concerti grossi] [Sound recording]
   Brandenberg concertos. Olympic
Records OL 8131/2. [1974]
   2 discs. 33 1/3 rpm. stereo. 12 in.
(The Classical collection)

   Boyd Neel Chamber Orchestra: Boyd Neel,
conductor.
   Manual sequence.
   Durations on label; program notes on
container.

   1. Concerti grossi--To 1800. I. Neel,
Boyd, 1905-   II. Boyd Neel Orchestra.
III. Title.

[1] Uniform title

[2] Medium designator

Fig. 9.28

Ukrainian songs. [Sound recording] SWS
   Records 200K 06-201K07 [1975]
   2 discs. 33 1/3 rpm. stereo. 12 in.

   Ivan Rudawsky, baritone; Ihor Bilohrud,
piano.
   Sung in Ukrainian.
   Durations on labels; biographical notes
on container.
   CONTENTS: v. 1. Blue flower.--Her fate.--The
fields.--Festival in Chyhyryn.--The mighty Dnipro
River.--Fly on my song.--I look at the sky and
dream.--Serenade.--In the pub.--Reapers.--Father
warned me.--Blow gentle wind across the Ukraine.
v. 2. Blow gentle wind across the Ukraine.--
Remind me, Bandura.--Prayer.--Mother mine.--Wheat
fields.--Longing for Ukraine.--Psalm.--Anniversary.
--The steppe.--The endless plain.--Blue flower.

   1. Songs, Ukrainian. 2. Folk-songs, Ukrainian.
I. Rudawsky, Ivan. II. Bilohrud, Ihor.

[1] Title entry

[2] Medium designator

Fig. 9.29

**Entry under
the author of
the original
work** ⟶ Andersen, Hans Christian.
   The little match girl and other tales.
 [Sound recording] Caedmon TC 1117. [196?]
   1 disc. 33 1/3 rpm. mono. 12 in.

   Read by Boris Karloff.
   Translated by Reginald Spink from the
author's Eventyr.
   CONTENTS: The swineherd.--The top and
the ball.--The red shoes.--Thumbelina.--
The little match girl.

   I. Karloff, Boris. II. Title.

10 CLASSIFICATION

INTRODUCTION

The books in libraries of any appreciable size are arranged according to some system, and the arrangement is generally referred to as **classification**. Classification provides formal access to the books. Many different arrangements of books have been used in the past from the **pinakes**, a catalog of general subject locations devised by Callimachus for the Alexandria Library, through classification by size, which was used in many early New England libraries, to today's subject classification systems, which use numbers, letters, or symbols, or a combination of the three.

No matter which scheme is chosen or how large the collection, the purpose of classification is to make each book readily available. This is especially important if the collection is heterogeneous. It is convenient and necessary—particularly in open-shelf collections, to which many libraries in the United States are committed—to have all histories of the United States together, or all books on cybernetics, or all symphony scores, simply so that the patron who may have one title in mind can find other, related works in the same location. He can also locate similar works if the one he wants is not on the shelf.

There are many different classification schemes. The ultimate aim of each scheme is to lead the patron to the books he requires, either through his own search (**open stacks**), or through the search of a library attendant or page whose duty it is to find books for the patron (**closed stacks**). Each system has its virtues; the open stack allows and encourages browsing and therefore stimulates intellectual awareness. The closed stack lessens the chances that books will be mishandled, misplaced, or stolen, but the patron must rely on the resources of the public service staff and the card catalog. The open stack necessitates a logical, comprehensible system of classification so that the patron might find together all books on his subject and on related aspects of his subject. The closed stack allows, theoretically at least, any sort of classification scheme, including the very simplest—that of merely assigning a consecutive number to each book as it is processed into the library collection. No matter what the classification scheme, the card catalog, as primary source of reference, must be complete and current. It provides access to a particular book by author, title, or subject and gives location through the call number.

PHILOSOPHICAL PROPERTIES OF CLASSIFICATION

It must be remembered that the term classification refers to two processes: making the scheme of classification, and using this scheme in the actual process of classifying a document. Before we can discuss theoretical problems of library classification, we must briefly touch on the classification of knowledge in general, or, as it is sometimes called, philosophical classification.

A classification scheme is defined simply as an **orderly** arrangement of categories of classes, a class being any group of entities sharing the same characteristic. A characteristic is an attribute by which concepts may be separated into groups or further subdivided by subjects. Thus, the purpose of classification is to bring together (or form classes of) entities that share common characteristics and to separate entities that do not share common characteristics; more simply stated, the purpose of classification is to bring together things that are alike and to separate things that are not alike.

As Shera and Egan indicated, "No theory of knowledge, and therefore no ordering of knowledge, is possible without taking into account the inherent ability of the human mind to form concepts, and to perceive beyond concepts the fundamental **categories** which pervade and organize the almost infinite number of possible specific concepts. Because classificatory processes of every kind are dependent upon this inherent intellectual ability, the classifier must begin with an explicit understanding of concept and category. . . . A **concept** is the recognition of a pattern of qualities, or a structure, which enables the mind to name the object in reality with recurrent consistency."[1]

All scientific knowledge, according to the Greek philosopher Aristotle, consists of the arrangement of particulars under class concepts or universals, and in the combination of these concepts into a system. The goal of science is a definition that explains the nature of a subject by its **essential** properties and by its **differentiating** properties, which mark it off from other groups. Thus, the ultimate goal of science would be a complete classification of objects of knowledge into class groups, exhibiting all the resemblances and differences in the properties of various classes.

This conception of science was clearly formulated by Aristotle. He said that the definition of a term or a class concept must be a complete statement of:

a)   the **essential attributes** of the class; for example, man is an animal with powers of rational speech;

b)   the **peculiar attributes** of the class; for example, man is capable of laughter;

c)   the **next higher genus**; for example, man is an animal;

d)   the **properties which differentiate** man from all other animal species; for example, man is capable of speech;

e)   **accidents** (that is, properties not part of the definition but common to the class and other classes); for example, man is a material object.

---

[1] Jesse H. Shera and Margaret E. Egan, *The Classified Catalog* (Chicago, American Library Association, 1956), p. 25.

Aristotelian categories are well known. In his attempt to classify universal knowledge, the philosopher defined ten classes (categories of modes of being) as follows:

1. Substance
2. Quantity
3. Quality
4. Relation
5. Place

6. Time
7. Situation or position
8. Possession or acquired character
9. Activity
10. Passivity

A more elaborate presentation of Aristotle's epistemology is found in the works of the German philosopher Immanuel Kant. Kant finds that there are always two factors in genuine knowledge—the raw materials, which are sense experiences, and the synthetic, organizing, or ordering activity of the mind. To the understanding or to the faculty of making judgments—that is, the faculty of forming the concepts and laws that constitute order and sequence—belong the native forms of judgment, or the universal ways in which the mind synthesizes or orders the contents of sense perception. These forms are the **categories**—that is, the fundamental and universal forms of thinking objects and their relations. Through the use of these categories, the mind builds up the material of sense perception into a systematized or orderly whole of intelligible experience. Kant's categories correspond to the classification of judgment forms in traditional logic. They are as follows:

1. Categories of quantity
    Unity
    Plurality
    Totality
2. Categories of quality
    Reality
    Negation
    Limitation
3. Categories of relation
    Inherence and subsistence, or substance
    Causality and dependence
    Community, or reciprocity of causal influence
4. Categories of modality
    Possibility — Impossibility
    Existence — Nonexistence
    Necessity — Contingency

In order to illustrate Kant's argument and theory it will suffice to show the application of a few of these categories:

1. **Unity**. The mind unites various sensations—for example, color, form, weight, size, taste, etc.—into the unity or identity of an orange.

2. **Plurality**. The mind, in order to count a bag of oranges, must repeat, say twelve times, its identification of unity and must add or synthesize each one to the previously recognized number, as it goes along.

3. **Substance**. The mind can recognize change only by reference to something permanent. Without consciousness of permanence there is no consciousness of change, and vice versa. Thus, when we think of any object—for example, a table—we can say its appearance changes only if we recognize an identical "it" that changes. If we go back to the old childhood home, we can say it has not changed much only if we recognize that we and other things have changed, while remaining recognizably the same.

4. **Causality**. A causal relation is one of necessary and irreversible sequence. "*A* is the cause of *B*" means that it is necessary that *A* should first occur if there is to be an occurrence of *B*.

Now, the use or application of any category means always synthesis, organization or unification, in some fashion, of the chaotic manifold of sense experience. Knowledge involves both analysis and synthesis. **We must first see things together before we can take them apart, and we cannot see things together unless we put them together.**

This seems to be one of the main problems of a logical classification. In view of the vast field of knowledge yet to be discovered, how successfully can we proceed with the mental grouping of "known" and often fragmentized pieces of information, fitting them into existing (or non-existing) patterns in our attempt at a synthesis?

As Sayers once said, we cannot reason, even in the simplest manner, unless we possess in a greater or lesser degree the power of classifying.[2] Knowledge in its broadest sense groups, divides, and registers thoughts, things, and ideas in an unlimited number. Not only do we classify tangible objects that we can see and touch, but we must try to classify and evaluate impressions, ideas, and notions that exist, have existed, or may exist. If classification per se is not knowledge, it is certainly the most important method of dealing with knowledge. It enables us to observe objects and to abstract from their various qualities those characteristics that they have in common and that show how they are mutually related. This is the process by which we arrive at all scientific generalization.

In this context we may mention **natural** and **artificial** classification. A natural classification exhibits the inherent properties of things classified. It depends on characteristics implied in homology, where inherent properties of things to be classified occur regularly and are inseparable from the object of classification. Natural classification conforms to the "order of nature" as closely as possible. Thus, it is philosophical classification. It uses all of the appropriate Aristotelian class concepts of essential attributes, peculiar attributes, the next higher genus, properties that differentiate, and accidents. An artificial classification is one in which only some accidental property of the things classified is adopted as the characteristic of arrangement.[3] Thus, artificial classification depends on analogy,

---

[2] Cf. W. C. Berwick Sayers, *A Manual of Classification for Librarians*, 4th ed., completely rev. and partly re-written by Arthur Maltby (London, Andre Deutsch, 1967), pp. 25-32.

[3] J. Mills, *A Modern Outline of Library Classification* (London, Chapman & Hall, 1968, c.1960), pp. 9-10.

where things are classified for specific purposes based on the arbitrary selection of an accidental trait inseparable from the objects to be classified. Classification solely by color or by size, for example, is accidental classification.

Types of philosophical classification may also be identified by the internal structure of the classification itself.[4] In this respect we may distinguish between hierarchical and referential classification. The hierarchical concept of classification is based on the assumption that the process of subdivision must exhibit as much as possible the "natural" hierarchy of the subject, proceeding from classes of greater extension and smaller intension to those of smaller extension and greater intension. The order of any subject, according to Bliss, is to put the general works first; these should be followed by works on general subjects treated specially, then by works on special subjects treated generally, and lastly by works on special subjects treated specially.

1. The general treated generally — Locomotives
2. The general treated specially — Loco-design
3. The special treated generally — Electric locomotives
4. The special treated specially — Electric loco-design

The following table designed by Bliss shows graded specifications that are applicable to the systematic subdivision of most subjects, general or special.[5]

General in scope
    Bibliographical
    Historical and critical
        Historical
        Method, scope, and relations of the subject to others
        Critical
        Biographical
        Ancillary: statistics, illustrations, etc.; documents, reports, etc.
    Miscellaneous
        Periodicals and serials of societies, etc.
        Collections, selections, readings, miscellanies, essays

General in scope and treatment
    Elementary, introductory
    Manuals, compends
    Treatises, principles, comprehensive studies
    Discourses

General in scope and special in treatment
    Theoretical treatises
    Aspects of general subject
    Treatment for special purposes, interests, professions, etc.
    Technical
    Experimental and laboratory

---

[4] Shera and Egan, *The Classified Catalog*, p. 38.

[5] Henry Evelyn Bliss, *The Organization of Knowledge in Libraries* (New York, H. W. Wilson, 1939), p. 93.

Special in scope and treatment
  Special subjects
  Special theories
  Aspects in special interests
  Special topics
  Special methods, experiments, etc.
  Statistical treatment
  Pamphlets of special content, and other special materials

The principles of hierarchical classification may be summarized as follows:

1. A hierarchical classification proceeds by assembling the groups of sciences of the principal fields of knowledge into main classes or divisions, which are dictated by the theory of knowledge accepted. Such classes have great extension and small intension.

2. The process is continued by the designation of differentiating qualities within each main class, and thus subclasses or subdivisions are made.

3. Each subdivision in turn is divided by further differentiating qualities to produce still further subdivisions, and still others successively to make sections and subsections, until further subdivision is impossible or impracticable.

4. Every subdivision of a class is subordinate to the class heading. The sum of these subdivisions is the whole meaning of the class term, but each single set of subdivisions may consist of classes of equal rank. These must be coordinated by likeness, or "collocated."[6]

It should be noted that many well-known library classification systems, such as Dewey Decimal Classification, follow a similar pattern.

Several authors writing about hierarchical classification have noted that the grouping of categories and topics in a hierarchical array is quite often predetermined not so much by their likeness to one another as by their subordination based on a common characteristic or trait chosen for a specific purpose. This second type of classification is based on an assumption that classification should show class relations of a given subject in a more convenient form than the traditional linear presentation. Shera and Egan define this type of classification as *referential* classification. Essentially, it is:

> a pragmatic and empirical system in which the constituent elements are related with reference to a single isolated trait, property, or use, without respect to other characteristics. Referential classification admits the possibility of regrouping the same universe of things according to a different trait, property, etc. Such a classification is predicated upon the obvious truth that any single unit may be meaningful in any number of different relationships, depending upon the immediate purpose. In referential classification it is the external relations, the environment, rather than the "essence" of concepts, that are all important to the act of classifying.[7]

---

[6] Shera and Egan, *The Classified Catalog*, pp. 38-39.

[7] Ibid., pp. 39-40.

Several existing classification schemes, such as the Universal Decimal Classification, Colon Classification, etc., show this approach. The cross-fertilization concepts in information retrieval that are based on the multidimensional approach have tended to be synthetic in nature; they rely on a minimum of enumeration. They will be briefly discussed in the context of existing library classification schemes; a detailed analysis of them, however, is outside the scope of this text and must be reserved for more advanced courses.

LIBRARY CLASSIFICATION

Several types of library catalogs existed in ancient civilization; such catalogs are, in fact, as old as organized collections of books themselves. The early systems of library arrangement were merely utilitarian in purpose. Many of the earlier catalogs were arranged by title, and some showed groupings by broad subjects, chronological arrangement, or arrangement by author, by order of accession, by size, or even by color of binding. The classified catalog has a very interesting history, but there is no need to go into this problem at this time.[8] For our purpose here, it is sufficient to say that the rapid growth of library collections and their use during the nineteenth century resulted in a definite need for better methods of book arrangement in library collections, so that their substantive content would be apparent to the user.

The history of modern library classification corresponds to the various attempts to adapt and modify the existing philosophical systems of classification of knowledge to the arrangement of materials and to users' needs. One of the best known early American classifiers was Thomas Jefferson, third President of the United States. He adapted certain elements of Bacon's classification of knowledge, not only to the collection of his own library, but also in connection with his plans for the reorganization of the College of William and Mary and the organization of the University of Virginia.

Bacon's classification[9] was based on the three basic faculties: history (natural, civil, literary, ecclesiastical) as the province of memory; philosophy (including theology) as that of reason; and poetry, fables, and the like, as that of imagination. Jefferson's classification was based on d'Alembert's modification of the Baconian system, which d'Alembert used in preparing the classification scheme for the *Encyclopédie ou dictionnaire raisonné des sciences des arts et des métiers* (1751-1765). The *Catalogue* of Benjamin Franklin's Library Company of Philadelphia (1789) was also arranged in the Bacon-d'Alembert tradition. Three years before Jefferson's *Catalogue of the Library of the United States* was installed in the Library of Congress, a variant of the Philadelphia scheme formed the basis of the arrangement of the 1812 *Catalogue of the Library of Congress.*[10]

---

[8]The history of the classed catalog is briefly discussed in the chapter on subject headings.

[9]Cf. Bacon's *Advancement of Learning* (1605) and *De augmentis scientarium* (1623) and Chapter 11, p. 258, of this text.

[10]L. E. LaMontagne, "Historical Background of Classification," in *The Subject Analysis of Library Materials* (New York, Columbia University School of Library Service, 1953), p. 20.

Among other early followers of the Baconian system were Thaddeus Mason Harris, librarian at Harvard (1791-1793); Edward William Johnson, librarian of the College of South Carolina and later of St. Louis Mercantile Library; and, finally, William Torrey Harris, a follower of Hegel, who inverted the Baconian system and who, after he succeeded Johnson in St. Louis, created an independent American classification in 1870. At the same time various adaptations of the Brunet utilitarian system of classification[11] existed in several American libraries as a direct result of the influence of the British Museum and the Bibliothèque Nationale, both partly arranged by Brunet.

In 1876, Melvil Dewey devised his famous Decimal Classification based, in the main, on W. T. Harris's system, with a decimal notation. Soon Dewey's classification was spreading its influence throughout the world. At the same time, Charles A. Cutter began his work in classification at the Boston Athenaeum. Cutter sought to devise not a classification of knowledge but a practical, utilitarian method for the arrangement of books. Nevertheless, his Expansive Classification, especially in the developmental pattern of its subordinate classes, shows the definite influence of Spencer and Comte.

At the beginning of the present century, when the Library of Congress had grown from several thousand books to nearly a million, it was apparent that the library would need a new classification system. After much deliberation, J. C. M. Hanson and Charles Martel decided to design an independent system governed by the actual content of the collection. This form of classification differs from a pure philosophical classification in that it is based on the collection of books themselves as entities. It is a utilitarian classification; in fact, it is a form of referential classification. Much of their work, however, closely follows the Cutter Expansive Classification in general outline.

Summing up this brief historical introduction, we may conclude that the established philosophical systems of classification of knowledge (with several modifications) formed the basic structure for most library classification systems. The distinction so often drawn between the classification of knowledge (philosophical classification) and the classification of books, showing them as two independent processes, seems to have confused the thinking of many librarians. The two processes have important interactions; even a par excellence utilitarian classification "based on books themselves" cannot divorce itself from the intellectual concept of a book as an expression of certain ideas, although structurally these ideas are presented in two different forms. While the philosophical classification arranges knowledge itself—registering, evaluating, and classifying thoughts, ideas, and concepts for the universal purpose of adequately representing the field of human learning—a book (or library) classification arranges the expression of knowledge as preserved in written records (with adjustments where they are needed because of the physical form of such records); the specific purpose of book classification is to provide an adequate subject approach to the existing collection. This concept is well expressed by Henry Bliss:

---

[11]*Table méthodique en forme de catalogue raisonné* consisted of five main classes: Theology, Jurisprudence, Sciences and Arts, Belles-Lettres, and History.

A classification of books is a structural organization of knowledge. If it is well constructed, it will serve with maximal efficiency for functional organizations of knowledge in grouping and re-grouping the books with regard to the various uses and the probable requirements. A classification is best qualified to serve thus, if it conforms fundamentally to the organizations of knowledge established in the scientific and educational consensus. If it does not, it will lack adequacy, efficiency, and educational value.

The distinction so often drawn between the classification of knowledge and the classification of books should not lead us to negative conclusions, such as those of the logician Jevons, the bibliographer Schneider, and the classificationer, Melvil Dewey. There are indeed two kinds of classification, on the one hand the logical, natural, and scientific, on the other hand the practical, the arbitrary, the purposive; but for library classification we should join these two hands; the two purposes should be combined. To make the classification conform to the scientific and educational organization of knowledge is to make it the more practical. A logical and scientific organization of knowledge should be adapted to the practical requirements, the various bibliographic services, and the necessary economies. It were well too that we should bear in mind that a library is, in a higher view, a temple of knowledge, and its classification should be, not a haphazard, ramshackle structure, but an internal edifice worthy of its environment and itself of intellectual and educational value.[12]

FUNCTIONAL PROPERTIES OF
TRADITIONAL CLASSIFICATION SCHEMES

As we indicated earlier, most traditional classification schemes are enumerative; by contrast, the more recent classification systems tend to be synthetic. In this introductory text our discussion of enumerative systems will be confined to their basic functional properties.

Books are written expressions of man's ideas; these ideas may be expressed from different viewpoints and on different levels. A subject may be treated in some books on a popular level while others provide a scientific treatment of it. Several subjects may be discussed in one book, or one subject may be discussed from several aspects. Also, readers require books for different purposes, and the subject treatment that satisfies one category of readers may not satisfy another. This is why

---

[12] Bliss, *The Organization of Knowledge in Libraries*, pp. 36-37.

books that attempt to synthesize any part of the total accumulation in the field, at any level, or from any particular point of view, tend to cut across the classes of the formal classification of knowledge in the field. In a very real sense, each book of this kind embodies a special classification in itself, constructed according to the purpose of the author and embodying only those parts of knowledge useful to that purpose.[13]

All printed schedules of book classification reflect adjustments made to take into account the physical form of books and other media of recorded information. A classification scheme designed for the arrangement of books and other materials provides detailed information as to the scope and sequence of subjects covered. It is well to remember that books on the shelf are arranged in one order only. Any book may be requested by author, title, subject, or form, but it can be arranged by only one of these. The concept of classification thus merges the functions of the public catalog and the shelflist. Briefly, the efficiency of the library catalog as an index to a given collection will depend on the basic factors as indicated by Cutter in his *Rules for a Dictionary Catalog,* as cited in Chapter 2 of this text. To make such principles workable, the library classification must contain certain elements; these are briefly stated here.

a)   Provision for a **generalia** or **general works class** to accommodate books that are too general for inclusion in any single class. Works included in this category usually overlap several traditional disciplines—for example, encyclopedias, dictionaries, general periodicals, etc.

b)   Provision for **form classes.** These classes abandon the predominant characteristic of classification, the subject of the book, in favor of the characteristic of form. Materials in this category are classed by their form. An example of a form class is Literature (Dewey Decimal Classification), where form is paramount.

c)   Provision for **form divisions** to accommodate books dealing with different subjects in the same form of presentation. The **standard subdivisions** used by Dewey Decimal Classification are good examples of such an approach and can be used for subdividing most of the topics. It should be recognized, however, that some of these form divisions or subdivisions are "modes of treatment" rather than form. So, for example, compends, outlines, dictionaries, or periodicals do treat of physical form; while other subdivisions are philosophical ("inner form" groups) dealing with theoretical or philosophical aspects of the subject, e.g., in Dewey Decimal Classification—01 Philosophy and Theory; —07 Study and Teaching; —09 History, etc.

d)   A **notation** to provide a shorthand symbol or code for a specific class, division, or subdivision in a classification scheme, thus providing a convenient means of reference to the arrangement and identification of subject categories.

e)   An **index** to provide a means of efficient reference to all the terms used in the classification schedules.

---

[13] Shera and Egan, *The Classified Catalog,* p. 45.

These last two important features of a classification schedule will be discussed in greater detail. In most library classification, the notation is a symbol that codifies a classification system; therefore, it must be simple, brief, and flexible. A notation may be composed of letters, numerals, arbitrary signs, or a mixture of them. In general, there are two basic types of notation:

a) **pure notation**, in which one kind of symbol, such as either letters **or** numerals, is used consistently;

b) **mixed notation**, which uses two or more kinds of symbols (e.g., a combination of letters and numerals).

Notation plays an important role in any classification scheme, especially with the adoption of relative location of shelf arrangement. Prior to the mid-nineteenth century, many libraries used a **fixed location** of materials; in this system, each book had one specific (fixed) location on the shelf in the library. **Relative location**, now commonly used in most libraries, is an arrangement of books according to their relationship to one another. The actual books may be moved from shelf to shelf without altering or disturbing their subject sequence. A notation that serves as a guide to book arrangement on the shelf helps to preserve such orderly sequence. A summary of some of the functions and properties of notation follows:

1) A notation stands in place of terms used in the classification, showing sequence of classes and, in some cases (e.g., Dewey Decimal Classification), subordination of subjects. Thus, the notation is not only a location device representing the terms of classification in a symbolic language, but it may also guide the user to the position of actual subjects in the hierarchy of the classification, indicating subject relationships.

2) A notation serves to connect the alphabetical order of terms listed in the index with the systematic order of classification.

3) In order to perform such guidance functions efficiently, a notation should be simple and brief, and should contain some mnemonic features; in addition, it must be flexible. As Sayers indicated, "Flexibility in a notation means that, as classification must permit the insertion of any new class or part of a class, so also the notation symbols must be capable of expansion to mark that insertion without dislocating the rest of the notation. This is the cardinal requirement of notation."[14]

Another important feature in the classification is its index. The index serves as an alphabetical list of terms mentioned in the classification scheme. One very common type of index is the relative index.

The **relative index** not only provides references in alphabetical order to all subjects and terms in the classification, but it also shows the relation of each subject to other related subjects or their aspects. Benjamin Custer, the current editor of the Dewey Decimal Classification, describes the relative index in his introduction to the 18th edition:

---

[14] Sayers, *A Manual of Classification*, p. 98.

The index is considered relative (and is traditionally known as the "relative index") because of its inverse relationship to the schedules. Whereas in the schedules the different aspects of a subject are scattered according to discipline, in the index they are brought together under the name of the subject, with their various locations in the schedules indicated.[15]

There is no doubt that a relative index is a useful classification aid for the beginning student of cataloging. This is particularly true because in the classification process it is important not only to locate specific topics in the classification schedules or in the index, but also to learn how to relate specific books to the rest of the collection. The key to successful cataloging is the realization that books are arranged according to specific subjects, but that they are also arranged in relation to the subjects of other books.

Classification schemes (as indicated earlier) vary widely. In addition to analysis of the subject matter of the book, a successful classification scheme may consist of such devices as classification by method of treatment or form of topics treated (though both these methods are vulnerable to the classifier's prejudices); classification according to an alphabetical arrangement of subjects (which allows little expansion room for new subjects); or classification according to a variety of bibliographical details, such as place of printing, publication date, or type of binding. Any or all of these may be justifiably and successfully used for a special collection (such as a rare book collection or a collection in a particular subject area or period). Assuming, however, that the library collection is neither highly specialized nor exceedingly rare, it is as well to list a few criteria for a successful classification scheme.

1. A classification scheme must be **inclusive** as well as **comprehensive**. That means it must encompass within its limits the whole field of knowledge as represented in books and other printed media of communication. A classification scheme must therefore include all subjects that are, have been, or may be the matter of books, allowing for any possible additions of knowledge. At the same time it must include "not only every book that has been or can be written but every *use* of books, either actual or potential."[16]

2. A classification scheme must be **systematic**. This means not only that the division of subjects and topics must be exhaustive—proceeding from "terms of great extension and small intension to terms of great intension and small extension"[17]—but that the subjects must be arranged systematically, to bring together the related subjects. The scheme must allow its users to locate whatever they want, easily and logically. A library using Dewey Decimal Classification, for example, will

---

[15] Benjamin A. Custer, "Editor's Introduction: Comments on Philosophy, Structure, Use," in Vol. 1 of *Dewey Decimal Classification and Relative Index*, devised by Melvil Dewey, Edition 18 (Lake Placid Club, N.Y., Forest Press, Inc. of Lake Placid Club Education Foundation, 1971), p. 42.

[16] Shera and Egan, *The Classified Catalog*, p. 46.

[17] Sayers, *A Manual of Classification*, p. 44.

classify all books on United States history into the general number 973; specific aspects of this subject, such as the Civil War, will be found together. All books on the Civil War will be found together as a specific aspect of United States history in general. In other words, a classification scheme must be so arranged that each aspect of a subject can be considered a separate yet related part of the subject, and it must be so arranged that new aspects can be added in a logical manner.

3. A classification scheme must be **flexible and expansive**. It must be constructed so that any new subject may be inserted without dislocating the general sequence of classification. It must allow for recognized knowledge in all its ramifications, and it must be capable of admitting new subjects or new aspects of well-established subjects. The flexibility of the notation is of first importance if the classification scheme is to be expansive and hospitable in the highest degree. It should also be current. Both Dewey Decimal Office and the Library of Congress, for example, send subscribing libraries periodic lists of all changes in their schedules, noting also additions and deletions. These notices and revisions are especially important in subject areas in which a great deal of new work is being done.

4. **Terminology** employed in the classification schedule must be clear and descriptive, with consistent meaning for both the user and the classifier. The arrangement of terms is of primary importance because the "uniqueness of the arrangement of terms is closely related to the property of significance of arrangement."[18]

Broad and Close Classification

Close classification means classing each subject as completely or as fully as possible, taking into consideration all available minute subdivisions as represented in the particular classification schedule. In **broad classification** the material is classed only in main divisions and subdivisions without using the minute breakdown of individual categories. One library, for example, may need to classify the King James Bible using Dewey Classification in 220.520 3, whereas a library with a small collection of books in this area may cut back to the broad number 220. Although neither policy can be defined with exactness, one may assume that smaller libraries tend to classify more broadly than do large and more specialized collections.[19] In most libraries, classification schedules are annotated, which provides the cataloger with guidance as to the particular library's policies. These policies cover the problems of close versus broad classification, but they also affect all major decisions concerning classification problems, local interpretation of specific numbers, adoption of new numbers from revised editions of classification schedules, etc.

---

[18] J. H. Shera, "Classification: Current Functions and Applications to the Subject Analysis of Library Materials," in Tauber, *The Subject Analysis of Library Materials*, p. 30.

[19] Many smaller libraries, for example, use the abridged edition of Dewey Decimal Classification, now in its 10th edition.

GENERAL PRINCIPLES OF
CLASSIFYING A BOOK

When classifying a book, the classifier must examine all aspects of it. If the book is notable for its literary form—if it is fiction, drama, poetry, or essays aesthetic enough to be considered belles lettres—it will be classified by form according to the author's nationality. If the book's subject is more important than the form used in the writing, it will be classified according to the subject.

These are general precepts. More specifically, the classifier will observe the principles summarized here:[20]

1. **Class the book first according to subject, then by the form in which the subject is represented, except in the generalia class and in literature, where form might be paramount.** This means that in most cases the classifier has to determine the subject matter of the book using classification schedules. This is no easy task, especially when a book does not cover a specific, easily recognized topic. Chapter 1 of this text provides a short summary of procedures used by catalogers in "reading a book technically." This approach is as helpful here as in descriptive cataloging; such elements as the preface, introduction, table of contents, or even the index may help the classifier to recognize the subject matter.

Following this principle of classifying a book first by subject, we should classify a book entitled *History of Mathematics* with mathematics and not with history, or *Nature in Italian Art, a Study of Landscape Backgrounds from Giotto to Tintoretto* under landscape painting, not under history of Italian art. In some cases, however, the subject treatment is elusive and the classifier must rely on his judgment. This situation is well described by Bliss and elaborated by Sayers:[21]

> If the book on Scotland is not mainly geographic and historical, but consists of descriptive and narrative chapters together with a melange of literary and scientific observations and reflections on the national traits and institutions, also considerable social philosophy in the last chapters, the judgment is indeed complex and the decisions may be uncertain.

Several other general principles need to be considered in order to select the proper alternative.

---

[20]This discussion summarizes the principles stated by several authors, including William Stetson Merrill, *Code for Classifiers, Principles Governing the Consistent Placing of Books in a System of Classification*, 2d ed. (Chicago, American Library Association, 1939) and W. C. Berwick Sayers, *A Manual of Classification for Libraries and Bibliographers*, 3d ed. (London, Andre Deutsch, 1955). These principles apply primarily to such linear classifications as Dewey Decimal. The reader will also observe that for the purpose of this discussion we selected Sayers' third edition and not the fourth, quoted earlier.

[21]Sayers, *A Manual of Classification*, 3rd ed., pp. 235-236.

2. **Class a book where it will be most useful.** This means that the classifier has to take into consideration the nature of the collection (see the discussion above of broad vs. close classification) and the needs of the user (which are obviously not casual needs). Generally speaking, this second principle is a part of the fundamental rule of classification—that characteristics chosen for classification are essential to the purpose of the classification. A number of questions can be raised in this context. What is the subject matter of the book and how does it relate to the nature of the collection? The procedures in a highly specialized library with a professional clientele will be different from those used in a public library. What is the form in which the subject is presented, or its method of treatment? For example, most bibliographies of a given subject will be classed with that subject. There they will be more useful to a patron who wants titles on a given subject already in the library collection, but who also, as is frequently the case, is interested in obtaining information about additional sources. Existing bibliographies can provide this information. Using the same general principle, Grove's *Dictionary of Music and Musicians* will be classed first by subject (e.g., 780 in the Dewey Decimal Classification) and then by form (0.3 is the number for dictionaries). Thus, using Dewey Decimal Classification this work will be classed in 780.3. In contrast to this approach, a literary work is classed first by form. Therefore, in the Dewey Decimal Classification the basic number for a volume of Arthur Miller's plays is 812 (8—for belles lettres; 1—for American; and 2—for drama).[22]

3. **Place a book in the most specific subject that will contain it, rather than in the general topic.** In this respect it is helpful to study the classification scheme, primarily in order to answer such questions as, What is the specific heading embracing the subject? or, How is this subject subdivided in the classification schedule? It is quite obvious that if a library assigns a single number to all books dealing with the history of France and fails to subdivide them by periods and places, the result—a discouragingly large assortment of volumes under one number—will impair the effectiveness of the collection. Using the Dewey Decimal Classification, James Truslow Adams's *Provincial Society, 1690-1763* will be classed in 973.3, the number for colonial history of the United States, and not in 973, the general number for United States history.

4. **When the book deals with two or three subjects, place it with the predominant subject or with the one treated first. When the book deals with more than three subjects, place it in the general class that combines all of them.** This principle requires little explanation. The subject that is treated most fully in the book will take predominance over secondary subjects. If the two subjects are coordinate—e.g., electricity and magnetism treated equally in the same volume—the book will be placed in the class for electricity. There are some refinements to this general principle. For example, if the work covers two subjects, one of which is represented as acting upon or influencing the other, such a work should be classed under the subject influenced or acted upon. A work discussing the French influence

---

[22] Dewey Decimal Classification is being used here to illustrate some of the basic principles of classification; the reader is advised to refer to the next chapter, on Dewey Decimal Classification, as necessary.

on English literature will be classed under English literature. Similarly, a book *Religious Aspects of Philosophy* (a work dealing with the philosophy of religion) will be classed under philosophy, not religion; religion is merely an aspect of the subject, while philosophy is actually the subject matter of the book.

5. **Class a book primarily according to the intent of the author.** Example: Rudolf Eucken's well-known book *Naturalism or Idealism* will be classed under idealism, the point of view advocated by the author.

It is sometimes necessary to insert new subjects in the classification schedule. Such decisions must be carefully recorded in the official schedule and new headings must be entered in the index to the classification scheme as well as in the shelf list. Many other general principles are, of course, used in classification procedures. Some of them relate specifically to certain classification schedules (for example, the Dewey Decimal Classification and the Library of Congress Classification occasionally provide alternative ways to classify a given work, and these problems are discussed in the following chapters).

CLASSIFICATION AS A FORM OF TRANSLATION

According to the late Indian classificationist Ranganathan, the actual intuitive process of classifying a book consists of eight steps.[23] Although these steps were designed to be used with Colon Classification, they may be applied to any system. The eight steps are:

    0. The raw title
    1. Expressive title
    2. Kernel title
    3. Analyzed title
    4. Transformed title
    5. Title in standard terms
    6. Title in kernel numbers
    7. Class number.

0. The **raw title** is the title appearing on the title page of the work being classified (for example, *A History of Modern Art*).

1. The **expressive title** is the cataloger's title based on the actual subject contents of the book. For instance, a perusal of *A History of Modern Art* might show that this work is really a history of art in Europe in the twentieth century.

2. The **kernel title** is the expressive title stated in nouns and descriptive adjectives only; e.g., History. Art. Europe. Twentieth century.

---

[23] A. Neelameghan, "Classification, Theory of," in *Encyclopedia of Library and Information Science*, Vol. 5 (New York, Marcel Dekker, 1971), pp. 167-173.

3. The **analyzed title** is the kernel title with the basic function of each kernel or element analyzed. This is a particularly important step in Colon Classification, but it can be applied to any scheme; e.g., History (Form division). Art (Main class). Europe (Geographic division). Twentieth century (Period division).

4. The **transformed title** is the analyzed title with the individual kernels and their respective labels rearranged into a sequence helpful to the user or according to the prescribed order of the particular classification system being used. In this example the Dewey Decimal Classification is used; e.g., Art (Main class). History (Form division). Europe (Geographic division). Twentieth century (Period division). This is a critical step because it establishes the order of the elements (or kernels) that make up the subject being classified. For instance, the order of any of the divisions in the above example might be changed if this were deemed necessary for a helpful sequence. In particular, the order of the geographic division and the period division might be reversed.

5. The **title in standard terms** is the replacement if necessary of any of the terms in the kernel title with their respective terms in the schedule of the classification system being used; e.g., Fine and decorative arts (Main class). Historical treatment (Form division). Europe (Geographic division). 20th century (Period division). In DDC, "Art" is called "fine and decorative arts"; "History" is "Historical treatment"; and "Twentieth century" is "20th century."

6. The **title in kernel numbers** is the replacement of the kernel terms with the appropriate notation from the classification system being used; e.g., 700 (Main class). −09 (Form division). −4 (Geographic division). −5 (Period division for Europe). The specific application of these numbers will be discussed in the following chapter.

7. The **class number** is generated by the removal of the basic functions from the title in kernel numbers; e.g., 709.45.

Neelameghan points out, "These steps keep close to theory. To the beginner, translating will give insight into the art of classifying. After some experience classifying will be done by reflex action without the need to cover each step consciously."[24] These eight steps are doubly valuable: not only are they used to generate the class number, but an analagous process may be applied to subject headings.

CONCLUSION

Critics have noted some of the limitations of existing classification systems used by most libraries today.[25] Such limitations are summarized here only as a basis for further study. A long-standing argument is the question of the logical arrangement of the various systems. Though a scheme may be logical within itself, it can also have inconsistencies. For example, in Dewey Decimal Classification, language is separated from literature and history from social sciences. Language is

---

[24] Ibid.

[25] A helpful list of articles and books on classification theory is provided in a brief bibliography: Phyllis A. Richmond, "Reading List in Classification Theory," in *Library Resources and Technical Services* 16 (Summer 1972): 364-382.

closely related to literature, but it is also used by all disciplines. The logic of Dewey is contained in the definitions under the ten major classes that define the scope of each class. Keeping the classification up to date causes problems of reorganization and relocations. As classification is expanded to include new subjects and to define others more specifically, notations tend to become more complex.

In conclusion it must be remembered that the two most popular classification schemes, Dewey Decimal and LC Classification, are linear and therefore uni-dimensional. Yet the relationships among books are multi-dimensional and cannot be represented as the projection of a straight line. Because the classification is linear, one classification number must be assigned to a book whether this book is concerned with one subject or many. A supplementary subject approach to classified materials through subject headings and connecting references was developed in an attempt to solve this problem.

11 DEWEY DECIMAL CLASSIFICATION

INTRODUCTION

The Dewey Decimal Classification is the most widely used library classification. It is also the oldest of the classification schemes in use today. Melvil[le Louis Kossuth] Dewey was born on December 10, 1851. (An advocate of spelling reform, he shortened the spelling of his forename to "Melvil," dropped his two middle forenames, and even attempted to change the spelling of his surname to "Dui.")

Upon graduation from Amherst in 1874, he became assistant college librarian there and he immersed himself in library affairs. As the founder of the first library school, at Columbia University, and throughout his career, he promoted librarianship by his teaching, writing, and speaking. He early recognized the need for an adequate classification scheme that would organize a collection for systematic use. He was aware of previous attempts and found them inadequate. In 1870, W. T. Harris, of the St. Louis public schools, suggested a general classification based on an inversion of the Baconian order. Bacon divided all knowledge into two broad categories: human knowledge, and divine knowledge or theology. As we pointed out in Chapter 10, he subdivided each of these two categories into history, poesy, and philosophy: history derived from memory, poesy from imagination, and philosophy from reason. Only the first category, human knowledge, was used by Bacon's followers, including Harris, who incorporated the second category, revealed theology, into the class "religion." Inverting the three main classes of the first category, Harris began his outline with Science (including philosophy, religion, etc.), then added Art (including fine arts, poetry, and pure fiction), and finally History (including geography, civil history, and biography). In general, Dewey's outline closely approximates that of Harris. A table comparing Bacon's outline with that of Harris and Dewey is provided on page 259.

Melvil Dewey never claimed that he originated decimals in classification, although earlier decimal systems were merely shelf locations and did not apply to the subject of a book.

What Dewey did claim as his invention, however, and with some justification, was his "Relative Index," compiled as a key to the "diverse material" included in his tables. Although this is valuable, the most significant contribution was perhaps the process of the decimal division itself. By introducing the numbers 0–9, which could be subdivided almost indefinitely, he established a basic classification principle.

Bacon		Harris	Dewey
Original	**Inverted**		

Bacon		Harris	Dewey
History	Philosophy	**Science**	
		Philosophy	General Works
		Religion	Philosophy
		Social and Political Science	Religion
		Natural Sciences and Useful Arts	Sociology
			Philology
			Science
			Useful Arts
Poesy	Poesy	**Art**	
		Fine Arts	Fine Arts
		Poetry	Literature
		Pure Fiction	
		Literary Miscellany	
Philosophy	History	**History**	
		Geography and Travel	History
		Civil History	Biography
		Biography	Geography and Travel
		Appendix	
		Miscellany	

The first edition of his system, prepared for the Amherst College Library, was published in 1876 under the title "A Classification and Subject Index for Cataloguing and Arranging the Books and Pamphlets of a Library." It included schedules to some 1,000 classes numbered decimally 000–999, a relative index, and prefatory matter—a total of 44 pages. The second edition, "revised and greatly enlarged," was published in 1885 under the title "Decimal Classification and Relative Index." Since that time, 16 more full editions and 10 abridgments have appeared. The 14th edition, published in 1942, was used as the standard edition for many years because of the unsuccessful index to the 15th edition (published in 1951). In 1958 the 16th edition appeared, with many changes and additions, and even more additions were introduced in the 17th edition (published in 1965) and the present 18th edition (published in 1971).

Dewey Decimal Classification is internationally known and is widely used by libraries in this country and abroad. Such widespread use is a tribute to Dewey, who formulated a classification adaptable enough to incorporate many new subjects and flexible enough to withstand the test of time.

The revisions of Dewey Decimal Classification, although necessary, cause administrative problems in that they require libraries to adopt new or expanded classification numbers, to relocate materials, etc. This problem was probably most dramatically demonstrated in the 17th edition, in that "keeping pace with knowledge" entailed a major departure from some of the standard features of the previous editions. A comparison between the 16th and 17th editions was presented in some detail in the second edition of this text, published in 1966. In the third completely revised edition, published in 1967, we discussed some major innovations in the 17th edition and some major weaknesses of its index. The first edition of the index to the 17th edition was later revised, in response to a number of critical comments in library literature. There is voluminous literature on this subject. The reader will be well advised to read the appropriate chapters in some of the textbooks included in the bibliography at the end of this volume, as well as some of the monographic works that summarize the development of the Dewey Decimal Classification.[1]

In December 1971, the 18th edition of the *Dewey Decimal Classification* was published by Forest Press; it introduced additional innovations and new features.

Auxiliary tables, used for the first time in the 17th edition, are now called "tables" (a term previously used for schedules), while the main classification schedules (now incorporated in the second volume) are simply called "schedules." These auxiliary tables (i.e., "tables") are of two kinds: applicable to all classes (like the Area Tables already introduced in the 17th edition) or limited to particular classes or subject areas—e.g., subdivisions of individual literatures. The 18th edition has seven tables (all in the first volume), which are identified as follows:

1. Standard subdivisions
2. Areas
3. Subdivisions of Individual Literatures
4. Subdivisions of Individual Languages
5. Racial, Ethnic, National Groups
6. Languages
7. Persons

---

[1] Of special interest are the following: Benjamin A. Custer, "Dewey Decimal Classification," *Encyclopedia of Library and Information Science*, Vol. 7 (New York, Marcel Dekker, 1972), pp. 128-142; and Winifred B. Linderman, "Dewey, Melvil," *Encyclopedia of Library and Information Science*, Vol. 7 (New York, Marcel Dekker, 1972), pp. 142-160. Also see Marty Bloomberg and Hans Weber, *An Introduction to Classification for Small and Medium-Sized Libraries* (Littleton, Colo., Libraries Unlimited, 1976); C. D. Batty, *An Introduction to the 18th ed. of the Dewey Decimal Classification* (Hamden, Conn., Archon Books, 1971); and his "A Close Look at Dewey 18: Alive and Well and Living in Albany," *Wilson Library Bulletin* 46 (April 1972): 711-717. There are also, of course, many articles on this subject in periodical literature. One of the best, dealing with the 10th abridged edition, is Lois Mai Chan, "The Tenth Abridged Dewey Decimal Classification . . . and Children's Room/School Library Collections," *School Library Journal* 20 (Sept. 15, 1973): 38-43.

This edition has a total of 396 relocations. The greatest number of these (164) are in Class 300, followed by Class 500 (74) and Class 600 (68). There are new schedules for two disciplines—340, Law, and 510, Mathematics (phoenix schedules). The obsolescent schedules are included in Volume 3, following the index, an arrangement that facilitates a possible reclassification of the law and mathematics collections. The concept of centered headings (introduced in an earlier edition) is retained, and explanatory notes indicate where to class comprehensive works and works of an interdisciplinary nature. For the first time, all unused and discontinued numbers are clearly indicated in the schedules; 210 of these discontinued numbers are listed.

An innovation in the 18th edition is the glossary of basic terms (over 70 terms are defined); the glossary will be most useful to beginning catalogers and to library school students.

The index to the 18th edition is competent; it continues the tradition of the 16th edition and the revised index to the 17th edition.

The first volume contains not only tables but also a brief historical sketch on Dewey Decimal Classification, Melvil Dewey's Introduction to the 12th Edition (a reprint with a few minor changes), and an informative Editor's Introduction that outlines major changes in this edition and provides concise instructions on the use of its new format. As was the case in the 17th edition, this introduction is written by Benjamin A. Custer; it contains many helpful examples that will assist the novice in the use of this edition.

This edition has replaced "divide like" notes with "add" instructions, a feature that is discussed in some detail on pages 273-275. It should be noted that Table 5, Racial, Ethnic and National Groups, is derived from the notation in Class 400 (Language), as is Table 6, Languages. The last table, Persons, is used for tracing trades and occupations and can be used with Table 5 and "add" instructions in order to provide a necessary specification by race, national origin, or social and economic characteristics.

As C. D. Batty indicated in his review in *Wilson Library Bulletin*,

> DC18's provision of separate tables of auxiliaries has three effects: it provides a much simpler method of general subdivision; it enables the tables of subdivision to be developed logically without subject class bias, and it frees the main schedules from considerable and possibly distracting built-in detail and annotation. The school librarian who uses full DC and also seeks simple and short notation is also aided by the ability to recognize more easily what is the base number and what is auxiliary.[2]

BASIC CONCEPTS

Dewey Decimal Classification is called "decimal" because it arranges all knowledge as represented by books into ten broad subject classes numbered from 0 to 9. Each of the classes from 100 to 900 consists of a group of related disciplines:

---

[2] Batty, "A Close Look at Dewey 18," p. 713.

Class 100–philosophy and related disciplines; Class 200–religion; Class 300–social sciences; Class 400–language; Class 500–pure sciences; Class 600–technology (applied sciences); etc. Together with class 000–generalities (general works) these subject classes embody the whole of human knowledge. Each class may be divided into ten divisions, each division into subdivisions, and so on.

Because the numbers are decimal, not consecutive, the order of progression is as follows:

333
333.001
333.01
333.1
333.13
333.2

The Dewey system, which uses only numbers for classification, is an example of **pure notation**. It is flexible only to the degree that numbers can be expanded for special aspects of general subjects; but the more specifically the cataloger classifies a book, the more likely it is that he will be forced to expand his combination of numbers. Thus, it is possible for a closely classified book to carry a Dewey number of 12 digits. Such a number, although quite correct, is most unwieldy; placing it on the spine of a book is difficult, and patrons cannot easily locate such a long sequence of numbers. It is for this and other reasons that many large libraries are turning from Dewey in favor of a more extensive yet more compact system, such as that of LC.

Nevertheless, the Dewey Decimal Classification scheme has many advantages. Its schedule is compact, consisting, in the 18th edition, of one volume for tables, a second volume for schedules of classes, and a third volume for the relative index. It makes use of many mnemonic devices that can be applied from one class to another (for example, –03 indicates a dictionary of some subject); thus the classifier, once he learns the system, can classify quite rapidly. It is flexible and allows for great detail of classification. The patron is more familiar with general aspects of Dewey Decimal Classification because it is the system most frequently used in public and school libraries. Furthermore, the Dewey scheme arranges subjects from the general to the specific in a logical order, which also very often carries over from one class to another.

The Dewey classification scheme is philosophical in both conception and intention. It is based on a systematic outline of knowledge that allows for subjects not yet known to man. Even so, the overall arrangement is not necessarily theoretical or logical. Dewey's intent was to provide a practical system for classifying books. It was consistent within its own limiting principles, containing in the 10 major classes only the subjects as defined under major headings.

Dewey successfully synthesized knowledge into 10 general classes (including one class–000–devised to provide for books too general to fit anywhere else).

The following numbers constitute subdivisions of the basic number. The Dewey classes are written in three digits as hundreds. Each class is divided into ten divisions (or subclasses); the first subclass covers the general works of the entire class, e.g.,

100–109	Philosophy (general works)
110	Metaphysics (speculative philosophy)
160	Logic
170	Ethics (moral philosophy)
	etc.

Each division (or subclass) is further subdivided into "sections" or sub-subclasses, again with the first section covering the general works on the entire division:

610	Medical sciences in general
611	Human anatomy, cytology, tissue biology
612	Human physiology
613	General and personal hygiene

611	Human anatomy—further subdivided:
611.1	Cardiovascular organs
611.2	Respiratory organs
611.3	Digestive organs
611.4	Lymphatic and glandular organs
	—further subdivided:

611.41	Spleen
611.42	Lymphatic system
611.43	Thymus gland
	etc.

Dewey Decimal Classification is built on the premise that there is no one class for any given subject. The basic arrangement is by discipline, and a given subject may appear in any number of disciplines. Various aspects of a specific subject are brought together by the relative index.

For example, a work on "family" as a subject can be classed in several disciplines depending on its emphasis. A work on "family as a social institution" can be classed in 301.42 (the basic number for marriage and family) and subdivided by several closely related social aspects—e.g., 301.421 Structure and functions of family; 301.422 Nature and forms of marriage (monogamy, polygamy, interracial, intercultural, interreligious marriage, etc.); 301.423 Family and social change (including effects upon family of urbanization, mobility, technology, industrialization, etc.). From the breakdown we can see that some aspects of the subject "family" are interrelated to another subject, "marriage," and these two subjects sometimes follow a similar pattern. Thus, legal aspects of both subjects will be classed in 346.016 (Marriage, including common law marriage, voidable marriage, marriage contracts) and ethical aspects in 173 (Ethics of family relationships: marriage, separation, divorce, responsibilities of parents for children and home life, etc.). Other special aspects of "family" (still in the sociological interpretation) are given in the section on Social welfare; e.g., works on social welfare assistance to families will be classed in 362.82; works on family influence on criminal prevention in 364.44. On the other hand, economic aspects of the subject, such as works on family budget and expenses, will be classed in 647.1; and historical aspects, such as family histories, in 929.2. There are, of course, many other aspects of this subject: material on religious aspects of the family is classed in 200's; health in 600's; a book dealing with family as a subject of art or literature, in 700's or 800's, etc. See the relative index for additional headings for the subject "family."

Dewey Decimal Classification is a hierarchical classification; it applies the principle of development from the general to the special-specific in disciplinary and subject relationships. This hierarchical structure is incorporated in the notation for a specific subject; notations display the hierarchical features in the successive lengthening of the basic number by one digit to achieve division:

620	Engineering and allied operations
621	Applied physics
621.1	Steam engineering
621.15	Engines
621.16	Stationary
621.165	Turbine

This hierarchical structure means that, in these subject relationships, what is true of the whole is true of the parts. Engineering is one of the applied sciences. Mechanical engineering is subordinated to engineering and steam as fluid-power engineering is a part of mechanical engineering, etc. It should be noted, however, that in certain places in the schedules the hierarchical structure cannot be closely observed; such a situation is shown in the tables by spans of additional digits, called **centered headings**. These are defined in the glossary to the 18th edition as: "A heading representing a concept for which there is no specific number in the hierarchy of notation, and which, therefore, covers a span of numbers." These centered headings are indicated in the schedules by a triangular mark—i.e., ▶342-345 Public law.

STANDARD SUBDIVISIONS

As it was noted in Chapter 10, Classification, all printed schedules of book classification have to provide for a dual approach to the classifying of books; i.e., some books will be classed on the basis of their physical form, while the placement of others will depend on their treatment of subject matter. The standard subdivisions used in the Dewey Decimal Classification provide examples of this dual approach. Some actually do treat physical form (e.g., dictionaries, encyclopedias, periodicals, etc.); others are "modes of treatment," covering theoretical or historical aspects of the subject, such as philosophy and theory, history, etc. The auxiliary table in the first volume of DDC 18 for standard subdivisions is Table 1. The following is a summary of that table.

Standard Subdivisions (Mnemonic)

01 — **Philosophy and theory.** An exposition of the subject treated from the theoretical point of view. Example:

> 701 — Philosophy of fine and decorative arts

02 — **Miscellany.** A subject treated briefly or in outline only, as in synopses, outlines, manuals, etc. This subdivision also includes material treated in tabular form, illustrations, directories, miscellaneous legal matters, inventories and identification marks, commercial miscellany, etc.

03 — **Dictionaries, encyclopedias, concordances.** Example:

> 720.3 — Dictionary of architecture

04 — **General special.** Reserved for special concepts that have general application; it is always indicated in the schedules, e.g.,

> 231.04 — God, Trinity, Godhead: General special

05 — **Serial publications.** Serial publications of a literary nature or in which the subject is treated in articles, papers, etc. Example:

> 720.5 — Architectural Record

06 — **Organizations.** Official publications of international, national, state, provincial, and local organizations such as reports, proceedings, regulations, membership lists, etc. Example:

> 720.6 — Transactions of the Royal Institute of
> British Architects

07 — **Study and Teaching.** Books on how to study and how to teach a subject; that is, methods of studying and teaching (including research). Example:

> 707 — Pearson's The New Art Education

08 — **Collections and Anthologies.** Including collected essays and lectures (formerly in 04). Essentially includes collections not planned as composite works. Example:

> 080 — Harvard Classics

09 — **Historical and Geographical Treatment.** Including historical periods not limited geographically, history and description by area and geographical treatment, history and description by continent, country, locality, etc. Example:

> 720.9 — Fletcher's History of Architecture

This number deals with the history of the subject in general, and can be geographically divided, e.g., 720.973 — History of Architecture in the United States.

There are further possibilities for subdividing within the standard subdivisions. For example, under 01—Philosophy and Theory are the following major topics:

012 — Classification
013 — Value
014 — Languages (Terminology) and communication
015 — Scientific principles
016 — Indexes
017 — Professional and occupational ethics
018 — Methodology
019 — Psychological principles

Unless specific instructions indicate otherwise, the standard subdivisions may be used with any number where they apply. Although each standard subdivision is preceded by a single-0, as 03 (dictionaries, encyclopedias, concordances), in many cases it is necessary to apply a double-0 or a triple-0 in order to introduce these standard subdivisions, because many of the —0 divisions have been utilized for special purposes within the tables. This can be determined from the study of the Dewey schedules; the instructions that cover these situations are explicit and should be followed carefully. A few examples will illustrate some of the basic principles.

a) Standard subdivisions contained as a part of a complete heading

In some parts of Dewey schedules, a concept that is ordinarily expressed as a standard subdivision has its own number—e.g., a dictionary of literature is classed in 803 (800 for literature, 803 for dictionary), rather than in 800.3 or 800.03.

b) 0-divisions utilized for specific purpose
Standard subdivision to be introduced by double-0

An example of the double-0 is found in 271 (Religious congregations and orders). Here the instruction is to use 271.001—271.009 for standard subdivisions. Single-0 is reserved for specific kinds of religious congregations (e.g., Contemplative 271.01, Teaching 271.03, Preaching 271.04, etc.). Therefore, a dictionary of religious congregations and orders in general is classed in 271.003.

c) 00-divisions utilized for special purposes (further hierarchical breakdown)
Standard subdivisions to be introduced by triple-0

An example of the triple-0 is found in 350 (Public administration). Here the instruction is to use 350.0001—350.0009 for standard subdivisions of this general subject. 350.001—350.009 are reserved for The Executive and 350.01—350.08 are used for specific executive departments and ministries. 350.1—350.9 encompasses specific aspects of public administration such as personnel management, registers of personnel, civil service examination, etc. Therefore, a dictionary of public administration in general is classed 350.0003.

Area Tables

When a given heading has particular geographic significance and the library has many books dealing with the subject, it is recommended that the classifier use the area table, which allows one to expand the number for that heading by area. This area table is Table 2, found in the first volume; area notations may be added to the basic numbers as required. It should be noted that this was one of the major changes introduced in the 17th edition of Dewey Decimal Classification. In the 16th edition geographic subdivision was allowed by means of a note to "Divide like 930–999." However, the use of these historical sequences to form a geographic number created some confusion. To simplify this matter in terms of number-building, the area table replaced 930–999 in creating regional subdivision, leaving the history numbers solely for history. The general arrangement of the area table is as follows:

−1	Regions, areas, places in general
−2	Persons regardless of area, region, place
−3	The ancient world
−4−9	The modern world
	−4 Europe
	−5 Asia, Orient, Far East
	−6 Africa
	−7 North America
	−8 South America
	−9 Other parts of the world and extraterrestrial worlds

For example, area −1 is used for the treatment of any subject by region, area or places in general—that is, those not limited by continent, country, or locality. This allows diverse elements that have natural ties as to region or groups to be brought together under certain subjects (e.g., frigid zones, temperate zones, types of vegetation, etc.). Area −1 notations may be added where they apply, in the same manner as the area notations described below.

Area notations −4−9 are for specific continents, modern world countries and localities. For example, area number −4, Europe, has the following summary:

−41	British Isles, including Scotland and Ireland
−42	England
−43	Central Europe, Germany
−44	France and Monaco
−45	Italy and adjacent territories
−46	Iberian Peninsula and adjacent islands, Spain
−47	Eastern Europe, Union of Soviet Socialist Republics
−48	Northern Europe, Scandinavia
−49	Other parts of Europe, etc.

The above example includes a recent revision of −41 and −42 in the area tables: formerly, −41 meant only Scotland and Ireland and −42 meant the entire British Isles. Now −41 means the British Isles, including Scotland and Ireland, and −42 means only England. Subdivision −411 has also been revised; instead of meaning

Northern Scotland it now means all of Scotland. The remaining subdivisions have not been changed. Below is an example of further subdivision using Table 2:

−41	British Isles. Scotland. Ireland.
−42	England.
−421	Greater London.
−4213	West London.
−42132	Westminster.
−42133	Hammersmith.
−42134	Kensington and Chelsea.

An example—a general treatise on higher education in Kensington, London—will illustrate the principles involved in using area tables. The number for higher education, as found in the index and the schedules, is 378. The direction in the schedule is "378.4−.9 for higher education by continent, country, locality in modern world," with a further instruction to "Add area notations 4−9 to 378." The index refers to area table −42134 as the number for Kensington, London. This number is then applied to 378 giving 378.42134 for higher education in Kensington, London. An analysis of this number shows:

378	Higher education
.4	Europe
.42	England
.421	Greater London
.4213	West London
.42134	Kensington and Chelsea
378.42134	Higher education in Kensington and Chelsea

There is no provision in Table 2 for separating Kensington and Chelsea, so this is the most specific number that can be applied.

Where specific instructions (as in 378.4−.9) are not given for geographical treatment in the schedules, the classifier can apply the standard subdivision −09 (historical and geographical treatment) with a single-0, double-0, or triple-0 to any number that can be logically developed. For example, for savings banks in Westminster, London, the procedure will be as follows: the specific number for savings banks is 332.21. The schedule shows that single-0 is not being used for any specific subdivisions, so the standard subdivision −09 may be used directly. Add the standard subdivision −09, then the area notation for Westminster, −42132. Thus, books on savings banks in Westminster, London, will be classed in 332.210942132. This number may be analyzed to show:

332.21	Savings banks
09	Standard subdivision for historical and geographical treatment
4	Europe
42	England
421	Greater London
4213	West London
42132	Westminster

332.210942132	Savings banks in Westminster

It should be noted by the beginning student that although both of these examples result in very long numbers, they are very simple to construct.

The 18th edition includes five additional auxiliary tables. These tables are used less frequently than the standard subdivisions or the area tables and often are limited to individual classes. They represent basic mnemonic features.

Individual Literatures

In Table 3, Subdivisions of Individual Literatures, a detailed and specialized development of standard subdivisions —08 for collections and —09 for historical and geographical treatment is given for base numbers 810—890. In addition, the table provides mnemonic form divisions for literature.

Form divisions for kinds of literature (mnemonic):

—1 — Poetry	(831 German poetry)
—2 — Drama	(842 French drama)
—3 — Fiction	(853 Italian fiction)
—4 — Essays	(864 Spanish essays)
—5 — Speeches	(845 French speeches)
—6 — Letters	(836 German letters)
—7 — Satire and humor	(847 French satire and humor)
—8 — Miscellany—sometimes used for author's whole works	(858 Italian miscellany)

Individual Languages

Table 4, Subdivisions of Individual Languages, is used with base numbers 420—490. This table is similar to Table 3, since it provides mnemonic form divisions for language.

Form divisions for languages (mnemonic)—apply to all:

−1 — Written and spoken codes (421 in English)
−2 — Etymology (422 in English; 432 in German)
−3 — Dictionaries (423 in English; 443 in French)
−4 — Not used
−5 — Structural system (former heading: Grammar.
425 in English; 455 in Italian)
−6 — Prosody (426 in English; 466 in Spanish)
−7 — Nonstandard language (427 Nonstandard English; 447 Nonstandard French)
−8 — Standard usage (428 Standard English usage; 458 Standard Italian usage)

Racial, Ethnic, National Groups

Table 5, Racial, Ethnic, National Groups, is used when directed in the schedules. The notations are added to base numbers in the schedules and in other auxiliary tables. This application is directly parallel to the use of Table 1 or Table 2. The summary of this table is:

−1 North Americans
−2 Anglo-Saxons, British, English
−3 Nordics
−4 Modern Latins
−5 Italians, Romanians, related groups
−6 Spanish and Portuguese
−7 Other Italic people
−8 Greeks and related groups
−9 Other racial, ethnic, national groups

An example to illustrate the use of this table could be a work dealing with special education for American Blacks. The number for special education as found in the index and the schedules is 371.9. The direction in the schedule for 371.97 (for exceptional students because of national, racial, or ethnic origin) states, "Add 'Racial, Ethnic, National Groups' notation 01−99 from Table 5 to base number 371.97." The number in Table 5 for American Blacks is −96073. Thus, the number for special education for American Blacks is 371.9796073. An analysis of this number is:

371.9	Special education
.97	Students exceptional because of racial, ethnic, national origin
9	Other racial, ethnic, national groups
96	Africans and people of African descent
0	Digit used to expand the notation, in this case geographically
073	United States
371.9796073	Special education for Black Americans

Languages

Table 6, Languages, is a basic mnemonic table used to indicate the particular national language. It is used as instructed in the tables and is particularly used in classes 400 and 800. The summary of these language mnemonics is:

−1	Indo-European languages
−2	English and Anglo-Saxon languages
−3	Germanic languages
−4	Romance languages (French and French related languages)
−5	Italian, Romanian, Rhaeto-Romanic
−6	Spanish and Portuguese
−7	Italic languages
−8	Hellenic languages
−9	Other languages

An example of the application of this table would be a Bible in French. The number in the index and the tables for the Bible is 220.5. For languages other than English, the schedule direction states "Add 'Languages' notation 3–9 from Table 6 to base number 220.5." The notation for French in Table 6 is −41. Thus, the number for a modern French Bible is 220.541. This may be analyzed:

220.5	Modern versions of the Bible
4	Romance languages
41	French

220.541   A modern version of the Bible in French

Persons

Table 7, Persons, is used when the schedules indicate to add the "Persons" notation to a base number. This table deals with various characteristics of persons, as the following summary shows.

−01	Individual persons in general	
−02	Groups of persons in general	
−03−08	Persons with nonoccupational characteristics	
	−03	Persons by racial, ethnic, national background (using Table 5 for subdivisions)
	−04	Persons by sex and kinship characteristics
	−05	Persons by age
	−06	Persons by social and economic characteristics
	−08	Persons by physical and mental characteristics
−09	Generalists and novices	
	(for example, librarians are −092)	

Table 7 (cont'd)

−1−9   Specialists
   −1   Persons occupied with philosophy
   −2   Persons occupied with religion
   −3   Persons occupied with social sciences
   −4   Persons occupied with linguistics
   −5   Persons occupied with pure sciences
   −6   Persons occupied with applied sciences
   −7   Persons occupied with the arts
              (for example, −78 musicians)
   −8   Persons occupied with creative writing and speaking
   −9   Persons occupied with geography, history, related
              disciplines

Obviously, from −09 to −9 this table is based on the ten main classes of DDC. A manual on sex instruction for polygamous persons may be used as an example of the use of this table. The number for sex instruction is 301.418. The directions in the schedule following this number state, "Add 'Persons' notation 03−99 from Table 7 to base number 301.418." The number in Table 7 for polygamous persons is "−0659." Thus, the number for a manual on sex instruction for polygamous persons is 301.4180659. An analysis of this number is:

301.418	Manuals on sex education
06	Persons by social and economic characteristics
065	By marriage status
0659	Polygamous persons
301.4180659	A manual on sex instruction for polygamous persons

Relative Index

The DDC "relative" index enumerates alphabetically all the main headings in the classification scheme, showing also synonyms and, to a large extent, the relation of each subject to other subjects. It should be noted that the index does not include all names of countries, cities, animals, and plants, and that frequently the full subdivisions are not included. Starting with the 14th edition, the relative index is quite comprehensive. It should be noted, however, that the relative index cannot be used as a substitute for schedules; rather, it is coordinated with them. It is limited for reasons of space. It will guide the classifier to some, but not all, aspects of a given subject by referring to specific numbers within the schedules. The classifier must always consult a particular topic or subject in the schedules for further instructions on selecting the appropriate number.

Broad and Close Classification

Since it has many opportunities for number-building, Dewey Decimal Classification can encompass the titles that large libraries may add in any subject. The needs of smaller libraries can also be met, through use of the abridged edition of *Dewey Decimal Classification.*

The classifier must remember that, in general, when he has relatively few books in a given subject area, he can resort to broad classification. Digits after the decimal point may be cut off at any appropriate place. The present policy of the Library of Congress is to provide LC cards with Dewey Decimal numbers of from one to three segments; smaller libraries can reduce the length of notations by dropping one or two segments. The segments are indicated by apostrophes; e.g., 016.91009'171'242 (Bibliography—Commonwealth of Nations—Description and travel).

Nevertheless, larger libraries that have more titles in a given subject area must make use of the opportunities for close classification. A small library in Rochester, New York, which has very few books on California history, may prefer to keep them all together under 979.4. On the other hand, a library in California with many books on that state's history may keep all books that deal with discovery and early exploration of California from 1542 to 1769, in 979.401; the Spanish period in California history (1769-1822) in 979.402; the Mexican period (1822-1848) in 979.403, etc. As it was indicated earlier, standard subdivisions or area notations may be added to certain numbers for further specificity.

Scope and "Add Instructions"

The body of schedules has several other instructional notes that will aid the classifier.

One such device is the **scope note**. This note, which appears directly after the statement of a major classification category, tells what is to be classed in that number. Under the centered heading 913—919, Geography of specific continents, countries, localities, we find the following instruction:

Scope: "Class here interdisciplinary works on geography and history of specific continents, countries, localities.

"If preferred, class in 930—990.

"Class comprehensive works, geography of and travel in more than one continent in 910; history of specific continents, countries, localities in 930—990; geography of and travel in areas, regions, places not limited by continent, country, locality in 910.09; historical geography in 911; graphic representations in 912."

This particular instruction not only tells us about the scope of a particular numerical sequence in the schedules but suggests alternative classification and provides a number of helpful further directions.

Other types of scope notes that frequently appear throughout the schedules are definitions of certain terms that will be helpful in understanding the scope of a particular subject. For example,

> "330   Economics
>   The science of human behavior as it relates to utilization of scarce means for satisfaction of needs and desires through production, distribution, consumption.
>   For commerce, see 380"

Still other subheadings are followed by notes enumerating specific qualifications, such as

> "331   Labor economics
>   Class here industrial relations
>   Class personnel management in 658.3"

> "331.1   Labor force and market
>   Class labor force and market with respect to specific classes of workers in 331.3—331.6"

It should be noted that another aid to the classifier was the **divide-like note**, which appeared quite frequently throughout each class in the 17th and older editions. The divide-like note, which served as a basis of number-building, was inserted under a simple number or a sequence of numbers. Basically it meant that an elaborate system of subdivision had been worked out elsewhere for a particular number, so that the classifier had to refer to another part of the schedules for instructions. The reader may recall a simple example of the divide-like note found in the sequence 430—490. The instruction was: "Divide each language identified by * like 421—428 (that is, English), e.g., Hebrew language dictionaries 492.43." In other words, languages other than English may use the corresponding subdivisions provided for English. The 18th edition no longer uses divide-like notes, which have been replaced by **add instructions**; these specify exactly what digits should be added to what base number. The add instructions are used with auxiliary tables, schedules, or a combination of the two ("add from both tables and schedules"), thereby providing an opportunity to expand certain numbers into subdivisions not enumerated in the schedules. Since this process of number-building is explained in some detail in the Editor's Introduction (see Volume 1, pp. 28-29), we will provide here only a brief summary of the most typical situations.

Auxiliary Tables 1 through 7 enable the classifier to expand existing numbers in the schedules into more specific subdivisions, a procedure that, with the addition of new auxiliary tables, now makes the expansion less cumbersome. For example, Table 3, Subdivisions of Individual Literatures, is used throughout 810—899. This eliminates the previously used divide-like notes, which required frequent back-and-forth page-turning in order to assign an appropriate number sequence. Similarly, Table 4, Subdivisions of Individual Languages, is used throughout 420—490, and Table 5, Racial, Ethnic, National Groups, is used frequently with "Areas" notation 109, from Table 2, which was introduced in the 17th edition. One example will illustrate this process. In both the 17th and the 18th editions, the number for ethnopsychology and national psychology is 155.8. The first subdivision provided in the schedules is for race differences (155.82), which requires no elaboration. The number for specific races is 155.84. In the 17th edition the reader will find a notation: "Divide like 420–490, e.g., psychology of Jews 155.84924." Under 155.84 the 18th edition has the following instructions: "Add 'Racial, Ethnic, National Groups' notation 01–99 from Table 5 to base number 155.84." Consulting this table in the first volume, the reader will find on page 403 a notation for Semites (–92) subdivided by particular ethnic groups, with –924 for Hebrews, Israelis, Jews. Thus, the process of number-building is more expedient and somewhat simplified.

In addition to the add instructions from auxiliary tables, such instructions are found in schedules. It should be noted that the base number is always provided in the instructions, indicating a sequence of numbers to be added. For example, under Botany, the number for Physiology of plants is 581.1, subdivided as 581.11 Circulation, 581.12 Respiration and transpiration, etc. Under 581.16 Reproduction (Propagation), we find the following: "Add to 581.16 the numbers following 574.16 in 574.162–574.166, e.g., Conjugation 581.1662." Thus, under 574.1 Physiology, we find a summary that provides us with 574.16 for Reproduction, and .162 for Parthenogenesis. To obtain the required number, the classifier adds 62 to the already established base number: 581.16+62.

Several other types of notes are useful in determining a needed classification number, and they occasionally clarify a given terminology with helpful examples. Thus, 693, Construction in specific materials and for specific purposes, has a number of subdivisions, including 693.98 Nonrigid materials. This particular subdivision is further explained with a note of "example: pneumatic construction." There are numerous "class here" notes throughout the schedules (e.g., 711.6, Area planning–structural elements: "Class here comprehensive works on plans and planning of specific elements. For utilities, see 711.7").

For the first time, all discontinued numbers are so indicated in the schedules. For example, 623.864, Flares and other portable lights for nautical craft "[.864] Flares and other portable lights, Number discontinued; class in 623.86."

There is also an increased number of optional provisions, with alternatives provided (e.g., 750.92, Painters, has the following note: "Use of this number is optional; prefer 759"). Also helpful are notes for interdisciplinary and comprehensive works (e.g., 669, Metallurgy: "Class here interdisciplinary works on metals. Use 669.001–669.009 for standard subdivisions. Class a specific aspect of metals with the subject, e.g., chemistry 546.3").

CONCLUSIONS

Using Dewey Decimal Classification–or, indeed, any classification system–presents several administrative problems. In the 18th edition of Dewey many long notations became necessary; the tendency to diminish mnemonic features resulted in subdivisions that contain five or six digits. Thus, a history of Jews in Germany is classed in 943.009 749 24. Librarians who wish to retain Dewey Decimal

Classification numbers of any length should write them on books and cards in several lines—e.g., Ralph C. and Estelle D. James's biography, *Hoffa and the Teamsters* (Princeton, N.J., Van Nostrand, 1965):

```
331
.8811
388
324
0924
```

Unfortunately, the abridged edition of Dewey only partially solves this problem. The 9th abridged edition contained 2,530 entries in the schedules and 308 in the tables, for a grand total of 2,838 entries (as compared to 17,132 entries in the schedules and 5,223 in the tables—a total of 22,355—for the 17th edition). The 18th edition has the following breakdown: total schedules, 18,980; tables, 7,161; grand total, 26,141. As we can see, the 18th edition shows a net increase of 3,786 entries. The 10th abridged edition contains 2,211 entries in the schedules and 311 entries in the tables, for a grand total of 2,542 entries. There are thus fewer entries in the 10th edition than in the 9th, as well as fewer opportunities to build numbers. The 10th edition is designed as an adaptation rather than an abridgment of the full edition. It is addressed to smaller libraries that will in all probability not wish to use the full edition. Besides length, there are at least 134 distinct variations between the 10th abridged and the 18th full edition. These are listed on pages 85-86 in the abridged edition, before the first summary. Furthermore, the 10th abridged uses only four of the seven auxiliary tables: standard subdivisions, areas, subdivisions for individual literatures, and subdivisions for individual languages. These four tables are all shortened in the 10th edition. Although the 10th edition is a more useful and practical edition in many aspects than the 9th edition, small libraries using LC printed cards and trying to segment DDC 18 numbers to become DDC 10 numbers have been somewhat critical of DDC 10's variations from the full edition.

The second problem, that of relocation, is not new. A tabulation of the number of relocations in the 18th edition shows 396, as compared with 746 in the 17th edition and 1,603 in the 16th edition.

Is it necessary for a library to reclassify immediately in certain areas? In a previous edition of this text we discussed this problem in some detail. As we considered the changes introduced in the 17th edition, we questioned whether it was necessary to reclassify in such areas as child psychology. Libraries with large collections in education and psychology may find this a difficult decision. The 18th edition has two completely revised schedules—Law and Mathematics. In the 17th edition, 345 was assigned to U.S. statutes and cases, 346 to British statutes and cases, and 349 to Statutes and cases not U.S. or British. In the 18th edition, all statutes, regulations and cases will be found in 348, the number not used in the 17th edition but previously used for religious law. Now 345 is allocated for Criminal law (343 in the previous edition); 343 is Miscellaneous public law; 344 is Social law (previously Martial law), etc. How many libraries with substantial collections of law material can afford to make all these changes? Similarly, the 510's, Mathematics, are completely new ("phoenix" schedule), and 511 (assigned in the 17th edition to Arithmetic) is now reserved for Generalities, while Arithmetic has been transferred to 513 (previously Synthetic geometry). 512, Algebra, is the same in both editions, although, of course, subdivisions are different. 514 is now Topology (Trigonometry in the 17th edition), 515 is Analysis (Descriptive geometry in the 17th edition), etc. For the convenience of classifiers the new edition contains in one list all the relocations made in the 18th edition, as well as all numbers discontinued in the new edition. Obsolescent schedules (340 and 510) are reprinted in the index volume; in the Editor's Introduction, classifiers "are urged to reclassify their collections in law and mathematics according to the new phoenix schedules." Tables of Concordance also included in this volume provide a correlation between numbers of the two editions, thus making this task easier.

Without any doubt, the 18th edition represents a substantial improvement. It is more up to date in terms of terminology and schedules, and the index contains an entry for every significant term in the schedules and tables. The numerous cross references in the index not only conserve space but also facilitate use of the index. All this is for the best. Nevertheless, most larger libraries face budgetary problems these days, and the adoption of the proposed changes may pose additional problems. As was pointed out in the third edition of this text, large libraries will probably continue to change to the Library of Congress Classification. Smaller libraries do not have much choice in this matter. They will continue to use Dewey Decimal Classification, the most popular classification not only in this country but in many foreign countries as well.

Work on the 19th edition is now going on at the Decimal Classification Office at the Library of Congress, again under the editorship of Benjamin Custer. The possible publication date of this edition is 1978 or 1979, with the 11th abridged to follow within a year or so. Possibly there will be three or more phoenix schedules: one on the political process, combining 324 and 329 into a single class, 324; another for sociology in the beginning of the 300's; and a third for music, being an adaptation of the scheme for music used in the *British Catalogue of Music* issued by the British National Bibliography. The first of these three phoenix schedules is already completed; the others are in progress. More detailed geographical area breakdowns are planned throughout, especially for Latin America and Africa. In addition, an official Spanish edition is presently being developed; an official French edition was published in 1974.

CUTTER NUMBERS

In order to provide a **call number**, or **book number**, that is distinctive to one book only and that indicates its place on the shelves, catalogers have devised a notation consisting of at least the classification number on the first line and the cutter, or author, number, plus the work mark, on the second line, thus:

> 813.4
> J27w

This combination is designated the call number for the book.

To accomplish this, most existing classification systems provide for an alphabetical progression within a classification.

The most famous alphabetical schedule is probably the combination of surnames and numerals devised by Charles Ammi Cutter. Cutter initially devised two-figure tables in a single alphabet of all consonants except the letter S, followed by an alphabet of vowels and the letter S. These two-figure tables were expanded to three-figure tables by Kate F. Sanborn. Since she did not use Cutter's two-figure tables as the basis for her tables, Cutter then expanded his own two-figure tables to three-figure tables. This means that there are three different Cutter tables: the two-figure Cutter tables, the three-figure Cutter-Sanborn tables, and the three-figure Cutter tables.

The purpose of cutter numbers is to allow alphabetical subdivision under individual class numbers. Cutter numbers are most commonly used to arrange material by authors' surnames; however, in some instances they are used to alphabetize material by subject, as in the case of biography. Cutter numbers are a part of the book number and not part of the class number.

The cutter number consists of the first letter (or letters) of the author's surname (or the subject) followed by the appropriate number (or numbers) from the Cutter table. For example, the English poet John Donne receives the cutter number D71 if the Cutter two-figure table is used. The two-figure table shows:

Doll	69	Foh
Dom	71	Folg
Doo	72	Foll

Donne is between "Dom" and "Doo." The instructions for this table call for choosing the preceding number rather than the following number. Thus, the cutter number from the two-figure table is "D71." The Cutter-Sanborn three-figure table shows:

Donk	684	Fonti
Donn	685	Fontr
Donner	686	Foo

The cutter number from the Cutter-Sanborn three-figure table is "D685," since Donne is between "Donn" and "Donner," and "685" is the preceding number. If the Cutter three-figure table is used, the expansion of the Cutter two-figure table may be observed:

Donk	718	Folk
Donnet	719	Folke
Doo	72	Foll

In this case, the cutter number would be "D718."

These three examples show that the Cutter three-figure table is an expansion of the Cutter two-figure table, while the Cutter-Sanborn three-figure table is not. These examples also demonstrate the typical three-column display used in Cutter tables. In this case the letters "D" and "F" share a single column of numbers. This type of display was used in all editions of the Cutter tables until 1969, when Paul K. Swanson of the Forbes Library, Northampton, Massachusetts, and Mrs. Ester M. Swift, editor of the H. R. Huntting Company (the distributor of the Cutter tables) revised this arrangement. The Swanson-Swift revision arranges the tables into a single continuous alphabet of two columns—one of the letters and the other of the numbers. The individual letter and figure combinations have not been changed. This arrangement appears to be easier to use and has been applied to all three versions of the Cutter tables. (*C. A. Cutter's Two-Figure Author Table*, Swanson-Swift revision, Huntting, Chicopee, Massachusetts, 1969; *C. A. Cutter's Three-Figure Author Table*, Swanson-Swift revision, Huntting, Chicopee, Massachusetts, 1969; *Cutter-Sanborn Three-Figure Author Table*, Swanson-Swift revision, Huntting, Chicopee, Massachusetts, 1969.)

The **work letter** (or **work mark**) is the first letter of the title of the work, exclusive of articles. It follows the cutter number on the second line of the call number. Thus, the complete call number of Henry James's novel *Wings of the Dove* is 813.4 J27w. Work letters do not inevitably insure that a book will be placed in alphabetical sequence within the author grouping; this depends upon the sequence of acquisition of the books. One additional letter from the title may be added if necessary. Thus, a copy of James's *Washington Square* might be classified 813.4 J27wa. If the third acquisition is a volume entitled *The Works of Henry James*, it can be classified 813.4 J27wo.

With an author such as Erle Stanley Gardner, who began the title of all of his Perry Mason mysteries with *The Case of the . . .* , such a scheme is not feasible. Depending on the library's policy, the cataloger can choose one of several alternatives. For example, he can ignore completely the common phrase "the case of the" and proceed directly to the distinctive part of the title; or he can use two work letters: "c" for "case," plus an additional letter for the distinctive title (e.g., *The Case of the Mischievous Doll* might be assigned the work letters "cm").

Biographies and criticism of a specific author pose a particular problem of library policy. Two procedures are common. In the Dewey schedule, 928 is the biography number for literary figures (920 for Biography; 8 for Literature). Thus, biographies of authors might be classified in 928, with subdivision for nationality. Another way of classifying biography is to use the standard biography subdivision, 092.

A third possibility is to classify biographies of authors with their work, in order to keep everything by and about a literary figure in one place. In such cases, a common method of distinguishing works "by" from works "about" an author is to insert an arbitrary letter—usually one toward the end of the alphabet—after the cutter number and to follow it with the initial of the author of the biography. This device puts all books about an author directly behind all books by him. Thus, if the letter "z" is chosen as the biographical letter, a biography or criticism of Henry James by Leon Edel would be cuttered J27zE; and it would follow, in shelf list order, J27w. If James had written a novel beginning with the letter "z" only the work letter "z" would be used for the novel; thus, the novel would still come before all criticism and biography.

The problem of a **variety of editions** occurs most frequently in literature, but classic works in all other fields are also reprinted by the same or another publisher, especially now that paperbacks have revived many worthwhile books that have been long out of print.

One cataloging practice is to assign the date of publication as part of the call number to all editions of a single work issued by the same publisher, and to assign a number following the work letter to all editions of the same work published by different publishers. Thus, the first acquired copy of *Wings of the Dove* would be classified 813.4 J27w. If the library acquired a second copy of the novel, issued by a different publisher, the number would be 813.4 J27w2. Assume that the second publisher was Modern Library, and that the library received another edition of the novel, also published by Modern Library in 1955. The call number might then be 813.4 J27w2 1955. A completely different edition published by a third publisher would be classified 813.4 J27w3.

12 LIBRARY OF CONGRESS CLASSIFICATION

INTRODUCTION

The earliest classification system used by the Library of Congress collection, founded in 1800, was by size (folios, quartos, octavos, etc.), subdivided by accession numbers. Since by 1812 the collection comprised about 3,000 volumes, a better method of classification was necessary. Works were classified under 18 subject categories based on a variation of the Bacon–d'Alembert system used by Benjamin Franklin's Library Company of Philadelphia. In 1814 the Library of Congress was burned by British soldiers. To re-establish it, Thomas Jefferson offered to sell his library of some 7,000 volumes to the Congress, which decided, after some debate, to accept it. Jefferson had cataloged and classified the collection himself. Forty-four main classes and divisions comprised this system, which was based on d'Alembert's modifications of the division of knowledge used by Bacon in *The Advancement of Learning* (1605) and *De augmentis scientarium* (1623). Jefferson's catalog was published in 1815 and his system, with some modifications, was used at the Library of Congress until the end of the nineteenth century.

By the beginning of the 1900s the Library of Congress collection ranked with those of the great national libraries of the world. In 1899 Dr. Herbert Putnam, the new librarian, decided to reorganize and reclassify the library in order to provide a more adequate and detailed system. At this time, of course, there were in existence the *Dewey Decimal Classification* and the first six expansions of Cutter's *Expansive Classification.* The Library of Congress did not adopt either of these two systems, but its debt to Cutter is obvious, and the experience that it gained from the study of both systems was profitable. The outline of the main classes and the structure of Z class (Bibliography) were based on Cutter's *Expansive Classification*, with minor deviations. The letters I, O, W, and X, which were used by Cutter, have not been used in the Library of Congress Classification.

Subject specialists developed the individual schedules, and most of the scheme appeared between 1899 and 1920. Each main class was separately published and has gone through several editions. The general design was based on the actual content of the Library itself.

The view of LC Classification as a series of special classification schedules is stated by Richard S. Angell, Chief of the Subject Cataloging Division:

> While in general outline and sequence of topics it has affinity with earlier systems, the Library's schedules basically represent a fresh start in the design of a system for its own particular purposes. The

schedules were developed one by one, by specialists working under a central direction, but with considerable independence. They were built up for the most part inductively, that is, by taking account of the collections of the Library as they existed and as they were expected to develop because of the Library's needs for comprehensive collections in all fields of knowledge.

From these origins and impulses the Library of Congress classification has developed into a comprehensive practical system for the arrangement and management of collections of books. With one obvious exception it is a complete system, embracing all of the areas of human knowledge, the various components of this universe of knowledge having been allocated to the respective schedules. The objective in the partitioning of this universe is to secure well-defined areas corresponding to the concepts by which the separate fields are taught and expounded, and on which developmental research is based. Within each area the objective is to provide an orderly and apprehendable arrangement of the volumes in an array which will make direct access to the collections useful and meaningful to qualified students and scholars, and helpful to the staff in the control and servicing of items wanted for reference or circulation. To the extent that this partitioning is successful, the classification as a whole becomes a seamless garment in that each of the parts exists basically for its place in the whole structure. At the same time the size and scope of the collections give each of the parts a considerable independence and self-sufficiency within its own field. This is particularly true of the manner in which certain common elements of a general classification scheme are treated in each of the parts of ours [schedules]. Geographical and chronological arrangements, for example, are framed in accordance with the needs of each subject field: that is, they are not carried out by means of a single division table as is the case in certain other classifications. This feature of the schedules has been both criticized and praised: criticized for resulting in extremely detailed and bulky schedules, praised for the freedom allowed in each schedule for development according to its subject field's own intrinsic structure.[1]

Individual volumes of schedules are frequently reviewed by special committees, and the committees make necessary revisions. This process of review insures that the system is readily adaptable and can absorb new subjects. For example, due to the large number of acquisitions of foreign materials by the Library of Congress, sections in the Class D (History) schedule for China, Japan, and Korea have been updated or completely revised. The same revision has occurred in Class PL, particularly in the sections for Chinese, Japanese, and Korean literatures. Unfortunately, there are exceptions to this procedure of frequent review, most notably in the area of East European materials. The Library of

---

[1] Richard S. Angell, "Development of Class K at the Library of Congress," *Law Library Journal* 57 (November 1964): 353-354.

Congress has very substantial holdings in this particular area, but the provisions for certain East European countries or nationalities are less than adequate.[2] At the present time, this situation is being slowly corrected; preliminary schedules have been prepared for Poland and other East European countries. It is hoped that the acquisition program under Public Law 480, which is bringing to the Library of Congress a large amount of foreign material, and the currently initiated program of shared cataloging will have a strong impact on the further development of the LC Classification schedules and on their currency. Since numbers and the letters of the alphabet can form hundreds of different combinations, it is obvious that LC can accommodate many subjects and aspects of subjects not yet known to mankind; thus, it is particularly valuable to large libraries or to libraries that house extensive special collections. Librarians of the many large university and research libraries in the United States and abroad find LC tailored to their requirements: its close classification and its inherent flexibility prove a great attraction. For these reasons, including the fact that printed cards are available for every book in the Library of Congress, many of these institutions have adopted the LC system. At present, this is an increasing trend.

The LC scheme is contained in 30 volumes, or **schedules**, with more than one schedule for broad subjects such as language. Subjects are designated by letters. The individual schedules are:

A.	– General Works, Polygraphy
B, pt. 1, B–BJ.	– Philosophy
B, pt. 2, BL–BX.	– Religion
C.	– Auxiliary Sciences of History
D.	– General and Old World History
E–F.	– American History
G.	– Geography, Anthropology, Folklore, Manners and Customs, Recreation
H.	– Social Sciences
J.	– Political Science
KD.	– Law of the United Kingdom and Ireland
KF.	– Law of the United States
L.	– Education
M.	– Music and Books on Music
N.	– Fine Arts
P–PA.	– Philology, Linguistics, Classical Philology, Classical Literature
PB–PH.	– Modern European Languages
PG, in part	– Russian Literature
PJ–PM.	– Languages and Literature of Asia, Africa, Oceania, America, Mixed Languages, Artificial Languages

---

[2]W. Veryha, "Library of Congress Classification and Subject Headings Relating to Slavic and Eastern Europe," *Library Resources and Technical Services* 16 (Fall 1972): 470-487. Similar problems exist in other areas; see, for example, Robert L. Mowery, "The Classification of African Literature by the Library of Congress," *Library Resources and Technical Services* 17 (Summer 1973): 340-352.

PN, PR, PS, PZ.	– Literature (General), English and American Literature, Fiction in English, Juvenile Literature
PQ, pt. 1.	– French Literature
PQ, pt. 2.	– Italian, Spanish, and Portuguese Literatures
PT, pt. 1.	– German Literature
PT, pt. 2.	– Dutch and Scandinavian Literatures
Q.	– Science
R.	– Medicine
S.	– Agriculture, Plant and Animal Industry, Fish Culture and Fisheries, Hunting Sports
T.	– Technology
U.	– Military Science
V.	– Naval Science
Z.	– Bibliography and Library Science

BASIC CONCEPTS

As has been noted, the LC scheme was planned to be a practical (utilitarian) classification of books in the Library of Congress. It is not, therefore, a theoretical or a philosophical classification. Rather, it is an enumerative classification whose numerous separate schedules are based entirely on the subject grouping of the collection of books in the Library of Congress. The order of main classes, with minor exceptions, is similar to Cutter's; the use of capital letters for main classes is also a feature found in Cutter. Cutter's author-marks are used in several classes for the alphabetical arrangement of works.

Because LC uses both letters and numbers, its notation is a mixed one, in contrast to the "pure" Dewey Decimal Classification, which uses numbers only. Single capital letters are assigned to the main classes, and double letters to the main divisions. These can be combined with numbers for more detailed subdivision.

The traditional disciplines are chosen as the main classes. There are 20 large classes, plus an additional class for general works, incorporated into 30 schedules. Besides these 30 basic schedules, there is one supplement for Language and Literature (PA—containing Byzantine and modern Greek literature). There is also a separately published partial index for P–PM subcategories in the Language and Literature class, and there is an outline of all schedules.

However, there is no official general index to the entire classification system. Most individual schedules have their own index. It should be noted also that indexes to individual schedules refer, generally speaking, only to class numbers in a given schedule; they do not refer to another schedule that might have related material. For example, the index in Class T (Technology) will provide numbers for engineering aspects of the automobile industry (classed in TL), but not for the economic aspects, since economic aspects of the automobile industry will be classed in schedule H. The lack of a general index to all classification schedules is a serious drawback for an inexperienced cataloger. Two general indexes to the classification were issued in 1974 by bodies other than the Library of Congress: a 15-volume index by the United States Historical Documents Institute, a commercial firm in Washington, D.C., and a large one-volume index issued by the Canadian Library

Association. Although both of these indexes are very helpful, neither replaces an official general index. In view of the heavy use of Library of Congress Classification by many large and even medium-sized libraries in this country, such a general index to LC Classification schedules should be prepared in the near future. A detailed relative index (similar to an index in the Dewey Decimal Classification) that indicates class numbers for all major aspects of a given subject or topic would enhance the use of Library of Congress Classification. Included in each schedule are synopses of main classes and larger divisions,[3] which serve as guides to the contents. Another kind of index, or a substitute for an index, to the entire LC Classification scheme consists of the suggested classification notations in the *Library of Congress Subject Headings* list and the LC *Subject Catalog.*

Frequent changes, additions, and revisions of LC Classification are published as follows:

1) They are published in the Library of Congress quarterly, *Library of Congress Additions and Changes.*

2) *Library of Congress Classification Schedules: A Cumulation of Additions and Changes through 1973* was published by Gale Research Company (1974) in 32 volumes.

3) From time to time supplementary pages to individual schedules are published. They are printed on leaves, with alternate blank pages, so that they can be clipped and tabbed into the original schedules. If the individual schedule is reprinted before it is revised, these supplementary pages are included at the end of the volume.

4) Any new editions of individual schedules incorporate new additions in the main body of the schedule.

A list of the schedules, their current editions, and the dates of these editions is given below:

A   General works: Polygraphy. 4th ed. (1973)
B   Philosophy and Religion.
     Part I. B—BJ: Philosophy. 2d ed. (1950) Reissue with supplementary pages, 1968
     Part II. BL—BX: Religion. 2d ed. (1962)
C   History: Auxiliary Sciences. 2d ed. (1948) Reissue with supplementary pages, 1967
D   History: General and Old World. 2d ed. (1959) Reissue with supplementary pages, 1966
E—F History: American. 3d ed. (1958) Reissue with supplementary pages, 1965
G   Geography, Anthropology, Folklore, etc. 3d ed. (1954) Reissue with supplementary pages, 1966
H   Social Sciences. 3d ed. (1950) Reissue with supplementary pages, 1965
J   Political Science. 2d ed. (1924) Reissue with supplementary pages, 1966

---

[3] Note that not all of the 30 schedules have an outline (e.g., PN, PR, PS, and PZ) and some do not have an index (PQ, pts. 1 and 2).

K   Law.
      KD: Law of United Kingdom and Ireland (1973)
      KF: Law of the United States. Prelim. ed. (1969)
L   Education. 3d ed. (1951) Reissue with supplementary pages, 1966
M   Music. 2d ed. (1917) Reissue with supplementary pages, 1968
N   Fine Arts. 4th ed. (1974)
P   Philology and Literature.
      P–PA: Philology. Classical Philology and Literature. (1928) Reissue with
          supplementary pages, 1968
      PA Supplement: Byzantine and Modern Greek Literature. Medieval and
          Modern Latin Literature. (1942) Reissue with supplementary pages,
          1968
      PB–PH: Modern European Languages. (1933) Reissue with supplementary
          pages, 1966
      PG: Russian Literature. (1948) Reissue with supplementary pages, 1965
      PJ–PM: Languages and Literatures of Asia, Africa, Oceania, America; Mixed
          Languages; Artificial Languages. (1935) Reissue with supplementary
          pages, 1965
      P–PM Supplement: Index to Languages and Dialects. 2d ed. (1957) Reissue
          with supplementary pages, 1965
      PN, PR, PS, PZ: Literature–General, English, American; Fiction, etc. (1915)
          Reissue with supplementary pages, 1964
      PQ, Part 1: French Literature. (1936) Reissue with supplementary pages,
          1966
      PQ, Part 2: Italian, Spanish, and Portuguese Literatures. (1937) Reissue with
          supplementary pages, 1965
      PT, Part 1: German Literature. (1938) Reissue with supplementary pages,
          1966
      PT, Part 2: Dutch and Scandinavian Literatures. (1942) Reissue with
          supplementary pages, 1965
Q   Science. 6th ed. (1973)
R   Medicine. 3d ed. (1952) Reissue with supplementary pages, 1966
S   Agriculture, etc. 3d ed. (1948) Reissue with supplementary pages, 1965
T   Technology. 5th ed. (1971)
U   Military Science. 4th ed. (1974)
V   Naval Science. 3d ed. (1974)
Z   Bibliography and Library Science. 4th ed. (1959) Reissue with supplementary
          pages, 1965

    All the schedules have similar formats, consisting of the following parts: a) a prefatory note, which gives a brief history of the schedule and quite frequently provides some comments on the scope; b) a synopsis, with a list of all double letters covered in the schedule; c) the main body of the schedule, containing classification tables; d) auxiliary tables; e) a detailed index; and f) supplementary pages of additions and changes.
    Although the Library of Congress Classification is very detailed and has many special tables for minutely subdividing more general topics, it offers little in terms

of mnemonic features, because even common form divisions are not always applicable to the whole classification system.

The general principle of arrangement within the classes follows approximately this pattern:

1. General form divisions
2. Theory, philosophy
3. History
4. Treatises
5. Law, regulations, state regulations
6. Study and teaching
7. Special subjects and subdivisions of subjects

Under individual subjects, the general arrangement is as listed above, although the sequence may not be the same in all classes. Within the sequence the order is approximately from general to specific, and arrangement is chronological wherever possible. Books that can be treated geographically can be subdivided by country, state, or city; this is accomplished by an alphabetical arrangement under one number or by the provision of special numbers. In philosophy, the social sciences, and political science, subjects are often associated by country instead of by topic.

Another kind of grouping of subjects may be found in such classes as B, Philosophy, and P, Literature, in which the schedules make room for individual authors and titles.

Like Dewey, LC has a general class, Class A, for works that do not fit into any special subject.

There are many auxiliary tables for logical and minute expansion of subjects and topics. They may be short simple tables incorporated in the body of the schedule itself or long complex tables that appear either at the end of the class or at the end of the schedule. A reference is made in the body of the schedule to the special tables to be used in each case where special arrangement is desirable. There are five types of auxiliary tables:

1. Form tables or divisions
2. Geographic tables
3. Chronological tables
4. Subject subdivision tables
5. Combination tables

General Form Divisions

Form subdivisions in LC Classification are adapted to the requirements of individual subjects. They are incorporated into the schedules or added in the form of separate tables, and they provide for subdivisions under periodicals, societies, collections, encyclopedias, dictionaries, official records, exhibitions, museums, yearbooks, etc. Neither history nor theory is considered as a form division; they will be discussed in the section on internal subdivisions. The examples below illustrate the use of form divisions adapted to the requirements of two disciplines. The subclass CR, Heraldry, shows the following breakdown at the beginning of this subject:

HERALDRY

Heraldry combined with genealogy classed with CS.

CR

→ 1   Periodicals. Societies.

→   Collected works.

4   Several authors.

5   Individual authors.

→ 7   Congresses, conventions, etc.

→ 9   Exhibitions.

→ 11   Directories.

→ 13   Dictionaries. Encyclopedias.

       Science, technique, theory, etc.

          History, *see* CR151–159.

       General works.

19   To 1800.

          1801–

21   Treatises.

23   Manuals.

27   Minor. Pamphlets, etc.

       General special. Special aspects, relations, etc.

29   Symbolism.

31   Heraldry and art, architecture, etc.

33   Heraldry and literature.

          Heraldry in Shakespeare, Scott, etc.

          Prefer the special author in PR, PQ, etc.

             e. g. PR3069.H4 for Shakespeare.

       Special.

41   Special branches, charges, etc., A–Z.

          e. g. Chess, collar, counter-charge, crest, crosses, doge's cap, double-headed eagle, fish, flowers (fleur-de-lis, rose, etc.), furs, goedendag, hatching, hatchments, helmets, heralds, linden, lion, liveries, marks of cadency, masons' marks, merchants' marks, mermaids, pomegranate, rebus, rest, signboards, tinctures, trademarks, triquetra, unicorn, urchin, water bouget, white horse, wreaths.

       Printers' marks, *see* Z235–236.

(43)   Armorial bindings and bookplates, *see* Z266–276 and Z993–996.

(45)   Armorial china, *see* NK4374.

Subclass CR, then, has the following form divisions: Periodicals; Societies; Collected Works; Congresses, Conventions, etc.; Exhibitions; Directories; Dictionaries; Encyclopedias.

Other subjects, such as printing (in subclass Book Industries and Trade, in Class Z), have slightly different form divisions.

BOOK INDUSTRIES AND TRADE

PRINTING

Z

116.A2	Treatises on the modern printed book.
.A3	General special.
	Arts and crafts literature, etc.
.A4	Pamphlets. Booklets, etc.
.A5–Z	General works on printing.
➡ 117	Bibliography.
➡ 118.A3	Collections. Series. Systematic encyclopedias, etc.
➡ .A5–Z	Dictionaries.
	Cf. Z 1006, Dictionaries of bibliographic terms.
➡ (.7)	Directories, *see* Z 282; and under country Z 293–543.
	e.g. Z 475 Directories of American booksellers, printers, etc.
➡ 119	Periodicals.
➡ .5	Yearbooks.
➡ 120	Societies. Trade unions.
➡ 121	Museums. Exhibitions.
122	Education and training. Schools.

These general form divisions usually precede all other divisions and are located at the beginning of a given subject. There are several exceptions to this general rule, however. For example, in schedule C (Auxiliary sciences of history) under CN, Epigraphy, we find that several inserted numbers separate the form division "dictionaries, terminology" (CN70) from other form divisions. In extracted form, the breakdown is as follows:

CN   Epigraphy

➡ 1	Periodicals. Societies.
➡ 15	Congresses.
➡ 20	Collected works.
➡ 25	Museums.
➡ 30	Private collections.
40	Philosophy. Theory.
50	Study and teaching.
55	History of epigraphy.
	Biography of epigraphists.
61	Collective.
62	Individual, A–Z.
➡ 70	Dictionaries. Terminology.

Obviously, CN50 (Study and teaching) and CN55-62 (for History) are not form divisions. Nevertheless, they are inserted here, at the very beginning of the subject classification for this topic.

Internal Subdivisions

Such terms as periodicals, encyclopedias, societies, etc., serve as general form divisions (also called external form divisions). Quite frequently these external form divisions are followed by internal subdivisions such as Theory, Philosophy, History, Study and teaching, Treatises, General works, etc. In the example above, CN50 (Study and teaching) is such an internal subdivision for Epigraphy, as is CN40 (Philosophy. Theory). The phrase "Philosophy. Theory" is used frequently as a single number (CN40) or it may have several numbers. For example, PN, Theory and philosophy of literature, has several numbers: PN50—Relation to history; PN51—Relation to sociology, economics and political science; PN52—Relation to education; PN53—Relation to art, etc. In some respects this internal subdivision may be compared to the standard subdivision "01" in the Dewey Decimal Classification.

The second internal subdivision, History, is used for historical subdivisions for almost any subject, as can be seen in the preceding examples. The historical breakdown of Socialism, Communism and Anarchism (Subclass HX) clearly illustrates the use of this caption. After general form divisions HX1 (Periodicals), HX11 (Societies), and HX13 (Congresses), the following numbers represent, in part, this internal subdivision:

HX   SOCIALISM. COMMUNISM. ANARCHISM   HX

	History.
21	General.
23	Biography (Collective).
	Individual classed with special period, HX 26–40 or with country, HX 84, 242, etc.
➤26	Ancient.
➤31	Medieval.
	Cf. HX 629, Medieval communism.
➤36	Modern.
➤38	French revolution.
➤39	19th century.
.5	Karl Marx.
➤40	20th century.

The captions "Treatises" and "General Works," which are used for comprehensive works on a given subject, require little explanation. Often they are also subdivided chronologically or by place or country. For example, HF, Business, has the following breakdown for general works:

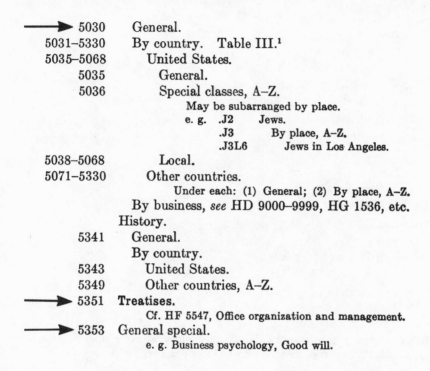

→ 5030	General.	
5031–5330	By country. Table III.[1]	
5035–5068	United States.	
5035	General.	
5036	Special classes, A–Z.	
	May be subarranged by place.	
	e. g. .J2 Jews.	
	.J3 By place, A–Z.	
	.J3L6 Jews in Los Angeles.	
5038–5068	Local.	
5071–5330	Other countries.	
	Under each: (1) General; (2) By place, A–Z.	
	By business, *see* HD 9000–9999, HG 1536, etc.	
	History.	
5341	General.	
	By country.	
5343	United States.	
5349	Other countries, A–Z.	
→ 5351	**Treatises.**	
	Cf. HF 5547, Office organization and management.	
→ 5353	General special.	
	e. g. Business psychology, Good will.	

The term "general" is often used in sequence with "general special," which means general or comprehensive works treated from a particular point of view–e.g., 5351 Treatises, and 5353 General Special (Business psychology). Additional comments on this caption are provided in the section on chronological tables.

The caption "Study and teaching" is similar to standard subdivision "07" in the Dewey Decimal Classification, and quite often it occurs as a single number. Occasionally several numbers will be provided for this internal subdivision (e.g., MT1–950, Study and teaching of music, or PR31–55, Study and teaching of English literature). Other captions are also used for internal subdivisions, such as Methodology, Biography, Popular works, Juvenile works, etc. They serve similar purposes and, generally speaking, follow a similar pattern.

Geographic Tables

There are no common geographical divisions as in Dewey; LC geographic tables are applied, with variations, to the classes as required. They usually follow this general pattern:

America
    North America
        United States
        British North America. Canada
        Mexico
    Central America
    West Indies
    South America
Europe
    Great Britain
    Continental countries
Asia
Africa
Australia and New Zealand
Pacific islands
Arctic regions
Antarctic regions

Within each region or country the arrangement is usually alphabetical. In general, geographic division is made according to three basic principles:

1) Numbers are assigned to a place in the regular notation.

2) A series of numbers is left vacant and the classifier is referred to a special table where the countries are listed. These numbers will fill the vacancies.

3) Subdivision can be made alphabetically by country.

The structure of geographic tables varies from a simple arrangement to the more detailed and complex tables provided in several schedules.

Simple arrangement:

SB   Plant culture and horticulture.
        History and conditions.
           By country.
83   United States
→85   States, A—W.
→87   Other countries, A—Z.

The schedule for Class H, Social Sciences, provides a good example of **floating geographic tables**, which may be used to divide subjects in other places. These include tables for American cities and states and a table of foreign countries. Like form divisions, the geographic divisions are repeated under every topic that justifies their use. The special geographic tables, which are alphabetically arranged, are not mnemonic and the letters used do not have a constant meaning.

Chronological Tables

Many chronological tables are usually found under the historical divisions of the subjects. They are brief and self-explanatory. **Period subdivisions** subdivide the history of each discipline and its subdivisions and aspects whenever necessary. These divisions, like all the others, are adapted to a number of subjects and vary in their structure.

RJ		Pediatrics
		History
36		General
37		General special
→38		Ancient
→39		Medieval
→40		Modern
42		By country, A–Z.

Another typical example of chronological subdivision will be found in Class H, Social Sciences. For example, the topic HJ, Public Finance, has the following numbers under Greece (Modern):

	Greece (Modern).
	General works. History.
2731	General.
→2733	Early to 1832.
→2735	1832–1900.
→2737	1901–
2738	Special.
2739	Provinces (Nomarchies), A–Z.

Please note that such captions as History (also Treatises), as we noted before, often make use of the terms "general" and "general special." The term "general" means comprehensive works in a particular subject category, and the term "general special" (as in Pediatrics) means general or comprehensive works treated from a particular point of view or connoting a specific aspect. This concept is not always clear, which is why, in the newly developed Class K, Law, the phrase "general special" is not used; instead, the more descriptive phrase "particular aspects" is substituted.

Subject Subdivision Tables and Combination Tables

Generally speaking, the basic arrangement in LC Classification is by discipline. Quite frequently a discipline may be subdivided alphabetically. For example, in Class Z, Biography and Library Science, we find the following subdivision for works on cataloging and subject headings:

695	**Cataloging. Subject headings.**
.A1	**Bibliography.**
.A3–Z	**General works.**
.1 ⟶	**By subject, A–Z.**
.A25	Aeronautics.
.A4	Agriculture.
.C5	Chemistry.
.C6	Children's material.
.D4	Decoration and ornament.
.E2	Economics.
.E3	Education.
	European War (World War I), 1914– 1918, *see* .W7.
.F5	Finance.
.F8	Freemasons.
.G4	Geographic names.
.G7	Government publications.
.H6	History (Local).
.H8	Housing.
.I3	Industry. Business.
.L12	Labor.
.L3	Law.
.L6	Literature.
	Cf. Z 695.1.O7, Oriental literature.
.M42	Mathematics.
.M48	Medicine.
.M6	Military science.
(.M95)	Music, *see* ML 111.
.N3	Naval art and science.
.N4	The Negro.
.O7	Oriental literature.
.P3	Packaging.

In the same schedule, subject bibliography on architecture will show not only subject subdivisions but subdivisions by country:

Architecture.

5941	General bibliography.
5942	City planning, municipal improvement, etc.

> Cf. Z 5943.D7, Domestic architecture.
> Z 7164.H8, Housing.

5943	Special topics, A–Z.

.C56	Church architecture.
(.C7)	College buildings, *see* .U5.
.D7	Domestic architecture.
.F3	Farm buildings.
.P7	Prefabricated buildings.
.U5	University and college buildings.

➤5944	By country, A–Z.
5945	Catalogs.

Occasionally, place or country takes precedence over subject since it is assumed that the user's interest is primarily concerned with the area, and only secondarily with the subject matter on institutions in that particular area. This area approach is illustrated by the arrangement in Class J. Here, works on government and politics of individual countries are first arranged by country and then subdivided by subject. Other examples of country collocation can be found in Subclass HE, Transportation and Communication. This particular subject is subdivided into several subcategories—e.g., traffic engineering, roads and highways, streets, water transportation, railways, etc. One of such topics, traffic surveys and regulations, is subdivided as follows:

Traffic surveys and regulations.

> Cf. HE 4201–5720.

369	General works.
370	General special.

> e. g. Street and traffic signs.

	By country.
	United States.
371.A2–3	General.
.A4-W	By state.
372	Local, A–Z.

> Subarranged by date.

373	Other countries, A–Z.

> Under each:
> (1) General works.
> (2) By region, state, etc., A–Z.
> (3) By place, A–Z.
>
> e. g. France: .F6, General works; .F7A–Z, Departments;
> .F71–89, Cities, e. g. .F8, Paris.

An example of a subject subdivision table is given in JK, Constitutional History of United States. It should be noted, however, that there are very few pure subject subdivision tables, because they are usually combined with one or two other types of tables. Illustrations of such combination tables are provided above; they occur in many schedules.

Other Features

Occasionally, Library of Congress Classification schedules use divide-like notes in order to save space. Generally speaking, they are simple to use. An example of such a note may be found in Class A (General Works, Polygraphy) under AG (Dictionaries):

AG
1–91   **Dictionaries. Minor encyclopedias** (including popular and juvenile).
            1: International. Polyglot.
⟶   5–91: Arranged like AE5–91.
                    e. g. AG5.M4   Mee, The book of knowledge.
            6: Not used.

Under AE 5–91 we find a detailed subdivision for encyclopedias (e.g., AE11–Austrian, AE15–Belgian, AE19–Dutch, etc.), which can be adapted for subdivisions of dictionaries.

Quite frequently LC schedules provide alternative class numbers for libraries that prefer not to follow LC practice. Such numbers are enclosed in parentheses. For example, in the schedule HM, Sociology, numbers 31 and 32 are alternative class numbers:

24   Philosophy. Theory. Method.
25   Relation to social work.
                Cf. HN 29; HV 40.
26   Relation to philosophy.
                Cf. B 63, Relation of philosophy to sociology.
27   Relation to psychology.
                Cf. BF 57, Relation of psychology to sociology.
30   Relation to ethics.
                Cf. BJ 51, Relation of ethics to sociology.
⟶ (31)   Relation to religion, *see* BL 60.
⟶ (32)   Relation to education, *see* LC 189–191.
33   Relation to politics.
                Cf. JA 76, Relation of political science to sociology.
34   Relation to law.
35   Relation to economics.

In both cases (BL60–Religion and LC189-191–Education), libraries that use LC Classification schedules may prefer to bring all material together instead of following Library of Congress practice.

Other helpful devices include **scope notes** (more clearly written than in Dewey Decimal Classification) and many cross references.[4]

LC NOTATION AND AUTHOR NUMBERS

As was indicated earlier, LC Classification uses a mixed notation consisting of letters and numbers. Like the Dewey Decimal Classification, notation consists of two principal parts: a class number and an author number. Thus, the LC call number will consist of a class number, an author number, and added symbols describing a particular work and its edition, if necessary.

The main classes are designated by capital letters; the subclasses, with the exception of the early Classes Z and E–F, by two capital letters; divisions and subdivisions by integral numbers in ordinary sequence. Decimal numbers are used for further expansion of individual class numbers, topics, and geographic subdivisions.

Q		Science (General)
QA		Mathematics
QB		Astronomy
QC		Physics
	81–119	Weights and measures
	122–168	Experimental mechanics
	811–849	Terrestrial magnetism
	851–999	Meteorology

Cutter numbers are used for topics arranged in one alphabet that do not follow the logical arrangement, such as biographies, simple arrangement of countries, provinces, cities, lists of minerals, etc.

QE		Geology
	389	Special groups of minerals
	.1	Native elements
	.2	Sulphides, etc.
	.3	Sulpho salts
	.4	Haloids
	391	Description of special minerals, A–Z
		e.g. .A5 Amber
		.B35 Barite
		(cutter numbers)

---

[4]The reader should be referred to John Phillip Immroth's *A Guide to the Library of Congress Classification*, 3d ed. (Littleton, Colo., Libraries Unlimited, 1976) for a more detailed discussion of these features in relation to individual schedules.

Internal Notation

In general, the arrangement of the material within each class is alphabetical, by author and title. This is because the elaborate classification schedules keep the number of books in each class to a minimum. Thus, in all classes, with the exception of Subclass PZ, Fiction in English (individual authors) and Juvenile literature, LC notation does not use three-figure Cutter numbers for authors. The Library of Congress author symbols are composed of initial letters followed by arabic numbers. The numbers are used decimally and are assigned on the basis of the tables given below, in a manner that preserves the alphabetical order of names within a class.

1. After the initial letter **S**

for the second letter:	a	ch	e	hi	mop	t	u
use number:	2	3	4	5	6	7-8	9

2. After the initial letters **Qu**

for the third letter:	a	e	i	o	r	y
use number:	3	4	5	6	7	9

3. After other initial consonants

for the second letter:	a	e	i	o	r	u	y
use number:	3	4	5	6	7	8	9

4. After initial vowels

for the second letter:	b	d	lm	n	p	r	st	uy
use number:	2	3	4	5	6	7	8	9

Letters not included in the foregoing tables are assigned the next higher or lower number as required by previous assignments in the particular class. Examples:

1. Names beginning with the letter **S**:

Sabine	.S15	Seaton	.S4	Steel	.S7
Saint	.S2	Shank	.S45	Storch	.S75
Schaefer	.S3	Shipley	.S5	Sturges	.S8
Schwedel	.S37	Smith	.S6	Sullivan	.S9

2. Names beginning with the letters **Qu**:

Quabbe	.Q3	Quick	.Q5	Qureshi	.Q7
Queener	.Q4	Quoist	.Q6	Quynn	.Q9

3. Names beginning with other consonants:

Carter	.C3	Cinelli	.C5	Crocket	.C7
Cecil	.C4	Corbett	.C6	Croft	.C73
Childs	.C45	Cox	.C65	Cullen	.C8
				Cyprus	.C9

4. Names beginning with vowels:

Abernathy	.A2	Ames	.A5	Arundel	.A78
Adams	.A3	Appleby	.A6	Atwater	.A87
Aldrich	.A4	Archer	.A7	Austin	.A9

Since the tables provide only a general framework for the assignment of author numbers, it should be noted that the symbol for a particular name is constant **only** within a single class.

The following example illustrates the construction of such notation:

Fig. 12.1

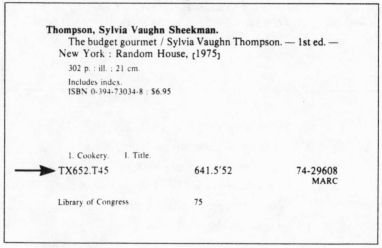

Thompson, Sylvia Vaughn Sheekman.
  The budget gourmet / Sylvia Vaughn Thompson. — 1st ed. —
New York : Random House, ₁1975₁

302 p. : ill. ; 21 cm.

Includes index.
ISBN 0-394-73034-8 : $6.95

1. Cookery.   1. Title.
➤ TX652.T45   641.5'52   74-29608
                                                     MARC

Library of Congress   75

T	Technology
TX	Home Economics
652	Cookery—General special (in this case gourmet cooking on a budget)
.T45	The author number for Thompson

The same plan is used to determine the notation for subjects, topics, biographies, countries, states, etc., that are arranged alphabetically under a single topic.

Fig. 12.2

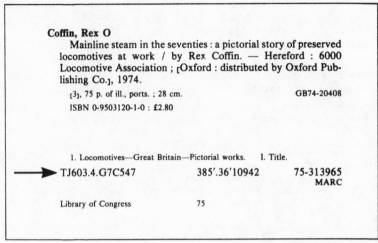

Coffin, Rex O
　　Mainline steam in the seventies : a pictorial story of preserved locomotives at work / by Rex Coffin. — Hereford : 6000 Locomotive Association ; [Oxford : distributed by Oxford Publishing Co.], 1974.
　　　　[3], 75 p. of ill., ports. ; 28 cm.　　　　　　　　GB74-20408
　　　　ISBN 0-9503120-1-0 : £2.80

　　1. Locomotives—Great Britain—Pictorial works.　I. Title.
　　TJ603.4.G7C547　　　　　　385'.36'10942　　　　75-313965
　　　　　　　　　　　　　　　　　　　　　　　　　　　　　　MARC

　　Library of Congress　　　　　　　75

T	Technology
TJ	Mechanical engineering and machinery
603	Locomotives–general works
.4	Geographic areas other than the United States, subdivided A–Z.
G7	Cutter number for Great Britain
C547	Author number for Coffin

Official Cutter Numbers

The "official cutter number" is applied, in the arrangement of books on the shelves, to publications of government organizations, institutions, societies, and other corporate bodies. It is also used for personal authors when they constitute the subject represented by class or subdivision. This device keeps the group of all works for which the particular corporate body or personal author is responsible ahead of descriptive or critical works by other authors. Quite frequently this type of cutter number (e.g., .A1, .A2, etc.) is incorporated in individual tables.

HA　　　　　　Statistics
　　　　　　　　United States
730　　　　　　　　Cities, A–Z
　　　　　　　　　　　Under each:
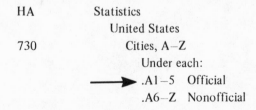
　　　　　　　　　　　.A1–5　Official
　　　　　　　　　　　.A6–Z　Nonofficial

Official cutter numbers are also used as form or common subject subdivisions placed at the beginning of a class:

HB	Economic theory
	History of economics
101–129	By country
	Under each:
⟶ .A2	History
⟶ .A3	Collective biography
.A5–Z	Individual biography

CONCLUSIONS

Unlike Dewey, LC does not use literary forms for individual authors in Class P, Literature. LC classifies first by original language, then by the period, and finally by the authors, regardless of form. Exceptions are made for Elizabethan drama and for fiction in English. The fact that LC ignores division by form is a very satisfactory feature in larger libraries, which usually prefer to have all the works of an author and all the works about him grouped together. In Class P, Literature, there is also a list of authors for whom detailed treatment is provided; students should pay particular attention to the various tables (23 different form tables to use with individual authors) that may have to be consulted.

In general, the recurring pattern within each literature group is as follows:

1) History and criticism, subdivided chronologically, and then by form
2) Collections or anthologies, subdivided by form
3) Individual authors, subdivided chronologically.

In turn, the pattern below is followed for individual authors:

1) Collective works
2) Individual works
3) Biography and criticism.

Collective and individual biography is usually classed with subject, although, like the Dewey 900s, biographies may be placed in the general category CT, a part of History.

In conclusion, it should be emphasized that LC Classification is the most detailed and comprehensive classification scheme ever published; because of its structure, however, it also has a great deal of flexibility and potential for possible future expansion. Expansion room is provided by gaps left in the notation, by the use of decimals, and by the use of author numbers in combinations of small letters with capital letters and numerals.

Constant revision maintains the currency of LC Classification. Because of its many provisions for the minute classification needed for large collections, it is important to large university and research libraries. Terminology is exact and explicit, and the definitions are an important aid to the cataloger. It must also be remembered that LC cards indicate the LC Classification numbers, a useful aid. Since LC lacks the mnemonic features of Dewey, however, catalogers must rely on the indexes or on the extensive outlines in the individual volumes of the main classes.

A beginning student of LC Classification may find it difficult to use the many auxiliary tables. Immroth's previously mentioned *A Guide to the Library of Congress Classification* will be very helpful in this respect, and other works can also provide partial assistance with this problem.[5]

---

[5] Cf. *The Use of the Library of Congress Classification.* Proceedings of the Institute on the Use of the Library of Congress Classification ... (Chicago, American Library Association, 1968); and an older work, Leo E. LaMontagne, *American Library Classification. With Special Reference to the Library of Congress* (Hamden, Conn., The Shoe String Press, 1961).

13 OTHER GENERAL CLASSIFICATION SYSTEMS

INTRODUCTION

This chapter provides a brief overview of some of the more important library classification systems other than the Dewey Decimal and Library of Congress Classifications. The systems introduced in this chapter are Cutter's Expansive Classification, James Duff Brown's Subject Classification, Bliss's Bibliographic Classification, the Universal Decimal Classification, and Ranganathan's Colon Classification. In order to demonstrate some of the differences and distinctive features of these systems, four comparative examples of classification problems are provided (beginning on page 314).[1]

EXPANSIVE CLASSIFICATION

Expansive Classification (EC) was devised by Charles Ammi Cutter while he was librarian of the Boston Athenaeum. Thelma Eaton has described the origin of EC:

> When Charles Ammi Cutter became librarian of the Boston Athenaeum that library used fixed location for shelf arrangement. Cutter did not attempt to change this until he had completed a dictionary catalogue. He had intended to use Dewey's classification as printed but upon examination he decided to modify it by adopting a larger base using the letters of the alphabet to designate classes, and by establishing a system of book numbers based on author entry.[2]

EC consists of seven distinct enumerative classification systems, with provisions for the use of such synthetic devices as form divisions and geographic divisions. The

---

[1] Another distinctive classification system is used by Harvard University Libraries. It is described in the published Widener shelflists, widely used by other large libraries in building their collections. This system is well adapted to area studies and should be discussed in advanced courses on classification theory.

[2] Thelma Eaton, "The Development of Classification in America," *The Role of Classification in the Modern American Library*; papers presented at an Institute conducted by the University of Illinois Graduate School of Library Science, November 1-4, 1959 (Champaign, Ill., Illini Union Bookstore, 1959), p. 17.

first six classification schedules were published from 1891 to 1893[3] and the seventh expansion, which was left unfinished at the time of the author's death in 1903, was issued in parts between 1896 and 1911.[4] Cutter described EC in 1897:

> It consists of seven tables of classification of progressive fulness, designed to meet the needs of a library at its successive stages of growth. The first table has few classes and no subdivisions. It is meant for a very small collection of books. The second has more classes and some subdivisions, but retains all the old classes with their previous marks. This is intended for the small collection, when it has swelled so much that it must be broken up into more parts. Now, the books which are put into the new classes must, of course, have new marks; but those in the old ones remain as they are—their marks need no change. In this way we go on, gradually increasing the number of classes and sub-classes, and yet in each transition from the simpler to the more complex scheme preserving all the old notation; so that there is only the absolutely necessary amount of alteration. It is as if an indestructible suit of clothes were made to grow with the growth of the youth who wears them. He would not have to go to a tailor now and then to get a new suit. So the rapidly-growing library does not have to get an entire rearrangement every ten or fifteen years, with entirely new class-marks. Passing through the third, fourth, fifth, and sixth, it comes finally to the seventh, which is full and minute enough for the British Museum, with a capacity of increase that would accommodate the British Museum raised to the tenth power; for there might be an eighth and a ninth and a tenth table, if need be. From this adaptation to growth comes the name *expansive*.[5]

The first classification outline consists of eight main classes. As Cutter pointed out, this rudimentary scheme was intended for a very small library. In his directions ("Introduction to the Smallest Library," pp. 1-3), Cutter writes:

> For arranging and marking a very small library in such a way that other books can be added to it without disturbing the arrangement, and with as little change as possible—divide your books into the following eight sections:

---

[3] Charles Ammi Cutter, *Expansive Classification, Part 1: The First Six Classifications* (Boston, Cutter, 1891-1893).

[4] Charles Ammi Cutter, *Expansive Classification, Part 2: Seventh Classification*, William Parker Cutter, ed. [Boston (and Northampton, Mass.), 1896-1911].

[5] Charles Ammi Cutter, "The Expansive Classification," *Transactions and Proceedings of the Second International Library Conference, London, July 13-16, 1897* (London, Morrison & Giblex, 1898), p. 84.

A   Works of reference and general works which include several of the following sections, and so could not go in any one.
B   Philosophy and Religion
E   Biography
F   History and Geography and Travels
H   Social Sciences
L   Natural Sciences and Arts
Y   Language and Literature
Y$_F$ Fiction.

. . . When you get your books sorted into eight sections, arrange them within each class alphabetically by the authors' names, except in Biography, which is to be arranged by the subjects, that is, by the names of those whose lives are told. In the sections Biography and Fiction, and in all classes in a library that is expected to grow rapidly, to distinguish different authors whose family names begin with the same letter, add to the initial a figure taken from Cutter's "Alphabetic order table," the method of using which will be fully explained further on.

In the second classification ("For a library that has grown larger"), Cutter already introduces 15 main classes (G for Geography and Travels, L for Physical Sciences, M for Natural History, etc.). The third classification has many more classes and subdivisions, and in the fifth the whole alphabet A-Z has been applied and all main classes are set out. In arranging the main classes Cutter claims to have followed an evolutionary or historical order. It is interesting to note that the main outline of the Library of Congress Classification is closely related to the Cutter scheme, as can be seen below:

Expansive		Library of Congress	
A.	General works	A.	General works
B.	Philosophy–Religion	B.	Philosophy–Religion
C.	Judaism and Christianity	C.	History–Auxiliary sciences
D.	Ecclesiastical history	D.	History and topography
E.	Biography		(except America)
F.	History	E–F.	America
G.	Geography	G.	Geography–Anthropology
H.	Social sciences	H.	Social sciences
I.	Sociology		
J.	Political science	J.	Political science
K.	Law	K.	Law
L.	Natural sciences	L.	Education
M.	Natural history	M.	Music
N.	Botany	N.	Fine arts
O–P.	Zoölogy	P.	Language and literature
Q.	Medicine	Q.	Science
R.	Technology	R.	Medicine

Expansive (cont'd)		**Library of Congress (cont'd)**	
S.	Engineering	S.	Agriculture
T.	Fabricative Arts	T.	Technology
U.	Combative and preservative arts	U.	Military science
V.	Athletic and recreative arts	V.	Naval science
W.	Fine arts		
X.	Philology		
Y.	Literature		
Z.	Book arts	Z.	Bibliography and library science

Like many other classification schemes, Cutter's system provides form divisions (designated numerically from 1 through 9—e.g., .1 Theory, .2 Bibliography, etc.); these form divisions are to be applied throughout the scheme. Another feature, a table of localities with two-figure numerical notations, consists of a series of numbers (11-99) and a list of countries and places to be used mainly for division of Geography and History. If, for example, 45 is the number for England and D is Church History, then D45 is English church history. Thus, the notation in *Expansive Classification* is mixed, consisting of capital letters (basic classes), small capital letters (subjects), and numerals. Cutter's summary of the notation of his first expansion is essentially applicable to the whole classification scheme; as he points out in his introduction (p. 7):

> The *Classification* consists of two parts (a) the *class mark*, which shows in what class the book belongs and (b) the *book mark*, which distinguishes that book from other books in the same class. The class mark in the series of classifications set forth here is the first notation: *a letter*, which may be followed by one or more letters when the class is a subject (as History, Philosophy, Science, the Arts) or a kind of literature (as fiction, drama, poetry); a *single figure*—to distinguish books written in certain form (as dictionaries, encyclopedias, etc.) from other works in the same class; *two figures*—to distinguish books relating to a place (as America, Africa, etc.) from other works in the same class.

For example, F is the class number of History and 30 is a local number for Europe. Therefore, Gibbon's *Decline and Fall of the Roman Empire* has the following number: F30·G35 (G35 is the author number for Gibbon). Since certain combinations of letters were reserved for subjects, it was possible for Cutter to provide a short notation for certain aspects of a particular discipline—e.g., chemical analysis, LOS (L—Science and Arts; LO—Chemistry; LOS—Analysis, chemical). Unfortunately, Cutter died before finishing his classification scheme, and the uncompleted seventh expansion was published after his death. Nevertheless, many of its best features were later used in the formulation of the Library of Congress Classification.[6]

EC does not expand consistently without notational change from the first to the seventh classification schedule. A book on corporal punishment of school children, for example, would be classed as follows using all seven classification schedules.

1st and 2nd classification:	H	Social sciences (including Sociology)
3rd classification:	I	Sociology
4th classification:	I	Sociology
	IK	Education
5th classification:	IK	Education
6th classification:	IK	Education
	IP	Pedagogics
7th classification:	IP	Pedagogics
	IPD	Discipline
	IPDC	Corporal punishment

In the above example the notation changes from H to I between the second and third expansion, and from IK to IP between the fifth and sixth expansion. All other changes are consistent additive notational expansions. Although the lack of consistency revealed here is theoretically a weakness of EC, it is unlikely that any library would expand from the first classification to the seventh.

The only part of EC that is still widely used today is the cutter-author mark or cutter number, which was originally developed to complete the notation of EC. Cutter numbers, which are usually used today with the Dewey Decimal Classification, are described in Chapter 11 of this textbook.

SUBJECT CLASSIFICATION

The *Subject Classification* of James Duff Brown (1862-1914) had little practical success. First published in 1894 as the Quinn-Brown scheme and somewhat modified in 1897 (*Adjustable Classification*), it was finally published in 1906 as *Subject Classification*. The second edition of *Subject Classification* was brought out in 1914 and the third edition (edited by J. D. Stewart) in 1939.[7] It consisted of eleven main classes in the following order:

---

[6] A detailed analysis of *Expansive Classification* is presented in H. E. Bliss, *The Organization of Knowledge in Libraries*, 2d ed. (New York, H. W. Wilson, 1939), Chapter XI; in W. C. B. Sayers, *A Manual of Classification*, 3d rev. ed. (London, Andre Deutsch, 1955), Chapter XV; and in John Phillip Immroth, "Expansive Classification," *Encyclopedia of Library and Information Science*, Vol. 8 (New York, Marcel Dekker, 1972), pp. 297-316.

[7] James Duff Brown, *Subject Classification: With Tables, Indexes, etc. for the Sub-division of Subjects*, Ed. 3, rev. and enl. by James Douglas Stewart (London, Grafton, 1939).

A   Generalia
B/D   Physical Sciences and Technology
E/F   Biological Sciences
G/H Ethnology and Medicine
I   Economic Biology and Domestic Arts
J/K   Philosophy and Religion
L   Social and Political Science
M   Language and Literature
N   Literary Forms
O/W History and Geography
X   Biography

The principle of the *Subject Classification* was to assemble everything relating to a topic at one constant place. Brown believed that every form of knowledge can be traced to a principle from which it develops. In the order of things first were factors of *Matter and Force* (Physical Sciences) which gave rise to *Life* (Biological Sciences, Ethnological Sciences and Medical Sciences); *Life* in time produced *Mind* (Philosophy and Religion, Social and Political Science), and finally *Record* (Language and Literature, Literary Forms, History, Geography and Biography). Brown's rather inflexible "scientific progression" lacked logical modulation from one class to another. It was adopted only in some smaller libraries in Great Britain, and primarily because of its simple notation: a single capital letter of the alphabet followed by numbers that can be treated decimally if required.[8]

BIBLIOGRAPHIC CLASSIFICATION

Unlike Dewey, who published his scheme within a few years, Henry Evelyn Bliss (1870-1955) spent some 30 years developing his ideas on bibliographical classification. He was for many years on the library staff of the College of the City of New York. His major work, *A Bibliographic Classification*, was published in four volumes between 1940 and 1953; a one-volume outline of his scheme, entitled *A System of Bibliographic Classification*, appeared in 1935.[9] A revised edition of BC is currently in progress, under the editorship of Jack Mills and sponsored by the Bliss Classification Association. The revised edition will be published in separate parts between 1975 and 1977.

Although, as will be seen, BC has many advantages, Bliss's classification scheme has had little success in establishing itself as a major competitor to the

---

[8] A detailed analysis of *Subject Classification* will be found in W. C. Berwick Sayers, *A Manual of Classification for Librarians*, 4th ed. (London, Andre Deutsch, 1967), pp. 166-179, and in J. Mills, *A Modern Outline of Library Classification* (London, Chapman & Hall, 1968, c1960), pp. 103-116.

[9] An abridged scheme for school libraries—*The Abridged Bliss Classification*—was published in 1967 by the School Library Association in London. In addition, Bliss published two major works on classification: *The Organization of Knowledge and the System of the Sciences* (New York, Holt, 1929), and *The Organization of Knowledge in Libraries* (New York, H. W. Wilson, 1933).

Dewey Decimal Classification and Library of Congress Classification. Nevertheless, the theoretical concepts developed by Bliss have influenced many other classification systems. One of the basic principles advocated by Bliss was the idea of "consensus." To use his own words, "Knowledge should be organized in consistency with the scientific and educational consensus, which is relatively stable and tends to become more so as theory and system become more definitely established in general and increasingly in detail."[10] Thus, according to Bliss, the most important part of the classification scheme was its order of basic and subordinate classes, determined by the scientific and educational consensus of educational requirements in the various branches of knowledge. In other words, the classes and schedules should arrange recorded knowledge in the order that has been found to be satisfactory by the expert scholars in a given discipline. The more closely a library classification reflects this consensus, the more efficient and flexible this classification scheme will be. The order of classes is based on three major principles: collocation of related subjects, subordination of special to general, and graduation of specialty. By collocation of related subjects, Bliss means placing closely related subjects in close proximity in the classified sequence—e.g., chemical technology is collocated with chemistry, plant pathology with plant eugenics, etc. By subordination, Bliss means placing related subjects according to the principle of decreasing extension, so that the general subject is followed by the more specific subject. Graduation by specialty, proceeding from the more general to the more specific, means that "the generalizations and laws of each more general science are true in some measure of all the more special sciences. . . . But the laws or truths of the more special sciences rarely apply to the more general sciences or solve their problems."[11] The notation of the scheme uses the alphabet in its full English form of 26 letters as the base for all classification by knowledge, reserving arabic numerals for considerations of form. An outline of the scheme is given below.

1–9		Anterior numeral classes (for special collections)
	A.	Philosophy and General Science
	B.	Physics
	C.	Chemistry
	D.	Astronomy, Geology, Geography
	E.	Biology
	F.	Botany
	G.	Zoology
	H.	Anthropology
	I.	Psychology
	J.	Education
	K.	Social Sciences
	L–O.	History, Social, Political and Economic, including Geography
	P.	Religion, Theology, and Ethics

---

[10] Henry Evelyn Bliss, *The Organization of Knowledge in Libraries*, 2d ed. (New York, H. W. Wilson, 1939), pp. 42-43.

[11] Ibid.

Q. Applied Social Sciences
R. Political Science
S. Law
T. Economics
U. Arts: Useful Arts
V. Fine Arts
W—Y. Literature and Language
Z. Bibliology, Bibliography, Libraries

The anterior numerical classes include subjects that other classification schemes place in the generalia class. Any of the numbers 1 through 9 can be prefixed to a particular class number—e.g., for a periodical in general technology, 6A2J (6—periodicals; A2J—Technology in general). Most notations are brief and consist of a combination of letters—e.g., UA is agriculture; UC, animal industries and products; UCJ, cattle; UCJD, dairying; and UCJF, milk production. According to Bliss, it is important in classifying a book to decide in what main classes it falls. The literature on concrete topics like "bees" is not kept in one place but is distributed according to the general "aspect" from which it is viewed. For example, a book on bees from a scientific aspect is provided for in class G (Zoology), whereas a book on beekeeping is to be classed in U (Useful Arts). Bliss uses both capital letters and lower case letters, the latter for geographic numbers and some other special tables (e.g., DL—regional geology, and DLi, geology of Italy). There are a number of auxiliary schedules for geographical subdivisions, historical periods, etc. Bliss classification schedules are famous for providing for different needs in different libraries, for their use of mnemonics, their brief notation, and their provision of alternatives. It is one of the most flexible classification systems ever produced.[12]

UNIVERSAL DECIMAL CLASSIFICATION

The UDC, an expansion of the Dewey Decimal Classification, was first published in French in 1899 as the *Manual du répertoire universel bibliographique*. Over the years it has been expanded in great detail by the Fédération Internationale de Documentation and published in several languages, including English.[13] UDC is primarily designed for subject indexing of all branches of knowledge, with decimal notation for specifying the classes of classification. The broader subject divisions

---

[12] A detailed description of *Bibliographic Classification* can be found in A. C. Foskett, *The Subject Approach to Information* (Hamden, Conn., Archon Books, 1969), pp. 185-196; and in Jack Mills's article in *Encyclopedia of Library and Information Science*, Vol. 2 (New York, Marcel Dekker, 1969), pp. 368-380.

[13] Fédération Internationale de Documentation, *Classification decimall universelle*, 2e éd. (Bruxelles, Institut International de Bibliographie, 1927-53), 4v.

_____, *Universal Decimal Classification. Complete English Edition*, 4th International Ed. (London, British Standards Institution, 1943–), in progress.

_____, *Universal Decimal Classification. Abridged English Edition*, 3d rev. 1961 (London, British Standards Institution, 1963).

are similar to those of the Dewey Decimal Classification, but in its detail and use of synthetic devices UDC has moved a long way from Dewey. The main classes of UDC are as follows:

0. Generalities of Knowledge
1. Philosophy, Metaphysics, Psychology
2. Religion, Theology
3. Social Sciences
5. Mathematics and Natural Sciences
6. Applied Sciences, Medicine, Technology
7. The Arts, Recreation, Entertainment, Sport
8. Literature, Belles-Lettres, Philology, Linguistics, Languages
9. Geography, Biography, History

Like the Dewey Decimal Classification, the basic notation of UDC consists of arabic numerals used decimally, based on the principle of proceeding from the general to the more particular or specific.

.3	Social Science. Sociology
.34	Law Jurisprudence
.347	Civil Law
.3477	Commercial Law

However, UDC achieves its great flexibility by providing a number of auxiliary devices in two basic groups: the common auxiliaries, which are applicable to all classes, and the special auxiliaries, which may have different meanings and which are used only in certain parts of UDC schedules. "Hospitality" is achieved in UDC with symbols of connection, addition, and consecutive extension, of which the first is the plus (+) sign. Example: 539.1+621.039, nuclear science and technology. This plus sign is used to connect two numbers to join different subjects. The slash (/) is used to join consecutive UDC numbers in order to indicate a broader heading (e.g., 624/628, all branches of civil engineering, or 22/28, the Christian religion). Any two independent class numbers in the scheme can be linked by a colon to form a more specific subject—e.g., 621.785 (the number for heat treatment) may be combined with 669.14 (the number for steel) to form 621.785:669.14, meaning "heat treatment of steel." By using the colon, the classifier can make numerous multiple entries with relative ease in order to achieve much-needed precision in subject description. The square brackets denote subordinate relation—e.g., mining statistics 622[31]. There are common auxiliaries of language: the equals sign specifies the language in which the document is written—e.g., 678(038)=82=20, Russian-English dictionary of rubbers and plastics. Place signs (1/9) are the usual geographic numbers of Dewey without the initial "9"; they are used within brackets—e.g., England [42], France [44]. Thus, 327[42:44] is used for International Relations between Britain and France. There are many other auxiliaries, such as common auxiliaries of time (denoted by inverted commas), alphabetical and numerical subdivisions, and many indicators to be used within the class in which they are enumerated. Space limitations preclude a detailed discussion here.[14] UDC, with its well-designed index, is the most important international classification scheme. It is widely used in a number of countries. UDC is certainly the most comprehensive classification; it has more than 100,000 divisions in the main tables, compared to about 11,000 in Dewey Decimal Classification.[15]

COLON CLASSIFICATION

In contrast to enumerative classifications, Colon Classification is an analytico-synthetic scheme. It was first introduced by S. R. Ranganathan in India. The first edition was published in 1933, and subsequent editions appeared in 1939, 1950, 1952, 1957, 1960, and 1963.[16] Dr. Ranganathan was one of the foremost theoreticians in the area of library classification, having published such works as *Prolegomena to Library Classification* (3rd ed. 1967), *Library Classification Fundamentals and Procedure* (1944), *Elements of Library Classification* (1953), and many other treatises, not to mention hundreds of articles and short essays, most of which deal with aspects of "facet" classification or indexing.

Ranganathan's influence can be compared to that of Dewey or Cutter in this country or James Duff Brown in Great Britain. A whole school of thought has developed from his basic concepts of classification, and there has recently been growing interest, particularly in Europe, in special "faceted" classification schemes.

It is almost impossible to present all the important features of Colon Classification in a brief discussion. Referring the reader to the voluminous literature on the subject,[17] we will limit our presentation here to the basic concepts embodied in this classification scheme. The aim of Colon Classification is to analyze the subject matter into constituent elements or facets. Thus, any field of knowledge (a class or subject) may be divided into subclasses (or subcategories) by the application of a characteristic of classification. For example, libraries may be

---

[14] Cf. *Guide to the Universal Decimal Classification* (London, British Standards Institution, 1963).

[15] A good critical presentation of UDC will be found in J. Mills, *The Universal Decimal Classification* (New Brunswick, N.J., Rutgers, The State University School of Library Science, 1964); and in A. C. Foskett, *The Universal Decimal Classification: The History, Present Status and Future Prospects of a Large General Classification Scheme* (Hamden, Conn., Linnet Books, 1973). Two other works on this subject are Jean Perrault, *An Introduction to U.D.C.* (Hamden, Conn., Archon Books, 1969), and his *Towards a Theory for U.D.C.: Essays Aimed at Structural Understanding and Operational Improvement* (Hamden, Conn., Archon Books, 1969).

[16] Shiyali Ramamrita Ranganathan, *Colon Classification*, 6th rev. ed. (London, Asia Publishing House, 1963). The seventh edition will appear in parts.

[17] The student will be well advised to read the following books on this subject: C. D. Batty, *Introduction to Colon Classification* (Hamden, Conn., Archon Books, 1966); B. I. Palmer and A. J. Wells, *The Fundamentals of Library Classification* (London, Allen & Unwin, 1951), which is rather dated but still one of the best presentations; and B. C. Vickery, *Classification and Indexing in Science*, 2d ed. (London, Butterworths, 1959). A sound discussion is A. Neelameghan, "Colon Classification," in *Encyclopedia of Library and Information Science*, Vol. 5 (New York: Marcel Dekker, 1971), pp. 316-340.

divided into categories of ownership (public, private, etc.), or according to educational status (school or special), physical status of user (hospital), subject covered (medicine), etc. The whole series of arrays based on a set of related characteristics is the "library facet." Similarly, the class "Literature" may be divided by the characteristic of language into such subcategories as Russian or French literature, or it may be subdivided by the characteristic of literary form into Poetry, Drama, etc. Each of these subcategories or subclasses is called a focus, and the totality or summation of the foci is called a facet of the class concerned. Any facet or isolate is a manifestation of five fundamental principles: Time, Space, Energy, Matter, and Personality. All subjects must be manifestations of one or more of these fundamental principles. Because facets are manifestations of fundamental principles, a faceted classification, in this case Colon, will allow for the easy interpolation of new subjects and topics in the general scheme since all new subjects represent some variation of the above-mentioned fundamental categories. Instead of listing subjects and their subdivisions as do all linear classification schemes, the Colon Classification lists a number of foci in the relevant facet of each main class. Thus, the sixth edition of Colon Classification consists of three parts: part one, the rules; part two, the schedules of classification; and part three, the schedules of classics and sacred books with special names. The schedule for Literature, Class O, is as follows:

Chapter O

Literature

O[P], [P2] [P3], [P4]

Foci in [P]

as the Language divisions in chapter 5

Foci in [P2]

1. Poetry
2. Drama
3. Fiction
4. Letters (literature written in the form of letters)
5. Oration
6. Other forms of prose
7. Campu

Foci in [P3]

1. To be got by (CD)

2. For authors born later than 1800, if the year of birth cannot be found at all, (CD) to be worked only to one digit. Thereafter, (AD) may be used.

Foci in [P4]

See rules in Chapter O of Part I.

Four major characteristics are applied for the subdivision of literature: Language, or "L"; Form, or "F"; Author, or "A"; and Work, or "W." Language is naturally the P facet, but literary form is P2 and author is P3. The number for author is arrived at from the table of the chronological divisions. Thus, O152,1J32 is for Hindi poet Tulsidas (O=Literature; 152=Hindi; 1=Poetry; J32=Birth date of Tulsidas).

The Colon Classification is equipped with numerous mnemonic and other notational devices. The following are a few of Ranganathan's more common devices: digit "2" is used for two dimensions—form, structure, constitution, etc. Digit "3" is used for heat, pathology, disease, etc. Digit "5" is used for aesthetics, emotion, etc. Digit "6" is used for finance, money, etc. The Colon Classification has a number of subject and alphabetical devices. The subject device (similar to "divide-like" notes) consists of using the appropriate class numbers for the formation or subdivision of a class or subject. The alphabetical device consists of using the first or the first two initial letters of the proper name, trade names, and certain technical nomenclature. Chronological devices, as we have already seen in literature, specify a new focus by means of date, with authors designated by their date of birth. From this brief discussion it is already apparent that the notation of Colon Classification is indeed mixed. The main classes are denoted usually by capital letters; arabic numbers are used for divisions in their facets; lower case letters are used for the common bibliographical forms and subject divisions, etc. In addition to symbols denoting classes or the foci within them, there are several connecting symbols (facet indicators): e.g., [P] is introduced by a comma, [M] by the semicolon, [E] by the colon, [S] by a period, and [T] by an apostrophe. Thus, the notation is lengthy and rather complex. In addition, there are four cumbersome indexes to the scheme and three orders to the main schedules. Colon Classification has not been widely used, even in India, because it is a difficult scheme to comprehend. Nevertheless, Ranganathan's ideas have provided a basis for current research on classification theory.

COMPARATIVE EXAMPLES

The following four examples of classification problems compare the results of using the five classification systems discussed in this chapter as well as the two systems previously discussed, DDC and LC. The order of each classification system in these examples is based solely on the order covered in this textbook: DDC, LC, EC, SC, BC, UDC, CC. These examples have been chosen to display various distinct features of the systems but they should not be interpreted as representative of all the qualities of any system. Although the notation in each example is analyzed, a detailed explanation of how to derive the notation is beyond the scope of this text.

Example 1

The first book chosen as an example is Langer's *Introduction to Symbolic Logic*, 1953. This example has been selected because it represents a single or simple subject: in this case, symbolic logic. Also, it is possible to consider this simple subject in relation to at least two separate main classes—i.e., Philosophy (as a subdivision of Logic), and Mathematics. In fact, as the following classifications show, this subject can be classed in Mathematics in one system and in Philosophy in another. If any of the systems allow this simple subject to be classed in one and only one notation, then **cross classification** is not present in the system, at least for this example. Cross classification occurs when a simple subject can be classed correctly in more than one location within one system. Cross classification is considered undesirable in a classification system.

DDC

The number for symbolic logic in DDC 18 is 511.3. Because this number is printed in the schedules, no number building is required here.

500	Pure sciences
510	Mathematics
511	Generalities
.3	Symbolic (mathematical) logic

511.3	Symbolic logic

It is interesting to note that in DDC 17 symbolic logic was classed 164, as a subdivision of logic in the class Philosophy. When the phoenix schedule for mathematics was developed for DDC 18, the decision was made to move symbolic logic to mathematics. Presently the number 164 is enclosed in brackets with a note directing the classifier to use 511.3. For this simple subject there is no cross classification in DDC.

LC

The Library of Congress notation for this example is BC 135. This number is found directly in the schedules and requires no use of auxiliary tables. The main schedules give two numbers for symbolic and mathematical logic:

131   Early works to 1800.

135   Later works, 1801–

Our example is obviously a "later work," so BC 135 is correct.

B	Philosophy
BC	Logic
135	Symbolic and mathematical logic– Later works, 1801–

BC 135	Symbolic and mathematical logic– Later works, 1801–

In this case, no appropriate location is given in the mathematics schedule, QA, so again there is no cross classification.

EC

Using the Expansive Classification in the seventh expansion, the notation for this example is BHS. Once again, this number is found directly in the schedules; in this case, the heading in the schedules is for "symbolic or algebraic logic."

B	Philosophy
BH	Logic
BHS	Symbolic or algebraic logic

Note the use of the mnemonic "S" as the last element of the notation; the "S" obviously relates to the word "symbolic"; this type of device often occurs in EC. No location can be found for this subject in the mathematics schedules.

SC

On the surface, Brown's *Subject Classification* might seem to be one of the better systems for this subject. In Brown's topical approach, the subclass for logic immediately precedes mathematics.

A 300	Logic
A 400	Mathematics

Both subjects are treated as subtopics in the class for generalia; further, both subjects also occur in the Categorical Tables, as follows:

.87	Logic
.91	Mathematics

These tables provide at least two possibilities for building a number for symbolic logic, since this particular subject is not listed in the SC schedules. An approximate number can be constructed as A 300.91 or as A 400.87. The numbers are built as follows:

A	Generalia
300	Logic
.91	Mathematical

A 300.91   Mathematical logic

A	Generalia
400	Mathematics
.87	Logic

A 400.87   Logical mathematics

This is not the most satisfactory solution; it demonstrates the fact that SC is not a highly specific or greatly detailed system.

BC

Bliss's *Bibliographic Classification* provides direct notation for symbolic logic printed in the schedule as ALS.

A	Philosophy
AL	Logic
ALS	Symbolic logic

In this notation two simple mnemonics are present—i.e., "L" for "Logic" and "S" for "Symbolic." The use of such simple mnemonics is a regular feature of BC. In addition to ALS, three other notations are related to our topic:

ALT	Mathematical, or Theoretical, Logic
ALU	Algebra of Logic
ALV	Relation of Logic to Mathematics

In the case of our particular book, ALS is the appropriate notation; but it should be noted that BC does provide more specific possibilities for this subject than do the other systems.

UDC

The Universal Decimal Classification uses the same basic number for this subject as DDC 17 did—namely, 164. In addition, however, the UDC common auxiliaries of form allow us to say that this is a comprehensive, advanced treatise by adding the notation (021).

16	Logic
164	Symbolic logic
(	Sign to introduce form or place divisions
(0	Digit to introduce form divisions
(02	Textbooks. Manuals. Monographs.
(021)	Comprehensive, advanced treatises

164(021) A comprehensive, advanced treatise on symbolic logic

CC

The number in Colon Classification is simply and directly found in the schedules as R14.

R	Philosophy
R1	Logic
R14	Symbolic

This is an extremely simple number in CC, but it must be remembered that this example is also simple. The remaining examples are more complex. Of the seven classification systems used in this example, DDC 18 is the only system to place symbolic logic in Mathematics; all the others (except for SC) place this first example in the Philosophy class. SC places it in the Generalia class—if, indeed, it can be placed in SC at all.

Example 2

The second example is Wilson Knight's *Principles of Shakespearian Production.* The expressive title for this work might well be "Stage presentations of the plays of Shakespeare." This example gives us our first complex subject; stage presentations are normally a subdivision of theatre, and Shakespeare is an author in English literature. Furthermore, Shakespeare has been deliberately chosen here because he is an author about whom one of the largest bodies of literature has been written and also because classification schemes, especially enumerative ones, often include a detailed breakdown for Shakespeare.

DDC

The number in the DDC schedules for Shakespeare is 822.33.

8	Literature
82	English literature
822	Drama
.3	Elizabethan period
.33	Shakespeare

However, the number for stage presentations is 792.02.

7	Arts
79	Recreational and performing arts
792	Theater (Stage presentations)
.02	Handbooks, techniques

This number is, of course, a general number for basic works on stage presentations and not specifically for Shakespearean presentations. In short, there is no single number for this complex subject in DDC 18. It is simply not specific enough for this example.

LC

For Shakespeare the Library of Congress Classification is far more specific, or enumerative, than any of the other systems. In fact, LC gives two possible choices: either PR 3091 or PR 3099. The range of numbers PR 3091-3112 is for the dramatic representation of Shakespeare's plays, as shown on the partial schedule on page 319.

PR

	Dramatic representation of Shakespeare's plays.
	General.
3091	English.
3092	Other.
	By period.
3095	Elizabethan.
3097	17th–18th centuries.
3099	19th–20th centuries.
	Separate plays, with text.
	By country.
	Cf. PR 2971.
3105	America.
3106	Great Britain.
3107	France.
3108	Germany.
3109	Other.
3112	Famous actors of Shakespearean parts.
	Cf. PN.

P	Language and literature
PR	English literature
PR 2750–3112	Shakespeare
PR 3091	English dramatic representation
or	
PR 3099	19th–20th century dramatic representation

Since the book deals with modern (i.e,, twentieth century) productions of Shakespeare, the latter number is perhaps more accurate. Both of these numbers occur within the same basic subdivision, so this is not an example of cross classification.

EC

Cutter provides a detailed special classification for Shakespeare in EC. The number is Y·S6V.

Y	Literature
·S	Shakespeare
6V	Performance

| Y·S6V | Shakespearean performance |

SC

Brown provides no detailed breakdown for Shakespeare. The biographical number, Brown's alphabetizing device, for Shakespeare is "7860." The number for Acting is N240. N240 seems to be the appropriate number in SC, since Shakespeare's plays are separated from criticism and biographical material.

N	Literary forms and texts
200	Drama
240	Acting

BC

YF is the section of BC provided for Shakespeare. From a special auxiliary table for sub-classification for any author, the letter "I" may be added for dramatization or theatrical production.

Y	Literature
YF	Shakespeare
I	Dramatization, or Theatrical production
YFI	Dramatization, or Theatrical production of Shakespeare

UDC

The schedule for literature in UDC is extremely brief and basically synthetic. It is, however, easy to use and, on the whole, accurate. Shakespeare may be specified by 822 Shak. The notation for theatre performance is 792.07. By the use of either of two UDC punctuation symbols, the plus sign or the colon, these two numbers may be linked together. The colon is used to show the relationship of one subject to another, while the plus sign is used to add one subject to another. In this case, then, we can say either Shakespeare's plays related to theatre performance or Shakespeare's plays and theatre performance. The former alternative appears to be more appropriate: 822 Shak. : 792.07.

8	Literature
2	English
2	Drama
Shak.	Shakespeare
:	Related to
7	Arts
9	Entertainment
2	Theatre
.07	Theatre- and stage-craft.
822 Shak. : 792.07	Shakespearean production

Although UDC is not as detailed for Shakespeare as DDC, these special symbols allow UDC to be more expressive than DDC in this particular example.

CC

The Colon Classification uses the basic literature table given on page 313 of this chapter. The Colon notation, for example, is O111, 2J64 0a NT. O111 is P; 2 is P2; J64 is P3.

O		Literature
111		Modern English
,		Indicator for P2
2		Drama
J		the 1500's
	64	1564, Shakespeare's year of birth
	0	Indicator for relations
	a	General relation, i.e., related to
	NT	Theatre

O 111, 2J64 0a NT   Shakespearean theatre

This example shows that highly enumerative systems such as LC, EC, and BC are capable of being more expressive (for Shakespeare, at least) than DDC or SC. Synthetic devices allow UDC and CC to be as expressive or nearly as expressive as the detailed enumerative systems.

Example 3

The third example is Noble's *Shakespeare's Biblical Knowledge and Use of the Book of Common Prayer.* This example allows the use of some of the material already explained in the second example. Furthermore, it is a three-part complex example: i.e., Shakespeare, the Bible, and the Book of Common Prayer. In this example, the principal subject is clearly Shakespeare, particularly Shakespeare's knowledge and use of two religious books.

DDC

As in Example 2, the number for Shakespeare in DDC is 822.33, and Shakespeare's knowledge may be further classed in 822.33F. The use of the letter "F" is from a special table of subdivisions in DDC 18 for Shakespeare. It means "Sources, allusions, learning." As a result of this special subdivision, the DDC notation in this case is no longer pure but rather becomes a mixed notation of numbers and letters. See example on page 322.

822.33	Shakespeare
F	Sources, allusions, learning

822.33F	A work dealing with Shakespeare's sources, allusions, or learning

DDC 18 makes no provision for further subdivision in relation to Shakespeare's knowledge or learning. Although there are, of course, separate numbers for both the Bible and the Book of Common Prayer, neither of these can be attached to 822.33F.

LC

Like the DDC notation, the most appropriate notation in LC cannot bring out all aspects of this particular book. The LC number is PR 3012.

PR 2750–3112	Shakespeare
PR 3000–3044	Treatment and knowledge of special subjects
3011	Religion
3012	The Bible

PR 3012	Shakespeare's treatment and knowledge of the Bible

EC

Cutter's EC provides two possible choices for this subject, with a special notation Y·S6U for Shakespeare's learning and his treatment of various subjects. This number is expanded either by simple mnemonics (such as "B" for the Bible) or by the use of the appropriate class number for the subject in its own schedules. The class number for the Bible is "CB" and the class number for the Book of Common Prayer is "CUEN" plus the date of the edition; in this case, the date of the edition of the Book of Common Prayer is 1559.

Y·S	Shakespeare
Y·S6U	Shakespeare's learning and his treatment of various subjects
CB	The Bible

Y·S6UCB	Shakespeare's knowledge and treatment of the Bible

Similarly,

Y·S6U	Shakespeare's learning and his treatment of various subjects
CUEN	The Book of Common Prayer
·1559	Date of the edition of the Book of Common Prayer

Y·S6UCUEN·1559	Shakespeare's knowledge and treatment of the Book of Common Prayer

This example shows an instance when a synthetic device in EC allows either of the related subjects to be expressed, but not both. It should also be noted that the second number is an extremely long one for EC notation.

SC

The basic number for biographical material in the Subject Classification is "X" plus the individual author's biographical number. Shakespeare is X 7860. The number for the Bible is K 110. The Book of Common Prayer may be expressed by the number for the Church of England, K 750, plus the categorical number for prayer books, .685. Brown's system, like the UDC, does allow the use of a plus sign to add two numbers together. His directions do not specify, however, whether three numbers can be added together. If they can, the number would be X 7860 + K 110 + K 750.685.

X	Biography
7860	Shakespeare's biographical number
+	Sign indicating composite work
K	Religion
110	The Bible
+	Sign indicating composite work
K 750	Church of England
.685	Liturgies

X 7860 + K 110 + K 750.685	Biographical material about Shakespeare in relation to the Bible and Church of England liturgies

Although all three subjects are expressed in this number, the concept of Shakespeare's knowledge or use does not appear; also, the Book of Common Prayer is not specifically indicated.

BC

The BC notation for this example is as expressive as the DDC notation. YFD is the notation meaning formative influences on the author's (i.e., Shakespeare's) mind and art. The specific subject of the influence cannot be specified.

YF	Shakespeare
D	Formative influences on the author's mind and art

YFD	Formative influences on Shakespeare's mind and art

UDC

UDC notation begins with the previously described notation for Shakespeare, 822 Shak. The number for the Bible is 22 (note that in DDC this would be treated as 220; in UDC, however, a final zero digit is dropped—even in the first three digits). The Book of Common Prayer is a construction problem. 264 is the number for worship and 264-12 is the number for missals. 283 is the Anglican Communion and (420) is the place number for England. When the UDC punctuation devices are used, the number that results is 822 Shak. : 22 + 264-12 [283(420)] .

822 Shak.	Shakespeare
:	Related to
22	The Bible
+	and
264	Worship
-12	Missals
[	Sign for subordinate relations
283	Anglican Communion
(	Place indicator
(420)]	England

822 Shak. : 22 + 264-12 [283(420)]	Shakespeare related to the Bible and the English Anglican Missal (i.e., the Book of Common Prayer).

Just as with the SC, this notation expresses all three subjects, but the concept of Shakespeare's knowledge or use does not appear.

CC

Even the highly synthetic Colon Classification cannot fully express this particular three-part subject. The number for Shakespeare as developed in Example 2 is O 111, 2J64. The number for the Bible is Q6:21, but the Book of Common Prayer can only be expressed as Christian worship, Q6:45. The following number may result: O 111, 2J64 0g Q6:21 0t45.

O 111, 2J64	Shakespeare
0	Zero, the indicator for relations
g	The influencing relation between classes
Q	Religion
Q6	Christianity
:	Required indicator for Class Q
21	The Bible
0	The indicator for relations
t	The general relations indicator within classes
45	Christian worship

O 111, 2J64 0g Q6:21 0t45	Shakespeare influenced by the Bible and Christian worship.

The phrase relations device allows this notation to express the idea of influencing. This may be seen as a closer expression of the original subject of Shakespeare's knowledge of the Bible; however, CC does not provide for the expression of the Book of Common Prayer any more precisely than "Christian worship."

Example 3 cannot be fully expressed by any of the systems; the detailed enumerative systems of LC, EC, and BC do not enumerate all the aspects of this subject. Each of the synthetic possibilities of UDC, SC, and CC lacks part of the expression. However, if this example dealt only with Shakespeare's influence by or his knowledge of the Bible, many of the systems could have readily accommodated it.

Example 4

The last example, which has often been used to demonstrate the expressiveness and flexibility of the Colon Classification, is a book on the influence of hereditary factors in the psychology of delinquent children. Like Example 3, this example contains three distinct parts: hereditary factors, psychology, and delinquent children.

DDC

There is a specific number in DDC for the psychology of delinquent and problem children, 155.453. However, there is also a separate number for evolutional psychology, with a note stating "Influence of heredity on personal characteristics," 155.7. This is once again a situation where there are two numbers that express the subject but there is no provision for combining them.

150	Psychology
155	Differential and genetic psychology
.4	Child psychology
.45	Exceptional children
.453	Delinquent and problem children

155.453	Psychology of delinquent and problem children

155	Differential and genetic psychology
.7	Evolutional psychology

155.7	Evolutional psychology

LC

Within the range of numbers for genetic psychology in LC, there is specific provision for child psychology and special topics, A–Z. Thus the following number can be constructed: BF 723.D35.

BF	Psychology
700–755	Genetic psychology
721–723	Child psychology
723	Special topics, A–Z
.D35	Delinquency

BF 723.D35   The genetic psychology of delinquent children

This notation appears to express the fourth example adequately.

EC

Genetic psychology is BK in Cutter's system; mental heredity and evolution is BKA; and child psychology is BKG. Furthermore, ICJ is used to express juvenile delinquency. EC has no provisions for combining any of these numbers. Since BKG is a subdivision of genetic psychology, it may be the most appropriate choice.

BK	Genetic psychology
BKG	Child psychology

The criminal or delinquency aspect cannot be provided for.

SC

This three-part subject creates an interesting problem in the Subject Classification, particularly with respect to its categorical tables. Psychology is classed as J 150 but also has the categorical number .626. Heredity is E 017, or the categorical number .381. Children have a separate class in SC in the G 110s as well as the categorical number .506. In the G 110 class, G 117 is specifically assigned to Juvenile Delinquency. In using SC one must decide whether to class this subject in psychology or in the special class for children. Since SC, unlike most of the other systems, is not based on traditional academic classes, either location may be considered appropriate; in fact, the separate location for material about children may be more appropriate to the spirit of SC. G 117.626 + E 017.506 is thus a possible notation.

G	Ethnology
G 110	Children
G 117	Juvenile delinquency
.626	Psychology
+	Sign indicating composite work
E	Biology
E 017	Heredity
.506	Children

G 117.626 + E 017.506	The psychology of delinquent children and the heredity of children.

In this case all three aspects of the subject are expressed, although the precise application is not—i.e., the influence of heredity on the psychology of delinquent children.

BC

BC provides three possible numbers which together adequately express the three parts of this subject. Child psychology is IV. QOE is Genetics in criminology (including heredity, breeding of delinquents and criminals); and QOF is the Psychology of delinquents and criminals. It should be noted that both of the QO numbers are from the subclass Criminology in the class Q for Applied social sciences (not class I for Psychology).

Q	Applied social science
QO	Criminology
QOE	Genetics in criminology

or

QO	Criminology
QOF	Psychology of delinquents and criminals

UDC

The notation for child psychology in UDC is 159.922.7; it should be noted that in UDC a decimal point is used for each group of three numbers unless some other punctuation symbol is used. The psychology of delinquents in the criminology subclass is 343.95, and the heredity of delinquents is 343.941. One possible notation would be 159.922.7 : 343.941.

159.922.7	Child psychology
:	related to
343.941	the heredity of delinquents

159.922.7 : 343.941	Child psychology related to the heredity of delinquents.

Similarly, 343.95 : 343.941 is another possibility:

343.95		Psychology of delinquents
:		related to
	343.941	the heredity of delinquents

343.95 : 343.941	Psychology of delinquents related to the heredity of delinquents.

Neither expression of the notation fully states the subject of Example 4. Particularly lacking is the idea of influence.

CC

This three-part subject with an influencing phase can be fully expressed by Colon Classification as S2–(T65) 0g G:61.

S				Psychology
S2				Adolescent
–				Superimposition device
	(T65)			Criminal (taken, i.e., superimposed, from Chapter T to be used as an attribute of "2" for adolescent)
		0		Relational symbol
			g	Influenced by
			G	Biology
			G:6	Genetics
			G:61	Heredity

S2–(T65) 0g G:61	The psychology of criminal children influenced by heredity.

This notation represents the fullest expression of this subject in its three parts and relations. This subject's relations can be expressed by CC because of its use of phase relations and, in this case, particularly the influencing phase.

14 SUBJECT HEADINGS

INTRODUCTION

Classification provides the library with a systematic arrangement of materials according to subject and form. In addition to classification, there is another approach to subject matter in a collection—namely, that of subject headings. At the risk of oversimplification, it can be stated that if classification provides a logical or systematic approach to subject matter, the subject headings give a topical approach, collecting aspects of a subject under its heading or name. When taken together, these two—classification schemes and subject headings—provide the patron with a dual subject approach to library materials, the classed and the alphabetical. Subject headings, then, add another dimension to the linear arrangement provided by classification.

The preceding chapters discussed some of the limitations of library classification. It was emphasized that these limitations are not only inherent in the philosophical characteristics of the classification process but are also imposed by the conflict between the dual natures of the book: it is both an intellectual *and* a physical entity. In practice, this means that the classifier may class the book in only one place; he must reach the best compromise between the content of the book and the printed classification schedule. Thus, a historical treatise may be classed in political or economic history, or even with social history or biography. In other words, the content of this particular treatise will not be sufficiently covered by classification alone, so there is an obvious need for the additional subject control provided by subject headings. Classification and subject headings are both integral parts of the classification process.

Classified Versus Alphabetical Approach to Information

There are many theoretically sound objectives of subject cataloging. Shera and Egan summarized them in the following points:[1]

"1. To provide access by subject to all relevant material.

2. To provide subject access to materials through all suitable principles of subject organization, e.g., matter, process, applications, etc.

---

[1] Jesse H. Shera and Margaret E. Egan, *The Classified Catalog* (Chicago, American Library Association, 1956), p. 10.

3. To bring together references to materials which treat substantially the same subject regardless of disparities in terminology, disparities which may have resulted from national differences, differences among groups of subject specialists, and/or from the changing nature of the concepts within the discipline itself.

4. To show affiliations among subject fields, affiliations which may depend upon similarities of matter studied, of method, or of point of view, or upon use or application of knowledge.

5. To provide entry to any subject field at any level of analysis, from the most general to the most specific.

6. To provide entry through any vocabulary common to any considerable group of users, specialized or lay.

7. To provide a formal description of the subject content of any bibliographic unit in the most precise, or specific, terms possible, whether the description be in the form of a word or brief phrase or in the form of a class number or symbol.

8. To provide means for the user to make selection from among all items in any particular category, according to any chosen set of criteria such as: most thorough, most recent, most elementary, etc."

Obviously, the classified arrangement of materials as represented in our traditional classified catalog can only partially satisfy these needs; the relative merits of these two systems have been much debated in library literature. Such discussion helps to isolate problems that are inherent in an attempt to decide *a priori* the advantages and disadvantages of the classified and the alphabetical approach to subject matter. Some of the main points may be summarized here.

The inquirer who wants information on a certain subject will approach the catalog with questions formulated in his *own* words which, in turn, must be *translated* or converted into the formal (predetermined) subject categories of the catalog. This communication between inquirer and catalog (with the possible assistance of the librarian, who can interpret the structure of the catalog) will take place regardless of the type of catalog to be consulted or the arrangement of its entries.

In the case of the classified catalog, the user's verbalization is converted into the retrieval channels of the catalog through the classification schedules, or through such helping devices as the alphabetical index to the classified catalog, author entries (if the inquirer remembers who wrote on a given subject), etc.

The alphabetical catalog might make the information retrieval process somewhat more expedient, but it is identical in principle to the classified catalog. The correlation between the vocabulary of the user and that of the catalog (i.e., questions formulated versus subject descriptors in the catalog) may be such that the user can go directly to the appropriate subject heading, where he will find relevant information. If not, however, he must either try a different term (i.e., adjust his vocabulary to that used in the catalog) or follow a cross reference that directs him to the proper place. This latter procedure is exactly equivalent to using the subject index to the classified catalog.[2]

---

[2] Our discussion is based on Jesse H. Shera and Margaret E. Egan's *The Classified Catalog*, pp. 14-21.

Each catalog—the alphabetical and the classified—requires a different pattern of communication. In the former, the information on a given subject is arranged alphabetically; thus, it is scattered throughout the entire catalog and requires a horizontal approach. The inquirer consults several places in the catalog in order to find most of the information on a given subject. The advantages of direct alphabetical access to information are somewhat dubious, because the inquirer can seldom be completely assured that he consulted **all** subject headings pertinent to his needs. In the classified catalog related classes (more general as well as more specific) are adjacent rather than scattered. Greater detail on these two approaches is provided in the following sections.

Classified Arrangement

The advantage of a classified (logical) arrangement lies in the simple fact that it brings together closely related classes and categories of material in a logical and orderly sequence (vertical approach), from general to more specific. Such an arrangement offers greater assurance for in-depth searching. Based on logical relationships rather than linguistic associations, this arrangement not only offers a better comprehension of subject matter but also directly stimulates the learning experience (which, at the risk of oversimplification, may be compared with the assumed values of browsing in an open-shelf library[3]). Directly related to this advantage is the fact that the user may browse not only from general to specific but also from specific to general.

A second advantage is that the classified array, being based on a classification system such as DDC or LC, has a controlled order of academic classes. The reader interested in psychology can initially consult and study a single section of the catalog.

A third advantage of a classified catalog is that multiple notations can potentially be used for complex or composite works such as those discussed in Examples 2-4 of the preceding chapter. There are cases when several class numbers appear to be appropriate choices for a given subject. A classified catalog allows one number to be used as the class number and the other(s) to be used as supplementary entries in the catalog. The DDC and BC numbers in Example 4 (Chapter 13) illustrate this.

On the other hand, the order of arrangement in the classified catalog is not a matter of common knowledge, as is the alphabet. As a result, the inquirer must have some knowledge of the classification system and the structure of a discipline, and quite frequently he must also use the subject index. In addition, the classification system in general has some inherent deficiencies, particularly when the system of organization within a subject field is made obsolete by advancing frontiers of knowledge.

---

[3] Unfortunately, the problems and values of browsing have not been sufficiently studied in library literature. One may raise here another question—why is the shelf list (which functions, for the most part, as a classified catalog) not generally accessible to the patron? If the shelf list benefits the cataloger and the reference librarian, it can conceivably stimulate the interest of an inquirer, if he has a sufficient grasp of knowledge in a given field of interest and if he is **willing** to learn the classification system.

If the classified catalog is to function adequately, it must have an alphabetical (A–Z) index. A reader may, in fact, use such an index to gain access either to the catalog or directly to the shelves. Since the index requires only an initial entry for each specific subject, maintaining it does not necessarily require a new entry for each new entry in the catalog. The index may be based on the published index to the classification scheme or on a list of subject headings, or it may be a specially generated index that uses a controlled vocabulary, such as a chain index.

A **chain index** is a direct and specific index based on the extracted vocabulary of a classification system. It retains all necessary context but deletes unnecessary context; all subheadings are superordinate terms. **Specific** means that the name of the subject being indexed is present in the index entry. **Direct** means that the specific name of the subject being indexed is the first element or alphabetizing element in the entry. **Superordinate terms** are higher hierarchical headings in the classification system being used. For example, the term "TP 605 Whiskey" from LC Class T, Technology, refers to the distilling of whiskey by the fermentation industries:

T	Technology
TP	Chemical technology
TP 500–659	Fermentation industries
TP 589–617	Distilling
TP 597–617	Distilled liquors
TP 605	Whiskey

The following chain index entries could result:

Whiskey: Fermentation industries, TP 605
Distilled liquors: Fermentation industries, TP 597–617
Distilling: Fermentation industries, TP 589–617
Fermentation industries: Chemical technology, TP 500–659
Chemical technology, TP
Technology, T

The term "whiskey" may be found in a different context in Class H, Social Sciences, under the number HD 9395. In this case, the index entry would be:

Whiskey: Economic history, HD 9395.

A major advantage of a chain index is that specific rules for controlling the vocabulary of the index may be generated based on the classification system being used.[4]

---

[4] Additional material on chain indexing may be found in Jack Mills, "Chain Indexing and the Classified Catalogue," *Library Association Record* 57 (April 1955): 141-148; and John Phillip Immroth, *Analysis of Vocabulary Control in Library of Congress Classification and Subject Headings* (Littleton, Colo., Libraries Unlimited, Inc., 1971), pp. 109-140, 156-172.

Alphabetical Arrangement

The advantage of the alphabetical arrangement is obviously its simplicity. Since the order of the alphabet is common knowledge to all, an alphabetical arrangement facilitates direct access to information. Also, consolidating author-title and subject entries into one alphabetical file makes the catalog easier to use. There is a greater freedom in the introduction of new groupings, because descriptive subject headings need not bear the same logical relationship to one another as do classes in the systematic arrangement. In addition, the subject descriptors in the context of machine information retrieval have a definite potential to develop a more efficient subject inventory of information, provided that we learn more in the future about the random access to subject matter.

On the other hand, the traditional alphabetical approach causes serious fragmentation of subject matter, and basic semantic problems often occur in subject headings. Additionally, there is a general weakness in the conceptual structure of subject headings per se, a problem that will be discussed in another section.

BASIC CONCEPTS
AND STRUCTURE OF SUBJECT HEADINGS

A book can be classified in only one place in the classification schedule. If a book treats two or more subjects, it is usually classified according to the most important one—with consideration of the nature of the collection and the needs of clientele it serves. However, through its subject headings the dictionary catalog provides an additional subject approach, covering other subjects or topics pertinent to the content of the book in hand and thus broadening the process of classification. In this context, then, we may define the assignment of subject headings as a process of abstraction that reduces the overall content of the book to a number of predetermined subject concepts. The subject headings of the dictionary catalog provide a systematic approach to all aspects of the subject. This is accomplished through an alphabetical list of terms and through interlocking references.

The interlocking references are generally called **cross references**. They hold a dictionary catalog together by directing the patron to various aspects of the subject, or by directing him from a heading that is not used to one that is. If the patron consults, for example, American History, he will be referred to United States—History. Suggesting the correct subject heading of several logical alternatives is only one purpose of cross references. They can also suggest a heading unknown to the inquirer that will lead him to additional material on his subject. They explain unknown terms and supply a logical alphabetical approach to the collection.

Many authors stress certain principles that should be helpful in determining the nature and semantics of such structured subject headings. These are here summarized as presented by David Haykin:[5]

---

[5] David J. Haykin, *Subject Headings: A Practical Guide* (Washington, Government Printing Office, 1951), pp. 7-11.

1. **The Reader as the Focus.** The reference to our lack of knowledge in regard to the approach of various classes and categories of readers to the subject catalog clearly points to the fundamental principle that the reader is the focus in all cataloging principles and practices.

2. **Unity.** A subject catalog must bring together under one heading all the books which deal principally or exclusively with the subject, whatever the terms applied to it by the authors of the books and whatever the varying terms applied to it at different times. The cataloger must, therefore, choose with care the term to be used and apply it uniformly to all the books on the subject. He must choose a term which is unambiguous and does not overlap in meaning other headings in the catalog, even where that involves defining the sense in which it is used as compared with, or distinguished from, other closely related headings.

3. **Usage.** The heading chosen must represent common usage or, at any rate, the usage of the class of reader for whom the material on the subject within which the heading falls is intended. Usage in an American library must inevitably mean current American usage. . . . Whether a popular term or a scientific one is to be chosen depends on several considerations. If the library serves a miscellaneous public, it must prefer the popular to the scientific term.

4. **Specificity.** The heading should be as specific as the topic it is intended to cover. As a corollary, the heading should not be broader than the topic; rather than use a broader heading, the cataloger should use two specific headings which will approximately cover it. . . . The subject heading must not be any broader than the subject matter of the books to which the heading is assigned.

Certain special problems of subject headings are noted here only as an introduction. Library literature is replete with detailed discussions on all aspects of these problems, and the interested student is referred to them.[6]

---

[6] It should be noted, however, that the literature on theoretical concepts of subject headings is practically non-existent. It would be only a slight exaggeration to say that Cutter's *Rules for a Dictionary Catalog*, the fourth and final edition of which appeared in 1904, still provides a solid basis on the theory and practice of subject headings. For a fuller understanding of theoretical as well as practical applications of subject headings, we recommend J. Pettee, *Subject Headings: The History and Theory of the Alphabetical Subject Approach to Books* (New York, H. W. Wilson, 1946); E. J. Coates, *Subject Catalogues: Headings and Structure* (London, Library Association, 1960); J. Metcalfe, *Alphabetical Subject Indication of Information* (New Brunswick, N.J., Graduate School of Library Service, Rutgers, The State University, 1965; Rutgers Series on Systems for the Intellectual Organization of Information, v.3); and J. Harris, *Subject Analysis: Computer Implications of Rigorous Definition* (Metuchen, N.J., Scarecrow Press, 1970). Of special interest to students will be an article by Lois Mai Chan, " 'American Poetry' but 'Satire, American': The Direct and Inverted Forms of Subject Headings Containing National Adjectives," *Library Resources and Technical Services* 17 (Summer 1973): 330-339. This article reveals a pattern of direct and inverted forms of subject headings that is based primarily on subject categories rather than the word-frequency discussed by Harris.

Change is inevitable. One must at least be aware of these patterns of change. In general, one can probably say that changes in subject headings hinge on the practical needs of the library patron. It is true that no one system of subject control can be everything to everyone; it is for this reason that supplementary services have been created for specific applications. For example, the specialist in any field has bibliographies that give him a deeper level of subject analysis than is possible in the catalog. Some highly specialized libraries have developed sophisticated classified catalogs for their research workers. Computerized information retrieval systems, including print-outs of bibliographies, are undoubtedly changing the form and function of subject cataloging.[7] These other approaches may serve to supplement the subject catalog or they may result in an entirely new form. One of the major attributes of the subject catalog—its currency and direct access to a large body of material—is being challenged by the use of computers to keep bibliographies up to date. In any event, the future is an exciting one for those who are interested in subject control. As the quantity of informational material is accumulating almost beyond count, more inventive means for subject control are being devised. The gap between control and material may never be closed entirely, but attempts are being made to minimize it.

The following summary contains a discussion of some of the most important problems encountered in construction and use of subject headings. A definition for subject headings can be found in the *A.L.A. Glossary of Library Terms*: "A word or a group of words indicating a subject under which all material dealing with the same theme is entered in a catalog or a bibliography, or is arranged in a file." Obviously, subject headings have dual objectives: to identify pertinent material on a given subject or topic, and to enable the inquirer to find material on related subjects. Both objectives pose problems of communication; both demand a set of subject headings that match, as far as possible, the terms likely to be in the minds of inquirers wishing to locate material on a given subject.

As Coates indicates,

> This would be fairly simple to achieve if there were an uncomplicated one-to-one relationship between concepts and words: that is to say, if there were a single word corresponding to each separate concept and a single concept corresponding to each separate word. In fact, we have on the one hand concepts that can be rendered by any one of a number of words, and on the other hand, concepts for which no single word equivalent exists in natural language.[8]

---

[7] For example, the Library of Congress provides an average of 1.5 to 3 subject headings for each non-fiction title cataloged; this is in comparison to about 13 descriptors per article indexed by MEDLARS.

[8] Coates, *Subject Catalogues: Headings and Structure*, p. 19.

The Choice of Subject Headings

Let us consider first the problem of choice of subject headings when a given concept has a number of different verbal equivalents. Here the cataloger must choose one subject heading from several synonymous or near synonymous headings. In choosing among synonymous headings Cutter recommends the following preferences:

a) most familiar to the general public
b) most used in other catalogs
c) one that has fewest meanings
d) comes first in the alphabet
e) brings the subject into the neighborhood of other related subjects.[9]

The author's usage and the patron's preference may predetermine the choice (with reference made from the others). Nevertheless, such decisions are not easy, especially if we realize that different writers may use different terms for the same subject. If the cataloger depends on the author's usage, he may enter the same subject under two different headings. The best safeguards are to use standard lists of preferred synonyms (as found, for example, in Sears or Library of Congress lists) or to use the results of classification.[10]

The opposite problem can also exist—i.e., there may be no single word that represents a given concept. Such concepts must be expressed by phrases (combinations of words), of which Cutter cites five varieties:

a) A noun preceded by an adjective—e.g., Regional planning;
b) A noun preceded by another noun used adjectively—e.g., Country life;
c) Two nouns connected by a preposition—e.g., Romanticism in music;
d) Two nouns connected by "and"—e.g., Religion and science;
e) A phrase or sentence—e.g., Firearms industry and trade.

Phrase headings, as Coates indicates, present certain disadvantages. Most inquirers consulting catalogs attempt to formulate topics as simple words, even in cases where a phrase would be needed in natural language.[11] There is also uncertainty as to the order in which the words of a phrase are cited in the subject heading. Does the heading retain the order of natural language or does it transpose the words for the sake of brevity? There is uncertainty as to which form of a phrase will represent the concept as subject heading. Nearly all phrases that consist of an adjective followed by a noun, or a noun used adjectively followed by a noun (e.g., Colonial

---

[9] C. A. Cutter, *Rules for a Dictionary Catalog*, 4th ed. (Washington, Government Printing Office, 1904), p. 70.

[10] The relationship between classification and the assignment of subject headings can be illustrated by the following: a particular title might be classed as History of Drama or as History of Theatre; the class that is chosen will determine the subject headings needed.

[11] Coates, *Subject Catalogues: Headings and Structure*, p. 19.

administration or Child psychology) can also be rendered as a more extended phrase consisting of a noun followed by a relational word (or words)—i.e., a preposition—followed by another noun (as Administration of colonies or Psychology of children). Both forms are permissible and common in ordinary language.[12]

The specific rules printed in Sears and Library of Congress lists of subject headings simplify but do not solve this problem, since they are purely arbitrary. The problem of communication still exists: many books are listed under subject headings that patrons would not immediately think of as the appropriate ones.

Location of Material on Related Subjects

One of the most important aspects of assigning subject headings is that of consistency. In general, this means that the cataloger will choose one subject heading, and one alone, for all books on that subject, and that he will refer to this chosen subject heading from all other possible headings.

Cross-references are essential to the proper functioning of subject headings. Not only do they provide the inquirer with assistance in finding needed information, but they guide him to related information on collateral subjects. In general, cross references refer from a larger to a smaller subject and, further, to "coordinate" and "illustrative" subjects. As an example, if the inquirer is trying to locate all material on civil engineering, under that heading he will probably find several entries that describe civil engineering in general. But the library contains more material on this topic scattered under more specific headings (e.g., Arches, Canals, Excavation, etc.). These specific headings can be brought to the attention of the inquirer by means of "see also" references. "See also" references suggest related topics. They refer from a term under which books are entered to a related term (under which books are also entered). They are ordinarily made from general to specific headings, or from one coordinate heading to another:

a) General to specific:

> Zoology
> > see also
> Birds
> Domestic animals
> Insects

b) Coordinate headings:

> Civil rights
> > see also
> Liberty

A closely related problem is the duplication of overlapping subjects. A **double entry** may be made under the special topic and also under the larger subject which

---

[12] Ibid., pp. 22-23.

embraces the special topic, (e.g., Buddhism—Japan and Japan—Religion), and the two subjects are then connected with "see also" references. Cutter's rule of "specific entry" does not forbid this practice; the decision depends on the nature of the collection and the needs of patrons.

Quite often the patron seeking specific information is directed toward collateral subjects. To facilitate this, the catalog must contain "see also" references from restricted to more general subjects in an upward direction. This practice, as we will see later, is followed by the Library of Congress (collateral subjects are frequently linked in both directions); the justification is that such non-specific entry policy assists patrons.

Briefly we should mention here again that in order to facilitate the use of subject headings it is also necessary to provide references which refer **from** a term or name under which no books are entered **to** the relevant term under which books are listed. Such references are called "see" references, and they are generally made in the case of synonymous terms, various forms of names of personal author and corporate body, and in all other cases when the term or phrase is not chosen for a heading, e.g.,

> Moral philosophy
> > see
> Ethics

> Psychology, Religious
> > see
> Religious psychology

In order to assure maximum consistency in the assignment of subject headings, a careful and up-to-date record of all administrative decisions must be kept, in one of two forms: a) a carefully annotated standard subject headings list (e.g., Sears or LC), or b) a separate subject authority file. By indicating the references already made by the library, such references provide the cataloger with the following information:

a) The synonymous terms from which "see" references have been made.
b) Scope notes describing the heading and distinguishing it from other headings, in those instances where one of two or more meanings of the term has been chosen for its use as a heading.
c) The less comprehensive, subordinate headings to which "see also" references have been made from more comprehensive headings.
d) The broader, more comprehensive headings, from which "see also" references have been made to the more specific headings.
e) The coordinate headings from which and to which "see also" references have been made from related headings.

In conclusion, it should be pointed out that only a very careful analysis of the individual library's needs can determine the limits at which cross references begin and end. A positive administrative solution to this problem will definitely increase the structured information service provided by the dictionary catalog.

Number of Subject Headings
and the Concept of "Specific Entry"

The number of subject headings to be made for a single book depends on many factors, some of which are economic. The larger the number of subject entries provided, the greater is the cost of classifying a title. Also, more subject entries mean more time to classify the book and more space required in the card catalog. On the other hand, the assignment of more headings per book makes the total resources of the library quickly available, and the policy of assigning many headings to the same book may bring out special aspects or bits of unusual or important information. This problem should be carefully evaluated in terms of economy or efficiency of subject approach in a given collection, but other factors must also be taken into consideration: the existence of specialized subject bibliographies or indexes, the library's policy regarding the use of analytical added entries for certain monographic works, research demands made on the library, nature of the collection, the acquisition policy for specialized materials, etc.

Each library that uses Library of Congress cards must decide how far it will go in adopting LC subject headings practice; this decision depends on the local needs of the particular library. A small public library, for example, can choose between the most specific term and the more inclusive one (between using the more inclusive term "trees" or the names of various kinds of trees such as elm, pine, oak, etc.). A larger collection will obviously need to use the more specific terms.

How specific is specific entry? On the subject of **specific entry**, Cutter said: "Enter a work under its subject heading, not under the heading of the class which includes that subject. . . . Put Lady Cust's book on 'the cat' under 'Cat,' not under Zoology or Mammals, or Domestic animals. . . . Some subjects have no name. They are spoken of by a phrase or phrases not definite enough to be used as headings. It is not always easy to decide what is a *distinct* subject."[13] Citing "movements of fluids in plants" as an example of a non-distinct subject, Cutter recommends entering it under a non-specific heading, Botany, Physiological. Recognizing the existing problems with subject names, Cutter concludes that "possible matters of investigation . . . must attain a certain individuality as objects of inquiry and be given some sort of *name*, otherwise we must assign them class-entry."[14]

One of the great weaknesses of the concept of specific entry is that subjects must be described in terms that are constantly changing. Material very often has to be cataloged long before a suitable term has been found in printed LC or other standard lists. This means that ambiguous vocabulary sometimes has to be accepted as a temporary solution. Many subjects now represent a cross-fertilization among once traditional disciplines. As Coates indicates, "new subjects are being generated around us all the time, and while subjects may still be more or less distinct, there can be no hard and fast separation of the 'distinct' subjects from the others."[15]

---

[13] Cutter, *Rules*, pp. 66-67.

[14] Ibid., Rule 161.

[15] Coates, *Subject Catalogues: Headings and Structure*, p. 32.

Two standard lists of subject headings are used in American libraries: *Sears List of Subject Headings* (10th ed., 1972) and the *Library of Congress Subject Headings* (8th ed., 1975). There are many other lists besides these two, including a large number of lists of subject headings designed for specialized collections and special libraries.[16]

FUTURE PROSPECTS

Many current automated information retrieval systems use specialized authority lists of terms called **thesauri**, which are in fact often very similar to lists of subject headings. The headings in these systems are usually called descriptors, and the "see also" references for superordinate terms are called broader terms (BT), subordinate terms are called narrower terms (NT), and coordinate terms are called related terms (RT). Also, chain indexes, already discussed in this chapter, have been used in various systems. As a matter of fact, a chain index was used in the construction of the alphabetical subject index to *The British National Bibliography* from 1950 to 1970. Since that time a different system, based on a set of working procedures rather than an established list of terms, has been used. This is called PRECIS, an acronym for the **PRE**served **C**ontext **I**ndexing **S**ystem. In his description of this system, Derek Austin states:

> The system is firmly based upon the concept of an open-ended vocabulary, which means that terms can be admitted into the index at any time, as soon as they have been encountered in literature. Once a term has been admitted, its relationships with other terms are handled in two different ways, distinguished as the syntactical and the semantic sides of the system.[17]

An indexing system similar to PRECIS is POPSI (**PO**stulate-based **P**ermuted **S**ubject **I**ndexing). This system was developed at the Documentation Research and Training Centre in Bangalore, India, where Ranganathan was the director until his death. Both systems are rotated pre-coordinate indexing systems, but POPSI has developed directly from classification schedules and chain indexing while PRECIS has not.[18]

Several mechanized systems are now being discussed in an attempt to automate the process of classification, primarily in two areas: a) automated

---

[16]Cf. *Guide to the SLA Loan Collection of Classification Schemes and Subject Heading Lists on Deposit at Western Reserve University as of March 20, 1961* (New York, Special Libraries Association, 1961).

[17]Derek Austin, "Progress in Documentation: The Development of PRECIS; A Theoretical and Technical History," *Journal of Documentation* 30 (March 1974): 47. This entire article is most useful for an understanding of PRECIS; it covers pages 47-102.

[18]G. Bhattacharyya and A. Neelameghan, "Postulate-Based Subject Heading for Dictionary Catalogue System," Documentation Research and Training Centre, *Annual Seminar* 7 (1969): 221-254; and G. Bhattacharyya, "Chain Procedure and Structuring of a Subject," *Library Science with a Slant to Documentation* 9 (1972): 585-635.

methods for devising a classification system, and b) automated methods of classifying documents.[19] Most traditional classification schemes are based on a logical division of the universe of knowledge. In contrast, the computer-based classification systems are empirical and descriptive, attempting to develop thesauri that must have one thing in common: a set of descriptors well suited to manipulation (e.g., a title or synthetic class number) that will generate a number of additional entries to a set pattern. A number of mathematical techniques are helpful in the subject analysis of a given document. To start with, it is possible to evaluate subject content of two documents by characterizing each document as a list of content word terms (keywords) that they share. Subsets may also be derived by means of the "theory of CLUMPS," which is based on a Boolean lattice model. Experimentation in this area at the Cambridge Language Research Unit seems promising.[20] Subsets may also be derived by factor analysis, which is a form of matrix algebra. For example, Borko and Bernick combined the factor analytic method for mathematically deriving a classification system with a factor score technique for automatically classifying documents into their proper categories.[21] Starting with the early work done by H. P. Luhn,[22] initial studies have indicated that these automatically produced categories are reasonably descriptive of the document collection.

The second aspect of automated classification research requires the design of specific mathematical procedures for computing the probability of a document's belonging to a designated category in order to automate the work of the classifier. These methods include Baysian prediction formulas,[23] factor scores (Borko and Bernick), latent class analysis (Baker), information theory measures (Trachtenberg), discriminant analysis (Williams), several types of linguistic analysis (Salton), and the use of citations (Garfield, Kessler). As Dr. Borko indicates, research in automatic indexing and classification of documents includes three areas of activity:

---

[19]There is much literature on this subject. The reader should probably start with *Classification Research*, Proceedings of the Second International Study Conference ... (Copenhagen, Munksgaard, 1965). The current companion volume to this is the *Proceedings* of the Third International Study Conference on Classification Research ... (Bombay, 1976). Another useful work is the symposium edited by Arthur Maltby, *Classification in the 1970's: A Discussion of Development and Prospects for the Major Schemes* (Hamden, Conn., Linnet Books, 1972). Also see "Classification: Theory and Practice," *Drexel Library Quarterly* 10 (October 1974): (no. 4) 1-120.

[20]Karen Sparck Jones, "CLUMPS, Theory of," *Encyclopedia of Library and Information Science*, Vol. 5 (New York, Marcel Dekker, 1971), pp. 208-224.

[21]H. Borko, "Research in Computer Based Classification Systems," in *Classification Research*, pp. 220-257.

[22]H. P. Luhn, *Keyword in Context Index for Technical Literature* (New York, IBM, 1959). For simple presentation of basic differences between Key-Word in Context (KWIC) indexing and Key-Word out of Context (KWOC) indexing, see A. C. Foskett's *The Subject Approach to Information*, 2d ed., rev. and enl. (Hamden, Conn., Linnet Books, 1972).

[23]M. E. Maron, "Automatic Indexing: An Experimental Inquiry," *Journal of ACM* 8 (July 1961): (3) 407-417.

a) Automatic methods of indexing: processing the natural language text of a document according to prescribed formulas which will identify key content words. Index terms can then be either automatically assigned or manually selected from machine produced lists of content words.

b) Automatic methods of deriving a classification system: mathematically analyzing the document collection so as to determine the number of descriptions of classes which are to be established.

c) Automatic methods of classifying documents: determining measures of document similarity based upon word content, plus specifying mathematical procedures for computing the probability of a document belonging to a particular category. In general, documents are designated as belonging to the same class if they are more similar to each other, as determined by the words they share in common, than they are to documents in any other class.[24]

All these procedures are still in an experimental stage, and no one method has achieved a full measure of success.

It is encouraging to note that at the present time a great deal of effort is invested in different methods of information retrieval, and the amount of research in this area increases each year. In this context one can mention the Cranfield Project I and II, concerned with investigating the cooperative efficiency of indexing systems; SYNTOL,[25] interested in developing a "meta-language" which would form a common ground between various systems; and others. Existing services based on computer applications are quite impressive. A detailed discussion of them should be an integral part of any advanced course in cataloging and classification. It is sufficient to say here that the possibility of producing a library catalog through computer use applies also to abstracting and indexing services, as evidenced in such projects as MEDLARS,[26] the application of the computer to produce the monthly index and annual cumulation for the *British Technology Index* and *Chemical Abstracts*, progress made with *Science Citation Index*, etc. Of special importance, of course, is the MARC Project, which is concerned with making cataloging information available in machine-readable form to all interested libraries. Originally started by the Library of Congress, the MARC Project will have important implications for the future of cataloging practices in this country. It is discussed in some detail in Chapter 17.

---

[24] A. Borko, "Research in Computer Based Classification Systems," p. 223.

[25] J. C. Gardin, *SYNTOL* (New Brunswick, N.J., Graduate School of Library Service, Rutgers, The State University, 1965).

[26] Cf. C. J. Austin's *MEDLARS, 1963-1967* (Bethesda, Md., National Library of Medicine, 1968).

15 LIBRARY OF CONGRESS SUBJECT HEADINGS

INTRODUCTION

The Library of Congress subject headings are used generally by large public libraries, by college and university libraries, and by special libraries, unless they have specialized subject lists of their own. Some smaller libraries also use LC subject headings on a selective basis, especially if they are using LC printed cards.

The new eighth edition contains in general the headings established and applied by the Library of Congress from 1897 through 1972. Subsequent additions and changes to these headings will be found in the quarterly *Supplement* for January-March 1973 and following quarterly and cumulative supplements. It should be noted that since January 1966 these supplements have been printed by automated techniques.

The basic volume includes nearly 50,000 subject headings with cross references, an extensive introduction to the use of the list, and a suggested LC Classification number for most of the main subject headings. It should be noted, however, that LC subject headings may be used with either LC Classification or any other classification system, especially Dewey Decimal Classification.

LC subject headings and LC Classification are developed for the multi-million volume collection of the Library of Congress. The main difference between LCSH and a set of subject headings such as Sears is that LC subject headings were prepared for use in an actual library—the Library of Congress—while the Sears list was prepared as a standard list of subject headings for small to medium-sized libraries in general. A further difference is that LC is constantly updated by quarterly and cumulative supplements, while the Sears list is revised infrequently; usually several years elapse before a new edition is issued. Finally, the LC list is much more comprehensive and detailed in its coverage than is Sears. The fact that many libraries use the LC printed cards, which indicate subject headings, should be an important factor in the consideration of adopting this list for a library. It is not recommended, however, that a library use more than one standard subject headings list, such as mixing LC and Sears subject headings in one catalog.

General Physical Characteristics of the List

All main headings in LCSH are in boldface type. The words "Indirect" and "Direct" refer to subdivision by place indirectly (in which case the name of a country or state is inserted between the subject and the name of the place within the country or state) or directly (without the interposition). More detailed discussion of this begins on page 355.

Subdivisions are printed in light face (medium) roman type. Most important subdivisions are included, although the general form divisions are omitted. Subdivisions for languages are given in full under English language. Subdivisions used under countries are given in full under the United States.

Symbols for indicating references to be made in the catalog are the following: sa—See also; x—Refer from (see); xx—Refer from (see also). This example illustrates the usage:

> **Nuclear geophysics**
> sa   Radioactive dating
> x   Nuclear geology
> xx   Geophysics

These references mean:

> Nuclear geophysics. See also Radioactive dating
> Nuclear geology. See Nuclear geophysics
> Geophysics. See also Nuclear geophysics

The symbol "sa" is read just as it is written; i.e.,

> **Nuclear geophysics**
> sa Radioactive dating

is read as

> **Nuclear geophysics**
> see also Radioactive dating.

The "x" and "xx" symbols, however, are read in inverted order—that is, beginning with the element following the "x" or "xx." Thus,

> **Nuclear geophysics**
> x   Nuclear geology

is read as

> Nuclear geology
> see **Nuclear geophysics**

and

> **Nuclear geophysics**
> xx Geophysics

is read as

> Geophysics
> see also **Nuclear geophysics**.

Some terms not used as subject headings are listed to provide reference to terms used, as shown below:

> Nuclear geology
> see **Nuclear geophysics**

Scope notes are provided when necessary for specifying range of subject matter and for drawing distinctions between related headings. A typical scope note is the one found under **Civil service** in LCSH 8.

Class numbers in parentheses follow many of the headings, as in this example:

> **Atomic mass.** (*Chemistry, QD466; Physics, QC173*)
> **Dilemma.** (*BC185*)
> **Dingal language.** (*PK2461–9*)

SPECIAL FEATURES
OF THE EIGHTH EDITION

The special features of the eighth edition of LCSH are a new filing arrangement for the subject headings list, designed for computer-generated bibliographic records, and an expanded introduction.

The new filing arrangement for LCSH 8 was designed by John C. Rather of the LC Technical Processes Research Office. This filing system is strictly word for word. Numbers given in digits precede alphabetic characters and are arranged in increasing numeric value. For example, the first subject heading in the eighth edition is:

4-H clubs.

In the seventh edition this subject heading was filed as if spelled out in the "f's" under "four." Abbreviations without interior punctuation file as words. Initials separated by punctuation are filed as separate words at the beginning of the alphabetic group.

OLD FORMAT	NEW FORMAT
C–coefficient	C–coefficient
CCPM test	C. F. & I. clause
C. F. & I. clause	C.O.D. shipments
C.O.D. shipments	Ca Gaba Indians
CTC system (Railroads)	Cazcan Indians
Ca Gaba Indians	CCPM test
Cazcan Indians	Crystals
Crystals	CTC system (Railroads)

Inverted headings indicated by a comma are filed before headings with parenthetical glosses.

OLD FORMAT	NEW FORMAT

Children   Children
Children (International law)   Children, Adopted
Children (Roman law)   Children, Vagrant
Children, Adopted   Children (International law)
Children, Vagrant   Children (Roman law)

All period subdivisions in LCSH 8 now have explicit dates to allow for computer filing.

OLD FORMAT	NEW FORMAT

Rome—History—Aboriginal and   **Rome**—History—To 510 B.C.
   early period   **United States**—History—Civil
U.S.—History—Civil War   War, 1861-1865
Italian poetry—Early to 1400   **Italian poetry**—To 1400

Finally, the order of subheadings is first by period (arranged chronologically from earliest to present), second by form and topic (alphabetically), and third by geographical division (also alphabetically).

The introduction to the LCSH 8 was prepared by Eugene Frosio, the principal subject cataloger of the Library of Congress. Besides a discussion of the filing rules, the introduction includes a list of headings omitted from the LCSH 8, a description of the formation of headings, and a detailed explanation of subdivision practice. Included in this explanation are a table of the headings that serve as patterns for sets of subdivisions, four pages of tables listing possible subdivisions under place names, and an annotated list of over 600 commonly used form and topical subdivisions.

The 72-page introduction is followed by nine pages of the *Subject Headings for Children's Literature* for the Annotated Card Program for Children's Literature, which is the second edition of this list. The introduction to these subject headings for children's literature explains their application, categories, subdivisions of general application, subdivisions and qualifying terms that are not used, and the use of names for these headings. At the present time cards for children's literature are annotated with a brief summary note, similar to the summary note for audiovisual media and special instructional material discussed in Chapter 9 of this textbook. The subject headings from the Children's Literature list are in brackets on the cards following the subject headings from LCSH. See Figs. 15.1 and 15.2.

Fig. 15.1

Fox, Mary Virginia.
    Lady for the defense : a biography of Belva Lockwood / Mary
Virginia Fox. — 1st ed. — New York : Harcourt Brace Jovano-
vich, ₁1975₎

    158 p. : port. ; 24 cm.

Subject
heading
from the
Children's
Literature
list

    Bibliography: p. 157-158.
    SUMMARY: A biography of the first woman lawyer to practice before the
United States Supreme Court who also was the first woman candidate for President.
    ISBN 0-15-243400-3

    1. Lockwood, Belva Ann Bennett, 1830-1917—Juvenile literature. ₁1. Lock-
wood, Belva Ann Bennett, 1830-1917. 2. Lawyers₎ I. Title.

    KF368.L58F69   340′.092′4   74-27460
                               ₁B₎ ₁92₎   MARC

    Library of Congress   74   AC

Fig. 15.2

McDonald, Lucile Saunders, 1898-
    The Arab Marco Polo, Ibn Battuta / Lucile McDonald. — 1st
ed. — Nashville : T. Nelson, ₁1975₎

    192 p. : maps ; 21 cm.

Subject
heading
from the
Children's
Literature
list

    SUMMARY: A biography of the fourteenth-century Muslim scholar who
traveled from his native Tangier to India and China, several times through the
Near East, and to black Africa.
    Includes index.
    ISBN 0-8407-6441-3

    1. Ibn Batuta, 1304-1377—Juvenile literature. ₁1. Ibn Bututa, 1304-1377.
2. Voyages and travels—Biography₎ I. Title.

    G93.I24M32   910′.92′4   75-4651
                             ₁B₎ ₁92₎   MARC

    Library of Congress   75   AC

The introduction to LCSH and the Subject Headings for Children's Literature are
both published separately in addition to being a part of the first volume of LCSH 8.

    For reasons of space, certain classes of subject headings are omitted from
LCSH 8, even though they are used on LC cards and, of course, by other libraries.
These categories are listed below:

    1) Names of persons, except those of Lincoln, Napoleon, Shakespeare,
Richard Wagner, Washington, and St. Thomas Aquinas. References can be made to
these for subdivisions needed for other names.

    2) Family names.

3) Gods and goddesses; legendary characters.

4) Most corporate bodies, including governments and their agencies, societies, institutions, and firms.

5) Places and regions, except when they form an integral part of other headings, when subdivisions under them must be shown (as in the case of historical periods), or when the scope of such a heading is indicated in a scope note.

6) Archaeological sites.

7) Natural features such as bays, capes, deserts, lakes, mountains, rivers, volcanos.

8) Structures such as aqueducts, bridges, canals, reservoirs; buildings, castles, historic houses, lighthouses; power plants.

9) Metropolitan areas; parkways, roads, squares, streets; city quarters.

10) Parks, forests and forest reserves, wildlife refuges.

11) Most sacred books, anonymous religious classics, and special prayers.

12) Works of art, motion pictures, and television programs.

13) Systematic names of families, genera, and species in botany and zoology; references from scientific to popular names.

14) Chemical compounds.

It should be noted that headings from any of these categories of names may appear in the list if they are used as examples cited under subject.

BASIC FORMS OF SUBJECT HEADINGS

The different forms of LC subject headings can be constructed in a variety of ways, ranging from a single noun to complex descriptive phrases.

Noun

This type of heading consists of a simple noun, in either singular or plural form, without a qualifying phrase to explain or limit it—e.g., **Ethics**, **Etching**, **Etchings**. Quite frequently "see" references are needed from synonymous terms or variant spelling—e.g., Ethology, see **Ethics**.

Headings with Qualifiers

This type of heading consists of an adjective or adjectival noun that precedes the noun modified. English language allows many different possibilities for this type of heading. The modifier can be a common adjective (**Ethnological jurisprudence**), a proper adjective (**Brownian movements**), an ethnic or geographic adjective (**Russian language**), a common or proper noun in the possessive case (**Machinists' tools**), or the modifier may be a common or proper noun used as an adjective but without an adjectival ending (**Electron optics**).

Inverted Headings with Qualifiers

These are used when it is important that the noun in an adjectival heading be in a prominent position, next to other headings beginning with the same noun—e.g., **Geography, Mathematical**. A "see" reference should be made from the uninverted form (Mathematical geography, see **Geography, Mathematical**).

Phrase Headings

Such headings consist of two nouns with or without modifiers, connected with a preposition or conjunction. In general, these headings may serve the following purposes:

1) To limit a concept or to render a more specific meaning, especially when a single word or a noun with modifiers cannot accomplish such a purpose—e.g., **Inmates of institutions**.

2) To express a relationship between two concepts—e.g., **Women as printers**.

3) To express a concept for which a phrase is commonly used in natural language—e.g., **Phonetics of the sentence**.

Inverted Phrase Headings

Such headings are used when the first element qualifies the second, which is also used in the catalog as an independent heading. The inversion is then equivalent to subdivision but it is used in place of subdivision in order to preserve the integrity of the commonly used phrase. It should be noted that, in principle, uninverted forms of headings are preferred because they reflect the order of natural language. It is also recommended that a "see" reference be prepared to direct the user from the uninverted form to the inverted form—e.g., Acids—Effect on plants, see **Plants, Effect of acids on**.

Compound Headings

Such headings are made up of two or more coordinate elements that serve, in general, the following purposes:

1) To express a relationship between two concepts—e.g., **Libraries and readers**.

2) To cover works on two opposite subjects that are treated together—e.g., **Good and evil**.

3) To define the scope of the subject in which the second noun explains the first—e.g., **Church and state**.

It should be noted that when such compound headings express a relationship or define the scope of a subject, a "see" reference is needed—e.g., State and church, see **Church and state**.

Composite Forms

This name is used for headings with a variety of combinations, such as: adjectives and prepositional phrases used to modify the noun, compound phrase headings that are more complex, phrase headings qualified by parenthetical elements, etc. Because a great many combinations are possible in this form, it is unfeasible to treat them separately in this introductory text. Typical examples of such headings include: **Church and social problems, Concertos (Trumpet with dance orchestra), First aid in illness and injury,** and **College and school drama.** Some composite headings require "see" references (e.g., College drama, see **College and school drama**; School drama, see **College and school drama**) and "see also" references (refer from: **College theater, Drama festivals, Drama in education**).

INDIVIDUAL NAMES AS SUBJECT HEADINGS

An individual name may be used as a subject heading for a critical, historical, or biographical work. Such subject entries assemble all of the separately cataloged material on a particular person or corporate body in one place in the catalog. Usually, to assist patrons who may look for this type of information under a broader heading, general or specific references are recommended, e.g., from a general heading **Authors, American,** or **English literature—Bio-bibliography,** etc. The type of reference required depends on the category of the individual names. The following categories of individual names are used as subject headings:

1) **Personal names.** Biographies, criticisms, bibliographies, certain literary works, and other types of works about a person may require a subject entry. The form of name used as a subject heading will follow the AACR headings for persons, as discussed in Chapter 4 in this text. If the literature about a person is voluminous, it is desirable to subdivide the name heading by the form of material; e.g.,

- Adaptations
- Allusions
- Anniversaries, etc.
- Bibliography
  etc.

The names of Lincoln, Napoleon, Shakespeare, Richard Wagner, Washington, and St. Thomas Aquinas are included in the LCSH in order to show by example the subdivisions that may be used under names of prominent individuals. It is common practice to omit the subject entry in a dictionary catalog under the name of the biographee for an autobiographical work.

2) **Corporate bodies.** A subject entry is required for historical material on corporate bodies and for material on their organization and function. The form of name used as a subject heading will again follow the AACR, as discussed in Chapter 5 of this text.

3) **Names of mythological, legendary, Biblical, and imaginary characters** may be used as subject headings exactly as those of real persons. The choice of form of name and necessary cross references are handled as they are for real persons.

4) **Proper names of other kinds.** Ships, famous buildings, or anything else so individualized as to bear a proper name may serve as a subject entry. Such names are usually qualified by a parenthetical expression that describes their nature—e.g., **Titan (Missile).**

5) **Individual works of literature.** An individual work of literature may require a subject heading if the work is a subject of criticism or commentaries. In the case of works by personal or corporate authors, the subject heading consists of the name of the author followed by the form of title used as a filing title; e.g., the subject entry for Shakespeare's *Hamlet* is:

> **Shakespeare, William. Hamlet.**

or

> **Shakespeare, William.**
> **Hamlet.**

but not

> Shakespeare, William
> The tragedie of Hamlet, prince of
> Denmarke

(*The Tragedie of Hamlet, prince of Denmarke* is the full title in the first folio.)

GEOGRAPHIC NAMES AS SUBJECT HEADINGS

In general, the same principles apply to geographic headings as to other subject headings. The Library of Congress uses the forms of geographic names as established by the U.S. Board on Geographic Names and its predecessors. In all cases special rules for geographic names as provided by AACR should be consulted.

Following the principle of usage, whenever possible a purely geographic name is preferred to a political one; use the form of name by which an area has continued to be known, even after a new political name has been adopted; e.g.,

> **Russia**, not Union of Soviet Socialist Republics
> **Great Britain**, not United Kingdom
> **United States**, not United States of America

This principle presents several problems, and it is not always used consistently—e.g., **Czechoslovak Republic** is used instead of Czechoslovakia, **Argentine Republic** instead of Argentina, etc. It should also be mentioned that if the form of name used in a subject heading is not the same as that chosen for the author entry, author and subject entries dealing with the same area will be separated.

According to the Library of Congress interpretation, the language of the heading is basically an aspect of usage. The usage in English speaking countries is preferred for well-known geographic areas or places (e.g., **Munich**, not München).

For little-known geographical names or for those that lack well-established English forms, the vernacular form of name is recommended.

Geographic headings may be qualified generically, geographically, and politically.

1) Generic qualifiers

Names of natural geographic features usually consist of a specific term and a generic term—e.g., **Volga River, Rocky Mountains**. If in the name of the geographic feature the generic term precedes the specific term, then the inverted form is used for the subject heading—e.g., **Mexico, Gulf of**.

2) Geographic qualifiers

A place name that is not readily identifiable requires as a qualifier the name of the major geographic or political area of which it is a part. Names of cities in the United States and Canada are followed by the name (or the usual abbreviation of the name) of the state or province; e.g.,

> **Littleton, Colo.**
> **London, Ont.**
> **Smolensk, Russia**

However, Library of Congress does not always follow this practice consistently.

3) Political qualifiers

If the name is used for different political and ecclesiastical jurisdictions in the same county or state, a qualification should follow the name (in parentheses).

> **New York (State)**
> **New York (City)**
> **New York (Archdiocese)**

This qualification may be extended to names and dates of different political jurisdictions:

Russia
> (No political qualifiers are used to refer to the Russian Empire prior to 1917.)

Russia (1917– . Provisional govt.)

Russia (1917–   . R.S.F.S.R.)
> **Note**: This name (R.S.F.S.R.), which actually stands only for the Russian Republic, is used for all other Soviet republics of that period.

Russia (1923–   . U.S.S.R.)
> **Note**: 1923 was the year when the Union of several Soviet republics (e.g., Russian, Ukrainian, Belorussian) was formed.

Changes in Geographic Names

As a rule the latest form of the name is preferred; however, if the material deals with the area during the period of an earlier name, the earlier name is preferred. This principle requires, of course, numerous cross references.

St. Petersburg
    sa Petrograd
    sa Leningrad

SUBJECT SUBDIVISION

In a large collection it is necessary to subdivide certain subjects into more specific topics or to show a particular aspect of a given subject. In general, there are four basic types of subdivisions: topical subdivisions, form subdivisions, period or chronological subdivisions, and geographic and local subdivisions.

Topical Subdivisions

Each heading may have special topic subdivisions appropriate to the particular subject. Topical subdivisions "limit the concept expressed by the heading to a special subtopic" (LCSH 8, p. xii). All subdivisions are introduced by a dash, which separates the subject heading from the subdivision. An example of a topical subdivision that limits the concept expressed by the heading is:

Jesus Christ—Nativity.

Topical subdivisions and form subdivisions are both included in the list of Most Commonly Used Subdivisions in the introduction to LCSH 8.

Form Subdivisions

Form subdivisions are used to indicate the form or arrangement of the subject matter in the book. Form subdivisions are always the last subdivision element to be attached to a subject heading. Headings without form subdivisions "should be interpreted as designating general discussions or treatises on the subject."

Examples:

Vocational education—Congresses
Jesus Christ—Nativity—Juvenile Literature

"Congresses" and "Juvenile Literature" are both examples of form subdivisions. Note that "Juvenile Literature" is the last subdivision element, as all form subdivisions should be.

354 / Library of Congress Subject Headings

The list of Most Commonly Used Subdivisions in the introduction to LCSH 8 contains over 600 topical or form subdivisions. This list represents one third of the LC file of usable subdivisions. Each subdivision in this list includes a general scope note in regard to usage of the particular subdivision.

Examples:

ABBREVIATIONS

Use as a form subdivision under topical headings for lists of abbreviations of words or phrases, e.g., **Engineering**—Abbreviations. If the work in hand is not in English, make a second entry under the subject heading **Abbreviations** qualified by the name of the language, e.g., **Abbreviations, German.**

 sa Acronyms
    Notation

ABSTRACTING AND INDEXING

Use under topical or geographic headings for discussions of methods used in abstracting or indexing works published on those topics.

 sa Indexes
  x Indexing

In addition to the subdivisions in this list, LC also applies other subdivisions, which are not listed in LCSH 8. These are called **free-floating subdivisions**. A list of these headings appeared in *Cataloging Service*, bulletin 114, Summer 1975, pages 9-10, with the statement that "this concept means that subdivisions so designated will appear on LC cards without the usage appearing in the printed list of subject headings. A free-floating subdivision is not a subdivision of general application which may be assigned indiscriminately under any subject without further regard for appropriateness."

Period or Chronological Subdivisions

The Library of Congress uses chronological and period subdivisions in many different ways. Only the most typical examples are discussed here.

Chronological subdivisions are applied as a heading for the history of a subject (e.g., histories of individual countries, places, etc.). In principle, period subdivisions should chronologically correspond with generally recognized epochs in the history of a particular country or should represent sufficient spaces of time frequently treated in standard works on this subject.

France–History – To 987
                – Capetians, 987-1328
                – Medieval period, 987-1515
                – 13th century
                – House of Valois, 1328-1589
                – Revolution, 1789-1799

Chronological or time subdivisions are often used to segregate material covering a certain period or published before a certain date:

Arithmetic – To 1846
            – 1846-1880

As already mentioned in this chapter, all period subdivisions in LCSH 8 must be expressed in explicit dates; those periods without a specific beginning date are expressed as "To date." For example, the period subdivision "Civil War" for the United States must now be qualified with the dates, 1861-1865; e.g., **Boston**–History–Civil War, 1861-1865. Previously the subdivision "Civil War" could be expressed without the dates. The only major exceptions to this are the descriptors "Ancient," "Medieval," and "Modern":

> **Philosophy, Ancient.**
> **Philosophy, Medieval.**
> **Philosophy, Modern.**

Geographic and Local Subdivisions

Many subject headings may be subdivided by the name of a country, a region, or another geographic locality. Such subdivisions are used primarily when the geographic element is of primary importance or when certain subjects indicate a geographic connotation. According to Library of Congress practice, scientific and technological terms in general do not require geographic subdivision because they do not possess a local connotation. For example, the heading **Geography, Mathematical** is not subdivided by place. There are important exceptions to this general principle, however. Some broad subjects in the field of science and technology, and especially in the area of natural sciences, *are* subdivided by place (e.g., **Geology**). Also, headings designating industries are subdivided by place (e.g., **Iron industry and trade**).

There are two methods of geographic subdivision: direct and indirect. Headings for which direct subdivision is indicated are followed immediately by the name of a specific place, without the interposition of the name of the country, state, or region–e.g., **Censorship** (Direct), which means **Censorship**–Paris and *not* **Censorship**–France–Paris.

Indirect subdivision indicates that the name of the relevant country is to be interposed between the subject heading and the name of any subordinate political, administrative, or geographical division within a country–assuming that the significance of certain subjects is inseparable from the larger area. In general, the previously mentioned broad subjects in the field of science, technology, and natural sciences are subdivided indirectly (e.g., **Geology**–Colorado–El Paso Co.).

Subdivision is always direct under the names of historic kingdoms and principalities, under members of federated states, and under other areas which historically formed a part of more than one state. The same principle applies to ecclesiastical jurisdictions that do not fall wholly within one political jurisdiction. In addition, direct subdivision is always used under the following categories:

1) United States, Canada, Great Britain: the names of the states, provinces, etc., are always used directly after the subject heading, with the names of counties, cities, and other subordinate units as further subdivisions; e.g.,

> **Music**–Colorado–Denver
> and not **Music**–U.S.–Colorado–Denver

2) Two cities–New York and Washington, D.C.–and the District of Columbia are always used as direct subdivisions. This is justified because of the amount of material the Library of Congress has on both cities. It should be noted here that any library might make the subdivision direct for any city on which its collection contains an extraordinary amount of material.

3) Certain other countries and states. The states, provinces, and major divisions of the following are entered directly after the subject heading:

> Australia   Germany, West
> Austria   Italy (Regions, only)
> France (Old provinces, only)   Netherlands
> Germany   USSR

> Example:

> **Music**–Victoria
> and not **Music**–Australia–Victoria

If, however, a subordinate locality such as a county or city in any of the above countries is used, the name of the country is also used–e.g., **Music**–Germany–Munich. The justification here is to identify a city or county by the addition of the name of the larger area, i.e., the country.

It is necessary to provide references from the subject followed by the name of place without the interpolation of the name of the country or larger geographic area; e.g., **Music**–Munich, see **Music**–Germany–Munich.

4) Certain headings subdivided indirectly are also used as subject subdivisions under names of cities–e.g., **Libraries** (Indirect);
thus,

> **Libraries**–Colorado–Arapahoe Co.

and

> **Denver**–Libraries

The tendency in Library of Congress practice has apparently been to use direct subdivision for place names, omitting the name of the country or state. Apart from the fact that this precludes any consistency in determining which headings are to be subdivided directly and which indirectly, the practice raises another problem—how to bring together a subject matter that is scattered under the names of cities, counties, rivers, and other geographical localities. According to Haykin, "the solution is that which the subject catalog affords in any subject field: if desired, references can be made from the subject heading subdivided by an inclusion area to all places within the area which have been used as subdivisions under that subject heading."[1]

Because of the cost involved, not all libraries follow this advice, a fact that contributes to some serious deficiencies in the system.

CROSS REFERENCES

As has already been seen, many subject headings are connected by cross references. There are three basic types of such syndetic devices: "see" references, "see also" references, and general references.

1) "See" references

A "see" reference is a reference from a term not used as a subject heading to the corresponding term that is used; e.g.,

> Ex-servicemen
> see
> **Veterans**

Often, a "see" reference is made from other than synonymous terms:

> Early printed books
> see
> **Bibliography**—Rare books
> **Incunabula**

2) "See also" references

A "see also" reference links related headings. In the LC list of subject headings a "see also" reference usually refers from a general subject heading to a more specific subject heading, or from one subject heading to another related (coordinate) subject heading.

Science	**Astronomy**	**Earth**
see also	see also	see also
Astronomy	**Earth**	**Geology**

---

[1] David Judson Haykin, *Subject Headings: A Practical Guide* (Washington, Government Printing Office, 1951), p. 31.

However, references are not made from the more specific subject heading to the general. Thus, the following reference is **not** made:

> Earth
> > see also
> Science

3) General references
"See also" references usually refer to particular headings to be found in the catalog, and when they are so used they are called **specific references**. However, when they are made not to an individual heading but instead to the specific members of a class or broader category, such "see also" references are called **general references**.

> **Birds**
> > see also
> **Cage-birds; Game and
> game birds; Humming-
> birds; Water-birds;** *and
> similar headings.*

Duplicate Entry

A **duplicate entry** is an entry that expresses a mutual opposition of two interests or points of view; e.g.,

> **United States**—Foreign relations—Italy
> **Italy**—Foreign relations—United States

or

> **English literature**—Translations from Chinese
> **Chinese literature**—Translations into English

16 SEARS LIST OF SUBJECT HEADINGS

INTRODUCTION

The Sears list, now in its tenth edition, is widely used by small public libraries and by school libraries. It is very much smaller in scope and more general in treatment than LC subject headings, but the format is similar, and a cataloger who works with one can adjust to the other.[1] Sears contains a very comprehensive introduction, "Suggestions for the Beginner in Subject Heading Work," to which the student is expected to refer.

The present edition, like its predecessors, follows the Library of Congress form of headings, with several modifications to meet the needs of smaller collections (e.g., Sears uses **"City planning"** rather than **"Cities and towns**–Planning"). New headings for this edition were suggested by libraries' responses to the editor's inquiries and by catalogers at the H. W. Wilson Company, who are responsible for the subject headings used in the Standard Catalog series. This edition also contains several new subject headings in the area of social sciences and the environment, and it incorporates *Subject Headings for Children's Literature*, issued by the Library of Congress. All headings were checked against the seventh edition of the *Subject Headings Used in the Dictionary Catalogs of the Library of Congress* and its supplements through November 1971.

The general philosophy of Sears subject headings is contained in two phrases, both of which the cataloger should remember as he makes the specific application that an individual book demands: the theory of specific heading and the theory of unique heading.

The **theory of specific heading** means that a specific heading is preferred to a general one. For a book about cats alone, **Cats** is to be preferred to **Domestic animals**. On the other hand, the heading Siamese cats or Seal-point Siamese cats is probably too specific for most libraries (except, perhaps, for a veterinary library). The cataloger must know his library, must know its emphases, and must be prepared to assign subject headings accordingly.

The **theory of unique heading** means that one subject heading, and one alone, is chosen for all books on that subject, and reference is made to the chosen subject heading from all other possibilities. The choice of subject headings, then, must be logical and consistent, and cross references should be inserted wherever they are applicable in order to anticipate the patron's approach.

---

[1] For more detailed discussion of the structure of subject headings refer to Chapter 14, Subject Headings, and Chapter 15, LC Subject Headings.

There are a few general principles that will help the cataloger to construct subject headings:

1) Prefer the English word or phrase unless a foreign one best expresses the idea (e.g., *laissez-faire*).

2) Try to use terms that are used in other libraries as well, unless the library in question is highly specialized or otherwise unique.

3) Try to use terms that will cover the field—i.e., terms that will apply to more than one book.

4) Try to use no more than three subject headings. This is not an arbitrary rule, however; some books may require more than three.

STRUCTURE OF SUBJECT HEADINGS

Like LC subject headings, Sears subject headings consist of a variety of forms, ranging from a single noun to a complex descriptive phrase.

The **single noun** is the most desirable form of subject heading, if it is specific enough to fit the book at hand. **Geometry** and **Horses** are examples of subject headings specific enough to fit most books on either subject. **Geometry** is more appropriate than **Mathematics**, which also includes algebra, calculus, and arithmetic. The criterion must always be: What is the patron likely to consult? Single nouns that are ambiguous must be qualified, and parentheses are conventionally used for this, as in **Life** (Biology) and **Life** (Theology). The **singular and plural forms** of a noun have different meanings. Thus, **Essay** indicates a book on the literary form and how to write it, while **Essays** indicates a collection of short, prose nonfictional pieces.

Some subject headings take the form of a noun modified by a descriptive **adjective**: **Constitutional law**; **National characteristics**. Obviously "law" by itself is too broad a topic and "characteristics," by itself, has no specific meaning.

Sometimes a subject heading is inverted, so that the noun, or main word, stands first. This allows it to be filed with other aspects of the same main subject (e.g., **Art, Abstract**). There is no absolute standard for inverting words or phrases; the cataloger must try to predict the form that will be most useful, and he should make cross references from the form not chosen. These cross references are usually indicated in the printed list of subject headings.

Compound phrases, made up of two nouns of equal value, are joined by a conjunction. A subject heading such as **"Education and crime"** is legitimate because books have been written on the relationship between the two topics, with neither topic subordinate to the other.

a) Some of the compound phrases used for subject headings may join related subjects: **Clocks and watches; Puppets and puppet plays.** Usually both of the ideas expressed in the subject heading are covered in a single book on the topic.

b) Some compound phrases link opposites (**Joy and sorrow, Good and evil**) because a book treating one considers the other as well.

c) Some compound phrases are so constructed because the most important word is susceptible to different interpretations. In this case the qualifying noun is added to dispel ambiguity. It is not enough to use Files as a subject heading: **Files and filing** must be distinguished from **Files and rasps**.

TYPES OF SUBDIVISIONS

Subdivisions of a subject heading indicate a more specialized aspect of a broad subject or a particular point of view. They are generally set off from the broad subject by a dash. Their primary purpose is to group similar books together, especially if the general subject is broad, or if the books about it are numerous (for example, **Education**). A patron seeking books on a specific topic in education has to examine two or three trays of cards unless **Education** is subdivided into specific, easily handled subtopics. There are several types of subdivisions.

1) **Form divisions** are used, like the Dewey Decimal Classification form divisions, to indicate the physical or philosophical form of the book, such as "dictionaries," "indexes," etc. Sears lists a table of form divisions that are appropriate to all major subjects.

2) **Special topic divisions** cannot be transferred from one subject to another. They are used to distinguish special aspects of certain topics, such as **Children**—Care and hygiene, or **Airplanes**—Piloting. (Obviously, one could not reasonably use **Children**—Piloting or **Airplanes**—Care and hygiene.) Any standard list of subject headings includes the appropriate topic divisions after the main subject entry, for they are not mnemonic in nature and usually cannot be memorized.

3) **Time divisions**, which apply most frequently to history, are used to define a specific chronology. They may be inverted (**History, Ancient**) or they may be set off from the main subject with a dash (**U.S.**—History—Civil War; **Church history**—primitive and early church).

4) **Geographic divisions** are used in two ways: area—subject or subject—area. Area—subject (i.e., **U.S.**—Description and travel) is chosen if the important part of the book is the area. In such cases, the subdivision is meaningless unless it refers to a specific place.

The Sears list indicates, by means of a parenthetical phrase, that a subject in science, technology, or economics can be divided geographically. If a book deals with geology in general, the simple heading **Geology** is used; but if it deals with a specific geologic region, a geographic subdivision may be added: **Geology**—Colorado; **Geology**—Bolivia. The unit chosen for subdivision may be any political or geographical unit that is applicable to the book, although, in the instances where a division for city may be used, the Sears note reads "(May subdiv. geog. country or state.)."

Sears uses a slightly different note for a book about music or art. Unless the book is comprehensive, a geographical interest is presumed. (However, a book that treats a specific aspect of the subject, such as **Harmony**, cuts across geographical lines.) The Sears list reads: "**Music** (May subdiv. geog. adjective form, e.g., **Music, American**)." Following this instruction, the cataloger adds the adjective form of the geographic area.

Science, technology, and the fine arts are usually assigned subject headings that are subdivided geographically. History, geography, politics, and some of the other social sciences are usually assigned area or geographical headings that are divided by subject. Thus, the real subject of a book about Colorado history (and the subject that the patron will most likely consult) is "**Colorado**," not "history." In fact, the subject heading **History** is used, in Sears, only for general works on history as an intellectual discipline.

If the subject is an institution (such as a library), the real subject may be either the institution or the area. The Sears list specifies: "**Libraries** (May subdiv. geog. country or state.)." This precludes division by city, and the "see also" note includes the phrase "names of cities with the subdivision 'Libraries' (e.g., **Chicago**–Libraries)." This means that a discussion of the libraries of a state or country will carry the subject heading "**Libraries**," subdivided by the state or the country; works on the libraries of one city, however, will have the name of the city as the major subject heading, subdivided by the topic, "libraries."

Generally, individual works of belles lettres (novels, plays, and poetry) are not assigned subject headings. Some libraries, however, prefer to make subject headings for fictionalized biography written in the form of a novel, a play, or a poem. Thus, the subject heading for a novel about the Civil War might be: **U.S.**–History–Civil War–Fiction.

PHYSICAL CHARACTERISTICS
AND FORMAT OF SEARS

In the Sears lists, subject headings to be used are printed in boldface type. If a subject heading is not printed in boldface, it is not to be used. After a major broad subject, such as **History**, there is a paragraph explaining when **History** is to be used as the subject heading instead of a geographical or political subdivision. This paragraph is called a **scope note**; it describes the scope or extent of the subject heading and it makes references to other possible, more specific, subject headings (e.g., "Works limited to the study and criticism of sources . . . are entered under **Historiography**").

Following the scope note are the words "see also" in italics. They precede a list in boldface of major aspects of history, such as **Anthropogeography**, **Colonization**, etc. Each boldface entry in this list is a legitimate subject heading. If a book deals with anthropogeography, the cataloger should not stop at the appropriate note under **History**; he should "see also" **Anthropogeography**, where he will be referred to more specific aspects of that subject, if he needs them.

Subdivisions of a subject are entered alphabetically in the Sears list; inverted phrases are interfiled with those of normal word order. Many of the subdivisions are printed in light face (medium) type, which indicates that they are not to be used, but all such entries refer to subject headings that may be used.

The letter "x" before a term means that a "see" reference should be made **from** each such term **to** the heading under which it is placed. Terms preceded by an "x" are never used as subject headings. The letters "xx" before a term mean that a "see also" reference should be made **from** this term **to** the term under which it is placed:

Algae
> x   Sea mosses; Seaweeds
> xx **Marine plants**

What this means is:

> Sea mosses, *see* **Algae**
> Seaweeds, *see* **Algae**
> **Marine plants**, *see also* **Algae**

Such devices as the "x" and the "xx" are valuable to the cataloger when he consults the list for subject headings for a specific book; they are valuable also to the patron who consults the card catalog, for the cataloger must record the "see" and the "see also" information for the patron's convenience. The cataloger usually proceeds in this way: If he has a book on seaweeds, he consults the Sears list under seaweeds and is instructed to "see **Algae**." Consulting **Algae**, he finds:

> **Algae**
> > x   Sea mosses; Seaweeds
> > xx **Marine plants**

Marine plants is in boldface, which means that it is a possible subject heading but not an appropriate subject heading for a book on seaweeds. If it were, the reference would have been from Seaweeds to **Marine plants**, rather than to **Algae**.

So **Algae** is the appropriate subject heading. In order to help the patron who might consult the catalog under Seaweeds, however, a cross-reference card must be made for the public catalog. It will look like this:

> SEAWEEDS
> > see
> ALGAE

If the library already contains books that carry the subject heading **Marine plants**, the cataloger makes another cross-reference card:

> MARINE PLANTS
> > see also
> ALGAE

This card will file behind all of the subject cards for **Marine plants**, thus suggesting to the patron further possibilities for search.

The cataloger does **not** make a card reading "Algae, see also Marine plants," since the topic of marine plants includes algae. An important rule in the construction of subject headings is: **Refer from general to specific or from equal to equal, never from specific to general.** The logic of this rule is obvious; the patron who consults a rather specific topic has no need to be referred to a broader one, whereas the patron who consults a broad topic may well want to know all of its ramifications. References from the specific to the general can send the patron in a circular search.

If the subject heading **Algae** is being used for the first time in the library, the cataloger must indicate the fact of its use to his colleagues. Several methods are possible.

A most efficient and highly recommended method of keeping a current record of subject headings is to use the printed list as a **subject authority file** by check-marking it or by making a subject authority card file. This is an alphabetical record of all subject headings used in the public catalog, as well as all "see" and "see also" references. The official card for Algae will look like this:

> ALGAE
>   x   Sea mosses
>   Seaweeds
>   xx Marine plants

The official card for Sea mosses (and for Seaweeds) will look like this:

> SEA MOSSES   SEAWEEDS
>   see   see
> ALGAE   ALGAE

The official card for Marine plants will look like this:

> MARINE PLANTS
>   see also
> ALGAE

The larger the library, the more books there will be that include an aspect of Marine plants   (the most comprehensive aspect so far of the topic under consideration). Each book acquired will undergo the procedure described above in order to receive a subject heading. Therefore, as books on new aspects of the topic are assigned subject headings, the official card for Marine plants might eventually look like this:

> MARINE PLANTS
>   see also   Algae
>   Fresh-water plants
>
>   x   Aquatic plants
>   Marine flora
>   Water plants
>
>   xx   Fresh-water plants
>   Geographic distribution of animals and plants
>   Marine biology
>   Plants

The "see also" indicates subjects used in the catalog, with reference **from** Marine plants. Each of these is more specific than **Marine plants**. The "x" indicates subjects not used in the catalog, although a card is made for each of them, referring the patron to the subject heading **Marine plants**. The "xx" indicates subjects used in the catalog, with a card made for each of them to "see also" **Marine plants**. Each of these subject headings is equal to or more general than **Marine plants**.

Note: The cataloger will not make references if the library does not have a book under the subject heading referred to. That is, if no book has been assigned the subject heading **Fresh-water plants**, then neither the public catalog nor the official subject catalog will include such a reference. When such a book is added to the collection, the appropriate notation is made on cards in both files.

A library may choose to consider the public catalog as its authority file. This is possible if the catalog department is located very near the public catalog and if changes in the cards can be made so quickly that patrons will not be inconvenienced. A separate record must, however, be kept for the convenience of the other catalogers. The most popular method of record-keeping is to place a check mark after the subject heading in the catalog department's official copy of Sears or LCSH. After the cataloger makes his "see" and "see also" cards for the public catalog, he checks those entries in his printed list. In this way, a colleague cataloging another book about seaweeds, for example, will not make cards that will duplicate previous work. Each edition of Sears carries a full-page illustration of a possible system of checking, and the novice would do well to consult it.

These procedures may seem complicated to the beginning cataloger, but his reaction is a natural one. Cataloging—and especially the assigning of subject headings—is a discipline that is probably completely new to him. Unlike other disciplines, it has no logical progression other than the progression of knowledge itself. Nothing in previous studies has led to it. Even the assigning of a classification number to a book is a less forbidding prospect to the novice, for he has at least been given some sort of orientation to the Dewey system, and he can see for himself the division of knowledge and why it should exist.

Subject headings are, however, not difficult once the cataloger has learned to handle them. Both Sears and LCSH are very explicit in their directions; both are prefaced by comprehensive and intelligible introductions. Both contain lists of subdivisions with specific instructions for their use. If they are followed consistently, they will provide a useful reference guide for the patron as well as the reference librarian.

The beginning cataloger should study the list with which he is to work. He should choose a subject in which he, personally, is interested, and trace it throughout the list, observing the interrelation of "see also" (sa), "x," and "xx" references. He has other aids. He should become familiar with the reference tools in his library. They amplify subjects and clarify aspects of them that are not well understood, especially in an age when no one can expect to know everything.

He should also study the library's shelf list and public catalog. The former is invaluable for suggesting subject headings if the cataloger already has a classification number in mind (classification schemes such as Dewey and LC do not offer standard subject headings). The public catalog is invaluable for suggesting classification numbers if the cataloger has a subject heading in mind. Neither is a completely reliable reference: books are very often written about more than one subject, and the vagaries of individual catalogers may mislead. But both are generally helpful, and both serve to indicate to the cataloger the practices of his library. If he is to catalog successfully, the cataloger must know what his library does and work within this frame of reference.

17 CENTRALIZED SERVICES AND CATALOGING ROUTINES

CENTRALIZED PROCESSING

Because of the problems facing librarians today, such as the great increase in volume of published material, the emphasis on rapid transfer of written communication from producers to consumers, and the resultant need for more and better library service, traditional patterns of library organization are undergoing change. For reasons of economy and efficiency, certain library procedures have been centralized into larger operational units. In a large university, for example, one catalog department usually processes all the books for all libraries on the campus; in large public library systems, cataloging for all branches is handled in one unit. Further development of this concept can be seen in centralized processing on a regional as well as on a state or even national basis.

Though centralized processing cannot be considered new (the Library of Congress began to distribute printed cards in 1901), it has been given great emphasis in the years since World War II, especially after the passage of the Library Services Act. Federal financial support further strengthened centralized processing, while preliminary descriptive surveys seemed to indicate the economic advantages of such operations, often somewhat optimistically. Because of the voluminous literature on this subject, we do not need to detail here the historical development of processing centers in the United States.[1] For the purpose of this discussion, **centralized processing** might be defined very broadly as any cooperative effort that results in the centralization of any or all of the technical processes necessary to get material ready for use. Such centers can be classified into three broad categories by the type of services rendered: 1) units responsible for complete technical processing; 2) units for ordering, cataloging and classifying; and 3) units for cataloging and classification only.

Centralized processing on a regional basis has been established in metropolitan areas and county systems for years. The more recent trend is to apply certain concepts of centralized processing to libraries of different types, which are not only separate administrative units and consequently may not belong to the same administrative system, but which may even be located in different geographical regions. In this context we usually use the term centralized processing to mean that a central agency orders, catalogs, and physically prepares library materials for use by a number of independent libraries or library systems.

---

[1] Cf. J. R. Hunt, "The Historical Development of Processing Centers in the United States," *Library Resources and Technical Services* 8 (Winter 1964): 54-59.

Sarah Vann, describing the structure of centralized processing centers, groups them into three arbitrary categories:[2]

1) The Autonomous Type. The autonomous center is directed by a board of trustees representing member libraries and is fully supported by its membership. The center may be cooperative in that the budget is divided among its members or in that member libraries contract to pay a certain fee.

2) The Neo-departmental Type. The neo-departmental type central processing center functions within an existing local, county or state agency which assumes administrative and, in large part, financial responsibility for the service. "Neo-departmental" indicates that, while the center functions within the administrative confines of the agency, its responsibilities exceed those of other departments since the needs of the members of the center may be considered in a perspective broader than that of the needs of the specific library with which it is associated.

3) The Multiple Service Type Encompassing Processing. The multiple service program usually functions within a federated or cooperative structure and offers such services as, advice on budgeting, building and staffing; guidance in book selection and weeding; and processing. Such a program, while long demonstrated, in part, within the federated structure of the Wayne County Library System in Michigan, was too much of an innovation for ready adoption into the traditionally autonomous local pattern.

Some of the factors that determine the character of a processing center or the type of services rendered are: 1) population to be served; 2) standards of previous cataloging practice; 3) types of services desired by member libraries (e.g., complete processing versus cataloging only); 4) size of member library budgets; 5) size and competency of professional staff; 6) amount and types of state aid and federal support available for setting up such centers, at least in initial stages; and finally, 7) the willingness to adopt uniform policies and procedures which quite often predetermine the efficiency and economics of a given operation.

Librarians cite many different reasons for establishing a system of centralized processing. These are usually directly related to local needs or predominant practices and to the results of critical studies of existing processing centers. The literature on this subject sometimes reveals very little about theoretically desirable models in terms of optimum requirements for setting up operation or the management and product cost of processing centers. Instead, the literature offers only descriptions of specific operations within a given system. Some of the reports are of the how-we-do-it-in-our-system type, and they attempt no generalization at all.[3]

---

[2] Sarah K. Vann, "Southeastern Pennsylvania Processing Center Feasibility Study: A Summary," *Library Resources and Technical Services* 10 (Fall 1966): 462-463.

[3] "Guidelines for Centralized Technical Services," prepared by the ALA Resources and Technical Services Division, Regional Processing Committee, can serve as a classic example of such a "pragmatic" approach. Cf. *Library Resources and Technical Services* 10 (Spring 1966): 233-240.

There are, of course, certain theoretical advantages in setting up a centralized processing pattern for member libraries. Some of the advantages are:

1) increased efficiency in processing a greater amount of material at less cost;
2) higher quality of cataloging practice;
3) centralization and simplification of business routines;
4) better utilization of professional staff;
5) utilization of more sophisticated equipment;
6) possible creation of union catalog.

The last advantage, the possible creation of a union catalog, is not only necessary for a successful centralized processing center but also can be valuable as a centralized bibliographic research center. A **union catalog** is a catalog that lists, completely or in part, the holdings of all the cooperating libraries. Ruth Patrick, in *Guidelines for Library Cooperation*, lists five different types of union catalogs: 1) complete union catalogs; 2) selective union catalogs and lists; 3) exchange of acquisition lists, catalog cards, and/or bibliographies; 4) lists of collection resources of the member libraries; and 5) union lists of serials.[4] The most typical selective union catalog developed by a centralized processing center is a limited chronological one—i.e., there are cards in the union catalog for everything cataloged by the center since its inception, but no cards for material cataloged prior to the development of the center. As Patrick points out, a complete union catalog may well be possible in the future:

> To produce a union catalog of the retrospective holdings of several large libraries would be an expensive undertaking. The advisable strategy on this activity seems to be to wait until the Library of Congress or the larger academic libraries have converted their retrospective holdings into machine-readable form, and to use their records instead of keyboarding the same bibliographic data in each individual library.[5]

There are, of course, basic problems in establishing and developing a centralized processing center. Many variables in practices have to be identified and, if necessary, eliminated. This in turn requires intensive study, both before and after decision-making, about whether the processing center can be justified economically. Such studies are not only required at the planning stage, to "justify" establishment of a processing unit, but they should also be an integral part of everyday operation in order to remedy possible deficiencies in the operational system. Initial descriptive reports of center activities, especially in the area of cost analysis, are rarely supplemented by critical self-appraisal and follow-up studies after the experimental period. Another problem is the excessive fragmentation of services rendered. Efficiency of operation is quite often the function of size. The theoretical "optimum" volume of materials processed in a given center has to be carefully

---

[4] Ruth Patrick, *Guidelines for Library Cooperation: Development of Academic Library Consortia* (Santa Monica, Calif., Systems Development Corporation, 1972), pp. 161-171.

[5] Ibid., pp. 165-166.

studied; in addition, however, combining several different types of libraries (e.g., school and public) within one system may result in problems that can seldom be solved by a highly structured apparatus. Such problems are serious, and they require intensive studies and extensive cooperative effort if the concept of centralized processing is to achieve the greatest possible advantage. Solution of these problems may lead to a new look at technical services in general and may bring about a reappraisal and a redefinition of now-undisputed practices of our cataloging routines.

PRINTED CATALOG CARDS

Most libraries do, and should, use printed cards when they are available. Not only is this practice in most instances more economical than original cataloging and typing of cards, but it also provides a standardized card form that conforms to all the major principles of descriptive cataloging and classification. This is not to say that there is no need for a professional cataloger if printed cards are used. The cataloger must still classify, even though the printed cards give the suggested Dewey or LC numbers. The set of cards must be checked against the book to ensure that there are no errors or variations in descriptive cataloging. Suggested subject headings must be carefully considered to verify that they are the ones utilized by the library, and, if necessary, new headings must be added. After these initial steps, a clerk can type the call numbers and the added entries on the set of cards. In addition, references to unused form of name, title, or subject headings must be checked and "see," "see also," or other reference cards must be added to the catalog as required.

Bibliographic Services of the
Library of Congress

Since 1901 the Library of Congress has made its own catalog cards available to libraries. At the present time the LC card distribution service is only one of many LC bibliographic services, among which are the distribution of proofsheets of LC cards; the Cataloging in Publication program (CIP); the publication of catalogs, including the *National Union Catalog* (NUC), bibliographies, and cataloging tools; the maintenance of the National Union Catalog on cards; and the generation and distribution of Machine Readable Cataloging records (MARC tapes).

LC Cards

LC printed cards offer complete coverage for materials, both foreign and domestic, cataloged by the Library of Congress. When the Higher Education Act of 1965 (Public Law 480) was signed into law, the Library of Congress was charged with acquiring, cataloging, and distributing cataloging information for all materials of research value published in foreign countries. In order to expedite this program several foreign offices of the Library of Congress were opened abroad.[6] In general, these offices accept the ISBD descriptive cataloging of each national bibliography as the standard, with the modifications needed for consistency with Library of Congress form of entries. Cataloging information from this program is identified on the card by initials of the foreign office (e.g., GB, C, F, GFR, USSR, Aus, It, Sw, etc.). The National Program for Acquisition and Cataloging (NPAC) of the Shared Cataloging Division, with increasing cooperation of national libraries and national bibliographies abroad, significantly increases the output and international coverage of LC cards.

The pamphlet *Catalog Cards* (published by the Cataloging Distribution Service Division of the Library of Congress) contains general information concerning the method of ordering, including an explanation of code formulas for the number of cards wanted. Orders for LC cards are prepared on standard order slips furnished free of charge to subscribers. See Fig. 17.1. In general, ordering by LC card number rather than by author or title is the most satisfactory method. This number is supplied in various standard bibliographies, such as the *Cumulative Book Index* (CBI), the *Weekly Record* (WR), *American Book Publishing Record* (BPR), *Library Journal* (LJ), etc., and on the verso of the title page of most current books.

Fig. 17.1—Sample Order Form

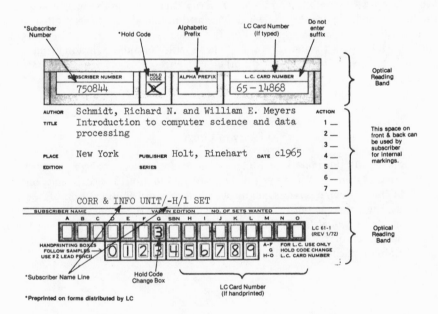

---

[6]*Annual Report of the Librarian of Congress* (Washington, Library of Congress; free to libraries) provides recent statistical data on publications acquired through the Public Law 480 Program.

Proofsheets

In addition to ordering individual LC cards, many libraries subscribe to the LC proofsheet service. **Proofsheets** are paper copies of LC cards issued on long "proofsheets" with five cards to a sheet. Proofsheets are classed by broad subject categories which agree in general with the main classes of LC Classification. Proofsheets are used in book selection, acquisitions, as a means of obtaining LC card numbers, and as copy for reproducing catalog cards. Proofsheets are issued only for material that is currently being cataloged by LC; they do not include motion pictures, filmstrips, and many other audiovisual media. Separate cards cut from proofsheets are called **proof slips**.[7]

Cataloging in Publication

Many current American books carry partial bibliographic description on the verso of the title page; this is the result of a program called **Cataloging in Publication** (CIP). William J. Welsh, Director of the Processing Department of the Library of Congress, describes this LC service as follows:

> Briefly expressed, the CIP entry will contain everything now on an LC printed card except for the information between the end of the title proper and the beginning of the series statement. Spelled out, the following information will be supplied: author, title, series statement, notes, subject and added entries, LC classification number, DC classification number, and LC card number. The entry will normally appear on the verso of the title page, printed in a format similar to the LC catalog card format. Entries for children's books will add annotations of the type now carried on our catalog cards for juvenile literature. Typography of the cataloging entry will probably match that of the book.[8]

Approximately 1,000 publishers are currently taking part in the CIP program. Each publisher submits galley proofs to the Library of Congress for preliminary cataloging, prior to publication of a book. CIP cataloging is useful for libraries that do original cataloging instead of ordering LC cards, as a source of LC card numbers, for the preliminary sorting of books at the receiving station of a library, and for libraries doing preliminary cataloging, or **fast-cat**, prior to the receipt of LC cards. Fig. 17.2 is an example of CIP preliminary cataloging. See also the verso of the title page of this textbook as an example of CIP data reproduced by a publisher.

---

[7] Samuel T. Waters and Salvatore L. Costabile, "The Proof of the Pudding: Using Library of Congress Proof Slips," *College and Research Libraries* 28 (March 1967): 87-91. This article describes a system for making maximum use of proof slips.

[8] William J. Welsh, "Report on Library of Congress Plans for Cataloging in Publication," *Library Resources and Technical Services* 15 (Winter 1971): 25-26.

Fig. 17.2

Library of Congress Cataloging in Publication Data

```
Morehead, Joe, 1931-
   Introduction to United States public documents.

   (Library science text series)
   Includes bibliographical references and index.
   1.  United States--Government publications.
2.  United States.  Government Printing Office.
I.  Title.
Z1223.Z7M67              015'.73              74-23628
ISBN 0-87287-106-1 lib. bdg.
```

Publications of the Library of Congress

Bibliographic information can also be obtained from the printed catalogs of the Library of Congress, especially the *National Union Catalog* (NUC). These catalogs consist of photographically reduced Library of Congress catalog cards. The purpose of the NUC is stated below.

> The *National Union Catalog* is designed as a current and cumulative continuation of *A Catalog of Books Represented by Library of Congress Printed Cards* and its supplements. It represents the works cataloged by the Library of Congress and by the libraries contributing to its cooperative cataloging program during the period of its coverage. In addition, it includes entries for monographic publications issued in 1956 and thereafter reported by about 950 North American libraries and not represented by LC printed cards. It constitutes a reference and research tool for a large part of the world's production of significant books as acquired and cataloged by the Library of Congress and a number of other North American libraries. For monographic works published since 1956 it indicates at least one library where the publication is held and serves thereby, at least for these imprints, as a National Union Catalog. It serves also, by indicating the LC card number, as a tool for the ordering of LC printed cards. It is supplemented by the other parts of the *Library of Congress Catalogs*.[9]

---

[9] United States Library of Congress, *The National Union Catalog: A Cumulative Author List Representing Library of Congress Printed Cards and Titles Reported by Other American Libraries.* Compiled by the Library of Congress with cooperation of the Resources Committee of the Resources and Technical Services Division, American Library Association, December 1972 (Washington, Library of Congress, 1972), page v.

Some of the other publications of the Library of Congress that are used by catalogers include the LC Classification Schedules, the *Library of Congress Subject Headings*, *New Serial Titles*, *Monographic Series*, and *Name Headings with References.*

Machine-Readable Cataloging (MARC)

Bibliographic descriptions are available through LC cards, proofsheets, CIP information, and NUC, but they are also available in machine-readable formats. The importance of the Library of Congress for cataloging practices became even more evident with the introduction of the MARC Distribution Service. The initial study of the recording of cataloging data in machine-readable form began in 1964; since that time, an extensive experimentation has been conducted in the MARC I and MARC II Pilot Projects.[10] At the present time the MARC Distribution Service provides, on a weekly basis, magnetic tapes containing bibliographical records in the MARC II communication format for all English and French language monographs currently cataloged at the Library of Congress. The corresponding LC printed cards for these titles have the notation "MARC" below the card number, and all additions and corrections to these printed cards are also issued as part of the distribution service. The subscription price for this weekly service is $1,200.00 per year. By 1974 some 427,000 records for books had been produced and distributed since the inauguration of the service in March 1969.

MARC tapes are available for films, maps, and serials, on a monthly basis. Subscriptions are $400.00 per year for each form. The following quotation by Henriette Avram, the principal developer of MARC, describes the origin and purpose of the computer-based system.

> The MARC Distribution Service grew out of a pilot project to test the feasibility of centrally producing and distributing machine-readable catalog records, The First Conference on Machine-Readable Catalog Copy in 1964, attended by representatives of the Library of Congress, universities, research agencies, government agencies, and private industry. Consensus was that early availability of machine-readable catalog copy as a by-product of LC's cataloging operations would be desirable. Since the record would be used for a variety of purposes in

---

[10]There is much literature on this subject, and the reader will be well advised to consult the following: Library of Congress. Information Systems Office. *Format Recognition; Process for MARC Records: A Logical Design* (Chicago, American Library Association, 1970); H. D. Avram, *The MARC Pilot Project: A Final Report on a Project Sponsored by the Council on Library Resources* (Washington, Library of Congress, 1968); H. D. Avram and others, *The MARC II Format: A Communications Format for Bibliographical Data* (Washington, Library of Congress, 1968); Library of Congress. MARC Development Office. *Information on the MARC System* (Washington, Library of Congress, 1974).

many libraries, agreement on data elements to be encoded was desirable, and the design of the machine-readable record by LC was probably the best means of standardization.

The pilot project resulted in: (1) a standard interchange format (ANSI standard), (2) the definition of standard records for several forms of material, and (3) the inception of the MARC Distribution Service beginning with the provision of English-Language Catalog Records in 1969. Expansion to other languages and other forms of material is planned for the future. While the implementation of systems for the utilization of MARC has been slow no one has suggested that the MARC Distribution Service (or the card division distribution service) be abandoned in favor of decentralized production of catalog records by many institutions.[11]

Ohio College Library Center (OCLC)

One direct result of LC's development and distribution of MARC tapes has been the establishment of regional bibliographic and shared cataloging networks. The Ohio College Library Center (OCLC) has become perhaps the most successful of the regional library networks. Incorporated under the laws of Ohio in 1967, since 1973 its membership has been open to all non-profit academic and non-academic libraries in the state. In addition, libraries and networks outside Ohio may participate as affiliates in OCLC's shared cataloging system.

OCLC fulfills four functions for its member libraries. It is a partial union catalog, a shared cataloging system, a pre-order search and acquisitions tool, and a generator of catalog cards. It is now a fully operational on-line system, meaning that all member libraries have direct access through cathode-ray terminals to the machine-readable data base maintained in the Center's Columbus headquarters. OCLC's data begins with MARC tapes, all records of which are incorporated into its own bibliographic data base; hence, any member may directly access OCLC for catalog data for any book on MARC tapes. Further, OCLC is a **shared** cataloging system. All member libraries may and do input the results of their own original cataloging into the system.

This aspect of the total system assumes major importance when it is remembered that OCLC members include such institutions as the Ohio State University, a major research library, and Oberlin College, a four-year school of the first rank and one with marked and distinctive research interests of its own. These and all other of the member libraries (577 as of August 1975) regularly contribute their own original catalog copy to the system. Once made a part of the system, these original catalog records are then accessible to all other member libraries. As of

---

[11] Henriette D. Avram and Josephine Pulsifer, "Bibliographic Series for a National Network," *Proceedings of the Conference on Interlibrary Communications and Information Networks*, sponsored by the American Library Association and U.S. Office of Education, Bureau of Libraries and Educational Technology, held at Airlie House, Warrenton, Virginia, September 28, 1970–October 2, 1970 (Chicago, American Library Association, 1971), p. 95.

January 1973, it was estimated by OCLC that the Center was adding an average of 300 records a day from MARC II tapes and 600 records daily from the original contributions of member libraries; thus, at least two-thirds of OCLC's data base is not derived from MARC.

The details of OCLC's program for producing and dispatching finished catalog copy are described in Hopkins' excellent article in LRTS,[12] as can the details of how OCLC fashions its catalog copy in accordance with the member library's own specifications.

By accessing the OCLC data base through any recognized MARC field (e.g., LC card order number, author-title for any given book), a member library can see flashed on its cathode-ray screen a complete catalog record plus coded references to the libraries that own it. Hence the system functions both as a partial union catalog and as a guide to interlibrary loan operations. Moreover, knowledge of existing locations for target books can and frequently does enter into acquisition decisions. Libraries may refrain from purchasing a given book when they know that one or more nearby libraries already own it.

Commercial Cataloging Services

There are several types of commercial cataloging services. Many jobbers supply cards or even cataloging kits for material ordered through them. Among these jobbers are Baker & Taylor, Blackwell of North America, Josten's, Bro-Dart, Demco-Alesco, and many others. Fig. 17.3 is an example of a Baker & Taylor card.

Fig. 17.3

```
PS          Bernhard, Robert.
3552            The Ullman code : a novel / by
E7314       Robert Bernhard. — New York :
            Putnam, [1974] c1975.
            242 p. ; 22 cm.


            ISBN 0-399-11417-3



            I. Title.
PZ4.B5247U13                        813'.5'4
[PS3552.E7314]
                                            74-16575
                        O                      MARC
Library of Congress
00073 *03059201   800458    B  ©THE BAKER & TAYLOR CO.   5074
```

---

[12]Judith Hopkins, "The Ohio College Library Center," *Library Resources and Technical Services* 17 (Summer 1973): 308-319.

Jobbers that provide cataloging kits may also offer complete processing services. This means that the material is ready for shelving when the library receives it.

Fig. 17.4–LJ Cards–processing kit

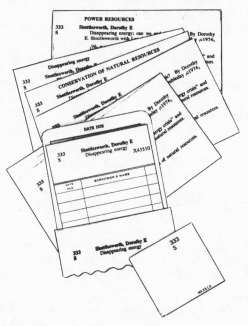

Most commercial services provide the library with a choice of LC or Dewey Decimal Classification and LC or Sears subject headings. Bro-Dart, for example, offers two types of services for the books ordered from them. The service for school or small public libraries uses Abridged Dewey and Sears. The service for larger libraries, called "Tech-Serv," provides LC subject headings and either LC or unabridged Dewey Decimal Classification.

In addition the cataloging kits available from jobbers, catalog cards or processing kits for books and other materials can also be obtained from several commercial firms. These firms provide such kits for items that the library has obtained from another source—e.g., directly from the publisher, through a jobber, or through a bookstore.

The *Library Journal/School Library Journal* "Annual Buyer's Guide 1975" lists 14 different commercial firms that offer cataloging services and/or book processing kits. The *LJ/SLJ* "Annual Buyer's Guide" usually appears in the September 1 issue of *Library Journal* and the September issue of *School Library Journal.* The extent and cost of commercial cataloging and/or processing services vary with each commercial agency. The cataloger should carefully consider all possibilities before subscribing to any single service. Some services are limited to juvenile books; some services are available only if the library purchases the book as well as its processing from the agency (these firms function both as jobbers and as commercial processing agencies); and some services are available only for pre-selected books and other materials. The cataloger must consider the flexibility of the subscription agreement and the number of options available, and he should compare the costs and availability of cards, kits, or shelf-ready books.

Finally, it should be noted that some publishers furnish sets of printed cards with their books, and some producers of audiovisual media provide card sets with each item. The introduction of the CIP program has lessened the advantages of this practice, and several publishers have ceased to provide catalog cards for their books.

REPRODUCING CATALOG CARDS

The reproduction of catalog cards is a complex technological problem that has many factors that directly or indirectly influence administrative decisions. In general, libraries can choose from several alternatives.

1) They may buy printed cards in sets of unit cards (e.g., LC cards) and adapt them for use in their libraries. In such libraries the reproduction of catalog cards is limited to original cataloging.

2) They may reproduce their own sets of unit cards from original cataloging.

3) They may obtain LC cataloging information using LC proofsheets, CIP information, *National Union Catalog*, *American Book Publishing Record*, etc., and reproduce their own cards.

4) They may use MARC tapes or machine-readable data provided by OCLC or other similar entities.

A further alternative, since most libraries still have to do some original cataloging, is to combine some of the above-mentioned approaches in order to arrive at the most economical method for a particular library. This is why most larger libraries still maintain some card reproduction equipment.

It should be noted that many commercial services will reproduce any number of copies not only from typed cards but also from LC cards, proofsheets, or camera prints. Several of these services that are well known are University Products, Inc., Library Reproduction Service, and General Microfilm Company.

Information on choosing the equipment and methods of catalog card reproduction has been summarized well in numerous writings.[13] Smaller libraries might find it advisable to invest in a small stencil duplicator. Medium-sized and larger libraries, of course, have a much larger volume of catalog card reproduction. If such libraries do not subscribe to commercial services or use LC or some regional cooperative services, then they will probably require more expensive equipment than that used by small libraries. Some of the methods and types of equipment used in larger libraries are indicated below.

1) Full size stencil duplicators are based on the same principles as the smaller machines but are faster; the library must prepare the stencils.

---

[13] Cf. G. Fry, *Catalog Card Reproduction*. Report based on study conducted by G. Fry and Associates, Inc. (Chicago, Library Technology Project of the American Library Association, 1965; L.T.P. Publications, No. 9). A more recent survey on card reproduction can be found in Arlene T. Dowell's *Cataloging with Copy: The Decision-Maker's Handbook* (Littleton, Colo., Libraries Unlimited, 1976).

2) Offset presses are used not only for card stock but for other printing work; these multilithing duplicators cost more than stencil machines, but they are larger and faster. Masters must be prepared.

3) Xerox or electrostatic copying can be used to reproduce LC cards, LC proof slips, and typed cards.

4) Magnetic tape typewriter (e.g., IBM Magnetic Tape Selectric Typewriter, the MT/ST) and the Flexowriter can be used either to reproduce cards or to prepare cards from original cataloging.

5) Catalog cards can be generated by computer.

The consideration of appropriate reproduction policy is based on several variable factors. These will be summarized here only briefly, since no two libraries' cataloging information and card needs are the same. Furthermore, no single process of card reproduction can meet the needs of all libraries. The administrative decisions are based, in general, on the following factors:

1) The percentage of available printed catalog cards applicable to the library's collection.

2) The quality of cataloging information needed.

3) The number of copies needed.

4) Delivery time (insertion of temporary records is expensive).

5) Card preparation for foreign language materials.

Small libraries that type all their cards may be wasting time and money, because it is quite expensive to type and proofread every card. For such libraries, ready-made cards might be more economical, since the actual reproduction of cards would then be limited to those for titles requiring original cataloging or to those needed to provide cross references not obtainable from commercial sources. Smaller libraries might also find it advisable to subscribe to centralized or cooperative processing services described above, since these firms offer services beyond the provision of printed cards.

It should be noted, however, that all libraries must type some cards. This is true for small libraries, which do a minimum amount of original cataloging, as well as for large libraries with elaborate card reproduction processes. The decision as to when the library should begin reproducing catalog cards on a large scale is elusive and variable. It depends not only on the number of cards needed per set (economic considerations) but also on the diversity and complexity of cataloging information needed, possible variations from standard cataloging practices, etc.

CATALOGING ROUTINES AND RECORDS

The efficiency of the library's catalog and the overall quality of cataloging are affected not only by the care and standards applied to cataloging each item but by several other important factors. The first of these is the organization and routines set up to handle each phase of the cataloging process; another is the provision for recording cataloging decisions and local practice and for keeping all vital catalog department files and records current; and last is the need to maintain and edit the catalog. Each of these areas requires careful study and policy decision. Here we will briefly consider the major responsibilities and summarize certain routines that vary in pattern from library to library. Organizational structure and the identification and assignment of non-professional routines to clerks and para-professionals are not within the scope of this text.[14]

Descriptive Cataloging

The cataloging process may be divided into three major responsibilities: descriptive cataloging, classifying, and assigning subject headings. Descriptive cataloging is performed on two levels: with LC cards or proof slips, and without LC cards. If LC cards are available, the cataloger checks the book against the card noting any changes and additions on a **work slip** for the typist (some libraries use a part of a multiple copy order form for this). Unless a change is made on the card, it can serve as the official card for the book being cataloged. In cases where LC cards are out of stock or otherwise not immediately available, the entry for the book can provide the cataloging copy; the information from NUC is copied to a work slip. Original cataloging must be done for books without LC copy. In these cases the cataloger prepares the official card. For any of these methods, the cataloger marks the work slip for main entry and for the cross references that should be made.

Classification

Classifying the book and assigning a call number (i.e., classification number), author number (cutter) and work mark (for title) are the next major steps. The classification number as it appears on the LC copy is either accepted or checked and adapted to the classification numbers in the collection, depending on established policy for the particular library. The author or book number is assigned and the shelf list is consulted to assure that a number is not duplicated. A temporary slip (e.g., the temporary card provided in most multiple order forms) is filed in the shelf list until a permanent shelf list card has been prepared. The call number is added to the work slip and penciled on the title page of the book.

Subject Cataloging and Other Responsibilities

The third major responsibility is that of accepting or assigning subject headings and other needed tracings and references. If LC copy is used, subject headings are checked and accepted according to local library policy and additional headings are assigned as required; the book is then sent to the preparation department for processing.

Other recurring responsibilities of the cataloger involve recataloging, cancelling, and reinstating and transferring cards for books already in the collection. Recataloging takes place on two levels. It may result from a changeover from one

---

[14]See Marty Bloomberg and G. Edward Evans, *Introduction to Technical Services for Library Technicians*, 2nd ed. (Littleton, Colo., Libraries Unlimited, 1974), pp. 133-134.

classification scheme to another, a change that can involve a special collection or the entire holdings of a library. More frequently, recataloging results from the relocation of class numbers within the same classification scheme (e.g., numbers relocated in the most recent edition of Dewey[15]), or from the change of form of entry (e.g., with adoption of AACR[16]). Copy numbers (i.e., "Cop. 1," "Cop. 2," etc.) for weeded (discarded) or lost books must be cancelled on the shelf list, a simple but necessary procedure and copy numbers for missing books that are later found must be reinstated on the shelf list card. If the discarded item is the last copy or only copy of a title, however, all library records must be cancelled. All cards—main entry, added entry, subject entry, and analyticals—shown on the main entry tracing must be removed from the catalog and all references in authority files checked. Any special cross references made for the title which would no longer be in use must be cancelled in the records and removed from the catalog. In effect, the cancellation of a title of which there is only one copy involves reversing the procedures used in cataloging the title to assure complete clearance of library records. If this is not accomplished accurately, a blind reference will occur in the catalog.

Records and Files in the Catalog Department

The catalog department maintains certain essential files: the shelf list, "in process" files, official catalog, name authority file, series authority file, and subject authority file.

Shelf List

The shelf list, the most important official library record, is usually kept in the catalog department. It is a complete list of all titles in the collection arranged by classification number as the books stand on the shelves. The primary purpose of the shelf list is to indicate the individual titles by class; it also shows the number of volumes and copies of each title. Notations of cost, accession or copy number, date of acquisition, missing copies, copies withdrawn—anything pertinent to the status of the title—may be noted on the shelf list card as dictated by the requirements of each library. The shelf list card may be a unit card since the tracings shown are useful for the cataloger. This file is used not only by the cataloger, but also by the reference staff and others; the classified arrangement shows what titles are in the collection for a specific class number but it also displays, within certain limitations, related materials more general and more specific on either side of the class referred to. As indicated above, catalogers consult the shelf list to verify their library's use of a particular class number, and in this respect it may be considered an important

---

[15]G. Edward Evans, "Dewey: Necessity or Luxury?" *Library Journal* 91 (September 15, 1966): 4038-4046.

[16]Joseph A. Rosenthal, "The Administrative Implications of the New Rules," *Library Resources and Technical Services* 10 (Fall 1966): 437-444.

classification aid. A temporary shelf list card is inserted in the file for each book being cataloged in order to avoid duplication of numbers and to provide temporary (though not necessarily complete) information about the new title. Additional cards may be filed in the shelf list explaining or describing the library's decisions as to scope and use of particular class numbers. For a unit card used as a shelf list card see Fig. 17.5.

Fig. 17.5

PR
6039
.032
Z9
1974

Wilson, Colin, 1931-
    Tree by Tolkien / by Colin Wilson. — Santa Barbara, Calif.
: Capra Press, 1974.
    47 p. : ill. ; 18 cm. — (Yes! Capra chapbook series ; 20)
    ISBN 0-912264-97-7. ISBN 0-912264-96-9 pbk. : $2.50

c.1 Baker & Taylor 11-5-74 $7.50--missing 9-30-75
c.2 Capra Press   10-9-75 $11.00

    I. Tolkien, John Ronald Renel, 1892-1973—Criticism and interpretation.
II. Title.

    PR6039.032Z9 1974   823'.9'12   75-314340
                                                MARC

    Library of Congress   75

Note: This shelf list card indicates that the library holds two copies of the title and that both added entries have been used. The added entries on an LC card that are actually used are checked by the cataloger on the official card, of which the shelf list card is a copy. Additional information included shows the purchase source, date and price of each copy, and the fact that Copy 1 is missing.[17]

In Process Files

Certain areas of acquisitions and cataloging overlap somewhat. Each library's requirements must be studied to eliminate duplication of record keeping, verification, etc.; this is a continuous administrative responsibility. However, some record, whether maintained by the cataloger or by the order librarian, must be kept to show "books in process"—i.e., the exact status of every book once it is received in the library but before permanent catalog cards are filed. Libraries that use multiple order forms to order books can keep part of such a form for the "in process" file. The form of the in-process file varies; some libraries use the original requisition card for this purpose once the book has been received in the library. Since the correct main entry may not be established until after the book is

---

[17]For additional examples of shelf list cards and explanations see Bloomberg and Evans, *Introduction to Technical Services*, pp. 189-192.

cataloged, it is recommended that in-process files be arranged by title rather than author. In addition, many libraries maintain a separate LC card order file; besides the card orders, this file contains LC card sets that arrive before the book itself.

Official Catalogs

Some libraries maintain an official catalog, kept in the catalog department, for the use of the library staff only. The character of this catalog varies considerably. Essentially, it is a tool of convenience, duplicating to a certain extent information found in the public catalog or in the shelf list. Quite frequently the official catalog is limited to one card per title cataloged (main entry card) and it serves as authority file for recording the accepted form of the main entry, including the tracing of all used subject headings, added entries, series, etc. In some libraries it also includes the location of books in departmental libraries or special collections. Since the official catalog is not used by the public, it may show certain additional non-bibliographic details for the guidance of the staff, such as administrative decisions pertaining to the use of cross references, analytical cards, and other notes of reference. Authority cards and subject entries can be made a part of this file.

While the shelf list approach is numerical and is based on the location of books as they stand on the shelves, the official catalog fully complements the shelf list through its alphabetical approach. Nevertheless, because of the high cost of maintaining it, many libraries do not have a separate official catalog, but use instead the public catalog and the shelf list as the main authority files. It is often such factors as the library's size, the poor architectural planning of the building, the decision to keep technical processes away from the public area, or responsibility for the cataloging in more than one library unit, which necessitate the maintenance of a separate official catalog.

Authority Files

Other cataloging aids are prepared and maintained by the catalog department. Author authority files are records of main entries prescribed for use by a particular library. Many libraries use the NUC as their author authority file. The purpose of an authority file is to control and maintain uniformity in the use of main entry, subject headings, cross references, etc. Many libraries use the public catalog as the authority file. Nevertheless, some information that needs to be available to the cataloger does not lend itself to inclusion in the public catalog. In this case an authority card record that interfiles all needed decisions or any combination of individual files may be developed—e.g., name authority file, subject and cross reference authority file, series authority file, or a general "decisions" file. Each card in such files carries the author name or subject heading and refers to additional names or headings in use plus all "see" and general reference cards made for the public catalog; decisions such as whether certain sets are cataloged and classed together or separately, etc., may also be recorded. This information is necessary in cataloging new material to assure uniformity of entry, to avoid duplication of work, and also to insure cancellation of all references and tracings when the withdrawal of a title from the collection may affect these items.

Some libraries maintain very carefully verified name authority files. The Library of Congress maintains an extensive name authority file.

Name Authority Cards

Name authority cards are prepared in order to establish the correct main entry heading for a particular author. Name authority cards bring together under one heading pseudonyms, shortened forenames, variations in surnames, and variant forms of the name of a corporate body. The steps outlined below demonstrate how to develop such an authority card. It is important to understand the process of verification of the author. **Verification** means determining the existence of an author and the form of his name as well as the correct title of the particular work for which the card is being made. Verification usually means consulting one or more bibliographic sources, as discussed under step two.

Step One: The book being cataloged—

Prepare a card with the following information from the title page of the book being cataloged:

1) the author's name as it appears on the title page of the book being cataloged;
2) the title of the book being cataloged;
3) the date of publication of the book being cataloged.

See Fig. 17.6 for the three parts of step one; note that the author's name is written on the line called "**Book Cat.**" which means the book being cataloged.

Fig. 17.6

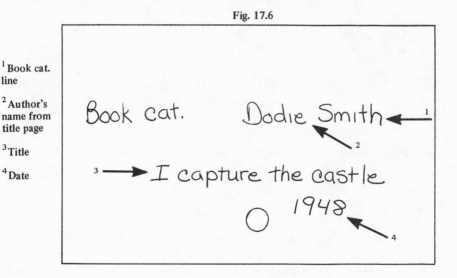

¹ Book cat. line

² Author's name from title page

³ Title

⁴ Date

Step Two: Verification of the author—

Consult the verification source or sources necessary for this particular author.[18] (CBI is a common verification source, as are NUC and BPR; if these sources fail to provide the author's name, then various biographical dictionaries and directories can be consulted.)

1) List the source and date of the verification source on the card, below the Book Cat. line.

2) Place the verified name at the top of the card in the appropriate order (i.e., for European names list the surname first, followed by forenames, followed by dates of birth and death).

3) When the author has been verified, place a first check mark under the Book Cat. line before the source of verification. If the author's dates have been found, place a lower case "d" at the third space from the first check. If the title of the book has been found in the source, place a second check after the first (or author's) check mark. If the particular edition of the book being cataloged is listed in the source, place a third check between the second check and the letter "d."

4) Indicate any necessary cross references in the lower left-hand corner of the card; if the form of the name on the Book Cat. line is different from the verified form, cross references may need to be made. Fig. 17.7 is an example of a verification card completed through step two.

Fig. 17.7

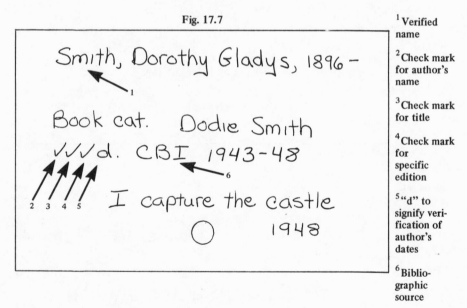

[1] Verified name

[2] Check mark for author's name

[3] Check mark for title

[4] Check mark for specific edition

[5] "d" to signify verification of author's dates

[6] Bibliographic source

---

[18] For an extensive discussion of verification sources, see Bloomberg and Evans, *Introduction to Technical Services*, pp. 44-65.

Step Three: Completion of the name authority card—

1) If the author's name on the Book Cat. line exactly matches the verified form of the author's name, cancel or remove the entire Book Cat. line.

2) If the verified form does not match, retain the entire Book Cat. line.

3) Type the card for the name authority file.

See Fig. 17.8 for step three.

Fig. 17.8

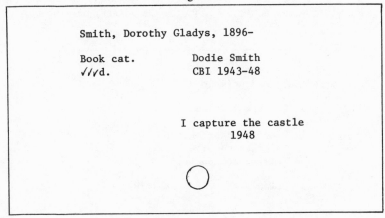

```
        Smith, Dorothy Gladys, 1896-

        Book cat.          Dodie Smith
        √√√d.              CBI 1943-48



                           I capture the castle
                                 1948
```

Step Four: Verification of additional names—

Any additional names on the title page (joint authors, editors, translators, illustrators, etc.) that the cataloger wants to use as added entries for a particular book must also be verified in the above manner. In addition, the following line must appear above the title line on the name authority card: "a.e. for [the verified main entry]." Fig. 17.9 is an example of a verified additional entry.

Fig. 17.9

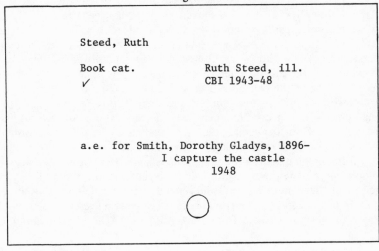

```
        Steed, Ruth

        Book cat.          Ruth Steed, ill.
        √                  CBI 1943-48



        a.e. for Smith, Dorothy Gladys, 1896-
                 I capture the castle
                       1948
```

Subject Authority Cards

LC and Sears subject headings lists are frequently marked and annotated to record local practice and are used as subject authority files. This procedure is simple, but transferring annotations from one cumulation or edition to another and updating all copies in a large department are costly procedures for some libraries. The choice and development of authority files and the form in which the information is recorded varies from library to library depending on individual cataloging requirements. Fig. 17.10 is a sample subject authority card.

Fig. 17.10

```
Literature and science

     sa  Science fiction

      x  Poetry and science
         Science and literature
         Science and poetry

     xx  Science and the humanities




                                   LC 7th ed.
```

Maintaining and Editing the Catalog

The public catalog is maintained and edited by the catalog department. Attention to physical elements such as repair of damaged drawers or replacement of worn and soiled cards is important. Certain aids such as drawer labels, guide cards, and instructions for use of the catalog inside and outside the file require careful consideration and should be altered whenever improvements can be presumed. Expansion of the catalog requires occasional shifting of cards.

Editing of the catalog is necessary to eliminate unnecessary entries as well as to suggest improvements and to plan for future growth and development. Inaccuracies and errors find their way into any catalog; old entries may not have been pulled from the catalog during cancellation of a title. Inconsistent headings, misleading or blind references may exist, and there may be errors in filing, omission of cards for some titles, wrong call numbers, etc. The normal and increasingly rapid obsolescence of terminology for some subject headings, the need for addition and review of "see" and "see also" and general references dictates constant revision and editing of the catalog. The complexity of connecting references from old rules for entry to new rules (e.g., from ALA rules to AACR when a library adopts this change) presents serious problems, as indicated by Rosenthal.[19] Changes in filing rules also present problems, and some entries need to be refiled in order to keep pace with changing needs of the library and its users.

FILING

The conventional file order for dictionary catalogs is alphabetical **word by word** arrangement with some modifications and exceptions (e.g., when a numerical or chronological arrangement is preferred). Catalog filing rules as generally adopted are not strictly alphabetical, as will be shown later. Some degree of arbitrary grouping is evident in most arrangements, especially in those designed for research libraries (e.g., LC filing rules). Moreover, various sets of rules for filing are in use; some libraries adapt standard rules for their own use while many libraries, such as special libraries, develop filing rules tailored to their unique requirements. Filing rules for use in a divided catalog may be much simpler than those used in a dictionary catalog. Experiments with computer mechanization of filing are being carried out, and it is hoped that they will result in simplification of file organization. It has been determined that mechanizing filing in its present form is too complex to be feasible.[20]

Arbitrary groupings, exceptions made from strict alphabetical order, and other complexities of filing are directly related to the construction of subject headings and form of catalog entries. In particular, conflicts in form of entry between the old *ALA Cataloging Rules* and AACR have resulted in filing problems, since most libraries retain old entries in their catalogs. Some libraries have attempted to file old and new forms of the same entry together, while others file all entries exactly as they appear on the card. In either case, ample use of cross references is necessary.

The *ALA Rules for Filing Catalog Cards* (2nd ed., 1968) is a current guide to filing.[21] A simplified discussion of these rules follows. Since there are many alternate filing systems and established rules, we have provided a critical comparative discussion of one alternate approach following the examples of ALA's 1968 filing rules. The reader should also consult Chapter 15 of this book for a brief discussion of the filing arrangement of LCSH 8. The following simplified rules and some of the examples are from those compiled by ALA for word-by-word arrangement.

---

[19] Rosenthal, "The Administrative Implications of the New Rules," p. 437.

[20] Kelley L. Cartwright, "Mechanization and Library Filing Rules," in *Advances in Librarianship*, v.1 (New York, Academic Press, 1970), p. 59.

[21] Cf. Pauline Seely, "ALA Filing Rules—New Edition," *Library Resources and Technical Services* 11 (Summer 1967): 377-379; also, Pauline Seely, "ALA Rules for Filing Catalog Cards: Differences Between 2d and 1st Editions (Arranged by 2d Ed. Rule Numbers)," *Library Resources and Technical Services* 13 (Spring 1969): 291-294; a modification of these ALA 1968 Rules for a three-way divided catalog is found in Grant W. Morse, *Filing Rules: A Three-Way Divided Catalog* (Hamden, Conn., Linnet Books, 1971).

ALA Filing Rules

Alphabetical Position of Entries

1. All entries are arranged letter by letter to the end of each word through the entry. Alphabetizing begins with the first word in the top line of the entry, then goes to the second word, etc.

1   2   3   '4   5 6 7

Charles Louis de Bourbon, Duke of Parma

2. File "nothing before something." Space between words is considered "nothing." This also is termed as, file "blank to Z"; the space or blank between words determines the end of each filing element—e.g., New York before Newark. In this way, short words file before longer words beginning with the same letters. (Filing A–Z, letter by letter, disregards blanks—e.g., Newark before New York.)

3. All punctuation and parentheses are ignored. Arrange elisions, contractions, and possessives as written. Do not supply missing letters.

Life	Who is who
Life–a bowl of rice	Whoa, Grandma!
"Life after death"	Who'd be a doctor?
Life, its true genesis	Whodunit
Life! physical and spiritual	Who's who

4. Every word in the entry, including articles and prepositions, is regarded.

Work for **a** man
Work for **Julia**
Work for **the** beginner

Exception: Disregard **initial articles** in all languages and file by the following word (in English: A, An, The).

The **man** of his time
A **man** of the age
Les **miserables**

5. Disregard all letter modifications such as umlaut, cedilla, tilde, all accent marks, etc. File ü as u, ç as c, etc.

6. Each initial is treated as a one-letter word. Combinations of initials are arranged in straight alphabetical sequence as if each initial were a one-letter word, regardless of variations in spacing or punctuation. Arrange acronyms as words (Unesco or FORTRAN) unless they are written in capitals with periods or spaces, in which case file as initials. See examples on page 389.

A.A.	U.D.F.
A apple pie	U.N.E.S.C.O., see Unesco
The **ABC** about collecting	U.R.S.S.
A B C and X Y Z	Unemployment
Aabel, Marie	Unesco fellowship handbook

7. Abbreviations are arranged as spelled in full in the language of the entry. **Exception**: File Mrs. and Ms. as written (but file Mr. as Mister).

Dr. Christian's office	The Great Brink's holdup
Doctor come quickly	Great Britain – Description and
Doktor Brents Wandlung	travel
Dr. Mabuse der Spieler	Great Britain on trial
	Great Britain or little England

8. Numerals in titles of books, dates, corporate names, cross references, etc., are arranged as spelled in the language of entry. Spell as if spoken. Use "and" before last element in compound numbers.

100 American poems	[one hundred]
101 best games for teens	[one hundred and one]
1,999 laughs	[one thousand nine hundred and
	ninety nine]
B–58 Bomber	[fifty-eight]
Europe since 1815	[eighteen fifteen]

9. Words spelled in different ways are interfiled as if spelled one way. **Note**: Some other filing rules file as spelled any words that have variant spelling. Cross references are made from the word to variant forms.

      Color   see also the word spelled
           Colour

Names spelled in different ways are arranged separately, regardless of how slight the difference. References between variant spellings are desirable.

      Andersen   see also the spellings Anderson, Anderssen, Andersson
      Andersen, Anders
      Andersen, Hans Christian
      Anderson   see also the spellings Andersen, Anderssen, Andersson
      Anderson, Arthur

10. Hyphenated words are filed as a) **separate words** when parts are complete forms—i.e., when each part can stand alone as a word in the context of the combined word; b) **one word** when forms begin with a prefix or combining form such as: anti–, bi–, co–, electro–, ex–, inter–, pan–, post–, etc. This applies whether the combined form is written with or without a hyphen. Explanatory references are made in the catalog. See examples on page 390.

Pan—

> Words beginning with the above combining form are alphabetized as one word

Pan in ambush
Panama
Pan American Bureau
Pan-American Congress

11. Compound words written as two separate words, hyphenated, and as a single word are interfiled under the one-word form, with an explanatory reference under the two-word form:

Camp dramatics
Camp fire

> For entries beginning with the above words, written with or without a hyphen, see the one-word form "Campfire."

Campbell
Campfire

> Here are filed all entries beginning with the words "Campfire," "Camp fire," and "Camp-fire."

Camp-fire and cotton-field
Camp Fire Girls
CAMPFIRE PROGRAMS
Camp-fire verse

12. Compound proper names are filed as separate words.

Hall & Patterson	Saint among the Hurons
Hall Co., Rex	St. Petersburg
Hall-Edwards,	Saint Vincent
Hall of fame	San Francisco
Hall Williams,	Sanborn

13. Proper names with a prefix are spelled as written but filed as one word. **Note:** ALA rules recommend an exception for M' and Mc to arrange as if spelled Mac. This is not recommended for libraries that want a simplified arrangement.

De Alberti,	Vanderbilt,	Mabee,
Defoe,	Van der Veer,	MacGregor,
De la Roche,	Vanderwalker,	Mack,
Delpero,	Vander Zaden,	MacVittie,
De Marco,		Maxwell,
		McTarnaghan,
		Mead,

Order of Different Headings
Beginning with the Same Word

1A. A simplified arrangement advocated by some school librarians and others is to interfile all entries, regardless of kind, in the manner of the telephone book.[22]

The Green	The green years
Green, Agnes	Greenaway, Kate
Green mansions	GREENBACKS
Green, William	Greenbaum, Joseph
(next column)	GREENE, NATHANIEL

1B. Arrangement recommended by ALA filing rules is to file entries with the same word, or combination of words, in two main groups:

    a) single surname entries, followed by
    b) all other entries arranged alphabetically disregarding kind of entry, form of heading, and punctuation.

Love, David T		LOVE – LETTERS
LOVE, DAVID T		LOVE, MATERIAL
Love, Zachary		LOVE POETRY
Love	[title]	LOVE – QUOTATIONS
Adams, P.		Love songs, old and new
		LOVE (THEOLOGY)
LOVE	[subject]	Love your neighbor
James, S		
Love and beauty		
(next column)		

Single surnames are arranged 1) surname only, 2) surname with dates only, 3) surname with designation, forenames or initials:

Smith,	Smith, John, surgeon
Smith, d. 1769	Smith, John, 1563–1616
Smith, Captain	Smith, John, 1798–1888
Smith, Sir John	Smith, John, b. 1823
(next column)	

Given name entries are filed **after** single surnames, interfiled with all other entries (see 1B.b above). Disregard numerals unless needed to distinguish between identical names. See examples on page 392.

---

[22]Joseph T. Popecki, "A Filing System for the Machine Age," *Library Resources and Technical Services* 9 (Summer 1965): 333-337.

Charles, William
Charles   [title]
Charles Ann, Sister
Charles City, Iowa
Charles de Blois
Charles Douglas, freedom fighter   [title]
Charles, Duke of Burgundy
CHARLES FAMILY
Charles III, King of France
Charles I, King of Great Britain

Homer, Winslow
Homer
Homer and history

2. Entries under an author are arranged in two groups:

   a) **works by the author**, main and added entries interfiled. For added
      entries disregard author main entry, file by title of main entry.
   b) **works about the author**, alphabetically by subdivision.

Pennell, Joseph, 1857–1926.
   The adventures of an illustrator.

Pennell, Joseph, 1857–1926, illus.
Van Rennselaer, Mariana Griswold
   English Cathedrals . . .

Pennell, Joseph, 1857–1926.
   Our journey to the Hebrides.

PENNELL, JOSEPH, 1857–1926.
Fraser, J
   The travels of an artist.

3. Arrange all entries beginning with the same geographical place name after
the same name as a single surname; interfile with all other kinds of entries (see 1B.b
above). Ignore all punctuation and parentheses. Different kinds of entries under the
same heading are grouped in this order:

   1) Author without subheading, subarranged by title.
   2) Subject without subdivision, and identical titles interfiled, subarranged by main entries.
   3) Heading with subdivisions, subdivisions interfiled alphabetically
with each other and with titles, etc.

Lincoln, William Sever
Lincoln and Ann Rutledge
LINCOLN, BATTLE OF, 1217
LINCOLN CO., KY.
LINCOLN, ENG.
Lincoln, Neb.
LINCOLN, NEB. – BIOGRAPHY
Lincoln plays

London, Jack
London
LONDON
London and Londoners
LONDON – DESCRIPTION
LONDON (DOG)
London, Ky.
London. National Gallery

4. Subject entries follow the same word used as a single surname (see 1B.b above). Arrange a subject, its subdivisions, etc., in the following order:

1) Subject without subdivision, interfile with identical ᶜtitles, alphabetically by their main entries.

2) Period divisions are arranged chronologically by the first date in heading.

3) All form, subject and geographical subdivisions, inverted subject headings, parenthetical terms, and phrase subject headings are interfiled word by word with titles and other headings beginning with the same word. Disregard all punctuation.

Period division note: Open dates (1865–   ) and periods beginning with the same year are arranged so as to bring the longest period first, and precede other periods beginning with the same or later years, e.g.,

> 1865–
> 1865–1961
> 1865–1898

Periods expressed in words[23] (–Colonial Period) or in words and dates (–Confederation, 1783–1789) are arranged chronologically, **not** alphabetically.

Subdivisions for language and literature, such as, –OLD FRENCH, –18TH CENTURY, etc., are period subdivisions and are arranged chronologically. However, the divisions –ANCIENT –MEDIEVAL, etc., are arranged **alphabetically** not chronologically even when followed by a date (History, – MODERN – 20TH CENTURY).

Exception: Arrange divisions –ANCIENT, –MODERN, etc., **chronologically** when used as further divisions of the subdivisions –HISTORY or –HISTORY AND CRITICISM (e.g., MUSIC – HISTORY AND CRITICISM – ANCIENT).

Detail of Period Division (using Sears Subject Headings)

```
U.S. – HISTORY
U.S. – HISTORY – COLONIAL PERIOD          [chronological]
               – FRENCH AND INDIAN WAR, 1755–1763
               – REVOLUTION
               – REVOLUTION – CAMPAIGNS AND BATTLES
               – 1783–1865
               – CIVIL WAR
               – 1865–1898
```

---

[23] Please note that all subject headings from LCSH 8 with period divisions include dates; *supra* Chapter 15 of this textbook, pp. 354–355.

Detail of Period Division (cont'd)

```
U.S.  -  HISTORY  -  WAR OF 1898
                  -  20TH CENTURY
                  -  1933–1945
U.S.  -  HISTORY  -  BIO–BIBLIOGRAPHY          [alphabetical]
U.S.  -  HISTORY  -  DESCRIPTION AND TRAVEL
U.S.  -  HISTORY  -  DICTIONARIES
U.S.  -  HISTORY  -  INDEXES
U.S.  -  HISTORY  -  PERIODICALS
U.S.  -  HISTORY  -  PHILOSOPHY
U.S.  -  HISTORY  -  SOCIETIES
U.S.  -  HISTORY  -  STUDY AND TEACHING
```

References

File "see" references in their alphabetical places according to the above rules as they apply; disregard the words "see" and "see also" and headings or notes following them. Arrange a "see" or an explanatory reference **before** the same word as an entry, except that a surname always takes precedence.

> DOCTORS,   [see PHYSICIANS]
>
> The doctors
> Gregor, P

File a subject "see also" reference **after** the last entry under the same words, whether that entry is a subject or a title, and **before** a subdivision of the subject or a longer entry.

> CHILDREN
> CHILDREN,   see also . . .
> CHILDREN – CARE AND HYGIENE

Alternate Filing Rules

The ALA (1968) filing rules were produced in response to a feeling that the traditional rules had become too complex and too awkward, and that they were overly concerned with fine theoretical distinctions. None of this was helpful to the user, who needs a simple system if he is to manipulate a card catalog quickly and easily. The traditional rules had been embodied in the first edition of the ALA filing rules.[24] Not everyone agrees with the 1968 ALA Committee, however. In

---

[24]American Library Association, *ALA Rules for Filing Catalog Cards* (Chicago, American Library Association, 1942).

fact, most libraries disagree so much that they have not fully implemented the new rules. Two considerations govern libraries' decisions regarding the rules. The first is cost. Obviously it would be prohibitively expensive for an established library of 1,000,000 volumes—all of which are documented by catalog cards arranged according to traditional rules—to change over to the new rules.

In addition, it has become increasingly clear that there is a direct relationship between the size of the collection and the need for complexity in filing rules. Rather argues the case for a flexible filing arrangement persuasively when he says,

> Filing arrangement is the capstone of the system of bibliographic control that begins with descriptive cataloging and includes subject analysis and classification. The entire effort to achieve bibliographic control necessarily reaches its fulfillment in the means of displaying catalog information to users. If the arrangement of the file violates the form or meaning of the headings, users will be hampered in their efforts to use the catalog successfully.[25]

Rather's article is essential reading for those who want to understand the complexities of the problem. In general two observations can be made: large libraries cannot adopt the new filing rules without major modification; and all libraries must formulate and make available to their publics a precise statement of the rules governing the arrangement of cards in their catalogs.

The 1942 ALA rules and the current practice among research libraries agree that to some extent the 1968 ALA rules do "violate the form or meaning of the headings." To prove the point, we have rearranged the same terms listed in 1B.b (page 391) according to the rules of the Library of Congress, all major research libraries, and the formulation of 1942.

1. Love, David T.
2. LOVE, DAVID T.
3. Love, Zachary
4. LOVE [subject]
   James, S.
5. LOVE – LETTERS
6. LOVE – QUOTATIONS
7. LOVE, MATERIAL
8. LOVE (THEOLOGY)
9. Love [title]
   Adams, P.
10. Love and beauty
11. LOVE POETRY
12. Love songs, old and new
13. Love your neighbor

Compare this arrangement closely with that given in 1B.b. Refer back to 1B.b and note that the 1968 rule states that entries beginning with the same initial element (in this case, "love") are to be filed in two main groups: first, single surname entries, followed by "all other entries arranged alphabetically **disregarding kind of entry, form of heading, and punctuation.**" Here we confront the issue squarely. Research library rules agree that for fields with identical initial elements

---

[25] John C. Rather, "Filing Arrangement in the Library of Congress Catalogs," *Library Resources and Technical Services* 16 (Spring 1972): 240-261.

single-surname entries do begin the sequence, but—and here is a crucial difference—succeeding entries are to be arranged in precisely this order: place entries, corporate body entries, subject entries, and finally title entries.

The example given above is imperfect in that it contains no Place or Corporate Body entries, but otherwise it is a satisfactory example of the traditional rule. Entry 1 is for David T. Love as an author; entry 2, for the same man as a subject. Entry 3 is for another "Love" as author. Entries 4–8 are **subject** (all caps) entries for LOVE in which this word is the initial element of a progressively subdivided series of entries. Entries 9 and 10 are title entries. Entry 11 is another subject entry, followed by 12 and 13, further title entries.

To further illustrate the rule governing sequence of entries by type, we have added place and corporate body entry to the "love" series, as follows:

1. Love, David T.
2. LOVE, DAVID T.
3. Love, Zachary
4. Love Co., Oklahoma
5. The Love Corporation
6. LOVE [subject]
   James, S.
7. LOVE – LETTERS
8. LOVE – QUOTATIONS
9. LOVE, MATERIAL
10. LOVE (THEOLOGY)
11. Love [title]
    Adams, P.
12. Love and beauty
13. LOVE POETRY
14. Love songs, old and new
15. Love your neighbor

Another major 1942 rule requires that subject entries beginning with the same initial element be arranged by type as signified by differing marks of punctuation, in the following mandatory order:

1. The subject alone, unqualified; i.e., LOVE
2. The subject followed by a dash (–); i.e.,
   LOVE – LETTERS
   LOVE – QUOTATIONS
3. The subject followed by a comma (,); i.e., LOVE, MATERIAL
4. The subject followed by a parenthetical (e.g., specificatory) gloss;
   i.e., LOVE (THEOLOGY)

This rule, of course, is further elaborated when period divisions are introduced. There are many further rules that are used in complex filing arrangements. For details, see the Rather article cited above.

Analysis shows the effects of these two sophisticated 1942 rules. All subjects built up from the main idea of LOVE are grouped together. They are **not** interspersed among, and irrelevantly interrupted by, extraneous author, place, corporate body, and title entries. One of the fundamental differences between the 1968 and the traditional rules is that the latter encourage systematic subject searching, whereas the former do not. Remember, however, that what determines the advisability of adopting the 1968 rules, speaking practically, is size of collection. Any library under 200,000 volumes can probably use the new rules; libraries containing collections larger than this almost certainly cannot.

In addition to the 1942 rules and the Rather article already cited, the reader should refer to the rules used by the Library of Congress.[26]

CATALOGING AND CLASSIFICATION AIDS

Fortunately many aids are available today to make the cataloger's task an easier one. The library's interest in bibliography and biography has provided important reference tools that will help the cataloger verify personal names and corporate bodies; additional tools help the cataloger decide on classification and choose subject headings. In fact, some of these will even furnish complete cataloging information as found on the printed LC cards.

The beginning cataloger must know the principles and rules for cataloging and classification before he can make intelligent use of these aids. For this reason introductory cataloging courses emphasize original cataloging in which the student does the descriptive cataloging and classification himself, even though in the actual on-the-job situation the shelf list and printed cards (when available) are generally used, and a basic main entry may be obtained from several sources. The listing of cataloging aids that follows, arranged by subject categories, does not pretend to be comprehensive. It suggests only certain types of material available for consultation and indicates the range of information covered by individual categories.

General Textbooks

Haykin, D. J. *Subject Headings: A Practical Guide*. Washington, Government Printing Office, 1951.

Immroth, J. P. *A Guide to the Library of Congress Classification*. 3rd ed. Littleton, Colo., Libraries Unlimited, 1976.

Mann, M. *Introduction to Cataloging and Classification of Books*. 2nd ed. Chicago, American Library Association, 1943.

Merrill, W. S. *Code for Classifiers*. 2nd ed. Chicago, American Library Association, 1939.

Additional titles are listed in the bibliography. It should be noted that these textbooks might be somewhat outdated because of such recent changes as the revisions of AACR, revisions of LCSH and Sears subject heading lists, and new editions of *Dewey Decimal Classification*. Nevertheless, they will help the beginning cataloger locate material on basic principles of cataloging and classification. In addition, it should not be overlooked that introductory material in LCSH and the Sears list and the "Editor's Introduction" to the *Dewey Decimal Classification* might be very helpful.

---

[26] U.S. Library of Congress, Card Catalog Division, *Filing Rules for the Dictionary Catalogs of the Library of Congress* (Washington, Government Printing Office, 1956).

National Bibliographies and National Union Catalogs

The following tools are useful for verifying main entries and providing information on descriptive cataloging and classification:

Library of Congress. *Catalog of Books Represented by Library of Congress Printed Cards* . . . Ann Arbor, Mich., Edwards Brothers, 1942–1955. 191v. (Title varies.)

Library of Congress. *The National Union Catalog: A Cumulative Author List Representing Library of Congress Printed Cards and Titles Reported by Other American Libraries.* Jan. 1956– . Washington, Government Printing Office, 1956– . (Title varies.)

Library of Congress. *Library of Congress Catalog; Books: Subjects, 1950–1954.* Ann Arbor, Mich., J. W. Edwards, 1955. 20v. 1955–1959. Paterson, N.J., Pageant Books, 1960. 22v.

National Union Catalog: Pre-1956 Imprints. London, Mansell, 1968– . (In progress.)

Union List of Serials in Libraries of the United States and Canada. 3rd ed. New York, H. W. Wilson, 1965. 5v.

New Serial Titles: A Union List of Serials Commencing Publication after December 31, 1949. Washington, Library of Congress, 1953– .

These are undoubtedly the most important of all cataloging aids. A library that has these basic sets, supplements, and current volumes will have invaluable information for the cataloger. Since the Library of Congress is the largest library in the United States, its catalog provides main entries for most of the works in the average library. Here at hand, then, would be a main entry furnishing the verified author entry (person or a corporate body), information on descriptive cataloging, tracings for added entries, necessary cross references, LC Classification number (and usually a suggested Dewey Classification number), and the LC card number, which is important to those who purchase LC cards. For verification of main entries, several foreign national bibliographies as well as catalogs published by the British Museum, French Bibliothèque Nationale, etc., might also be useful.

Additional Aids

For verifying main entries and for providing tracings and a suggested Dewey Decimal Classification number:

Weekly Record. New York, R. R. Bowker, 1974– .

BPR: American Book Publishing Record. New York, R. R. Bowker, 1960– .

Standard Catalog for Public Libraries. 6th ed. New York, H. W. Wilson, 1973. Supplements.

Senior High School Library Catalog. 10th ed. New York, H. W. Wilson, 1972. Supplements.

Junior High School Library Catalog. 3rd ed. New York, H. W. Wilson, 1975. Supplements.

Children's Catalog. 12th ed. New York, H. W. Wilson, 1971. Supplements.

Fiction Catalog. 8th ed. New York, H. W. Wilson, 1970. Supplements.

For verifying author entry (personal and corporate body) in addition to those titles mentioned in the two previous categories:

Cumulative Book Index: A World List of Books in the English Language. New York, H. W. Wilson, 1898– .

Book Review Digest, 1905– . New York, H. W. Wilson, 1905– .

United States Government Organization Manual, 1935– . Washington, Government Printing Office, 1935– .

U.S. Superintendent of Documents. *Monthly Catalog of United States Government Publications.* Washington, Government Printing Office, 1895– .

A.L.A. Booklist, 1905– . Chicago, American Library Association, 1905– .

For suggested Dewey Classification numbers and subject headings:

Weekly Record
BPR: American Book Publishing Record
Book Review Digest
A.L.A. Booklist
H. W. Wilson Company's Standard Catalogs

For LC card number (important for those libraries purchasing LC cards):

Weekly Record
BPR: American Book Publishing Record
Cumulative Book Index
Book Review Digest
Library Journal
A.L.A. Booklist
H. W. Wilson Company's Standard Catalogs
Individual publishers' catalogs

General Biographical Directories

These are used for verifying names, dates, and other biographical data:

Contemporary Authors. Detroit, Gale Research, 1962– .

Current Biography: Who's News and Why. New York, H. W. Wilson, 1940– .

Dictionary of American Biography, edited by Allen Johnson and Dumas Malone. New York, Scribner's, 1928–1936. 20v. Index and 3 supplements.

Dictionary of National Biography, edited by Leslie Stephen and Sidney Lee. London, Smith, Elder, 1885–1901. 63v. and 6 supplements. Additional supplements to 1960. Reissued in 22v. by Oxford University Press, 1938.

The New York Times Obituaries Index 1858–1968. New York, New York Times, 1970.

The New Century Cyclopedia of Names. New York, Appleton-Century-Crofts, 1954. 3v.

Webster's Biographical Dictionary. Springfield, Mass., Merriam, 1972.

Who's Who in America: A Biographical Dictionary of Notable Living Men and Women. Chicago, Marquis, 1899– .

Who's Who: An Annual Biographical Dictionary. London, Black, 1849– .

In addition, catalogers use many specialized biographical directories for the purpose of verification, such as *American Men of Science, Directory of American Scholars, Twentieth Century Authors, Who's Who in Education,* etc. Many special handbooks, gazetteers and general reference tools, including encyclopedias, are also useful for verification.

Geographical Names

Library of Congress. *Library of Congress Catalog: A Cumulative List of Works Represented by Library of Congress Printed Cards: Maps and Atlases.* v.1–3. Washington, Library of Congress, 1953–1955.

U.S. Geographic Board. *Sixth Report,* 1890–1932. Washington, Government Printing Office, 1933– .

Please note that the basic sources for standard forms of geographic names for American libraries are the publications of the U.S. Board on Geographic Names and its predecessors, the Board on Geographic Names (1934–1947) and the Geographic Board (1890–1934). The principal sources for foreign names are the *Gazetteers* of the present Board. Many foreign gazetteers and geographical reference sources will supplement this information.

Additional Sources

The following serial publications of the Library of Congress are all useful to the cataloger:

Library of Congress. *Information Bulletin.* Washington, Library of Congress, 1942– (weekly).

Library of Congress. Decimal Classification Division. *Dewey Decimal Classification: Additions, Notes and Decisions.* Washington, Library of Congress, 1959– (irregular).

Library of Congress. Processing Department. *Cataloging Service.* Washington, Library of Congress, 1945– (quarterly).

Library of Congress. Subject Cataloging Division. *L.C. Classification–Additions and Changes.* Washington, Library of Congress, 1928– (quarterly).

Library of Congress Subject Headings Supplement. Washington, Library of Congress, 1908– (quarterly).

GLOSSARY OF
SELECTED TERMS AND ABBREVIATIONS

AACR. The *Anglo-American Cataloging Rules.*

Accession number. A number assigned to each book as it is received in the library. Accession numbers may be assigned through continuous numbering (e.g., 30291, 30292) or a coded system (67-201, 67-202, etc.).

Accompanying materials. Dependent materials, such as answer books, teacher's manuals, atlases, portfolios of plates, slides, and phonodiscs.

Add instructions. Notes in classification schedules that specify what digits to add to what base number; they replace divide-like notes in DDC.

Added entry. A secondary entry—i.e., any other than the main entry. An added entry card duplicates the main entry card except that it has an additional heading to represent in the catalog a subject, joint author, illustrator, editor, compiler, translator, collaborator, series, etc. (Subject entry is excluded from this definition in LC usage.)

Alternative title. A second title introduced by "or" or its equivalent—e.g., *Hypatia: or, New foes with an old face.*

Analytical entry. An entry for a part of a work or for a whole work contained in a series or a collection for which a comprehensive entry is made. Author-title analytics may be made in the form of added entries.

Anonymous work. One in which the author's name does not appear anywhere in the book; a work of unknown authorship.

Area. A major section of a catalog entry—e.g., edition area or collation area.

Artifact. See **Realia.**

Author. The person or corporate body chiefly responsible for the intellectual or artistic content of a work—e.g., writer of a book, compiler of a bibliography, composer of a musical work, artist, photographer, etc.

Author number. See **Book number.**

Author-title added entry. In the tracings, an added entry that includes author and title of a work.

Authority file. A record of the correct forms of names, series, or subjects used in the catalog. The purpose of the authority file is to keep entries uniform.

b&w. Black and white.

BC. Bibliographic Classification.

Binder's title. The title stamped on the spine of the original binding.

Body of the entry. The first paragraph of a catalog entry; it includes the title and statement of authorship area, the edition area, and the imprint area.

Book catalog. A catalog printed and bound in the form of a book.

Book number. The symbols, usually a combination of letters and numbers, used to distinguish books with the same classification number in order to maintain the alphabetical order (by author) of books on the shelves; also called an author number. Cutter number is another term used, deriving from the widespread use of Cutter-Sanborn Tables to devise book number symbols.

Books in sets. See **Monographs in collected sets.**

Bound-with. Two or more works, each with a separate title page and separate pagination, bound together without a composite title page.

Byname. A secondary name, such as a nickname, epithet, or sobriquet.

Call number. The notation used to identify and locate a particular book on the shelves; it consists of the classification number and author number, and it may also include a work number (work mark).

Canadian Rules. The rules contained in *Nonbook Materials* by Jean Riddle Weihs, Shirley Lewis, and Janet Macdonald (Ottawa, Canadian Library Association, 1973).

Caption title. A brief title printed on the leaf directly preceding the text of a book.

Card catalog. A catalog whose entries are prepared on standard 7.5x12.5 cm. cards and filed in trays or drawers.

Cartouche. A scroll-shaped or other ornamental design, with a space containing an inscription, as on an old map.

Catalog. A list of books, maps, recordings, coins, or any other medium that comprises a collection. It may be arranged by alphabet, by number, or by subject.

Cataloging. The process of describing an item in the collection and assigning a classification number. See also **Descriptive cataloging** and **Subject cataloging.**

CC. Colon Classification.

Centralized processing. Any cooperative effort that results in the centralization of one or more of the technical processes involved in getting material ready for use in a library.

Chain index. A direct and specific index based on the extracted vocabulary of a classification system. It retains all necessary context but deletes unnecessary context; all subheadings are superordinate terms.

Chart. A sheet that presents data usually arranged in tabular or graphic form; includes flipcharts.

Choice of entry. The process of selecting the main entry or heading. See also **Form of entry.**

CIP. Cataloging in Publication, a program sponsored by the Library of Congress and cooperating publishers; a partial bibliographic description is provided on the verso of the title page of a book.

Classified catalog. A catalog arranged by subject according to some classification scheme.

Classification number. The number assigned to an item of a collection to show the subject area and to indicate its location in the collection.

Classification schedule. The printed scheme of a particular classification system.

cm. Centimeters.

Collation area. The section of a catalog entry that includes pagination or number of volumes, illustrative material (if any), and size.

Collection. Three or more works or parts of works by one author published together; or two or more works or parts of works by more than one author published together. Each work in a collection was originally written independently or as part of an independent publication.

Colophon. A statement at the end of the printed text of a book that indicates the name of the printer, place of printing, and often the name of the type face and the type of paper used in printing the book.

Compiler. One who brings together written or printed matter from the works of various authors or the works of a single author.

Composite work. An original work produced by the collaboration of two or more authors in which the contribution of each forms a separate and distinct part.

Compound name. A name formed from two or more proper names which are usually connected by a hyphen, a conjunction, or a preposition.

Computer-produced catalog. A catalog based on machine-readable cataloging records.

col. Color or colored.

Continuation. 1) A work issued as a supplement to an earlier one. 2) A part issued in continuance of a book, a serial, or a series.

Continuation card. An additional card for a catalog entry on which is written any information for which there is no space on the preceding card. Also called extension card.

Continuations of sets. Non-serial sets in process of publication.

Continuous paging. The term used for the pagination of a work in more than one volume when the numbering continues sequentially through the entire work.

Copyright. The exclusive right to publish a work for a specified number of years. The copyright date is printed on the title page or the verso of the title page.

Corporate body. An organization or group of persons who are identified by a name and who act as an entity.

Cover title. The title printed on the original cover of a book or pamphlet—i.e., on the publisher's binding.

Credits. A note used in cataloging motion pictures which lists the persons (other than members of the cast) involved in the creative or technical production of the work, such as producers, directors, writers, etc.

Cross reference. A reference made from one entry in a catalog to another: "see" reference and "see also" reference.

Cutter number. See **Book number.**

Dash-on. A dash is used to represent the author heading for a dependent supplement.

DDC. Dewey Decimal Classification.

Descriptive cataloging. The phase of the cataloging process concerned with the identification and description of library material and the recording of this information in the form of a catalog entry.

Dictionary catalog. A catalog in which all the entries (author, title, added entries) are arranged in one alphabet.

Diorama. A three-dimensional representation of a scene.

Divided catalog. Card catalog separated into two or more parts, usually author/title and subject.

EC. Expansive Classification.

ed. Editor(s) or edition(s).

Edition. All the impressions of a work printed at any time or times from one setting of type. Also, one of the successive forms in which a literary text is issued either by the author or by a subsequent editor.

Edition area. Includes the following elements: named and/or numbered edition statement, author statement relating to a particular edition, and illustration statement, if any.

Editor. One who prepares for publication or supervises the publication of a work or collection of works or articles that are not his own. Responsibility may extend to revising, providing commentaries and introductory matter, etc.

Element. A sub-section of an area in the catalog entry; for example, the alternative title is an element of the title and statement of authorship area.

End papers. See **Lining papers.**

Entry. A record of a bibliographic entity in a catalog.

Entry word. The word by which the entry is arranged in the catalog, usually the first word (other than an article) of the heading. Also called filing word.

Explanatory reference. A reference that gives the detailed guidance necessary for effective use of the headings involved.

Extension card. See **Continuation card.**

Facsimile. An edition whose chief purpose is to provide a nearly exact copy of the edition being replicated; may include a new title page, new imprint, or additional title page or imprint.

Filing word. See **Entry word.**

Filmstrip. A length of film (usually 35mm) on which still images are recorded; it is intended for projection frame by frame.

First indention. The ninth typewriter space from the left edge of a catalog card.

Flash card. A card bearing an image (words, numbers, etc.) designed to be shown briefly (i.e., "flashed") in a teaching presentation.

Flipchart. A set of charts hinged together on one side.

Form division. See **Standard subdivision.**

Form of entry. The specific spelling and wording used to record an entry on a catalog card.

Form subheading. A specific word or series of words consistently used in particular subheadings, e.g., "Laws, statutes, etc."

fr. Frames.

Gathering. A physical section of a book, produced by folding a sheet of paper or several sheets of paper; gatherings are sewn together when a book is bound.

Geographic name. The place name usually used in reference to a geographic area. It is not necessarily the political name. See also **Political name.**

Guide card. A labeled card with a noticeable projection that distinguishes it from other catalog cards. It is inserted in a card catalog to help the user find a desired place or heading in the catalog.

Half title. A brief title printed on a separate leaf preceding the main title page.

Hanging indention. This form of indention is used when the main entry is under title; the title begins at first indention and all succeeding lines of the body of the card begin at second indention.

Head title. A title provided at the top (or head) of the first page of the text.

Heading. A name, word, or phrase at the top of the catalog card used as the primary identification element. As a catalog entry, the heading provides access to elements of the bibliographic description or to the subject matter of a work—e.g., authorship, subject content, series, title, etc.

Holdings statement. The publication record of a serial. It does not necessarily indicate the volumes of a series held by a library.

ill. Illustration(s) or illustrator(s).

Imprint. The place, the name of the publisher, and the date of publication on the catalog card (in that order).

Imprint area. Includes the following elements: place of publication, name of publisher, date of publication (including copyright date, if necessary), place of printing if place of publication is not known, and name of printer if name of publisher is not known.

in. Inches.

Informal notes. Informal notes consist of statements quoted from the work or other sources, or stated by the cataloger in his own words, or a combination of the two. Informal notes deal with the identification or description of the work.

ips. Inches per second.

ISBD. International Standard Bibliographic Description.

ISBD(M). An internationally accepted format for the representation of descriptive information in bibliographic records of monographic publications.

ISBD(S). An internationally accepted format for the representation of descriptive information in bibliographic records of serial publications.

ISBN. International Standard Book Number, a distinctive and unique number assigned to a book. ISBNs are used internationally; the U.S. agency for ISBNs is R. R. Bowker Company.

ISDS. International Serials Data System, a network of national and international centers sponsored by Unesco. The centers develop and maintain registers of serial publications; this includes the assignment of ISSNs and key title.

ISSN. International Standard Serial Number, a distinctive number assigned by ISDS.

Joint author. A person who collaborates with one or more associates to produce a work in which the individual contributions of the authors cannot be distinguished.

Joint pseudonym. The use of a single pseudonym by two or more authors writing together; e.g., Ellery Queen is the joint pseudonym of Frederic Dannay and Manfred B. Lee.

Kit. A package of more than one medium designed for use as a unit; if one of the media is so clearly the principal one that all others must be considered as auxiliary or accompanying, the package is not considered as a kit.

LC. Library of Congress or Library of Congress Classification.

LCSH. *Library of Congress Subject Headings.*

Leaf. A single thickness of paper; i.e., two pages.

Lining papers. The end sheets that join the bulk of the book to the covers of the book.

Main entry card. A full catalog entry, usually the author entry, which gives all the information necessary for the complete identification of a work. This entry also bears the tracing of all the other headings under which the work is entered in the catalog.

MARC. Machine Readable Cataloging, a program of the Library of Congress, which distributes machine readable cataloging in LC format.

Medium designator. A generic term indicating the category of material to which a work belongs (e.g., sound recording).

Microform. Usually a reproduction photographically reduced to a size difficult or impossible to read with the naked eye; some microforms are not reproductions but original editions.

min. Minutes.

Mixed notation. A notation that combines two or more kinds of symbols, such as a combination of letters and numbers.

mm. Millimeters.

Mnemonic devices. Devices intended to aid or assist the memory.

Mock-up. A model, generally full-sized, designed to simulate a device, process, or activity.

Model. A three-dimensional representation of a real thing; includes mock-ups.

mono. Monophonic.

Monograph. A complete bibliographic unit; it may be issued in successive parts at regular or irregular intervals, but it is *not* intended to continue indefinitely. It may be a single work or a collection that is not a serial.

Monographic series. A series of monographs with a collective title.

Monographs in collected sets. Collections or compilations by one or more authors issued in two or more volumes.

Name authority file. A file of the name (author) headings used in a given catalog, and the references made to them from other forms.

Nonbook materials. One type of special materials. Among nonbook materials are maps, globes, motion pictures, filmstrips, videorecordings, sound recordings, etc.

Non-periodical. Any serial that is not a periodical. Non-periodicals include memoirs of societies, transactions, proceedings, yearbooks, studies, almanacs, annuals, and any series classed together instead of separately.

Notation. A system of numbers and/or letters used to represent a classification scheme.

Notes area. Reserved for recording catalog data that cannot be incorporated in the preceding parts of the card. Each note is usually recorded in a separate area.

NUC. The *National Union Catalog*, a publication in the *Library of Congress Catalogs* series.

OCLC. Ohio College Library Center, a regional library network. Among other services, it provides a machine-readable data base for cataloging.

Open entry. A part of the descriptive cataloging not completed at the time of cataloging. Used for uncompleted works such as serials, series, etc.

Other title. A title other than the title proper (and parallel title)—e.g., an alternative title.

Parallel title. The title proper written in another language or in another script.

Partial title. A secondary part of the title as given on the title page. It may be a catch-word title, a subtitle, or an alternative title.

Periodical. A publication with a distinctive title which appears in successive numbers or parts at stated or regular intervals and which is intended to continue indefinitely. Usually each issue contains articles by several contributors. Newspapers and memoirs, proceedings, journals, etc., of corporate bodies primarily related to their internal affairs are not included in this definition. See also **Serial** and **Monograph**.

Phonograph records. See **Sound recordings.**

Plate. An illustrative leaf that is not included in the pagination of the text; it is not an integral part of a text gathering; it is often printed on paper different from that used for the text.

Political name. The proper name of a geographical area according to the law. This name often changes with a change in government.

Preface. A book part that precedes the text; in the preface the author explains to the reader his intent, his plan, his development of the subject, or his acknowledgment for any assistance he may have received.

Preliminaries. The half title page, any added title pages, the verso of the title page, the cover title, the binder's title, and the spine.

Printer's imprint. The place of printing and the name of the printer.

Proof slips. Individual paper copies of LC catalog cards cut from proofsheets.

Proofsheets. Paper copies of LC catalog cards, issued on long sheets with five cards to a sheet.

Pseudonym. A false name assumed by an author to conceal his identity.

Pseudo-serial. A frequently reissued and revised publication which at first publication is usually treated as a monographic work.

Publisher. The person, corporate body, or firm responsible for issuing printed matter.

Publisher series. A series of books whose only link may be the collective title assigned by the publisher.

Pure notation. A notation that consistently uses only one kind of symbol (e.g., either letters *or* numbers, but not both).

quad. Quadraphonic.

Realia. Actual objects (artifacts, specimens, etc.) rather than replicas.

Recto. The right-hand page of an open book (see also **Verso**).

Relative index. An index to a classification scheme that not only provides alphabetical references to the subjects and terms in the classification but also shows some of the relations between subjects and aspects of subjects.

Replica. See **Model.**

Romanization. The representation of the characters of a non-roman alphabet by roman characters.

rpm. Revolutions per minute.

Running title. A title repeated at the top of each page or alternate page of the book; it may be the title of the book, a chapter, or a section. Also called running head.

s.l. Place of publication unknown (*sine loco*).

s.n. Name of publisher unknown (*sine nomine*).

SC. Subject Classification.

sd. Sound.

Second indention. Thirteen typewriter spaces from the left edge of a catalog card. It is used 1) for title statement in body of card; 2) for added entries; 3) for collation; and 4) for the beginning of the notes paragraph.

Secondary entry. All entries other than the main entry added to a unit card. See also **Added entry.**

"See also" reference. A reference indicating related entries or headings.

"See" reference. A direction from a heading not used to a heading that is used.

Serial. A publication issued in successive parts at regular or irregular intervals and intended to continue indefinitely. Included are periodicals, newspapers, proceedings, reports, memoirs, annuals, and numbered monographic series. See also **Periodical** and **Monograph.**

Series. A number of separate works, usually related in subject or form, that are issued successively. They are usually issued by the same publisher and in uniform style, with a collective title that may appear at the head of the title page, on the half title page, or on the cover.

Series area. The area of a catalog card that gives series information.

Series authority file. A file of series entries used in a catalog with the record of references made to them from other forms.

Series title. The collective title given to volumes or parts issued in a series.

Shared authorship. More than one author is responsible for the work.

Sheaf catalog. A catalog whose entries are prepared on standardized slips of paper that are then inserted into a looseleaf binder.

Shelf list. A record of the books in a library; entries are arranged in the order of the books on the shelves.

si. Silent.

Slide. A segment of film or other transparent material on which a still image is recorded; the film is mounted in cardboard or plastic and is viewed through a slide viewer or projector.

Sound recordings. Aural records including discs (i.e., phonograph records), cartridges, cassettes, cylinders, etc.

Special materials. Any library materials that are not handled as monographs. Special materials include serials, pamphlets, and nonbook materials.

Specimen. See **Realia.**

Spine. The part of the cover or binding that conceals the sewed or bound edge of a book; it usually bears the binder's title and frequently the author's name and the publisher.

Standard subdivisions. Divisions used in DDC that apply to the form a work takes. Form may be physical (as in a periodical or a dictionary) or it may be philosophical (such as a philosophy or history of a subject). Formerly called form divisions.

stereo. Stereophonic.

Subject authority file. A file of the subject headings used in a given catalog, with the record of the references made to them.

Subject cataloging. The assignment of classification numbers and subject headings to the items of a library collection.

Subject entry. The catalog entry for a work under the subject heading.

Subject heading. A word or group of words indicating a subject.

Subject subdivision. A restrictive word or group of words added to a subject heading to limit it to a more specific meaning.

Subsidiary authors. Authors other than the principal author, including revisers, editors, translators, writers of prefaces, and illustrators.

Subtitle. A secondary title, often used to expand or limit the title proper.

Superimposition. A policy decision of the Library of Congress regarding AACR: for choice of entry the AACR are applied only to works new to the Library of Congress; for form of entry, AACR are applied only to names that are being established for the first time.

Thesaurus. A specialized authority list of terms used with automated information retrieval systems; very similar to a list of subject headings.

Third indention. Fifteen typewriter spaces from the left edge of a catalog card. It is used 1) to begin collation when volumes of a series are not completed; 2) for run-over on added entries; and 3) for run-over on author entry.

Title and statement of authorship area. The section of a catalog entry that gives the title of a work and information on its authorship.

Title entry. The catalog record of a work under the title. It may be a main entry or an added entry.

Title page. A page that occurs very near the beginning of the book and that contains the most complete bibliographic information about the book, such as the author's name, the fullest form of the book's title, the name and/or number of the book's edition, the name of the publisher, and the place and date of publication.

Title proper. The title found on the title page.

Tracing. The record on the main entry card of all the additional entries under which the work is listed in the catalog.

Transliteration. A representation of the characters of one alphabet by those of another. See also **Romanization.**

UDC. Universal Decimal Classification.

Uniform title. The title chosen for cataloging purposes when a work has appeared under varying titles.

Union catalog. A catalog that lists, completely or in part, the holdings of more than one library or collection.

Unit card. The basic catalog card, in the form of a main entry, which when duplicated may be used as a unit for all other entries for that work in the catalog by the addition of appropriate headings.

Verification. Determining the existence of an author and the form of his name as well as the correct title of a particular work; in short, using bibliographic sources to verify—i.e., prove—the existence of an author and/or work.

Vernacular name. A person's name in the form used in reference sources in his own country.

Verso. The left-hand page of an open book; the verso is the back side of a recto.

Verso of the title page. The page immediately following the title page; i.e., the page on the back side of the title page.

Videocassette. A videorecording on tape housed in a cassette.

Videodisc. A videorecording on a disc.

Videorecording. A recording originally generated in the form of electronic impulses and designed primarily for television playback. The term includes videocassettes, videodiscs, and videotapes.

Videotape. A videorecording on tape.

Volume. In the bibliographical sense, a book distinguished from other books by having its own title page and (usually) independent pagination or foliation.

Work mark. A letter (or letters) placed after the cutter number. A work mark may consist of one or two letters, the first of which is the first letter of the title of a work (exclusive of articles). Also called work number.

Work slip. A card or other form that accompanies a book throughout the cataloging and preparation processes. The cataloger notes on the work slip any directions and information needed to prepare catalog entries, cross references, etc.

BIBLIOGRAPHY

Advances in Librarianship. New York, Academic Press, 1970– . Annual.

American Library Association. *A.L.A. Rules for Filing Catalog Cards.* 2nd ed. Chicago, The Association, 1968.

A.L.A. Cataloging Rules for Author and Title Entries. 2nd ed. Chicago, American Library Association, 1949.

Anglo-American Cataloging Rules. North American Text. Chicago, American Library Association, 1967. Reissued with supplement, 1970.

Anglo-American Cataloging Rules: Chapter 6, Separately Published Monographs; Incorporating Chapter 9, "Photographic and Other Reproductions," and Revised to Accord with the International Standard Bibliographic Description (Monographs). North American Text. Chicago, American Library Association, 1974.

Anglo-American Cataloging Rules: Chapter 12 Revised, Audiovisual Media and Special Instructional Materials. North American Text. Chicago, American Library Association, 1975.

Anglo-American Cataloguing Rules. British Text. London, The Library Association, 1967.

Association of Research Libraries. *The Future of Card Catalogs: Report of a Program Sponsored by the Association of Research Libraries, January 18, 1975.* Washington, The Association, 1975.

Barden, B. R. *Book Numbers: A Manual for Students, with a Basic Code of Rules.* Chicago, American Library Association, 1937.

Bliss, Henry Evelyn. *A Bibliographic Classification: Extended by Systematic Auxiliary Schedules for Composite Specification and Notation.* New York, H. W. Wilson, 1940-1953. 4v. in 3.

_____. *The Organization of Knowledge in Libraries and the Subject Approach to Books.* New York, H. W. Wilson, 1939.

Bloomberg, Marty, and G. Edward Evans. *Introduction to Technical Services for Library Technicians.* 2nd ed. Littleton, Colo., Libraries Unlimited, 1974.

Boggs, S. W., and D. C. Lewis. *Classification and Cataloging of Maps and Atlases.* New York, Special Libraries Association, 1945.

Brown, James Duff. *Subject Classification: With Tables, Indexes, etc., for the Sub-Division of Subjects.* 3rd ed. rev. and enl. by James D. Stewart. London, Grafton, 1939.

Cataloging Rules of the American Library Association and the Library of Congress. Additions and Changes, 1949-1958. Washington, Library of Congress, 1959.

Classification Research. Proceedings of the Second International Study Conference ... 14-18 Sept. 1964. Copenhagen, Munksgaard, 1965.

Coates, E. J. *Subject Catalogues: Headings and Structure.* London, The Library Association, 1960.

Cutter, Charles Ammi. *C. A. Cutter's Two-Figure Author Table.* Swanson-Swift revision. Chicopee, Mass., Huntting, 1969.

_____. *C. A. Cutter's Three-Figure Author Table.* Swanson-Swift revision. Chicopee, Mass., Huntting, 1969.

_____. *Cutter-Sanborn Three-Figure Author Table.* Swanson-Swift revision. Chicopee, Mass., Huntting, 1969.

_____. *Expansive Classification, Part 1: The First Six Classifications.* Boston, C. A. Cutter, 1891-93.

_____. *Expansive Classification, Part 2: Seventh Classification.* Edited by William Parker Cutter. Boston, 1896-1911. 2v.

_____. *Rules for a Dictionary Catalog.* 4th ed. rewritten. Washington, Government Printing Office, 1904.

Dewey, Harry. *Fundamentals of Cataloging and Classification.* Madison, Wis., Capital Press, 1956-57. 2v.

Dewey, Melvil. *Dewey Decimal Classification and Relative Index.* 10th Abridged Edition. Lake Placid Club, N.Y., Forest Press, 1972.

_____. *Dewey Decimal Classification and Relative Index.* 18th ed. Lake Placid Club, N.Y., Forest Press, 1971.

Dowell, Arlene. *Cataloging with Copy: The Decision-Maker's Handbook.* Littleton, Colo., Libraries Unlimited, 1976.

Dunkin, Paul Shaner. *How to Catalog a Rare Book.* 2nd ed., rev. Chicago, American Library Association, 1973.

Encyclopedia of Library and Information Science. Ed. by Allen Kent and Harold Lancour. New York, Marcel Dekker, 1968– . In progress.

Foskett, A. C. *The Subject Approach to Information.* 2nd ed., rev. and enl. Hamden, Conn., Linnet Books, 1972.

_____. *The Universal Decimal Classification: The History, Present Status and Future Prospects of a Large General Classification Scheme.* Hamden, Conn., Linnet Books, 1973.

Fry, G. *Catalog Card Reproduction.* Report Based on Study Conducted by G. Fry and Associates, Inc. Chicago, Library Technology Project of the American Library Association, 1965 (L.T.P. Publications, No. 9).

Gaskell, Philip. *A New Introduction to Bibliography.* New York, Oxford University Press, 1972.

Gorman, Michael. *A Study of the Rules for Entry and Heading in the Anglo-American Cataloguing Rules, 1967 (British Text).* London, The Library Association, 1968.

Grove, Pearce S., and Evelyn G. Clement, eds. *Bibliographic Control of Nonprint Media.* Chicago, American Library Association, 1972.

Guide to the Universal Decimal Classification. London, British Standards Institution, 1963.

Harris, Jessica. *Subject Analysis: Computer Implications of Rigorous Definition.* Metuchen, N.J., Scarecrow Press, 1970.

Haykin, David J. *Subject Headings: A Practical Guide.* Washington, Government Printing Office, 1951.

Horner, John. *Special Cataloguing: With Particular Reference to Music, Films, Maps, Serials and the Multi-Media Computerised Catalogue.* Hamden, Conn., Linnet Books, 1973.

Immroth, John Phillip. *Analysis of Vocabulary Control in Library of Congress Classification and Subject Headings.* Littleton, Colo., Libraries Unlimited, 1971.

_____. *A Guide to the Library of Congress Classification.* 3rd ed. Littleton, Colo., Libraries Unlimited, 1976.

_____. "Library of Congress Classification," in *Encyclopedia of Library and Information Science*, Vol. 15. New York, Marcel Dekker, 1975. pp. 93-200.

International Conference on Cataloging Principles. Paris, 9th-18th October, 1961. *Report.* London, International Federation of Library Associations, 1963.

International Federation of Library Associations. *ISBD(M): International Standard Bibliographic Description for Monographic Publications.* 1st standard ed. London, IFLA Committee on Cataloging, 1974.

Kent, Allen, ed. *Resource Sharing in Libraries: Why, How, When, Next Action Steps.* New York, Marcel Dekker, 1974.

LaMontagne, L. E. *American Classification with Special Reference to the Library of Congress.* Hamden, Conn., Shoe String Press, 1961.

Library of Congress Classification Schedules: A Cumulation of Additions and Changes through 1973. Detroit, Gale Research Company, 1974. 32v.

Lubetzky, Seymour. *Cataloging Rules and Principles.* Washington, Library of Congress, 1953.

Maltby, Arthur, ed. *Classification in the 1970's: A Discussion of Development and Prospects for the Major Schemes.* Hamden, Conn., Linnet Books, 1972.

McKerrow, Ronald B. *An Introduction to Bibliography for Literary Students.* Oxford, Clarendon Press, 1928.

Mann, Margaret. *Introduction to Cataloging and the Classification of Books.* 2nd ed. Chicago, American Library Association, 1943.

Merrill, William Stenson. *Code for Classifiers: Principles Governing the Consistent Placing of Books in a System of Classification.* 2nd ed. Chicago, American Library Association, 1939.

Metcalfe, John. *Alphabetical Subject Indication of Information.* New Brunswick, N.J., Graduate School of Library Service, Rutgers, The State University, 1965.

_____. *Information Indexing and Subject Cataloging; Alphabetical: Classified: Coordinate: Mechanical.* New York, Scarecrow Press, 1957.

_____. *Subject Classifying and Indexing of Libraries and Literature.* New York, Scarecrow Press, 1959.

Mills, J. *A Modern Outline of Library Classification.* London, Chapman and Hall, 1968 (c.1960).

_____. *The Universal Decimal Classification.* New Brunswick, N.J., Graduate School of Library Service, Rutgers, The State University, 1964.

Music Library Association. *Code for Cataloging Music and Phonorecords.* Chicago, American Library Association, 1958.

Norris, Dorothy May. *A History of Cataloguing and Cataloguing Methods 1100-1850; With an Introductory Survey of Ancient Times.* London, Grafton, 1939.

Olding, R. K., ed. *Readings in Library Cataloguing.* Hamden, Conn., Shoe String Press, 1966.

Osborn, Andrew. "The Crisis in Cataloging," *Library Quarterly* 11 (October 1941): 393-411.

_____. *Serial Publications: Their Place and Treatment in Libraries.* 2nd ed., rev. Chicago, American Library Association, 1973.

Painter, Ann F., comp. *Reader in Classification and Descriptive Cataloging.* Washington, NCR Microcard Editions, 1972 (Reader Series in Library and Information Science).

Palmer, B. I. *Itself an Education: Six Lectures on Classification.* 2nd ed. London, The Library Association, 1971.

_____, and A. J. Wells. *The Fundamentals of Library Classification.* London, Allen & Unwin, 1951.

Patrick, Ruth. *Guidelines for Library Cooperation: Development of Academic Library Consortia.* Santa Monica, Calif., Systems Development Corporation, 1972.

Perrault, Jean. *An Introduction to U.D.C.* Hamden, Conn., Archon Books, 1969.

_____. *Towards a Theory for U.D.C.: Essays Aimed at Structural Understanding and Operational Improvement.* Hamden, Conn., Archon Books, 1969.

Pettee, Julia. *Subject Headings, the History and Theory of the Alphabetical Approach to Books.* New York, H. W. Wilson, 1946.

Ranganathan, Shiyali Ramamrita. *Colon Classification.* 6th rev. ed. London, Asia Publishing House, 1963.

Rowland, A. R., ed. *The Catalog and Cataloging.* Hamden, Conn., Shoe String Press, 1969.

Saheb-Ettaba, Caroline, and Roger B. McFarland. *ANSCR: Alpha-Numeric System for Classification of Recordings.* Williamsport, Pa., Bro-Dart, 1969.

Sayers, W. C. Berwick. *A Manual of Classification for Librarians.* 4th ed., completely rev. and partly re-written by Arthur Maltby. London, Andre Deutsch, 1967.

Sears, Minnie E. *Sears List of Subject Headings.* Edited by B. M. Westby. 10th ed. New York, H. W. Wilson, 1972.

Shera, J. H., and M. E. Egan. *Bibliographic Organization.* Papers presented before the Fifteenth Annual Conference of the Graduate Library School, July 24-29, 1950. Chicago, The University of Chicago Press, 1951.

_____. *The Classified Catalog: Basic Principles and Practices.* Chicago, American Library Association, 1956.

Soderland, K. W. "The Literature of Cataloging and Classification," in *Occasional Papers*, No. 58 Revised. Urbana, Ill., University of Illinois Graduate School of Library Science, April 1963.

State of the Library Art. Edited by Ralph R. Shaw. v.I, pt. 1: *Cataloging and Classification*, by Maurice F. Tauber; v.I, pt. 2: *Subject Headings*, by Carlyle J. Frarey; v.I, pt. 3: *Classification Systems*, by Maurice F. Tauber and Edith Wise. New Brunswick, N.J., Graduate School of Library Service, Rutgers, The State University, 1960-61.

Subject Retrieval in the Seventies: New Directions. Proceedings of an International Symposium ... Ed. by Hans (Hanan) Wellich and Thomas D. Wilson. Westport, Conn., Greenwood Publishing Co., 1972.

Swihart, S. J., and B. F. Hefley. *Computer Systems in the Library.* Los Angeles, Melville Publishing Co., 1973.

Tauber, Maurice F. *The Subject Analysis of Library Materials.* New York, School of Library Service, Columbia University, 1953.

_____. *Technical Services in Libraries: Acquisitions, Cataloging, Classification, Binding, Photographic Reproduction and Circulation Operations.* New York, Columbia University Press, 1954 (Columbia University Studies in Library Service, No. 7).

_____, and Hilda Feinberg. *Book Catalogs.* Metuchen, N.J., Scarecrow, 1971.

U.S. Library of Congress. *Filing Rules for the Dictionary Catalogs of the Library of Congress.* Washington, Government Printing Office, 1956.

_____. *Studies of Descriptive Cataloging.* Washington, Government Printing Office, 1946.

_____. Descriptive Cataloging Division. *Cooperative Cataloging Manual for the Use of Contributing Libraries.* Washington, Government Printing Office, 1944.

_____. _____. *Rules for Descriptive Cataloging.* Washington, Government Printing Office, 1949.

_____. Information Systems Office. *MARC Manuals Used by the Library of Congress.* 2nd ed. Chicago, American Library Association, 1970.

_____. _____. *Format Recognition. Process for MARC Records: A Logical Design.* Chicago, American Library Association, 1970.

_____. MARC Development Office. *Books: A MARC Format.* 5th ed. Washington, Library of Congress, 1972.

_____. _____. *Books: A MARC Format. Addenda.* (especially number 9). Washington, Library of Congress, 1972– .

_____. _____. *Serials: A MARC Format.* 2nd ed. Washington, Library of Congress, 1974.

_____. Processing Department. Subject Cataloging Division. *Library of Congress Subject Headings.* 8th ed. Washington, Government Printing Office, 1975.

_____. _____. _____. *Classification* [Schedules].

Universal Decimal Classification. Complete English ed. 4th international ed. London, British Standards Institution, 1943– . In progress.

The Use of the Library of Congress Classification. Proceedings of the Institute on the Use of the Library of Congress Classification ... Chicago, American Library Association, 1968.

Vickery, B. C. *Classification and Indexing in Science.* 2nd ed. London, Butterworths, 1959.

Viswanathan, C. G. *Cataloguing: Theory and Practice.* New York, Asia Publishing House, 1965.

Weihs, Jean Riddle, Shirley Lewis, and Janet Macdonald. *Nonbook Materials: The Organization of Integrated Collections.* 1st ed. Ottawa, Canadian Library Association, 1973.

INDEX